DEVOTIONS
BY
DAWN

INSPIRATION *for a* NEW BEGINNING

by
DAWN DAVIS

Foreword by Faith A. Davis

xulon
PRESS

www.xulonpress.com

CONTENTS

FOREWORD

*P*rior to her death, Dawn felt impressed by God to write a devotional book. She wanted it to be an audio devotional that people could listen to in their cars, at the gym, or whenever they had a few minutes. Despite fatigue and pain experienced as a result of various treatments and disease progression, Dawn did her best, despite her failing health, to get up every day and worked on this book.

In her final days, her eyesight began to fail, so she employed her niece to type and transcribe as she told her what to write. She was determined to share with the world her experiences, along with the faith that helped her through her life's journey. Dawn knew it would be an immense blessing to her readers.

In her final days, she requested that her book be completed. Thus, the completion of this book has been an emotional labor of love by her family. While editing and compiling the manuscript, we have been immensely blessed. Each person brought a different element to the writing process, which was necessary for completion.

Dawn Davis went to be with her Lord on December 6, 2007. Because of her hold on God's unchanging hand, she remained faithful to God throughout her fifteen-year battle with cancer. God honored her request and gave her seven more years to live than she asked for. The night before her death, she and her family had a praise and worship service. What a beautiful way to end her life — giving praise to God because of His faithfulness!

In 1 Thessalonians 4:16-17, we read, "For the Lord himself shall descend from heaven with a shout, with the voice of the archangel, and with the trump of God: and the dead in Christ shall rise first: Then we which are alive and remain shall be caught up together with them in the clouds, to meet the Lord in the air: and so shall we ever be with the Lord."

We know that Dawn has successfully finished her course here on earth. The question for us is: Are we eagerly anticipating Jesus' return with what is in our hearts, as well as by the way we live? He is going to take the faithful with Him. God help us all to be in that number.

Expect to be blessed

The finished book is made up of fifty devotions of varying length, originally designed for audio. The content was modified to be read in book form since she is no longer able to record the devotions. The devotions include scriptures, songs, an inspirational thought, and a prayer. Each devotion discusses a practical topic that applies to daily life, and provides new perspective on the privilege of being alive, given the condition of the author at the time of writing.

I encourage you to take a journey with us, and gain a perspective of praise despite life's circumstances.

We're alive, so let's thank God for another day to live for Him!

Faith A. Davis

INTRODUCTION

evotions by Dawn is an inspirational book written by Collette "Dawn" Davis. Each devotional shares a nugget that can be used to navigate life's challenges with a spirit of praise. Understanding the perspective of the author, despite her circumstances, is critical in order to experience the full impact of this book.

Dawn endured a long battle with breast cancer and was optimistic and full of praise throughout her illness. She wrote an article a few months before she passed, which was published in *Message Magazine* and titled "Jesus, My Tower of Strength." It is included here to begin to answer the question, Who is Dawn?

Jesus, My Tower of Strength

Wow! Has it been fifteen years already since my diagnosis of cancer? I am a cancer *survivor*. Here is a tidbit about my journey. My opportunity for great praise began in 1993. Somehow cancer found a way to invade my body. I was a triathlete, vegetarian, regular-exercising Christian young woman. Cancer was the last thing I suspected would be my malady. I was diagnosed with breast cancer, and after the initial shock passed, what began to matter to me most was not "Why me?" but "How can I use this challenge to bring glory to my God?" I was the one singing with exuberance, "I Am on the Battlefield for My Lord," "Victory Is Mine," and "We've Come This Far by Faith."

I talked to God about my survival. He asked me how much survival time I would be satisfied with if He granted my request. I asked Him to please be kind to me and allow me to see my youngest child graduate from high school—she was in the third grade at the time. A reasonable request, don't you think? I have three children and wanted the privilege of rearing them in a loving, happy, God-fearing home. God said to me, "I will do that for you." My faith latched onto His Word. I was cured. I took the recommended medical and herbal treatments and kept on living life with gusto and praise.

My daughters and I went skydiving. I left all my troubles in the sky with God. We had a blast! We went on family Caribbean vacations and frequent skiing outings. The children grew to know and love God. We were active participants in the church school and church youth programs. I focused on praise parties. No pity parties were allowed. The family's agenda was simple: laughter and living life to the fullest. Our family built memory after memory. I especially remember my fiftieth birthday party and our twenty-fifth anniversary cruise. We had high school graduation celebrations for my son and eldest daughter, and then my youngest daughter. The celebrations were grand.

Two months to the day before my youngest child's graduation, I felt bone pain. The cancer had resurfaced in my hip bones. My faith grew like an oak tree in the spring. God had given me exactly what I had asked for. He had answered my prayer. He had kept His Word. If He never does another thing for me, I know He answers prayer. When He asked me again how much time I wanted, I gave Him full reign to do whatever He wanted. I was assured of His love for me. I was also sure of His promises and

His ever-present helpfulness to me through every challenge—health or otherwise.

He is there with sustaining strength for trials and with help to regulate the mind. When I was diagnosed with cancer, like many survivors, I had to keep positive thoughts; if not, death threats would take over. There is concern that every ache or pain could be the cancer again. There are thoughts of loss of life and funerals that can frequently creep into the mind. These thoughts and concerns must be avoided like the plague. Being aware of the body's responses to treatment and medication is necessary, but figuring out how your family will survive minus you is not your territory of concern. Why take God's job away? He can do it all. I had to get that straight.

It is because of Christ's birth into this world that I know He understands my pain—debilitating pain. It is because of Christ's death that I can identify with someone Who stood bravely through unfairness, viciousness, and mistreatment. Jesus came here to teach me how a child of God can go through tough times and still have joy and happiness. Since Jesus did it, I can follow Him and do it also. Right? If you are in a similar challenge, so can you.

Thank God for the birth of His Son here on earth. He is truly my Tower of Strength! When I die, and we all will one day, I will go to be with Him and will one day have a new, cancer-free body. Because I have placed my faith in Him as my Savior, who can deliver me from sin, I will live eternally with Jesus— pain-free, cancer-free, and sin-free.

Thank You, Jesus, for Your birth and death on my behalf. I love You, Lord. I glorify You, Lord. I will praise Your name forevermore. You are worthy of all my praise and thanksgiving. Thank You for keeping me alive for seven more years already beyond what I originally asked You for. Awesome! Proverbs 9:11 says: "For by me thy days shall be multiplied, and the years of thy life shall be increased." You gave me that promise, Lord, and I am giving You one in return. I will praise Your name till I die. I will never give up my faith in You. When the time is right, You will gently lay me to rest.

Psalm 116:15 says, "Precious in the sight of the Lord is the death of his saints." Until that time I'm going to be Your shadow. Give me strength to walk like You. I also have to deal with developing a Christ like character along with this malady. Help me to accept the threatening words people send my way, just as You did. Help me to know when to speak and when to keep silent, just as You did. I'm learning, Jesus, that the center of my life is You, not my cancer. My response to life's trials will be praise to You. It is all because of You that I can stand and face each day with joy. Thank You, Jesus, for sustaining me. Psalm 3:5 says: "I laid me down and slept; I awaked; for the Lord sustained me."

It is because of Christ's birth that cancer, like any other challenge, is just something a soldier can and must overcome in this life. I decided to comfort other soldiers along the way. I decided not to complain or discourage others. I decided to share all my blessings from God and my praise with others. In doing this, I help to bring glory to my Commander-in-Chief Jesus Christ. "For unto you is born this day in the city of David a Saviour, which is Christ the Lord" (Luke 2:11). That is, bar none, the best Christmas gift ever.

Editorial note: Dawn Davis has metastatic breast cancer that has spread to the bone, lung, brain, liver, and kidney. She has lost sight in her left eye due to a tumor. She says the favor of God is what keeps her going.

Day 1

THE PURPLE FLOWER

I'm alive. Thank God for another day to live for Him.

"Behold, I will do a new thing; now it shall spring forth; shall ye not know it?
I will even make a way in the wilderness and rivers in the desert"
(Isaiah 43:19).

New every morning is thy love.

Our wakening and uprising prove;

Through sleep and darkness safely brought,

Restored to life and power and thought.

New mercies, each returning day,

Hover around us while we pray;

New perils passed, new sins forgiven,

New thoughts of God new hopes of heaven.

"New Every Morning is Thy Love," John Keble

*T*have a purple flower in my front yard. It is soft, delicate, beautiful, lavender, and it blooms every morning. By evening it's gone or

11

gone to sleep. By the next morning it is back. I'm amazed at its consistent behavior. Matthew 6:28-29 says, "Consider the lilies of the field how they grow." The lilies don't take on tomorrow's trouble. Just as I'm confident that my purple flower will bloom every day, you can be just as confident that God's Word is true and sure.

In Isaiah 35:4-6 we read, "Say to them that are of a fearful heart, be strong, fear not: behold, your God will come with vengeance, even God with a recompence; he will come and save you. Then the eyes of the blind shall be opened, and the ears of the deaf shall be unstopped. Then shall the lame man leap as a hart, and the tongue of the dumb sing: for in the wilderness shall waters break out, and streams in the desert."

God will do wonderful and amazing things because He keeps His promises. We have to start by believing God's Word. Let us pray together.

Lord,

We want to acknowledge You as the God of our lives. Thank You for even allowing us into this Your new day. We have resolved to spend a daily devotional time with You every day. Remind us, please, of our commitment. Give us a mind to remember that new every morning is Thy great love. Refresh us, revive us, repair us, and restore us through Your Word. Help us to trust You, and know that what You say in your Holy Word cannot change because You are God (Malachi 3:6). You keep Your promises.

Father, give us confidence in Your Word. Where our faith is shaky, help us to find an anchor, a Scripture passage to steady us, so that we can stand for You and be immovable. Help us keep our resolution to spend daily time with You. May each experience we go through today increase our faith. May we see You working things out on our behalf. Let this experience be a faith-strengthening one. Thank You for Your words to us—they are life.

Amen.

Day 2

SNOWSTORM EXPERIENCE

I'm alive! Thank God for another day to live for You.

"The apostles said to the Lord, 'Increase our faith!'" (Luke 17:5, NIV)

We've come this far by faith, leaning on the Lord;
Trusting in His Holy Word, He's never failed me yet.
Don't be discouraged, when trouble's in your life.
He'll bear your burdens, and move all misery and strife.
Thank God we've come this far by faith.

"We've Come This Far by Faith," Albert A. Goodman

*M*y younger daughter was to be inducted into the honor society. Her school was hosting a special induction ceremony. My oldest daughter had her honor society induction several weeks before, and the family made a big deal about it. We had pictures taken. We invited family and friends to a big dinner celebration. She even ate from a special plate. She was welcomed into the honor society and felt very important.

Now that it was my younger daughter's turn, I went to the teacher to find out the date. Alas, it conflicted with a trip to California that our family had already scheduled. I explained the dilemma to the teacher, not wanting my daughter to have to choose between California and her honor society program. The teacher told me it didn't really matter what the conflict was, because she was not going to change the date. It was already planned and they were behind in the event's preparations. The speaker had already committed, and there was no way she would change the date.

You know how mothers can be with their children when they want a special thing for them. I begged and pleaded, but the teacher would not budge. I said to her, "I guess I'll have to talk to my Father in heaven, because He is the one who can see my heart, knows what I want for my daughter, and knows what's good for her."

As I left, I told the teacher that I believed the honor society program would not take place on the date she had scheduled it because I was going to talk to my Father and He would change the date for me. She looked at me like she was thinking, *Yeah, I don't know, whatever you say.*

So I decided to go and talk to the Lord about it.

This is where my faith came in. I said, "Lord, as the apostles asked in Luke 17:5, give me more faith. If You want her to participate in this induction with her class, I need You to make it happen. We have already planned to go to California, tickets have been bought, and we are going."

After I left the teacher that day, I said to my prayer group, "This is a dilemma. I know it's nothing major. I know that it's not an urgent or deep need. But I would like for her to be a part of her induction service for the honor society."

We agreed we would all pray together. I went to prayer meeting at my church and I asked them to pray as well. They said, "Sure, we will pray."

I asked several groups from my church to pray. I told them that I really wanted my daughter to be a part of the honor society induction program, although I didn't want anything unforeseen to happen that would cause a problem for anybody.

We flew to California. I called to find out how things were going at home in Washington D.C. It was the end of March when the cherry blossoms usually bloom, and the weather warms. Instead, there was a snowstorm that shut the entire city down! Even the airports could not fly people in or out. The honor society induction ceremony had to be cancelled.

I said, "Lord, I knew You would do it, but I didn't know it would be in such a drastic way."

The snowstorm He sent to Washington, D.C., meant my daughter could participate in the honor society induction program with her class when it was rescheduled. Now this is the kind of thing that grows your faith.

Someone asked me, "Dawn, how do you know the Lord will do it?"

I asked Him. I just said to Him, "Lord, unless You see another reason why she shouldn't be inducted with her class, please make it happen. Since You told me whatever I want I should ask You for and You will give it to me." Talk about a faith-building experience. My faith grew!

While I was in California, I shared the experience with everybody I met. I even had a lady ask me to pray for her son. She said, "He's studying in school and not doing very well. Would you pray that he will do better?"

Right then, we prayed together and for several weeks afterward I prayed for her son. I believe God answered this prayer as well.

The faith of the teacher who had told me she would not change the date also grew. When she saw me in the school hallway, she asked me to pray for the honor society program. Talk about faith-building! My child's faith grew. The faith of all the people who had prayed for her and joined me in my request on her behalf grew. Whenever I talk of the snowstorm experience, my daughter immediately says, "I remember the miracle God did for me."

Not only did their faith grow, now your faith can also grow. Good job, God. All you have to do is take Him at His Word and ask Him to do what

He says He will do. You're an obedient child of God and you can count on Him. He's working it out for you.

Thank You, God, for always being willing to grow our faith.

When you ask for faith, you have to know that you are going to face a challenge—something you know you can't do on your own. Then when you see the results, you know it had to be God who did it for you. It's not something that just happened. It's not just by chance or happenstance. God doesn't work like that.

You are an obedient child of God. Ask Him to do what He says He will do. When you ask Him for something within His will, believing His Word say, "Lord, You said if we ask anything in Your name, believing in faith, we shall receive it." He can work with that. It's according to His will and He loves to do good things for His children, even more than parents love to give good gifts to their children.

I just wanted my child there for the program. God wants us to have salvation. He wants to save our souls. God wants to include us in His ministry. He wants to use us to bring other people to His kingdom. God wants our stories to be full of wonderful surprises so we can go to someone and say, "Take it to the Lord in faith and He will do it for you."

I would like to pray for us and ask God to give us more faith in Him. Let's thank Him for what He has done for us and ask Him to build our faith.

Holy One,

Some had a horrific day yesterday. Help them not to get discouraged. Whenever we launch out with You, the devil gets unhappy. Then he sets out to use his problem-creating tools and discouragement to get us down.

Lord, give us praise, a tool we need to use more often. When things seem like they are discouraging us and weighing us down, help us to remember the tool of praise.

Lord, give us a tool we can use to fight temptation, like the armor of God described in Ephesians 6. Let us remember the joy of the Lord is our strength (Nehemiah 8:10). We will not be moved. We will endure hardship like a good soldier (2 Timothy 2:3). That is how our faith is strengthened.

Help us to keep our daily devotions going so our faith in You can flourish. Take care of us all today. Take care of all that troubled us yesterday and that you brought us through. Keep us peaceful and standing by your strength and power today. Those of us who had a great or an all right day give You the glory. Lord, we know it's all because of You and we thank You for Your faithfulness.

In Jesus name, Amen.

Day 3

SING, SMILE, AND PRAY

I'm alive! Thank God for another day to live for Him.

"Yet the LORD will command his loving kindness in the day time, and in the
night his song shall be with me, and my prayer unto the God of my life"
(Psalm 42:8).

Sing, smile, and pray your burdens away.
For Jesus has promised to take them all.
Sing, smile, and pray your burdens away.

"Roll your Burdens Away," Wesley A. Crane

*R*ecently, I had surgery to get a biopsy. Doctors consider that a
minor procedure. But to those of us living the experience, nothing
about surgery is minor. They read us the disclaimers for anesthesia and
possible death. Still, the doctor says you need to have this procedure done.

Talk to God to get His take on it. If He says to move ahead with the
procedure, trust His Word. Not one of His promises will ever fail (1 Kings
8:56). His compassion is new every morning (Lamentations 3:22-23).

I was given a light anesthetic. I was in a twilight zone, not completely out, semi-conscious. Once I was awake and hearing the doctor's

confirmation that the procedure had been completed, I broke out into song. "Blessed assurance; Jesus is mine." I even asked the operating room team if they knew the song. I don't recall their answer, but I came out of the experience feeling happy I had shared the assurance of Jesus even when I was semi-conscious.

That's how the idea of a song in the night became real for me. No matter the difficulty, plan ahead to sing, smile, and pray. God will give you strength as your faith grows because of your daily devotions.

Lord,

It is not easy to smile, sing, and pray through trials. But we know You will give us the strength to do it. You fill us with songs of deliverance when we are fearful. Fill our hearts with a song, a smile, and a prayer all through this day, so our situation will be sweetened with heavenly sugar.

Keep us smiling so others will know Your joy is inside us.

Keep us smiling to confuse the devil.

Keep us smiling so that unhappiness cannot force itself on us.

Today we will smile at people we meet and infect them with the joy we got from our devotion time with You today. I pray for consistency in our lives so we can sing, smile, and pray continuously today and every day in Jesus' name.

Amen.

Day 4

LIVING IN THE LIGHT

I'm alive! Thank You, God, for another day to live for You.

"Thy word is a lamp unto my feet, and a light unto my path"
(Psalm 119:105).

Jesus bids us shine

With a pure, clear light,

Like a little candle

Burning in the night.

In this world of darkness

So let us shine

You in your small corner,

And I in mine.

"Jesus Bids Us Shine," Susan Bogert Warner

For a lamp or light to have any real value, there has to be darkness. The darker the surroundings, the greater the need for and value of light. Dark places breed fear. Getting around in thick darkness, one begins to depend on the sense of touch rather than sight. That is unnatural for the sighted person. Getting around in the dark can be very scary; you just can't see where you are going. The fear of bumping into something or taking a wrong step and losing your balance leaves you feeling vulnerable.

How does the darkness make us feel? We feel fear, vulnerability, unfamiliarity with surroundings, and just plain uncomfortable. We grope around, hoping for light to help us see where we are and where we are going.

We can all agree that even a small candle brings great relief because light dispels darkness. When circumstances of life darken our days and our future, we react with fear, doubt, and uncertainty, and we become vulnerable to depression.

I was paying my bills the other day and realized I did not have enough to meet the month's expenses. Clearly, some of you may agree with me that rough financial situations brings darkness emotionally. Some may even say, "My whole life is like that!"

Yet in God's Word, He promises to bring light to all our situations of darkness. He even says we will become lights to others—imagine that! How will God do that? Psalm 37:25 says, "I have been young, and now am old; yet have I not seen the righteous forsaken, nor his seed begging bread."

Somehow the bills got paid and I'm still here. How do I explain it? I can only say I was here with not enough and now I'm here and don't know how I was able to make it, except God. Ever been there? He has financial light and we must follow Him. According to Psalm 24:1, "The earth is the Lord's and the fullness thereof."

What about the darkness of ill health? Have you been there? A new pain or health problem arises and you can no longer do what you used to. Darkness and despair come in as uninvited guests. They have us grasping to find a way out of the problem. We often don't know what the final outcome will be, so we make up outcomes and wonder what we will do if this or that happens.

Here we go again: We can't see, so we try to grope our way through the darkness. But it is better to call upon Jesus. He is not intimidated by darkness. "But he knows the way that I take" (Job 23:10, NIV). He is the light. Go to Him and ask Him for the candle that will light your path. He is the one who created you. He can fix your health problems. He can lead you to the right doctor or medicine. Don't let the fear of this dark experience put out your light. But if it does, Jesus can light your candle again. Before long, you can be a light house for someone coming along your same road.

Lots of earthly maladies cause darkness. There is also the darkness of bad habits. You often want to do them and keep them in the dark. You don't want to be seen doing them in the light. That is a sign you need to change that habit. What you do in the dark always comes out in the light anyway. Save yourself the embarrassment and shame and self-correct. Ask God to give you His light to show you out of your dark way, and to set you up on a hill to help light someone else's way. Then His name will be glorified, you will have a testimony to give, and others can grow from your experience.

That is the way the Lord does His thing. Darkness might come in the form of grief that can come from pain and loss. The darkness of grief is very thick because there seems to be no other way besides the way you used to travel with your loved one. You had become so comfortable with that person. Now he or she is gone and you are left alone, groping in darkness.

Here again, the answer to the darkness is Jesus. He tells us He is the way, the truth, and the light (John 14:6); His Word is *the* lamp and light. Snuggle up and ask Him to turn your night into day by giving you His light. He says in Matthew 11:28, "Come unto me, all ye that labor and are heavy laden, and I will give you rest."

Then He will place you as the light of the world on a hill, just as a lighted city cannot be hidden (Matthew 5:14).

22

Isn't God miraculous? How does He do this? I guess it's called the mystery of godliness. I know that all you and I have to do is to have a willing heart to follow the Seed of righteousness. Let us pray for willingness to follow Jesus.

Dearest Jesus,

Giver of light and life, we Your children, are groping around in all kinds of darkness in our lives. We can't see one step in front of us. We need to see and follow Your path. Thank You for being a God who neither slumbers nor sleeps. Thank You for knowing the way out of our dark dilemmas.

Give us confidence in Your Word to know You will do what You say You will do. Direct our paths (Proverbs 3:6). Lead us not into temptation (Matthew 6:13). You said you are our light and our salvation; whom shall we fear? (Psalm 27:1) Give us more faith as we live daily, proving Your words through our lives.

Let our doubts and darkness disappear in the light of Your promises found in Your Word, the Bible. Let us choose You as our guide through dark times, and not some imposter pretending to be You—the devil. Lead us to where you want us to be. May we follow you to a brighter day and a better way. May we always have peace on our lips and joy and thanksgiving in our hearts.

In Jesus' shining name I pray, Amen.

Day 5

HOW TO BE BRAVE

I'm alive! Thanks, God, for another day to live for You.

"It is written, Man shall not live by bread alone, but by every word that proceedeth out of the mouth of God. Jesus said unto him, It is written again, Thou shalt not tempt the Lord thy God. Then saith Jesus unto him, Get thee hence, Satan: for it is written, Thou shalt worship the Lord thy God, and him only shalt thou serve" (Matthew 4:4, 7, 10).

Sing Hosanna

Give me oil in my lamp

Keep me burning

Keep me burning till the break of day

"Oil in My Lamp" by Eric Morris

The verses above were spoken by Jesus to the devil when he tried to tempt Him after His forty-day fast.

Wherever you work, there is at least one manual specific to your kind of job. A manual helps you to fix common problems. It gives instructions on how things should be handled if a particular situation arises. When you don't know how your company handles a problem, you go to the manual and get instructions. Usually, when you receive and follow the directions or instructions, you can solve the problem. At the very least, you followed the process according to company standards, policy, or protocol.

If a problem should arise in the medical profession and the desired outcome does not happen, the first question asked of the staff pertains to whether they followed the standard of care. If the standard of care was followed, usually the problem is not with the staff but is beyond their control. Since they followed the policy stated, the reasonable person standard, then the problem cannot be blamed on the staff for not following procedures.

When Jesus walked this earth, His mission was partly to leave us an example of how to make it through this world of woe. The Bible records some of Jesus' most troubling times, right after His experience in the wilderness. He had just completed a forty-day fast and he was weak, hungry, and worn. The devil loves to come when we are most vulnerable. For example, you are newly married and determined to do things God's way instead of living together, then here comes trouble! Just when you are determined to give up a bad habit, here comes an unusual situation bringing with it strong temptations to fall back in "the habit."

But let's see what Jesus did to overcome temptation in Matthew 4:1-11. He quoted the exact Scripture passages to offset the devil's use of incomplete Scripture. That kind of knowledge of Scripture is amazing. Satan uses *if* and Jesus comes back with the correct Bible quotation. Satan tries to tempt God. He uses *if* three times and Jesus replies, "It is written." Those *ifs* questioned His relationship with God. The second *if* questioned His Father's protection of His Son. The last *if* Satan tries to get the Creator to worship him. He uses anything to try to get us to doubt God.

I say let's fight the way Jesus did—with His Word. To do that, we must learn the Scriptures. We read in Psalm 119:11, "Thy word have I hid in mine heart, that I might not sin against thee."

Once you have Scripture in your mind and heart, when someone asks you to say something that you know is not the truth, you turn to the Bible. You read that the Bible tells us not to bear false witness. It says that lying lips are an abomination to the Lord, but they that deal truly are His delight (Proverbs 12:22).

What about the young lady dressed so provocatively you have to close your eyes not to notice the action? What Scripture could help now? Proverbs 2:19 says, "None that go unto her return again, neither take they hold of the path of life."

Are you ready to reject your Lord for a moment of earthly pleasure? I didn't think so.

The instruction on not judging in Matthew 7:1 will help you avoid your version of why you believe another person behaved badly. The truth is that you really don't know! Passing on your guess makes it difficult for the person to repent and come back to God. Do you want the Lord to judge you that way? Then make a decision to stop judging others, starting today. That is how we learn to be kind to others.

Pull out your Bible and say, "Satan, it is written." That gave you strength, didn't it? "The Lord is my helper I wouldn't fear what man will do to me" (Hebrews 13:6). "God can do exceeding abundantly above what we ask or think" (Ephesians 3:20). These powerful weapons are in Scripture, and they will help us hold on in our personal battle against "self." We can hold on because "It is written." And God keeps His Word.

Dear Lord,

Today we want to be brave in Your might when we face challenges. Our moods change to happy with good news and sad with bad news. Balance us out somewhere in the middle. Help us to remember You are in every situation with us. You keep us anchored in every storm, no matter how it rages. It is Your peace I seek and if, along the way today, I meet answered prayers and unexpected blessings, help me look up to the heavens and thank You for being faithful to us. All I need, You provide. Thank You, Father, for the courage you will give us to make it through *any* storm or strong wind today, no matter where it comes from. Let us find a hiding place in Your Word and stand on Your Word. I have confidence, and because I trust Your Word, I will be brave today.

In Jesus' worthy name, Amen!

Day 6

MOVING DAY

I'm alive! Thank You, God, for another day to live for You.

"In my Father's House are many mansions: if it were not so, I would have told you. I go to prepare a place for you. And if I go and prepare a place for you, I will come again, and receive you unto myself; that where I am, there ye may be also" (John 14:2-3).

Moving can be very hectic. If you are moving today, you have a lot of things to complete. You have to:

- Decide what goes and what gets dumped.
- Determine who gets what and how and when they will pick the things up.
- Overcome your own feelings and thoughts about memories. You may have lived there one year or fifty years. Of course, the longer you have lived in a place, the more attached you have become.

Wow, all that to do before the mover's come!

You also need to find safekeeping for your valuables while you are in transition. When you get to the next place, you worry if all of your belongings will be there intact.

How will all your possessions fit if you are moving in a pickup? Will stuff fall out the back of the truck? Do you have enough strong cord to hold everything? If you are moving to another country, how long will it be before you get your belongings? Will you manage all right until your crate arrives? Moving day is full of anxiety.

Let me tell you one of my moving day miracles. I moved from Maryland to Florida. A family friend, Mark, was to go to the house I sold, collect the discarded items, and go to a free dump on Sunday to unload. I received a call from Mark, saying he had loaded the truck and was at the county dump, but he didn't have county identification, and was unable to dump the trash. As I listened to him, anxiety filled my heart; but what could I do in Florida while he was at the dump in Maryland?

I sent up a prayer. *Lord, You know how hectic moving days are. I don't know how this is going to work out but Mark can't bring the stuff back to my house. I have to get rid of it. Help me know what to do.*

Right away a thought came to me. *Call another neighbor and see if he can find a way to meet Mark.* I thought about Marlon but he wasn't home. I called another neighbor, who also wasn't at home. I called CeCe, a neighbor I knew couldn't do it but I thought she might be able to help find someone who could. She had a cordless telephone and she went to the house of another neighbor, whom I had already called and had not answered the phone. She left her house with the phone in hand and went up the street to the other neighbor's. The first miracle was that her phone didn't cut off. Usually a phone doesn't have that much power to be able to go house to house.

Another neighbor, Marlon, was outside washing his car and this is why he hadn't answered the phone. She told him that someone in Florida wanted to talk to him. I explained my situation, and he said, "I'm on it, Dawn." I gave him Mark's phone number and told him he was sitting at the dump, waiting for someone to help.

Marlon jumped in his truck and drove to the dump. When he arrived, he and Mark drove in Mark's truck to the dumping grounds, and he showed his county identification to indicate that I had been his neighbor and lived right next door to him.

God put people in place and told me whom to call. Mark, Marlon, and CeCe's kindness coupled with God's favor all got the job done. Hence, His child could be worry free. What a story!

You will have your moving day story one day as well. Things will seem impossible, but just send up a prayer and ask God for patience to keep you from angry outbursts. Things will not be done your way and in your time. These are tricks of the enemy to make a wonderful moment miserable. Don't be tempted. Remember, God will give you the strength to make it through the day. On moving day, stand on the promises that cannot fail.

Oh, my Father,

Today all over the world people are moving. Some have to move and have nowhere to move to. Show up for them, Lord, and be their shelter. Talk to them and tell them where they can find housing. Open someone's heart on their behalf to take them in. Make a blessing happen for your sons and daughters who find themselves moving to nowhere.

For others who are dealing with feelings and emotions about the history they're leaving behind, make the transition less painful by reminding them that You left heaven to come here to save us, and it's going to be okay. If tempers flare up a bit, let apologies come just as fast. Help the families know that separation from the homestead causes grieving for all involved. Since we all grieve differently, teach us to be patient with each other.

Above all, remind us that nothing in this world is our home and that paradise with You will be ours if we are faithful in our own earthly home. You loved us so much that You gave your only Son for us (John 3:16).

Thank You for smoothing out some of the wrinkles of moving day. We give You glory because You gave us life. Lamentations 3:22-23 says, "It is of the Lord's mercies that we are not consumed, because his compassions fail not. They are new every morning: great is thy faithfulness."

Amen.

Day 7

MIND-BODY CONFLICT

I'm alive. Thank You, God, for another day to live for You.

"Thy word have I hid in my heart that I may not sin against Thee"
(Psalm 119:11).

The law of the Lord is perfect,

Converting the soul;

The testimony of the Lord is sure,

Making wise the simple.

More to be desired are they than gold.

Yea, than much fine gold:

Sweeter also than honey

And the honeycomb.

"The Law of the Lord is Perfect," Anonymous

*E*ver wonder why your body reacts when you are thinking about doing something wrong? Let me give you an example. Shortly after 9/11, I was traveling to California to my cousin's wedding. I brought a set of knives for their wedding present. I wrapped it nicely in wedding paper, and put a lovely bow on the box. I wanted it to stay well decorated during my air transit. Sometimes when things are checked in the baggage section, they get rearranged and torn up. I carefully packed the gift-wrapped knives in my carry-on luggage without a second thought.

The knives passed through the scanner without a glitch. I still had not remembered they were in the bag. I did not even remember the new law about no knives in carry-on bags. In those days, army personnel walked about the airport with guns. They were serious about carrying out the new law.

I waited to board the plane. I handed my ticket to the attendant and I was informed I had been chosen for a random search of my bag.

That's no problem, I thought.

When the TSA officer opened the suitcases to do the random search, I saw the wedding present. Suddenly, I recalled the new law and I began to shake. My knees got weak. *Will the TSA officer open the gift and find out what I have inside? Should I tell him now so he doesn't cart me off to jail for obviously disobeying the law?*

Then he simply asked me, "Is this a wedding gift?"

I said, "Yes."

He finished his search. He zipped up my carry-on bag and handed it back to me.

In the meantime, I was shaking like a leaf. I could hardly get my boarding card to the attendant. I don't know how I got through except that the Lord covered me in my ignorance. Anyone would have picked up that something wasn't right by my nervousness. My mind made my body react to what I knew was a broken law. Now I pack my carry-on luggage carefully. You can be sure that I follow all the guidelines. My conscience reminded me, both physically and mentally, that I was not in obedience to the law.

This is what God means when He says, "If you hide my words in your heart you won't sin against me" (Psalm 119:11). Whenever we think or act against what we know is right, our conscience is triggered inside. Our hearts start to beat fast and our mouths get dry. We begin to get fidgety and jumpy, or our knees get weak. Some or all of these are physical signs that tell us to back up because we aren't on the right path.

You are about to sin. You are about to bring disgrace to your heavenly Father. You are about to bring disgrace to your family and to yourself. Our minds start racing from one thought to the next. Our consciences play Ping-Pong with us. *Do I do this thing or not?*

When the behavior you are going to do is a good one, you still have the back and forth. But it doesn't come with the physical symptoms of nervousness and guilt. *Should I do this or not?* The nervous response happens because we have committed ourselves to obeying God's Word. Now we are about to do something contrary to what we promised God we would do. He sends in this response mechanism to help us remember that He can keep us from falling. He wants us to know that we don't have to obey the devil. He wants us to know that obedience and faithfulness to Him allows Him to bless us more than we can ever expect.

God is awesome. He offers to help us keep His commandments. He knows we must learn obedience if we are to remain His sons and daughters. We will go through a test from time to time. Whom we choose to listen to will determine whose side we are on—Christ's or Satan's.

"If we have not the Holy Spirit, we are none of His," Paul declares in Romans 8:9. We can obey by following the promptings of the Holy Spirit. One of the roles of the Holy Spirit is to guide us into all truth (see John 16:13). He convicts us when we are making wrong choices. He speaks to our hearts the words we have read in the Bible. He emphasizes the ones that will convince us to pass by the temptation before us. Now our faithfulness must kick in and we can honor God through obedience. God shines when you forsake evil and do good.

We also live more peaceful lives. We don't have to worry about the laws of man because the laws of God include the laws of man. Ever drive at 75 or 80 miles per hour in a 55-mile-per-hour speed limit area? When you see the police officer, what happens? If you are like me, you begin to think of what to say when you are stopped. Your knees get weak.

You think to yourself, "don't let him come behind me." Even if you are not stopped, your heart is almost pounding out of your chest. And you wonder where your legs are, right?

That means the Holy Spirit is saying to you, "Obey the laws of the land. Stop speeding.

Render unto Caesar what is Caesar's and unto God what is God's" (Matthew 22:21). Obeying the laws of man that do not conflict with the laws of God is obeying God as well. When a sinner is tempted to do wrong, God comes in with backup power to help the sinner change his ways by power of the Holy Spirit. Satan shows up, but God also shows up. Satan shows the reason he wants us to sin. God shows us why He wants us to be victorious.

The overcoming power is there for you. Choose right! Become familiar with right by studying and learning God's Word and hiding it in your heart. Meditate on it day and night. Now let us pray for power to overcome our besetting sins.

Dearest Jesus,

We thank You that You made us with a conscience. We thank You that You show up to do battle on our side when we are tempted. We ask for strength this day to do things Your way. When the devil shows up with his tricks and deception, please help us to see it. Reveal the trap to us. Don't let it spring on us suddenly and catch us off guard. We want to be your faithful, obedient sons and daughters.

When we feel the physical symptoms of sin coming on, remind us to choose the right way, the high way. The right way always brings pleasure and satisfaction to You, Lord, and to us. Give us strength to obey Your laws, the laws of the land, the laws of work, the laws of family, the laws of driving, and all laws. We really do know right from wrong. Your children are obedient to You because we are Your children.

Keep us abiding in Your arms today while we deal with our mind and body conflicts. Show up for us, Jesus. We need Your presence continually. We want to be Your letters to the world. These letters must let the world know how abiding, dependent children of God live.

In Jesus' name we pray, Amen.

Day 8

MY LITTLE NIECE

I'm alive. Thank You, God, for another day to live for You.

"The LORD is nigh unto them that are of a broken heart;

and saveth such as be of a contrite spirit"

(Psalm 34:18).

There's someone who loves every sinner

He's calling oh hear him today.

Tis Jesus our blessed redeemer

He's only a prayer away.

"He's Only a Prayer Away," Harold L. Graham

*T*t was a Sunday afternoon I'll never forget. I was getting my hair braided in the basement studio of my hairdresser. My family tried to reach me, but my cell phone did not get good reception in the basement. All the ladies in the shop were having great conversations, as you know can happen at the hairdresser's.

When I was finished, I got in my car and my phone told me I had a message, so I pulled into a nearby plaza. It was from my husband. "I am in the emergency room of the hospital and you need to come here now! Where have you been? It doesn't look good for our little niece."

As I called him back, I suddenly wanted a million questions answered over the phone, but he said, "Just come."

I'm so glad I waited in the plaza parking lot, or I would have been on the highway with even farther to drive before I could turn around and go to the hospital. Even in little things, God guides!

On the way to the hospital, my mind made up all kinds of scenarios. *My little niece is sick with an infection; she had an accident and got a blood clot somewhere and was in surgery getting it fixed.* I was trying to prepare myself for everything but the worst. You know how your mind can take you in a lot of different directions when a crisis hits.

I had to pray hard to stay focused on my driving. I had to pray for strength to face whatever was wrong with my little niece. I had to pray for strength to support her parents and strength to support my children. *Why am I praying this prayer anyway?* I asked myself. I did not know if I could even say it . . . you know the word I'm avoiding by now. I just prayed as I pulled up to the emergency room and took a deep breath.

"Lord," I prayed, "give me strength to be ready to face whatever I must go through."

When I arrived I was immediately ushered into a back conference room, but I passed through the emergency room lobby, there were many people I knew with very sad faces. I even saw one of the ladies who had been at the hairdresser with me and left about thirty minutes before I did. *This is not good.*

In the conference room, I was met with the news that my little niece had just died.

Ever had one of those unreal, crushing, crumbling, shattering, punishing, terrible, gut- wrenching, cruel moments in your life? The next thing I knew, my mind started banging out questions: *Did they (the hospital teams) do everything? Are they sure she is dead? Jesus, can You just come down here and raise her back to life? This can't be happening, not to my little niece! She is such a wonderful child. Respectful! Kind! Pleasant! Full of laughter! Athletic! A friend-to-the-friendless kind of child.*

After we said our goodbyes to my niece in the emergency area, which was the hardest thing I have ever had to do, the hospital chaplain invited us to the chapel. We sang songs of encouragement; we prayed, sang some more, and the pastor reminded us of four things:

1. The reason Jesus came and died on a cross is so the penalty for our sins would be paid, so my little niece can live again! She accepted Jesus into her young life.
2. He can and will comfort us, though we might hurt for a long time. That's the kind of work my Jesus does. Over the next months and years we would get to know Him as a God of comfort. The words I wanted to say were in my mind but I could not communicate them to anyone else. 2 Corinthians 1:4 says, "He comforts us in all our troubles so that we can comfort others. When they are troubled, we will be able to give them the same comfort God has given us" (NLT).
3. Jesus knows all about grief. He lost His friend Lazarus and cried when He heard of his death (John 11:35).
4. We must all one day go the way of the earth. From this life none of us will make it out alive. This is not a practice run.

I encourage you to live life like my little niece did and remember that in John 14:2 Jesus said, "In my Father's house are many mansions: if it were not so, I would have told you. I go to prepare a place for you."

Lord,

Many of my readers have had similar heartbreaks. Remind us that You came to end all this pain, even though we have to pass through the fingers of temporary death. Nothing can hold us because death could not hold You. Praise your name, oh, God of comfort, and keep my little niece secure until I can see her again.

Amen.

Day 9

EXPECT CHALLENGES

I'm alive. Thank You, God, for another day to live for You.

"And why take ye thought for raiment? Consider the lilies of the field,
how they grow; they toil not, neither do they spin: And yet I say unto
you, that even Solomon in all his glory was not arrayed like one of these"
(Matthew 6:28-29).

*C*heer up, my friends. I have a little-accepted fact for you today. Are
you ready? Here it comes: With life come challenges. We live with
the reality of those words every day, don't we? One of the challenges many
face is physical changes. You can thank God if you were born "normal,"
free of physical challenges. Your legs, arms, even your eyes and face work
fine, and all of your internal organs are working according to normal,
healthy standards. Your heart is beating, your lungs are clearing oxygen,
and your kidneys are putting out urine and clearing toxins. Your mouth and
stomach work well, maybe too well, as the weight inches upward. Overall,
most of us live in physically great bodies. That's good!

How do we deal with news of a disease in this perfect body? How does
one deal with the news that he or she has to lose an arm or leg?

You may begin journaling about your day, saying, "It was a blood-filled day. I never expected to even make it through the day." Or, "I didn't even know what hit me when the stroke took me away from life for three months. My face became twisted, and my words became unrecognizable to me and others. The words I wanted to say were in my mind and I could not communicate them to anyone else. My arms and legs were not cooperating with my brain. I asked, 'Lord, what is this?'"

Some have to deal with outwardly disfiguring and weakening conditions like multiple sclerosis or a discoloration of the skin caused by renal dialysis. Bell's Palsy causes one side of the face to droop. Cancer changes people as well. Many have involuntary hair and weight loss.

But I'll say it again: Cheer up, my friend! You have been called upon to help Your Savior bear His cross with an infirmity. Must Jesus bear the cross alone and all the world go free? Not at all. There is a cross for everyone and there is a cross for me. Jesus took beatings for our healing and for our salvation. Did you hear me? Our healing and salvation.

Some people get better and return to normal. When that's the case, "Praise God" should be your song every day! Share your story and thanksgiving. Some live on with the challenge; others may die. Remember, this life is not a practice run. None of us will make it out alive.

For those of us who must live our lives with altered body images, let me encourage you today. Look from the inside out. Don't worry about what people say to you or about you. Hurtful comments come from the mouths of people who have not experienced pain the way you are right now. "What's wrong with your eye?" "Look at her, she has no hair." "He has skin that looks blotchy." "Won't you hurry up? You are too slow." "He/she is so fat."

Remember, you are still who God made you to be—a beautiful person with a soul to save.

Instead of complaining, thank the parts of you that are working fine, such as your lung or kidney. "Thank you for doing the job of two, since one is not working. Thank God for giving me two lungs and kidneys, so when one fails there is another that can take over." Or how about, "Thank you stomach for digesting my food? Thank you legs, even though you limp, for not going away. Thank you for the role you play in helping me get around independently."

Remember, no matter how bad off you are dear friend, someone is overcoming a challenge worse than yours. Jesus says that when He comes back for us, He will give us new bodies. If we were all perfect, we might not want Him to come back.

He promises the lame will leap, the dumb will speak, and we will be given new bodies. We will get rid of our crutches and be without walkers. Our backs will straighten with the life of youth, and there will be no more hunching over. Memory will return; gravity will release the wrinkles!

If you have something you are patiently waiting on Jesus to fix, He will do His great work for you as He did when He was here. You may have to wait until He returns, but He hasn't broken one promise yet. Remain faithful and look from the inside out. That means reminding yourself that you still are you. You are the funny, friendly, beautiful, kind, giving, family-loving person you always were. That doesn't change, even if you have become grumpy and ornery. Let yesterday be the last of it.

Do a good deed, smile, read the Bible, and see how much God loves you. When you expect a challenge from life, the challenge becomes more bearable. You may not be the same as you were the day before, but God says you are more beautiful to Him than the lilies of the field. Encourage yourself today: God is faithful, and He has a reason for allowing you to experience your hardship.

In 2 Corinthians 12:7-10, Paul talks about his thorn in the side. Three times he asked the Lord to remove it. The Clear Word Bible explains that it was poor eyesight. He told God he needed to see to do His work more effectively. God might have said, You (Paul), would have too much pride, self, and boasting with eyesight. I need you to depend on Me, not on yourself.

Stay humble. We cannot get into heaven full of pride. These infirmities help keep pride away. God is wise. He is not random with challenges. He uses them to save us and others. When others see us praising God in spite of our trials, it gives them courage to make it through their trials. God is then glorified and praised. When you are weak, He is strong in you. God's grace will carry you through. Let us pray for strength to face all of life's challenges.

Dear Jesus, our loving Friend,

We know You are a healing God. We know healing comes from You. Help those of us bearing physical challenges to be prepared to tell our stories. When we arrive in heaven, You will want us to tell others of Your sustaining grace. As long as we have to bear up, keep us from complaining. We can gain strength from You and courage to go happily on our journey with praise and thanksgiving.

For those who receive complete healing, help their mouths to be full of praise and thanksgiving. Let the miracle You work for them be a living witness of Your greatness. May they comfort others who pass through a similar corridor of pain. May their stories be full of the wonder-working power found in the blood of Jesus. Help us to remember that it is by Your stripes, bleeding stripes, we are healed. If we have been healed, let us shout praises to You every day for being our substitute.

For those of us still pressing on the upward way carrying our maladies, let us hide them behind the cross You so willingly bore, and keep praising You. Keep praising God! We will find burdens lifted and made lighter at Calvary. On the cross of Calvary You suffered for us so that one day we, too, can all be challenge-free. Thank You, God, for all You do for me. I'll bear up for you, whatever the cost. I'll keep on trying; I'll keep on fighting; I'll never give up. In Your strength, grace, and mercy, I'll make it home someday.

In Jesus' strength I pray, Amen.

Day 10

STANDING ON GOD'S PROMISES

I'm alive. Thank God for another day to live for Him!

"I have desired His words more than my daily bread"

(Job 23:12, cwv).

Standing on the promises of Christ my king,

Through eternal ages let His praises ring;

Glory in the highest I will shout and sing,

Standing on the promises of God.

Standing, standing, standing on the promises of God.

"Standing on the Promises," R. Kelso Carter

That song has a nice cadence, rhymes well, and provides an upbeat tune to begin the day. I enjoy singing that song. The words we sing must ring true to us. If we are to mean what we say, we should also mean what we sing! Never thought of that one, huh? When we sing, the words have a way of hanging around in our conscious mind a bit longer than if we speak them. This is especially true if they come in a catchy tune.

Marketers count on that in the jingles they produce, hoping you will remember the jingle in the store and buy their products. It often works too well, especially with children. Ever been in the store and your children only want a particular brand of hotdog? That's what they heard and that's what they remember.

Let's use that to work in our favor in building confidence in God's Word. Play your favorite spiritual CD over and over while traveling in your car or at home instead of listening to other songs on the radio. Instead of reading a novel, maybe you can put some uplifting music on your iPod while you work out. Then memorize a Scripture verse or two every week. I find that I memorize Scripture easier when I know the story around it or the context it is taken from.

Let me give you an example. In 2 Chronicles 14, the story of King Asa, a good king of Israel, is told. He took down all the strange gods, their altars, and their images. He built up fences and cities in Judah and sought the Lord. Because of that the Lord was pleased. When an army came up against him, Asa prayed, "Oh, Lord, Thou art our God. Let not man prevail against us" (2 Chronicles 14:11). In 2 Chronicles 15:7, God promises, "Be strong therefore and let not your hands be weak for your work shall be rewarded!"

This is a promise. Plug your name into the text. Be strong, Dawn, Carolyn, Maryanna, Brenda, Brian, Cory, David, Linda, Steven, Faith. Let not your hands be weak. Maybe you're experiencing weak hands from a stroke or surgery. Your work (faith in God) shall be rewarded. Some will remember the "be strong" part of the passage—your work (faith in God) shall be rewarded.

Recite that Scripture during the day. Any time you get tempted to be weak, think of what King Asa did. He cried to the Lord, "Let no man prevail against me." He rested in the Lord. The Bible says the Lord smote the enemy before Asa and Judah, and the Lord's victory was Asa's victory also. What comfort, what promise we have when we are obedient to the Lord as Asa was.

That's what standing on the promises means. Take God at His Word, which cannot fail. If you do get weak, He has a promise for you in His Word. 2 Corinthians 12:9 says, "And He said my grace is sufficient for you, for my strength is made perfect in weakness."

God is strongest for you when you are weak and worn out for Him. Bear up, ol' soldier. The power of God rests upon you in your infirmities. The power of God rests upon you when you remain humble under emotional fire. God says, Come rest in my arms on my shoulder. I will carry you while I take care of your evil enemies.

Job sustained himself with the words of God. In Job 23:12 he says, "He esteems the words of God more than his necessary food." Do you get an idea of how much faith you need to overcome difficult trials? There are times you will need the words and strength from God more than you need food.

Start learning and reading now so you are always preparing for battle. Sharpen your sword and polish your shield. Reading this devotional daily gives you another weapon. If you find one devotional in particular to be strengthening for you, read it several times. Ask God to help you make the changes necessary to keep you in line with His plan for your life. Turn to Him when you are tempted to be weak. You will overcome and your work will be rewarded. Get ready for the reward of blessings today.

Lord,

We are trusting You with all the circumstances of our lives. This is a brand new day and we don't know what the day will bring. But we know someone who is the Alpha and Omega, the beginning and the end. We know someone who is from everlasting to everlasting and still God. You know the path I take before a word is on my lips. Take charge of my day today.

Lord, let no man prevail against Thee through me. I'm hiding in Thee; I'm standing on Your promises in order to make it today. Help me keep a prayer on each breath so I can keep You consciously close to me today. And I promise to give You praise.

In the dependable name of Jesus, Amen.

Day 11

MY SISTER AND I

I'm alive! Thank You, God, for another day to live for You!

"A friend loveth at all times and a brother is born for adversity"
(Proverbs 17:17).

My sister and I were very close growing up. We were close in age and many people thought we were twins. She is almost two years older than me. She always joked and said that she was the more beautiful of the two. Because my sister is shorter than I am, I would jokingly respond, "But why is beauty so short? You can't even see it."

Growing up, we shared secrets about boys we had a crush on, wedding plans, and children's names we liked. When we were in high school, I realized she would graduate a year before I would and leave me behind. I couldn't have that. So I completed my high school in three years. Off to college we went together (poor Dad).

After we were married, we shared ways that worked to make our marriages better. We were there for the births of each other's children. We went through disappointments and celebrated happy holidays together. We were close. Do you have a sister or brother like that?

Then the fateful day came when she had a massive stroke. She lived seven hundred miles away from me. As soon as I heard about her situation, I left work immediately. I caught the next plane out and was by her bedside by the afternoon. What I saw did not look good. The doctors offered little hope. But I know a man named Jesus who can heal the sick. In fact, this did not take Him by surprise. I told Him, "Please fix this situation to work best for all. If my sister lives or dies, my faith in You will not waiver."

I cried and cried when I saw my sister, the strong one of the family, sprawled out in the intensive care unit bed with tubes everywhere. That was traumatic. I'm sure some of you know exactly how I felt because you have had a close family member or friend with a similar experience. She was later sent to a specialty hospital for her condition in my hometown. And it gave me a chance to love her through her rehabilitation. I really thank God for that. Friends and family rallied around us both to foster recovery and help in any way needed. Some even gave financial support.

If you know someone going through a difficult time, offer your time, talent, or finances. Bless them with a cooked supper, and be sure to check food preferences because ill persons usually have dietary restrictions. Make yourself a blessing. If you are a hair care person, offer to provide that service for the sick. Go sing some uplifting songs if singing is your talent. Relieve the caregiver to have time away alone.

These are just a few examples. I am sure you can think of more. If you can't think of something, ask what you can do. Listen to God. He can give you ideas for things you can do. It will return to you ten to a hundred times.

Time has passed, and she is with her family where she wants to be. However, now I cannot have a close sister relationship with her as before, due to her new mental status, unresolved family issues, and distance apart. Oh, the pain I feel over this loss. She is still alive but I have had to make major emotional separation adjustments. For a long time, it felt like pulling glued paper apart. I had to go to God for strength every day so I could make it without crying. Guess what? God came through and is coming through every day.

I thank Him for letting me love so deeply in the first place. I thank Him for sparing her life for her family. I thank God for teaching me that He is the one I should love so deeply. God is never sick, dead, absent, or uncaring. It is after Jesus and Jesus only that I should be hungering and thirsting to fill the sister void in my life. 2 Corinthians 1:4 says, "Who comforts us in all our tribulation, that we may be able to comfort them which are in any trouble, by the comfort with which we ourselves are comforted of God" (AKJV).

We are blessed and comforted when in our pain we reach out to help others through their pain. God, You are awesome, and I'll love You forever. And I'll praise You for working all things together for our good. The scar is still there, and if I go brooding about my loss, I forget that God is planning. God takes away the pain only when His design for using it is fulfilled.

I don't want to forget God's mission. I will wait until He comes to make all things plain for me. My sister and I will be reunited physically and mentally in heaven. As for my sister, I pray that her pain is relieved and her mind is right. God is able to do that also. Her courage and resolve are stronger now than ever. She just wants to see Jesus and be with Him forever. I thank God for that.

My friend, if you are dealing with similar pain today, remember that family and friends are born for adversity, and we are to love anyway at all times, especially through crisis. God will give us the strength to make it through. There is no greater love than to love when one cannot get love in return when desire is deep. Let us pray together now for that greater love today.

Dear Lord,

The pain is thick and sickening and only You can remedy it for us. Wipe away those hot tears and replace them with sympathy and a resolve to be a supportive brother or sister to our disabled loved ones. Give us patient endurance and gentleness that can only come from You as we care for our afflicted loved ones. We need a double portion of kindness, patience, and knowledge to care for our sick loved one. We need to learn everything. We need to learn so that we can teach our handicapped loved one. It is not easy. Some of us will not be able to communicate with our loved one verbally and that is frustrating.

Lord, please help us to make the correct guess as to what they need. Give us strength to lift, pull, and carry wheelchairs and other supportive devices without injuring ourselves. Help us to remember that someday we will all need a brother or sister to lean on. Please keep us happy while we are working for our family or friend. Let us see them as You see them. Let us care for them as if we were caring for You, Jesus. You said, "As you have done it unto the least of these my brethren you have done it unto me" (Matthew 25:40). That keeps us a bit more loving and our task less burdensome.

When we think of all You suffered for us, surely we can carry a cross for You. All we ask, dear Lord, is for You to supply us with Your strength and remind us that Your perfect will, carried out, brings perfect rewards and blessings. At a time of need like this, I pray this prayer to You, God, because You know my situation.

I pray this in Jesus' name, Amen.

Day 12

UNLOCK THE BLESSINGS

I'm alive. Thank God for another day to live for Him!

"If I regard iniquity in my heart, the Lord will not hear me" (Psalm 66:18).

*P*eople say, "I pray all the time, and it seems God does not answer my prayers. Why is that?" I am not able to give all the answers to that question. The Bible gives answers, though. So I will point those out. Then you must evaluate your own life and see if you need to change anything so you can get your blessings.

The Bible makes it clear that if you do certain things, your prayers are hindered (Psalm 66:18). That is serious. You and I need to take heed because we do not want our blessings withheld, do we? Are we ready for some heart clearing work? We must give up cherished sins. Sin is knowing and willfully breaking any of God's commandments. These commandments can be found in Exodus 20:3-17 and throughout the Bible. Some sins, like habitual lying, are so deep in us; we lie and don't even realize we are lying.

Someone may ask, "What is your dress size?" That is a question that often produces a lie, especially if we are discontented with ourselves. "What time did you come in last night?" We lie when we don't want our parents to know how long we have been out. Before we breathe a cherished sin like lying takes hold of our tongues and out pops a lie. That is a blessing blocker, so we must weed it out.

Another thing that blocks our blessing is insincere worship. Isaiah 58:2-5 says that you fast and pray but still do your own thing. You act eager and delighted to know God's way. But day after day, no change is made in your behavior or your heart, to become more like Jesus. This means to love our fellow man, we must be more humble. We jump and shout hallelujah in church and laugh when our minister touches on our areas of weakness, with no plans for change. That is insincere worship.

Another way insincere worship shows up is when we hear a sermon or read a Scripture passage and say, "Hmm . . . I wish so and so were here. They need to hear this." The point is that *you* are here. *You* need to hear the message. *You* are the one that needs change. Instead of looking for the speck in your brother's eye, consider the large speck in your eye first.

God wants us to fix ourselves up. When you learn a new truth about yourself, stop trying to fix up someone else. Change your behavior. Others will get the message better by your example than by your explanation.

Another blessing blocker is an unforgiving spirit. Mark 11:25-26 says, "Whenever you stand praying, forgive, if you have anything against anyone, so that your Father who is in heaven will also forgive you your transgressions. But if you do not forgive, neither will your Father who is in heaven forgive your transgressions" (NASV).

Also, in Matthew 5:23-24, the Bible says if you are praying at the altar and remember that your brother has something against you (not you against your brother), leave your gift, go take care of the problem, then come back and pray. In other words, "Go kiss and make up," then come back and pray so your prayers can be answered and your blessings are not blocked. The Lord doesn't want to hear from you until your relationships with your fellow man are cleared up. He still works on your behalf and takes care of you, but, boy, do we block blessings. We miss out on a lot of gifts God's planned for us.

The next blessing blocker is the misuse of spiritual gifts. Matthew 25:4-30 talks of the talents God gives as money. It has a dual meaning of vocal talents, teaching, preaching, encouragement, or any of the spiritual gifts Paul talks about in Ephesians 4:11-13. God uses talents to edify the church and build up God's people. If you have a gift and refuse to use it for God's glory, you are blocking your blessings.

Imagine if we all used our gifts and talents to praise and honor God. This world would be a better place, wouldn't it? Heaven will be full of people who will use their talents to glorify God. So let's practice down here now. If you have talent you are using to glorify Satan, switch your commander-in-chief today. God keeps His promises; Satan cannot. Satan has nothing to give us in the end but death. Why sing, work or act for his kingdom when he has no reward for your allegiance?

This next blessing blocker hits home. It is unity in the home (see 1 Peter 3:6-7). Do you have family members in your home not speaking to one another? Do you have family members in your home speaking angrily at one another? Are games of avoidance played in your home? Is there laughter and togetherness in your home? Is there prayer time together? Are there lots of prayer and affirmations of each other? That is what God wants His children practicing down here. Husbands and fathers be tender, understanding, committed, and forgiving. Wives honor and love your husband, so your blessing might be received.

The final area I want to mention that hinders your blessings is lacking faith. James 1:6-7 says, "But when he asks, he must believe and not doubt, because he who doubts is like a wave of the sea, blown and tossed by the wind. That man should not think he will receive anything from the Lord" (NIV).

When Jesus was on earth healing the sick, He often told the followers whom He healed according to their faith. Some were healed, not by their own faith, but the faith of those who brought them to Jesus. We must be willing to change our ways so that God can pour out so much blessing that we don't have enough room to receive it.

Ask God for courage and determination to make these changes. You can begin by obeying and praying in Jesus' name. Remember, Jesus has an unlimited supply of grace and mercy. Ask according to God's will and don't doubt God's power to hear your cry for help to do His will. Then when you pray heaven's door will open wide. The prayers you pray get to God because your heart is not full of evil. The more we give of ourselves to Jesus to be cleaned up, the more prayers get answered. You will want to clean up more and more and begin to pray like David, "Create in me a clean heart, O God, and renew a right a spirit within me."

Ah, prayers like that Jesus loves to answer. We have a lot of praying to do to get evil out of our hearts.

Dear God,

We have discovered that we have some evil ways in us that minimize our prayers. We have cherished sins, insincere worship, unforgiving spirits, misused spiritual gifts, discord and strife in our homes, and a lack of faith in You. This causes doubt. Lord, we are sorry for going on this long in our sinful ways. Now that You have shown us what we have to do to unlock our blessings, please unblock our blessings. We pray for Your power. We can only change if You give us Your power. We cannot change ourselves. We need Your help. Lord, help us to see the ugliness in ourselves. Help us to see how much pain we cause You by continuing in our evil ways. Now that You have exposed us to ourselves, we are responsible to ask You for help to make changes.

Please, God, whatever it takes to clean out our hearts, do it. We want above anything else to be like You. We want You to recognize Yourself in us, so when You come You can take us back to heaven with You. Please give us a made up mind to do Your will. Remove us from our sinful ways and help us to depend on You as our new commander-in-chief. Thank You for being willing to take us all in and keep us in your arms while You work on our hearts. Thank You for Your grace and mercy that protects our salvation while You work on us. Thank You for the example of Jesus, Who shows us the way.

Thank You for Your undying love for us that never leaves us to flounder on our own without direction. Thank You for the Bible, which is full of Your words, promises, encouragement, and direction for us. Thank You for thinking about all we would need to make it through this world of woe before we were even born. You are some kind of God. We love You, we adore You, and we promise to serve You until we die.

In the worthy name of Jesus, Amen.

Day 13

LORD, TEACH US TO PRAY

I'm alive. Thank God for another day to live for Him!

"This, then, is how you should pray: 'Our Father in heaven, hallowed be
your name, your kingdom come, your will be done on earth as it is in
heaven. Give us today our daily bread. Forgive us our debts, as we also
have forgiven our debtors. And lead us not into temptation,
but deliver us from the evil one"
(Matthew 6:9-13, NIV).

*S*ome people have said to me, "Dawn, I don't know how to pray. You
say, 'Pray every day,' and I don't know what to say. I kneel down
and I fall asleep or I start thinking about a song on the radio or a television
show that I watched. Sometimes I just have to pray out loud the Lord's
prayer or a prayer I learned a long time ago. I can't just pray. To be honest,
sometimes I fall asleep on my knees."

Here is a little help for you. God's Word says in John 14:14, "If you ask
anything in my name, I will do it." The first thing to do is to ask for God's
help as you kneel to pray. Say a version of "Lord, I don't know how to talk
to You in prayer. Show me how."

Take thirty seconds—some will need more time—to pray for all the people who have asked you to pray for them. Keep prayer request lists going, if necessary. Take another thirty seconds to praise God. Then pray for your home and finally for yourself.

Don't keep your prayers selfish. I know we have a long way to go to be like the Lord, but intercessory prayer on behalf of others is necessary. Pray for the young people you know who may have left the Lord. Ask God for a loving and tender heart toward all His children. A special prayer you can ask the Lord for is acceptance of all people who are different from you. Pray for people you cannot figure out. Do you know people who are just difficult to get along with? Pray for them.

Pray for your pastors and your church leadership. Ask God to keep them from corruption and keep them preaching Bible-based truths that will give you strength on your Christian journey. Pray for your missionaries in foreign lands who are spreading God's Word. Pray for their provisions and protection. Pray for your world leaders, asking God to keep them sane. Ask God to guide their thoughts to what is best for their country and for the world.

Pray for the military. Pray for your sons and daughters in the military who are risking their lives every day for your freedom and mine. Pray protection for others, fighting in the danger zones of the world. Pray they will soon return home. Pray for people you know who are carrying extra crosses, like stroke, cancer, or kidney failure victims or people with multiple losses in their families, and for the newly divorced or widowed. Pray for the orphans, the homeless, and I'm sure you can add others to your list.

Praise God in your prayers. Acknowledge His sovereignty and grace. Thank Him for loving you and for giving you a desire to want to pray. Praise can go on and on as you feel it. Thank Him for His sacrifice for you. Acknowledge Him as your creator.

Next, pray for love in your home. Pray for each child and his or her needs. Pray for your immediate family. Do you have any family issues that only God can fix? Pray about those issues. Are you in an extended family with issues? Pray for each person in your extended family who needs your intercession. You will feel better and God will begin working on their behalf.

Now ask God for things that you need. Are you stretched as far as you can as an employee, parent, home engineer, spiritual leader for the family, etc.? Ask God to show you how to stop fretting. Ask Him to help you trust Him and give you faith to know that He is working things out for you.

Is there someone you have not forgiven? Do you hold someone in your heart, thinking, *I will never be bothered with that person again*? Really pray and ask God to give you His forgiving spirit. Remember, this is essential, so that your blessings from God are not blocked. Love does not hold grudges.

Power over my tongue is something that I ask for daily. I pray to remove or clean out selfishness and pride that may have grown up over- night in my heart. Ask for the house or the car or the material thing that you want if it is His will to work it out. Pray for salvation. Come boldly before the throne of God. If you need a loan or a mortgage for your home and the odds are stacked against you, pray. When you are a child of God, He wants to show off through you. Go to your Father and make your requests known to Him.

Pray for traveling mercies for the day while you and your family mem- bers are traveling. Things happen out there quickly. Within seconds you can go from life to death with any number of injuries in between. You need God driving beside you, so invite Him in. Pray to God to remind you often to take time to know Him better. Pray for a conviction to study His Word daily and to keep Him on your mind.

Finally, pray that you will give God glory. Pray in Jesus' name. Pray for strength to stay in the Christian race. Pray that sinfulness will not overtake you. Pray for spiritual growth. All in the praiseworthy name of Jesus.

In any of those areas, you can spend longer than thirty seconds if you need to. There are times when you are sorely distressed and you pray to God for victory. You may need several hours or a whole night in prayer. Jesus often spent whole nights in prayer, especially when the temptation was great. Remember, demons tremble when one soul is on their knees talking to the heavenly Father requesting some of His power to overcome the enemy. Satan is the one that makes you confused or sleepy. Don't fall prey to him. If you have to, write down the names of people you are praying for. Read the list out loud to God. He likes that. He already knows, but there is something about the request coming from one child of God for another child of God. He wants everyone blessed. Then everyone will be able to give a testimony of how someone prayed for them and look at them now. You will be blessed, having been a part of the praying group.

You'll be able to truthfully encourage a sister or a brother by saying you have been praying for them.

Form prayer groups in your church or become part of one already in place. See the wonderful things that can happen when you pray. Imagine the ripple effect when the whole church prays for a miracle and it happens. God is glorified. Our praises and hosannas go up to Him and join in with the angels' praise.

The prayers in the Bible are many; read some of them. Jesus prays for His disciples. Peter prays three little words, "Jesus, save me." We can find some of Daniel's prayer in Daniel 9:16. The Bible also includes great prayers of Hezekiah, Jehoshaphat, and Esther. All these prayers are very inspiring. See how your prayers can be more than just the same repetitive peanut butter and jelly sandwiches every day.

As you go deeper with God, you will start to pray from a broken heart, with conviction. You will pray with the faith that God will do what He says He will do. James 1:6 says, "But let him ask in faith, nothing wavering. For he that wavereth is like a wave of the sea driven with the wind and tossed."

Then hear God speak to you about which way to go in your life. Yes, He will speak to you! He will stand up and fight your battles for you. Yes, He will save you and your children. He will provide for you. Yes, He will show up in the courtroom and in the sickroom. That is just the way my Father is; that's just the way. Let us talk with Him now.

Dear God,

Thank You for making a way for us to talk to You directly. Thank You that we can confess our sins and our faults to You ourselves. Part of the reason You came to earth was to be our high priest forever and we thank You for that. Help us to let other prayer warriors know our prayer requests so they can intercede to You also. Keep us awake when we need to pray to You. Help us to pray without ceasing as we think of someone. Remind us to pray for that person by a whisper of their name. Instead of talking about people to another person, give us a prayer for them instead. Remind us that when we say "Our Father," it unites all Your children as brothers and sisters and You are pleased with that. Thank You for responding quickly to our prayers.

In your name, God the Father, Jesus the Son, and the Holy Spirit Who sends the power, Amen.

Day 14

LOOK FOR THE FLOWERS

I'm alive! Thank You, God, for another day to live for You.

"I am the rose of Sharon and the lily of the valleys"
(Song of Solomon 2:1).

Today let us practice appreciating the beauty of nature. For instance, there are several types of flowers all around us. Places where it is warm and moist all the time have abundantly more flowers than where it is dry and the seasons change. Everywhere a flower shows up or a flower blooms, it spreads beauty. God uses beauty to let us know He has made everything beautiful (Ecclesiastes 3:11). He comforts us and brings us joy through flowers.

Have you ever had a florist deliver flowers to you for one occasion or another? How did you feel towards your sender? Did you feel happy, special, rewarded, or appreciated? Now I encourage you to take it a step further and appreciate *the Maker* of those flowers. He sent His sunlight and rain to grow those flowers so your kind sender of the bouquet could have something to send you. Before you read the name tag as to who your earthly sender is, thank your heavenly sender.

Let me give you an example from my life of how God used His flowers to remind me He is by my side. Not long ago I had surgery on my throat. When I was finally brought back to my room, I found I was unable to catch my breath. Not being able to breathe can be a scary thing! I saw the room fill up with doctors and nurses and a red cart was dragged in. I heard them paging my doctor over the intercom to come to my room—now! I saw my mother's face as the nurse escorted her away, looking extremely worried. It took everything I had to be calm because anxiety in me would only make it harder to catch my breath.

Then the Lord did something very special for me. He sent someone to my bedside with a bouquet of flowers who said, "This is for you. You will be okay. You are loved." Immediately, I knew God was going to see me through this episode.

How did this ministering angel get into my room with flowers at such a crucial time? I'll never know. The nurses and doctors were scurrying around and here comes Jesus with a gift only He can create. He said that everything will be okay. What an assurance, what a gift. I really appreciate flowers now. I praise God when I see beauty. I soak it in and think what a dreary place the world would be without flowers. I thank God He reminded me of His love when He sent me my flowers. I will never forget Him or the angel He sent to deliver them.

You are a flower to the world today. You can send flowers or you can use your words like flowers to brighten someone's day. When someone gives you good news, say something like "You have just sprinkled my day with roses. Thank you for sharing your good news with me."

Or if you see someone looking very lonely today, say, "You look like a fresh bouquet of flowers." It brings the Creator's natural beauty into your compliment.

Jesus wants us to be flowering plants all around our world today. If it is winter where you are today and no natural flowers are blooming, become the bloom in your environment with your words and kind actions. We will be like Jesus since he is the Rose of Sharon and Lily of the Valley.

Aren't you glad we serve a God who creates beauty? You are beautiful. You are one of His special flowers. He took time to make you beautiful. Remember, He has made everything beautiful, including you.

Smile, shine, and beautify the world today, wherever you are. Infect someone with thoughts of beauty. Give someone a bouquet of flowers and tell him or her that the bouquet is from God through you.

If you receive a bouquet today, thank God for creating the flowers, and then appreciate your sender with words that beautify him or her. Aren't you glad God made such a splendid variety of flowers just for us? Let us pray and thank Him.

Dear beautiful Savior,

How beautiful You must be. You created this world and did not leave out the flowers. They bring so much joy to our eyes and spirits. May we become more grateful to You today by acknowledging your creative power and all the flowers around us. Let us pause to recognize and thank You when we see flowers.

When You send special deliveries like You did for me, remind us to give You praise with our own lips. Please, God, let us not be ungrateful; the world would be intolerable without the beauty of nature and flowers. Thank You for the beauty and color You give us in flowers. Thank You for what You say to us each time we see a flower. "I love you. You are special to me. Be happy today. Here's a reward for you from me."

Oh, Jesus, You are wonderful. Thank You for thinking ahead at creation. You knew that we would need beauty. Thank You for the beauty that remains in nature and flowers, even though this world is messed up because of our sins. You are an awesome God! Good looking out for us!

In Jesus' lovely name, Amen.

Day 15

FANTASY

I'm alive. Thank God for another day to live for Him!

"But godliness with contentment is great gain" (1 Timothy 6:6).

*E*ver wonder why life is so hard? I heard an answer once that sobered me. Are you ready? *You expected it to be easy.*

When you prepare for a hard exam, you get ready, you study, you stay up at night, you read over your material thoroughly, and you go in prepared. Now suppose you thought the same exam was going to be easy, a cake walk, and you went in and found you were not properly prepared — not only would you fail the exam, but you would also declare it a hard exam.

My friend, allow me to let you in on a secret so you are not unprepared. If you don't already know it, life is hard and you must toughen up and get ready for the battles. One of the reasons life tosses us about is that we expect easy street or entitlement. We think we'll automatically receive great outcomes! Life is often the opposite of that. Life is what happens *after* you plan.

Imagination plays a large role in our views of life. When we look at someone, in our minds we come up with who that person is and what he or she is about. We place him in a nice little category. For instance, you may see someone driving what you consider a fancy car. Your imagination says the person is rich, healthy, and has it going on. You may not know that the car is rented, deep debts are owed to the bank, the driver may be on the way to the doctor to see about ill health, or the driver could be in some kind of trouble or having family problems.

Instead of thinking about the real life situation, we fantasize. Suddenly, we become miserable because our car is not a "fancy one." Or we may not be on our way to success. Let me help to curb all those passions today.

Paul said, "Whatever situation you find yourself in be content" (Philippians 4:11). He also said, "If you have food and raiment, be content" (1 Timothy 6:8). When we start looking at other people and assume that they have it better than what we have it, we are in the coveting camp. Let's get out of there quickly!

The 10th Commandment says, "Thou shall not covet" (Exodus 20:17). *Life is wonderful where you are—make it so.* If you have health, rejoice. If you have ill health, at least you are alive and still can feel pain. Dead people are not so privileged. Do you have food in your belly? Even have extra supplies in the pantry? Be grateful. Thank God for His provision.

Some people are exposed to fantasy through watching television or listening to unhealthy music, in which the lyrics tell you to do wrong when you should do right. This is a form of fantasy. Take your spouse and say wonderful things about him or her until you see the real magic about what you say come true. That's reality.

Some fantasize that a smaller body size will bring happiness. I have seen large-bodied people lose weight and become unhappy because all they fantasized about with a small body did not happen. A happy life is being content with your size no matter what it is. Ask God for strength to do hard life changes that will make you become healthy. It takes more effort to be healthy than to lose weight. Drink water, eat healthier foods, consume fewer sweets, decrease junk food, eat smaller portions as your age goes up, and exercise. It can be hard for some.

A hard life for some is spending within your budget, not buying on credit because you think it will make your life better. It won't; that would be fantasy. But after going into debt you have to work hard to pay the bill and interest and you risk your happiness, spend more time away from your children and spouse working, and have less to give to God's causes.

Are you developing a shopping habit that is hard to break? Stop, my friend, and ask yourself if that item was necessary in the bigger scheme of things. Put your money or credit card back in your pocket, and keep it there. I have heard of people getting the diamond they had wanted for so long, and when they wear it no one even notices it.

Somehow we think the media, our dreams, or the fascination for things in our heads is reality. That is not reality. Life is taking the kids to school every day and picking them up in the afternoon. It is running to their school from work during lunchtime to see that they get their lunch that they forgot at home—the same lunch you got up early to prepare for them. Life is forgiving your spouse for some off-the-wall remark because we often say not-so-smart things too. Forgiveness is a must. That is life. Hard life. The rewards are more satisfaction and contentment though. Easy, no; doable, yes.

Get those "life is easy" fantasy ideas out of your head and prepare for a hard exam. In 2 Timothy 2:3 we read, "Endure hardness, as a good soldier of Jesus Christ." Pray your way through your struggles. Sing when fantasies come into your head and the deceiver tells you that you don't have to put up with this or that. Yes, you do! That is the stuff that builds character. That's the overcoming you have to do to get to the tree of life in paradise. If you don't pass your test in this round, God will have to keep giving you the same exam over and over again until you get it. Learn to depend on Him.

Don't try to force your dreamed-up fantasy to happen with a dreamed- up answer. You only get onto slippery slopes, hard times, and depression. My prayer for you today is in our Scripture, 1 Timothy 6:6: "Godliness with contentment is great gain."

Here is my prayer for you today:

Lord,

I thank You for my position and station in life. It is not bad when I look at it. Yes, I see that I have areas to work on. Make that part of my growth today, Lord. Give me the reassurance that in Your power I can conquer all my fantasies. Help me learn the lessons You are trying to teach me. It is not about having more, but it is about using what I have wisely and with satisfaction. You will work the rest out because of my faithfulness and obedience to You.

Help me not to look at what everyone else has and desire to have it too. Curb my appetite of covetousness. Remind me that You are the monarch of this universe and You can do what You say You can do. You can keep me contented with what You have given me. You can keep us in perfect peace if our minds are stayed on you (Isaiah 26:3).

Lord, keep our minds from wild imaginations today and help us live in reality. We praise You and thank You for Your sure Word because that is reality.

In Jesus' name we pray, Amen.

Day 16

TIME IS EVERYTHING

I'm alive! Thank You, God, for another day to live for You!

"To everything there is a season, and a time to every purpose under the heaven: A time to be born, and a time to die; a time to plant, and a time to pluck up that which is planted; A time to kill, and a time to heal; a time to break down, and a time to build up; A time to weep, and a time to laugh; a time to mourn, and a time to dance; A time to cast away stones, and a time to gather stones together; a time to embrace, and a time to refrain from embracing; A time to get, and a time to lose; a time to keep, and a time to cast away; A time to rend, and a time to sew; a time to keep silence, and a time to speak; A time to love, and a time to hate;

a time of war, and a time of peace"

(Ecclesiastes 3:1-8).

$\mathcal{T}$he Scripture begins by saying, "To everything there is a season, a time for every purpose under heaven . . . a time to be born and a time to die, a time to plant and a time to pluck up what was planted, a time to kill and a time to heal, a time to laugh," etc. You can read the rest of the verses and think on them as they relate to your life situation later. The point I want to make in this thought today is that no situation you are in is permanent. Don't latch on to someone or something forever. The Bible puts in the disclaimer for you to be forewarned, just as there is a time to be born, there is a time coming to die.

When things like death come, they can really throw us. We often feel it came too soon, no matter what age. While we are without problems, we often do not consider that change can and will come. We set ourselves up for hard falls when we don't appreciate both sides of life. For example, there is a time to win and a time to lose. So expect it. No one will always win. As sure as there is winning, there is losing. It's called balance and counterbalance. Do you have your expectations so well polished that when the opposite happens, you blame God? He told us we would have a time to laugh and a time to cry.

Here is something I often think of to keep me constant during the changes life brings. Life is not a snapshot; it is a video. Sometimes people commit suicide because of financial losses that turn out not to be as bad as the person thought. One mother who lost a daughter to suicide told me her daughter needed about twenty thousand dollars to pay off her debt. She found herself bound in financial woes and could not see her way out. Her job, which she felt was the only way she could earn income, gave her only enough to fall behind one hundred dollars or more every month. She could not take the threats from the bill collectors and was behind in taxes.

Some of you know that the tax situation can be a never-ending saga of you owe, now you also owe interest. This young lady just felt hopeless. She had complete dependence on self, things, and not on God. That was a setup for suicide. The mother told me later during the week her daughter died she received a check from an inheritance much over the amount owed. So her loss of life was a waste to her family and community. She looked at life as a snapshot of her circumstances.

Solomon wrote in Ecclesiastes that there is a time to gain and a time to lose. When life gives you a downer, hold on. *It won't and can't last forever. It's just a test to build your testimony.* If you never have a problem, you won't know that God can solve problems. You will never know what faith in God can do. Through it all, learn to depend on God and Jesus. Learn to depend on His Word. Yes, God will take care of His faithful children. You, however, will need to make some changes. It is for that very reason you got the trial. Trials often force us to make changes that in the long run make us better people. Trials make us ponder. With successes, we often take things for granted.

My friend, are you at a snapshot crossroad in life? Then roll the video. That is not a permanent place. Don't make permanent decisions, permanent plans, or take a permanent position in crisis. Learn today something very real about life—it changes. You can change with it. Be prepared and know that as sure as there is up, there is down. As sure as there is peacetime there is wartime.

God gives us a formula for getting through each of the seasons of our lives. It's simple: depend on Him. He will see you through. He knew the end of your life before you were born. He knows your purpose and what will make you happiest and most successful. He knows how much you can bear and what is too much for you. He only allows what you can carry to be a burden for you. 1 Corinthians 10:13 says, "No temptation has overtaken you that is not common to man" (esv). That means several people will be dealing with your same situation. But God is faithful and will not allow you to be tempted beyond what you are able. But with the temptation—now hear this—He will make a way of escape that you may be able to bear it. Temptation resisted builds your character with strength and endurance. God won't always explain, but He will sustain.

Hear our prayer today, Lord,

As we come to You today, some of us are on the upside of life and some of us are on the down side of life. Whatever side we're on, I know You're proud of us because we are coming to You to work things out. Please remind us that You have an escape route for all our possible problems. Let us not short circuit our lives by thinking death is the only way out of a problem. If someone is thinking that today, remind him or her that You already died for them and now they must live for You.

Thank You for the precious promises in Your Word that confirm that You are present in each life. May we be flexible soldiers, knowing there is a time for everything. You are orderly with the seasons of the year. So Lord, we know you will be just as orderly with the seasons of our lives. Give us patience with ourselves. Teach us patience to wait on You as we learn to trust You.

In the timely name of Jesus, Amen.

Day 17

A BAD DAY

I'm alive. Thank You, God, for another day to live for You!

"Be strong and of a good courage, fear not, nor be afraid of them: for the LORD thy God, he it is that doth go with thee; he will not fail thee, nor forsake thee" (Deuteronomy 31:6).

*H*ey, friend, are you going through a particularly rough time right now? Are your eyes brimming with hot tears? Is your body broken and painful? Did you have a relationship that has left you broken and stranded? Has your child just done the unimaginable? Has all the money you thought that you had disappeared? Did you just lose a loved one, the dearest person on earth to you?

I know there are days like this. God said so and mama said so. At times in our lives when we can't find answers, we often feel our biggest need for God. Some of us jump Him and demand answers. Some lose confidence in His abilities to take care of our needs. Some of us just trust to see what the end will be. None of those responses is right or wrong; they are just our responses to an awful day. The next step, however, makes all the difference in how we make it through a bad day.

First, we must remember that Jesus had a very bad day also. One week the people sang His praises, "Hosanna to the son of David" (Matthew 21:9). The next week the same lips were saying, "Crucify Him." That day ended very badly for Jesus (Mark 15:13-14). Since we have a high priest who was tempted in all points and is acquainted with our struggles and loves us through our trials, I recommend Him strongly to you today. Here is what He did on His bad day.

Number one, He took care of His mother. Expand that for yourself; take care of your family relationships. These people are in your life to teach unconditional love and forgiveness. Your family deserves your best self, but we often give family members our worst self. We get up in the morning and grunt at family members. We leave for work and smile at our coworkers and say, "Good morning, everyone." We even give out a few hugs. Yet we fail to smile, hug, or even say goodbye to those we live with called family. You are not assured that you will meet them alive at the end of the day. Life is uncertain; it is death that is certain. So take care of your family like Jesus did of His mother.

Number two, He forgave the people responsible for crucifying Him. It seems to me that forgiveness must become a way of life if we are to pass the test for the next life. In this life, we must follow His example when having bad days. It also seems that the sooner we forgive, the sooner we free up our emotions to enjoy happiness while we live and when we die. We make room for healthy emotions like love and peace. We leave the vengeance to God, who claims it anyway (Deuteronomy 32:35).

Number three, He said, "I thirst." Drink a lot of water when you're having a bad day. There are other destructive behaviors you can choose, but water is from God. We cannot make water and it is good for us to drink. So drink fresh water and see if doesn't help. Take care of yourself and get some rest as well. Get rest even if you don't sleep. Stress uses up a lot of energy. I also recommend getting fresh air and exercise if you can. Take a walk around the block. Breathe deeply. Jesus did not have the luxury of doing all these things on His bad day. But He made it possible for you to do all of this on your bad day. As a side note here, Jesus did not ask for alcohol, He refused vinegar, and He asked for what would quench His thirst. What a wonderful thing!

Number four, He took His doubt to His Father. Yes, Jesus needed reassurance and so will you. He said, "Father, why have You forsaken me?" There will be times you cannot feel the band of angels around you. Know that the Father has dispatched them to you to lift, strengthen, and encourage you. It is then that you realize that God is carrying you as He did His Son on the cross. You would not have made it without Him either. God is in the business of sustaining.

Number five, He stopped dying long enough to reward the thief on the cross who confessed. The thief had done wrong. Jesus told that thief he would be with Him in paradise. Imagine that even if your bad day has you facing consequences for your own wrongdoing, Jesus will still forgive you and at the eleventh hour, if you confess Him as your Savior and give Him your submitted will, He will offer paradise. Call on the Lord to remember you. And I tell you He shall not forget you. He didn't forget the thief on the cross, and He won't forget you. Remember, we are talking about Jesus' very bad day. A day far beyond even the one you are having today. He made it and so can you.

Number six, He commended His spirit into God's hands. He kept the line of communication open between Himself and His Father. Don't close God out of your bad day. He is the only one who can save you. The rest of the people around you will only be around you until their world gets shattered or they get tired of your burden. Those who hang on, you must pay or pay back. So your best bet is putting yourself into the hands of your

Father, who can save and sustain you and in the end take you to a place He is preparing for you. God calls it paradise. That must be some place, for God to call it paradise. Hold on, friends—don't try to go running off to paradise until He calls you.

Finally, number seven, Jesus said, "It is finished." Your pain will not last forever. The crucifixion ended, and so will your days of tears and emotional upheaval. Jesus promises, "My peace I leave with you, My peace I give unto you. Let not your heart be troubled neither let it be afraid" (John 14:27).

Jesus made it through by leaning heavily on His Father, and so must you. That is the only way not to sink in despair. Know that some days are just bombs. Remember that Jesus is in heaven now, preparing a place for those who obey and believe in Him. Until then, use His method and get out of the clutches of despair. Wipe those tears away. God collects them in a bottle anyway. He sends you comforting angels and is there beside you Himself. Encourage yourself in the Lord.

Dear Lord,

Today is a very bad day. Tears cannot express the pain my heart is feeling. I am broken and battered. I need Your strength. Comfort me and place me in Your arms of safety. My strength is gone. O God, what shall I do? What steps should I take? Where do I go from here? I am helpless. I have just reviewed how You went through Your bad day. Help me to find strength as I read the Scripture about Your triumph. Give me patience and bear with me as I am humanly weak. Join Your strength with mine so I can have perfect strength in You.

I am willing to go through whatever I must go through. I just need the reassurance that You will never leave me nor forsake me. Thank You for Your Word—it is my strength and my rock. In Jesus' sustaining name I pray, in Your arms I stay, Amen.

Day 18

HE SEES ME

I'm alive. Thank God for another day to live for Him!

"And he saw them toiling in rowing; for the wind was contrary unto them:
and about the fourth watch of the night he cometh unto them,
walking upon the sea . . ." (Mark 6:48).

*J*esus sees you. Let us put it another way: God has His eye on you. The thought for today is that God is not letting you out of His sight. Did you get it?! Are you feeling like you are being watched by an all-seeing God? Well, you are today and every day.

Mark 6 is very special to me. When my sister had her stroke I was reading this chapter. I felt so supported and understood by God. It gave me courage to go on struggling with her and the unusual situation I found myself in. In Mark 6, Jesus had just sent His disciples on to get ready for their next day at work. He had just fed five thousand plus people and was about to do some healing in a nearby village. Jesus stayed behind to pray. This reminded me to pray often, before a miracle, after a miracle, and during a miracle.

Storms that erupt don't care about you. Winds of life like to just blow and become contrary. The disciples of Jesus were not exempt from contrary winds. The Bible says that at about the fourth watch, I guess at about 4 a.m., Jesus was alone on the mountain. They all left Him and Jesus was praying. The winds on the sea were not allowing any forward movement for the disciples. I hear that weather on the sea can change quickly. One minute things can be calm and peaceful and the next large breakers can form and strong winds can bring fear for life for experienced seamen. This was one of those crises for the disciples.

Now here is the part that really caught my attention. Jesus is on the mountain praying and He sees the disciples on the night sea, struggling at four in the morning and He comes to them by any means necessary. This, of course, was Jesus bouncing on the water. Oh, what a God we serve! I was struggling with my sister and God came bouncing to my rescue. He gave me insight as to where the best healthcare facility would be and allowed things to work out for her to be at that facility. This was a big miracle in her life and mine.

You know how we plan our days; *I'm going to stop at the grocery store before I visit my friends.* Somewhere between you getting food and visiting, do you need a visit from Jesus? Were you struggling last night with some problem you felt is getting the best of you? Jesus is prayed up and bouncing over to you in your sea of struggle because He sees you and you need Him. He sent you on a mission and you were obeying. Count on your Savior showing up because He sees you and cares. I can just imagine the tender eyes of God looking over His children today. When you struggle He sees you.

God can be no different towards us than He was to His disciples because He is God. God's love cannot change. It is constant towards His children. He told the disciples to get in the boat. When they obeyed, then Jesus came walking on the water. This means to me that whatever way He comes to us, there are no limits. Jesus came at four o'clock in the morning. That means that no time is inconvenient. He got in the ship and the wind ceased. With His presence, He brings peace, calm, and normal, tolerable conditions.

In Mark 6:50, He also said to be of good cheer and be not afraid. "I am here." This means to me, be happy in your struggles. God is already there. He saw us in the boat. He saw us struggling with contrary situations. He came to us when we didn't even call Him in our situation. He came anyway. He wants us to know that He is God and He can calm the sea in our lives.

Because of His presence there is lack of fear and good cheer. He can do the same in your life today, my friend, because Jesus sees everything. Psalm 34:15 says, "The eyes of the Lord are upon the righteous." If you want God's eyes on you today, pray with me and let's ask Him, shall we?

Dearest ever-seeing, ever-knowing God,

We come to you today humbled, knowing Your eyes are on us. Thank You for that. We will think on that today as we go about our activities. We will do our best in all we do, knowing that makes You happy. We will obey just as the disciples obeyed, because we want You to show up in the storms of our lives and bring peace, good cheer, and fearlessness. Thank You for Your Word and the stories of Your life that bring us great courage. Help us to share this thought with someone else today so that he or she can rest in Your promise that Your eyes are always on us and Your rescue missions are in place as needed. Thank You, Lord, for being in our tomorrows and our yesterdays. We love You and depend on You. Show up in our storms today.

In the all- seeing name of Jesus, Amen.

Day 19

FORSAKE ME NOT

I'm alive! Thank You, God, for another day to live for You.

"…Then all the disciples forsook Him, and fled" (Matthew 26:56).

*L*et me set the scene for you. The disciples were Jesus' closest companions while He was on earth. He was always with one, some, or all of His boys. They shared stories, planned business, laughed, and joked. Jesus always made sure there was food for them, as they sometimes worked long hours. They went boating and fishing together. The disciples got to know a lot about Jesus. Similarly, He knew everything about them. Some disciples thought He would become president. When they saw His following, they wanted the position of vice president, treasurer, or head of some department. The boys were close friends. Jesus held private parties for His disciples and told them ahead of time things that were going to happen. It seemed that Jesus had brothers who would cover His back.

Then that awful moment came. Jesus had warned that this moment would come. The capturing mobsters came to take Him for trial and death by crucifixion. Of course, the disciples were all present and around Him. The businessman/treasurer led the mob to Him. He had it all financially figured out. That is why the business people out there should not mix greed with speed and need. The results can be betrayal of those who trusted you and serious personal loss. Take it from Judas, he knows. There is nothing new under the sun. Whatever awful plan you have to get over on someone else, has been tried. If betrayal was on your agenda today, change that. It is not worth your soul.

What did the rest of the disciples do when they saw their buddy tied up and surrounded by mobsters? Their mouths fell open as Jesus was taken away like a common criminal. The Bible says, "They all ran away!"

Ever watch the old western movies when the law man tries to hold back citizens who want to go after criminals themselves and forget about justice? They get rowdy, get weapons, and get ready to take matters into their own hands. They say, "There is no justice in the law." This is the way the mobsters came to get Jesus. What did Jesus do? First, He healed a man's ear. It had been cut off by Peter's best efforts to keep the Pharisees and the chief priests away from Jesus. Then Jesus willingly submitted to go where they would take Him.

Where are you today, my friend? Do the mobsters of circumstance have you down? Do you feel deserted by your family and friends through no fault of your own? Even if you feel that you deserve consequences for your actions, desertion by those you love is still a heavy cross. Now you can empathize a little with what the Savior experienced that Thursday night. Have you ever said, "I will never leave the Lord like that?" I pray for you to hold fast.

Read Matthew 26:40-41, and review some of the reasons the disciples fled. When they should have been praying, they were fast asleep. Jesus woke them up after one of His prayer sessions and asked the disciples to pray with Him a little bit because they were about to be hit hard. He went back to praying and, with heavy eyes, they went back to sleep. Prayer gives stamina to stand up in the battles of life. Pray as you walk. Pray in preparation for battle. Pray for release from fear that will keep you from fleeing in the face of your worst temptation or enemy.

The disciples did not have enough staying power in the heat of this battle. They all fled. Don't be too hard on yourself if you have done that. Let us not keep on fleeing after today's devotion. Jesus knows your heart. He knows your frame. He went up the hill carrying that old rugged cross so that you would have the chance to face the enemy squarely. Friend, please pray before the battle is on, or intense, for staying power. Ask the Savior to help you stay with Him through your fiercest trial.

I'm wondering what fleeing means in today's language since the literal biblical situation is not what we deal with on a day to day basis. I have some idea and you can add your own ideas with the Holy Spirit's help. He will enlighten you about your situation. How about your ministry? God has asked you to do a task for Him. He has gifted and empowered you. Do you sit on your gift, or run from it, because of fear of the unknown?

My friend, that sounds like a disciple fleeing. God can do what He sets you up to do. Another area I often run from, and maybe you do also, is forgiveness of a family member who has hurt me. We say we will follow the Lord; we go to church, pray, and do ministry, while our hearts are blocked with pain and betrayal we just cannot let go of. Those are only two examples of fleeing.

What are you going to do today to turn the "running away from God" around? Peter wept bitterly. John later came to the cross. All the disciples eventually repented of their sins and came together in the upper room. Judas, who could not accept forgiveness, is the exception. He became a powerful example of someone who rejected Christ. Don't flee when you're scared; cleave to God. Let us pray and ask God for more strength than we have now.

Dearest Jesus, friend and mighty warrior for Your children,

I come this day on behalf of all Your children who have stepped away, deserted You, or are planning on deserting You today. Please remind them that You gave Your life for us. You know how to bear up under a heavy cross. God, oh, God, give us power over self-preservation and help us give that assignment back to You. You do a better job with that than we ever could. Please give us experiences that will show us that we can be victors when we come up against demons. Here we will learn to stand and resist the devil. Help us learn to stand. Your Word says that if we do this, the devil will flee from us (James 4:7).

Remind us not to let You carry our cross and Yours by Yourself. There is a cross for all and there is also one for me. Give us Your strength to bear up. Lord, You develop leaders by trials so help us not to develop fear of the outcome. Keep us following You by taking up our crosses cheerfully. The disciples finally got it; help us to understand too. What a difference they made in the world. What a positive difference we too can make when You are in the equation.

In the precious name of Jesus I pray, Amen.

Day 20

JUST PRAY

I'm alive. Thank You, God, for another day to live for You!

"...The effectual fervent prayer of a righteous man |woman| availeth much" (James 5:16, brackets added).

*T*oday I just feel the urge to pray. There are many hurting people reading this devotional who just need a prayer going up for them today. So let's talk to the One who can make a difference in our lives. The first group I would like to pray for is the workers and the managers.

Father in heaven, today I am called to be in charge, a manager on my job. Management may be a new post for some, while it may be a routine job for others. Some of Your children have to make hard decisions today. It may be about the direction of the company, hiring or firing of employees, or the financial downturns that challenge the company. The very jobs of some of Your servants may be in jeopardy. This may not even be their doing.

Lord, some are severely accused by others of mismanagement. Some may be overloaded with too much responsibility for one person to carry. The load is overwhelming. Some are under legal fire just because of the title they hold. Others are trying to hold onto a job while facing a severe family crisis. Yet the job demands time away from home.

Lord, it can get convoluted. We come to You, the God who knows how to untwist all these tangled webs and turn these big problems into testimonies. Help these dear praying managers to come to You with their cups empty and ask You to show them that Jesus can fill it up. You said You would talk to us and tell us which way to go (Isaiah 30:21).

You said You would order our steps (Psalm 37:23). You said You know where we live (Revelation 2:13). You said You can supply all our needs (Philippians 4:19). Fill us up today, Lord, so that we can say the right words. Remind us to take the right actions and obey Your voice so that You can be our guide. Leadership is demanding and if You have entrusted us with this assignment, then, Lord, we trust You to bring us through.

For workers who may be facing unemployment or slander of character, Lord, step in. Clarify the misunderstandings in our workplaces, I pray. Let there be fewer assumptions like what others may be thinking and more actual communicating. Ask questions like, "What were you thinking?" "How did you get to that conclusion?" Let there be less speaking and more listening (James 1:19).

Thank You for stopping by here today to fulfill our deepest needs. Since You have great plans for us, let me accept this challenge and recognize it as a stepping stone for greater things.

For those of us in new jobs today not understanding what is asked of them, let them remember that we can ask someone who knows the job and not be ashamed of not knowing. Remind us that it is better to ask than to make regrettable mistakes. God, please also give us wisdom and direction (James 1:5). This is our request in Your name.

This next prayer is for our city and government leaders.

Lord, today as the day breaks upon our cities, we are as unsure about the outcome of this day as we are about ourselves. Today we come asking You to overrule with Your purpose in our cities. Protect them from violence and natural disasters, many caused by our own sins. Lord, please help us to clean up our cities physically also. Let us not litter and make them look untidy. Help us keep our garbage until we get to a proper dump. Remind us that cleanliness is next to godliness. We live in this city and we need Your presence today. Your children can make this city a better place because You live here through us.

Lord, there are corrupt leaders planning and scheming to elevate themselves at the expense of their city. Since You are the one who placed them in charge, You can straighten them out.

We also ask you to bless the poor and homeless today who struggle to find food. Help those of us who can give a dollar to not judge how it might be used, but that those asking might be blessed by our giving. We know we will be storing up treasures in heaven when we give cheerfully.

We pray for Your protection of abused children. Lord, if there is child abuse or neglect going on in any home, please protect the children. Intervene today on their behalf. Let someone come to the home that can relieve the suffering, even if You have to come Yourself, please come. Send an angel undercover to change around the minds of the abusers from serving self to serving You. Even this prayer can do it if it is seen by the eyes of the right reader with power of the Holy Spirit. You did it for Paul; You can do it again.

Lord, be with our low income workers, for those working with struggling families or delivering healthcare to the indigent. Help our violence prevention organizations that depend on You so much. Stimulate the generosity of others to fund a much needed cause. Grant financial relief today so there will be enough generosity in our hearts to give. Let us not hoard in bank accounts, come up with greedy schemes, and build bigger barns to store our wealth in. There are people here to the right and left of us who don't have enough money to eat or to pay rent. Reduce the wastefulness of all of us.

Help us not to think of ourselves today, but of how we can make our city better by what we do. Lord, You be spirit for us and we will be flesh for You. Our hands will rock the orphan babies; our feet will visit the nursing homes. Our lips will help the teachers with slow learning students; our hearts will reach out with a donation to help in someone's world today. Show us who, show us where, and show us how to make the best contribution. Compel us and convince us when it is You telling us to contribute.

We pray for the safety of youth in cities. For someone who faces a death trap today, disarm it, we pray. Let the person who was spared see that it was You Who locked the gun or kept him or her away from that sure death trap. Help the youth of our cities see that they need to get back to God and to order their lives. Keep them from harm's way until they realize that the devil would love to have us all dead today. It is You, God, Who sustains us and we must call on You in obedience in order to find Your favor.

The final prayer I pray today is on behalf of our expectant moms and dads.

Dear Lord, a little life is growing in my womb. I am called upon to be the vessel You chose to give this baby life. I don't know who or what this little person will grow up to become. But I know I will need Your help with this big job.

Some are struggling to carry the baby to full term. They can't seem to hold onto it alone. But today, God please help the baby to hold on. Others want to abort their babies, Lord, help these women to know that only You can create life. And if You gave them the life in their wombs, You can see them through. You already have plans and purposes for this child.

Lord, prepare these moms and dads for the self-sacrificing tasks that will have to happen to bring up these children You have placed in their hands. Give them a nurturing place. Many feel they are not up for the financial challenge. Remind them that the earth is Yours and the fullness thereof… (Psalm 24:1). Teach us faith. You can supply all our needs. Help us to obey. That way we can teach our children to obey. Lord, when delivery day comes, please attend to Your women through the valley of the shadow of death. Please deliver healthy babies, and we will give You praise. If there are complications, we count on You to bring the moms and dads though it with sustained courage.

Should there be loss of life for mom, baby, or both, we count on You to be a God of grief recovery. Take our hands, precious Lord, and lead these families through. If there is a problem, Lord, You knew it was coming. You prepared a way so that we would be able to bear up. Save our bitter tears and let us not be afraid to trust You now even though we cannot understand. We know that You love us no matter the storm.

In Jesus' name, Amen.

Day 21

BLIND

I'm alive. Thank You, God, for another day to live for You!

"He answered, 'Whether he is a sinner I do not know. One thing I do
know, that though I was blind, now I see'"
(John 9:25, ESV).

*T*was rebuked by a six-month-old preemie baby today. She showed so
much courage that it brought tears to my eyes. Her grandma showed
me pictures of what this little one-pound preemie had come through. Now
she is seven pounds and only needs a little bit of oxygen. I looked at
the baby girl doing baby girl things. She was stretching, quickly smiling,
opening and closing her eyes, almost like a game for people to try and get
a quick picture with her eyes open. She was yawning and kicking her feet.
I suppose she was feeling very good today.

However, what I saw today did not tell the story of the night she bled
so much that the doctors gave up hope for her life. I did not see the hole
in her heart where she had to have surgery to keep her alive. I didn't see
the painful needles she had to bear in her flesh every few hours when she
had to have her blood drawn. I did not see the times she had to eat and she
couldn't because her stomach regurgitated the ounce-size feedings she was

receiving. I was not there when the sweep of infection almost took her body to sure death. I was not there to see the abundance of tubes everywhere that kept her life supported.

What I saw today was an overcomer of difficult circumstances. What I saw was one who endures. What I saw was a non-complainer. What I saw was Jesus reflected in a child. And He said: "I tell you the truth, unless you change and become like little children, you will never enter the kingdom of heaven" (Matthew 18:3, NIV). This little baby girl learned early that it's so sweet to trust in Jesus. Her panic moments were nonexistent. She just did what she had to do every day to make it. Today was a stretching, smiling, all-dressed-up-receiving-hugs day. Every day was not like that.

I parallel this experience with a new challenge I am facing. Recently, I was called to the cross of losing sight in my left eye. My vision was blurry and I knew this would be a problem. I would have to do things with one eye that I used to do with two. When people ask me how I am doing with this, I say, "I am trusting God through the storm." Every day I lose more and more sight in my left eye. Still, I am not like my baby girl, living for today. God knows what I need and will direct me to what I need to do. I only pray I will be willing to do what He wants me to with one eye. God knew a long time ago that this day would come. And He needs me to be strong to share my story with you and help you overcome your struggles. Then you can help someone else overcome theirs.

How does He accomplish this? He starts with the baby's problems. He helps her through, and then He goes to mine. He clears my head by using the baby's strength. He lets me know that He has this eyesight problem under His care.

Now He is using me to tell you that whatever new ailment, or old one, you are going through, don't rehearse the difficulty unless you are talking to your medical provider, but pray for strength to bear up under the mission.

It won't be the final end of the story. There is more joy to come. Wait for it. Whenever the Lord arrives on the scene, He often says, "Be of good cheer." Cheer is miles of smiles, happiness, thankfulness, and encouragement to others! Cheer is Jesus, blessed Jesus, in your heart. When you are tempted to engage in self-pity, remember the newborn babies fighting for their lives in the neo-natal intensive care units all across the world.

Dear mom and dad, if your baby is in such a state today, I give you Jesus. He gives the peace that passes all understanding. I give you Jesus, your child's Savior and my Friend. May God's peace support and surround you as you bear up. I know it is hard watching your child struggle and my prayer is with you.

Lord,

Life is often harder than we planned it. I know if we could choose, all the babies in the world would be born healthy, bouncy baby boys and girls. We have so corrupted the world with our sins that death must result. We are truly sorry, Lord, and in our state of confession and obedience, we ask that You visit the neo-natal intensive care units of the world. Strengthen the young babies struggling for breath. Strengthen their families and parents as they watch their undeserving child suffer. Give them courage to understand that You know the way that is best for them and the child.

May the experience make us all the more sensitive to the pain and agony that sin causes. May those looking on be cheerleaders like You were. Every time You showed up, You said to be of good cheer. Today, may some baby, the medical team thought might not make it through the night, survive and thrive. Let there be several extra miracles today.

You said, "Yet ye have not, because ye ask not" (James 4:2). I'm asking today on behalf of these infants who depend on us to ask on their behalf. Thank You for Your promise of compassion. Thank You that You are a sovereign God. You will never make a mistake. We accept Your perfect plan, whatever the outcome. Thank You, Lord, for another opportunity to talk to You about what hurts our hearts and thank You for listening.

In Jesus' name, Amen.

Day 22

JUDGING

I'm alive. Thank God for another day to live for Him!

"Judge not, that ye be not judged. For with what judgment ye judge,

ye shall be judged: and with what measure ye mete,

it shall be measured to you again" (Matthew 7:1-2).

*T*oday's thought and prayers are for the judges on the judicial benches of the world. You, judge, are called to do something written in the above Scripture that we are told not to do. Before you get concerned, let me clarify. This does not refer to your role on the bench. We must have judging in a society to keep the rules working. You are a valuable, irreplaceable person in this society. Men, women, all of us, refuse to obey God's simple rules. Therefore men come up with tons of rules to have a civilized society. All these rules are made up by men trying to get us to conform to God's simple laws. These laws can be found in His Word, the Bible.

Here are a few of God's rules. Do to everyone today as you would want someone to do to you. Look in Luke 6:31 and you will see that it is already in the Bible. Since God is your Father, treat everyone as your blood sister and brother. Don't we all address the Lord in our prayers as our Father? Don't harm yourself or others.

These three rules alone would reduce the law books on the shelves by half. Not to mention the ones in the commandments. Do not steal, do not lie, do not take your neighbor's spouse, do not kill, and take your eyes off what other people have. But because of society's unwillingness to follow God's simple rules, we give our judges the arduous task of learning volumes of books and translating the contents into prison sentences, probation times, death row, and all sorts of creative sentencing. This is their best effort to keep order in society. Our judges need our prayers today and every day.

My daughter worked for a very nice judge. I met him personally. He is a father, a grandfather, and a very nice man. Off the bench, he is an ordinary friendly human being. On the bench, he is different. He has to review documents on behalf of the person being tried. That person broke a rule of society and has to be punished.

My only caution to you judges is to ask God to lead you in your sentencing every day. Because of your position, you can easily become proud and think more highly of yourself than you ought to. It doesn't take much to become filled with self and self- pride and say, "my knowledge," "my power," and "my way is the way." Your standards become how you give out punishments. You could be in danger of getting punishment equal to what you unjustly pass out. You see so much evil and evildoers coming before you that judging becomes easy. You smell the bad guys and girls out before they come to you. After all, you have been doing this every day. Keep in mind that there are those who have tender hearts that broke and deserve punishment. These hearts can also be rehabilitated with a second chance. Ask the Lord to help you see those as well and judge tenderly. How will you know which ones deserve what treatment? God will tell you, if you listen for His voice and obey. You make a big difference in the lives of those you judge. Do not be alarmed if you ask for God's direction and find yourself sentencing someone in a way other than you would have sentenced him or her on your own.

Lord,

Live in the mind of the judges across the world today, and keep them from pride and self-sufficiency. Take care of their needs so the sentences rolling from the bench are well thought out. Let the sentencing not speak out of the judge's own issues or experiences. Lord, our judges are human like the rest of us. They need Your divine light to guide them in their sentencing. Show them what the sentence should be. Take away any prejudice or hatred for any group of people they may have in their hearts. Let there be fairness. Take out intimidation and bribery from them so there can be equality in their sentences. Take away fear as they deal with high-profile cases, where the outcome may even cost them their jobs or their life. Help them to know that integrity is better in all cases. Help them to know that You are present for them and will show up with good cheer and favor.

Give them wisdom like You gave Solomon to judge fairly in 1 Kings 3:16-27. He made a good decision between two women fighting over a baby. Please, Jesus, protect the judges and their families from hardship due to their role as a judge and otherwise. Remind them of Your love for them. Help the people of the land who know they have been granted undeserved favor to stop and thank You.

May the defendants make an effort to send back letters of thanks and appreciation for giving them another chance. May they take the undeserved blessings given to them by You and help others not make similar mistakes. May they include the good things that are now happening in their lives in their letters. May our judges get some special words of encouragement that will invigorate them in their thankless jobs. Thank You that judges across the world serve as they do.

Now for those who will face the judges today be kind to them, Lord. These judges are only doing the job that we pay them to do. Help them to remember that if they have done something wrong, they must pay the consequences. Help them to accept their sentences with humility and, with Your help, to change. The judge is not the cause of their problem. He only interprets the law.

Lord, we pray for fairness and equality and help us to go and sin no more. Today, Lord, someone deserves a hard sentence. But allow the price You paid on Calvary to be the ransom. Let that person know that it is because of Your prayers on his behalf and Your sacrifice on the cross that he has been granted leniency.

Some people may be planning to do an evil deed that may land them in the hand of evil judges. Please, God, help them reconsider their plans for today. Help them rethink the mischief and consider whether it is worth the penalty that the wrong may bring. Foil the plans, I pray.

And, Lord, a final word for the judges, please give them Your peace as they sleep each night after a day of sentencing and penalties.

I pray in Jesus' name, Amen.

Day 23

WAGES

I'm alive. Thank You, God, for another day to live for You!

"The wages of sin is death, but the gift of God is eternal life through Jesus Christ our Lord" (Romans 6:23).

*W*ages are payments for work done. In other words, at the end of the day or pay period, the wage earner gets what is due him or her in spendable portions. Our Bible verse says, "The wages of sin is death." Sometimes we don't think of life with a death component. We think of death in the grave, but living with death all around you should make you detest sin and not want to be a part of it.

Death is separation from life filled with sin. This is what I believe God wants us to see as the words of the Scripture spring off the page and into our hearts. To me, death means no more divorces, broken homes, or messed up relationships due to selfishness. No more rapes, drugs, gunshot killings, or crimes. It also eliminates the need for jail bonds and insurance. Death means no more broken bones, arthritis, or pain. No more sleeplessness, pests, or roaches. No more debt collectors, no more running away, no more spending on credit, no more fires, no more terrorists. It also means no more nights of crying, no more world hunger, no more disobedient children and parents, no more despair and doubt, no more jealousy, no more disconnected phones, water, electricity, or gas. It means no more house foreclosures or evictions, no more taxes and bankruptcy, no more asthma, high blood pressure, cancer, diabetes, kidney dialysis, wheelchairs, hospitals, or cemeteries. It means no more lawsuits.

Can you imagine a world like that? What a wonderful world that would be! That was just to name a few of our problems. I could go on and on but I'm sure you get the picture. It is because of our sins, and we have brought all of these sins on ourselves.

How does God help us out of all of this? The same verse gives us a *but*, which is a cancelling preposition. All that goes on before the *but* can no longer affect us in the end, if we do something very simple. Accept the gift of Jesus Christ our Lord, and the result will be eternal life. That is what we will get in exchange for death.

We will get eternal life, mansions, paradise, unspeakable joy, personal talks with Jesus and angels, fruits from the tree of life, and streets of gold. We will be able to live in a city with rainbow foundations, clear jasper walls, huge pearl gates, and a diamond in the sky. We will get clear skies. We will have nights filled with sleep and not tears. We will get visits to other parts of the universe. What joy, what unspeakable joy awaits us. Put down the wages of sin, and take on the gift of eternal life.

Who is this, the One Who promises all this? Can He keep His promise? It is Jesus Christ, King of kings and Lord of lords. He was here on earth for a short time and changed the course of time from B.C. to A.D. He is the One who hung on the cross so our sins could be paid in full by a worthy deliverer.

Who is Jesus? Isaiah 40:8 says, "The grass withereth, the flower fadeth: but the word of our God shall stand forever." You can be sure Jesus can back up His promises. He is able to keep His promises and they are sure. Your decision today as you rush through your busy tasks is which gift will you receive? Will you receive gifts that bring death or will you accept the gift of eternal life? To accept eternal life means you accept Jesus. To accept Jesus, you must accept His ways. You must also accept His truth and His life. That means you will be kind to those around you today, starting in your home. Isn't that Jesus' way? You will accept His way because you want to do things like Jesus did. Remember, if we follow in His footsteps we will never be lost because He knows the way.

When tempted to tell a lie that only we know is a lie, even a lie as small as our dress size or our weight, we will stop and choose death or life. To tell the truth is the way of life; to lie is the way of death. When tempted to say unkind words about a driver who just cut us off in traffic, we will stop and think. We will choose words of life and not of death. When faced with sudden failing health or when we are facing death, we will not doubt God but trust His promises. He is always faithful to the faithful and will choose those who are faithful over doubters for the gift of eternal life.

Today, friend, you can choose the wages of sin by your responses, or you can choose eternal life. Which one will it be? Each action has the power of life or the power of death. Please be aware of that. Obeying God brings life; disobeying God brings death and suffering. You can take that to the bank. Let's pray and ask God for strength to make eternal life choices today.

Dear God,

The One who makes impossible things possible, we come to You today asking for strength to make choices that will lead to eternal life instead of permanent death. Many of us have been making death choices for so long that we cannot see how to get out of this trap.

Lord, You have the answers. If there is anything we are doing to our body that we know causes disease, help us to decide to stop it today. Help us to know that death can even be in the food placed on the fork that we place in our mouths every day. Give us willingness to exercise and keep our bodies purified. Death may come from our slanderous, dangerous tongues that we use against others because of our own weakness and pride. Lord, thank You for showing us a more excellent way. And now give us strength to do things right.

Let us not just be hearers of Your Word but doers of Your Word. We want eternal life; we want paradise and mansions, we really do. We know we must follow Your lead to get there. So I ask for strength and endurance today to do just that. Keep us praying for strength to do right. Let us clap our hands in thanksgiving that You made a way out of all the death traps set for us. Let us sing praises when we have overcome some of our sins. Put a smile on our faces when we make an eternal life move. Let us feel free to cry out to You, Holy One, when we are struggling with some long-cherished vice. We know we have to give it up. Please, give us victory so we can make eternal life choices. Help us to see that our sins not only affect us, but others. Nature is destroyed by our sins, and our environment, our children, our innocent and poor suffer because of our sinning.

Lord, take all of that away today. We want no part of the wages of sin. Clean us up and purify us. We want to become eternal life people. We want to be in the mansions that You have gone to prepare for us. Wasn't that what You said You were up there preparing for us? Thank You, Lord, for leaving the blueprints for living right. Thank You for backing them up with Your blood on Calvary. Thank You for the promise of eternal life and paradise.

In the worthy name of Jesus, Amen.

Day 24

BEATINGS AND FALSE WITNESS

I'm alive and I thank God for another day to live for Him!

"And the Lord said, Simon, Simon, [put your name here] behold, Satan
hath desired to have you, that he may sift you as wheat:
But I have prayed for thee, that thy faith fail not: and
when thou art converted, strengthen thy brethren
(Luke 22:31-32, brackets added).

*H*ard times, very hard times, will come to everyone sometime. How
do I know that? Followers of Jesus who accept Him as their Savior
must follow His example. Let us review together the trials of Jesus. I hope
this will help you bear up under the struggle. Matthew 10:22 says, "And
ye shall be hated of all men for my name's sake: but he that endureth to the
end shall be saved." You and I know how awful it feels to be hated. Bear
up—more hate will be coming your way.

In Mark 8:31, Jesus says that the Son of man will be rejected and killed.
Have you ever been rejected? The group doesn't want you around anymore.
You cannot play softball well, so you are rejected by your teammates and
kicked off the team. Prepare for the world to reject you because you want
to obey God and follow His commandments.

Jesus was cursed at, despised, and rejected. To be cursed out is painful. Sometimes the accusations are from a false source. To be called dirty things and have your name spoken of in a dirty way is demoralizing. God endured it, and you will have to as well. Jesus was blindfolded, slapped in the face, and then ridiculed. This is because He said that He was the Son of God.

We need a double portion of the Holy Spirit not to retaliate. Jesus took all this for us. 1 Peter 24 tells us all about Jesus' suffering. Read it for yourself and grow tender towards your Savior. Jesus was beaten and bloodied across His back twice. He had done no evil, but evil showed up and showed how cruelly it can behave. You or I may be called upon to take beatings we do not deserve. Cruel people find this way to take out their anger on others. Of course, we know Satan is behind all this. He hoped it would be too much for Jesus. It was at this time that Jesus prayed and prayed. He prayed for His persecutors and He prayed for you and me.

When our time of rejection comes, we must be as faithful. Jesus was betrayed and backstabbed by a close friend. You hug or embrace someone close to you to express genuine love and concern. In return, they hug you back, then stab you in the back with a dagger, and leave you wounded bleeding and in pain. This backstabbing can be done emotionally. As Christians, sometimes even the people we worship with turn on us for being faithful to God. Even our own family members can become backstabbers. They can make up lies and spread them about us. True disciples of God expect this. Mark 14:57 says that some bore false witness against Jesus.

Here is a disgusting thing hateful people did to a non-retaliating Jesus. They spat in His face and ripped out His beard. No one stood up for Jesus. The Scripture in Isaiah 50:6 said this would happen to Jesus. Matthew 26:67 records these disgusting things happening to Jesus. Even at this, Jesus did not retaliate. We are Jesus' disciples and must expect equal treatment.

Be prepared to follow Jesus all the way. Prepare now by learning how Jesus prepared for His worst moment. He prayed and prayed and prayed. He knew His Father would take care of His accusers. He still loved all these mean people (Psalm 109:4). He wanted all to be saved in His kingdom. He even asked His Father to forgive them.

When Jesus was beaten, falsely accused, spat upon, de-bearded, crowned with prickly bush mashed into His brow, and crucified, He never murmured a word against His perpetrators. That is what we should be working towards. We are kingly bound disciples so we must endure our persecution. Some will get it early; others will get it late. Bearing up under your trials is how we learn to be like Jesus. Some will get lots of trials; some will get a few. Do not compare yourself with others; you are not God. You do not make the decisions as to who can take more or less.

Keep in mind that God suffered more than any one of us will be called on to suffer. We know it will come, so let us become very familiar with Scripture and know how Jesus wants us to live. The reason for the trials we have to endure is so that Jesus will know who His true followers are. Affliction will not take place in heaven. He wants to know that all the people He brings to His Father want to live in heaven with them.

The great news is there are some rewards He promises to those who endure faithfully. Revelation 2:10 tells us if we endure we will receive a crown of life. John 14:2-3 says, "In my Father's house are many mansions: if it were not so, I would have told you. I go to prepare a place for you. And if I go and prepare a place for you, I will come again, and receive you unto myself; that where I am, there ye may be also."

Where is Jesus now? He is at the right hand of the Father in heaven (Mark 16:19). This is incredible—I am not making it up. I just took excerpts from the Bible and put this thought together for you today.

If you are hearing this for the first time, get a Bible and read Matthew, Mark, Luke, and John. Those are the first four books of the New Testament called the Gospels. If you know all these things already, happy are you. If you respond as Jesus did in His trials during your trials, then happy are you. Thank God for the example and promises of Jesus.

I feel ready to study about the strength that I can have over self. I know that the strength Jesus left me in the form of the Holy Spirit can make me an overcomer. The Holy Spirit will also help all of us remain faithful disciples. I love to tell the story of Jesus and His love. Just try Jesus.

Let's pray and ask God to give us a lovely spirit even when we are beaten and lied about.

Lord,

It is so hard to lay self aside when we are attacked by falsehood. You know what it is like; You have been there. We need to be ready to say to the world, "I am a disciple of Christ." We are weak and we will stumble about lying ourselves. Yet we yearn to become more like You, Jesus. Help us want to change and to be your faithful and truthful representatives.

This world is so full of evil. Help us to be bright lights of right living in this evil world. Remind us that You can and will take care of our tormentors. That is a job You have given Yourself. You did not take Your tormentors out. You could have, but You left that up to Your Father, Who says, "Vengeance is mine" (Hebrews 10:30).

God, thank You for the painful experiences we have to bear up under. We now know they are preparing us for kingdom living. Thank You for being such a kind God and only giving us what we can bear (1 Corinthians 10:13). Get us ready for the warfare, and strengthen our resolve to do right in all our dealings.

Give us Your power to put Satan out of business in our homes. When we are on the job, let us not fail to let others know we are God's obedient children. May we not be afraid to stand for right even when those around us are coercing us to do wrong. Thank You, Lord, for Your power and Your victory. You have given us a lot of power against the enemy. Let us use Your good Word, the Bible, as our two-edged sword (Hebrews 4:12).

In Jesus' trustworthy name, Amen.

Day 25

CONSIDER THE POOR

I'm alive! Thank You, God, for another day to live for You!

"Blessed is he that considers the poor: the LORD will deliver him in time of trouble. The LORD will preserve him, and keep him alive; and he shall be blessed on the earth: and you will not deliver him to the will of his enemies" (Psalm 41:1-3, NKJV).

*W*hat a promise! There is a blessing that comes from God to the one who does something to help the poor. Those blessing include deliverance when you are in trouble. It means a long life for you, longer than you may have had if you had not been kind to the poor. You will receive God's blessings here on earth and they will come in many forms. Divine protection from our enemies is also promised. A lot of blessings will come to you just for reaching out to the poor. The Bible really says so!

However, the motive for considering the poor cannot be what you will receive; instead, the motive should be unselfish giving. This will develop in the heart of a man or woman who considers the poor. Jesus was all about relieving poverty when He was on earth. When you act on behalf of Jesus, you do His will. Soon you will find yourself growing to be more and more like your Savior.

You may say, "Dawn, I am not sure how to help poor people, I am poor also; what can I do?" God is not so much interested in the gift but in the condition of the heart of the giver. Was the gift driven by a political setup? Will townspeople say, "He gave so many dollars, so the town should elect him as mayor and name the town after him"? Is there a hidden selfish reason for your gift? God is looking for the giver to be compassionate and caring about the well-being of the poor. Please do not turn your nose up and think you are above needy people. Poverty can come to any one of us suddenly.

In Luke 21:1-3 Jesus takes note of a widow giving her two mites. He mentioned that she gave more than the rich worshipers. She gave all she had, financially as well as spiritually. Whenever this story is read, note is to be taken of this trusting child of God. She depended on God to sustain her. She gave Him back all she had.

God is able to get His message of salvation and heaven to the poor easier than He can get the same message to the wealthy. I wonder if it is because wealthy people depend on their money to pay for everything. Some even believe that money can do more for them than God. You and I, as disciples of Christ, know better. We must practice unselfishness so that others can learn through our testimony that God provides everything for His children. He may use His willing servants, but He can also use a fish or even a bird. The Bible tells stories of all this.

God prefers to use people to provide for His people. Let us stop asking questions like, "Why is there so much poverty in such and such a place?" Instead, start asking God how you can become part of the solution. You may have a home, and you can let some weary soul stay awhile and find rest. You can offer a good warm bowl of soup for a hungry soul at your door. There are soup kitchens all around large cities. Offer your help; provide supplies, help serve, help cook the meal. I'm sure volunteers are needed in those areas. Don't wait to be asked to help; ask what you can do. Tell the overseer you are there to help. Tell the shelter you brought blankets or beds.

Find out if your church or community group has a way they lend help regularly. Join in their community service. Do something, my friend, do something. Make hats and scarves to give to those who are in need of warm clothes. We are often ready to throw out a coin to the man on the corner. But how many of us are willing to invest time and encouragement to people who are poverty-stricken. This will discipline us as followers of Jesus. The poor are often looked down upon in society. Find creative ways to introduce the poor to Christ. Visit with one or two families regularly. Assess their needs. Find a way to relieve them and encourage them often. You will know those who are poor or lonely. God will reveal them to you if you ask Him.

Isaiah 58:6-14 gives us a word from the Lord as to how He wants us to treat the poor. The Clear Word Bible expresses well what is acceptable to God: remove chains of injustice, untie heavy burdens, and let the oppressed go free. Ever notice that it is the poor people struggling to make ends meet, being assessed bank fees, credit card fees, and so on? The already oppressed get the worst oppression added. The oppression on the poor population will eventually get a sore rebuke from God. His disciples need to lift the spirits and the burdens of the brokenhearted. They share their food with the hungry. Giving a turkey at Thanksgiving or four dented cans of beans at Christmas does not cut it.

Isaiah 58 says we are to expend ourselves on the behalf of the hungry. We are to give clothes to those who have nothing. We are not to give our worst clothes or discarded clothes, but our best or brand new clothes.

Please read Isaiah 58 when you can meditate on it. The Lord will show you how you can become a bigger blessing to His poor population all around you. Blessings of God will follow you because of your unselfishness. These blessings include health that will come to you quickly and speedily. Maybe your illness will clear up as you take on Christ.

Immerse yourself in the Isaiah 58 principles. Depression is promised to clear up also and you will be kept strong and well. When you need the Lord, He will show up and say, "Here I am." God is not asking us to do anything He cannot do. He just wants us to develop unselfishness. He wants us to share His glory using our hands and our deeds. God can take care of His children with or without us. However, we are blessed when we become part of the salvation of others. We become participants in God's saving plan. We also benefit with health and wealth. Our mental well-being is strengthened. We are also promised protection and the presence of God whenever we call. He will show up for us. Look how love goes around. The Father is glorified, Jesus is satisfied, you are sanctified, and people around you are blessed.

This is the way the Father likes things to be done. Everyone is full of joy. Healing is going on. Please take God literally here. Ask Him to help you get rid of meanness and selfishness. Ask God to help you with the Isaiah 58 principles and see if some of those diseases you have are not cured. You may be busy thinking herbs and medicines will cure you, and they are not bad. However, you need to treat your fellow men better for spiritual and physical healing to occur.

The tongue must be tamed as part of helping the poor. Don't leave the home you just ministered to and tell your colleagues about the smell there. Don't speak of the untidiness or the pests you may have seen there. If God showed it to you, then order pest control. Hire a housekeeper. This becomes your assignment. Let God see what you will do with it.

That judgmental finger must be folded and pointed to your own self. Plead with God to keep you from assuming what another person is thinking then spreading that as fact. We don't know what another person is thinking because we are not God. We need to keep from sharing negative words your wounded pride. Your self-unimportance was exposed. Your feelings of inferiority were exposed. Your inability to deal with your own weakness is all exposed. Don't go blaming the messenger; that is Scripture, God's Word, 1 Corinthians 13:5. Read as many translations as you can and the meaning will be expanded even further.

To love like Christ, one must put self-interest aside. The interest of others must be on the front burner. This takes conscious thought and prayer. It will not happen overnight.

Each day, we must ask God to help us focus on others. When we look in the mirror, do we see a rude, evil, boastful individual? This should be an indicator that love is gone and self is all puffed up. Self begins to feel more important than it really is. When some good soul crosses your puffed-up path and says something that validates your already puffed-up self, more air is pumped into you. You are fine with that person. An example would be, "You look extra special today, sir," and up goes the puff. The girls say something like, "You are so handsome," and up goes the self-puff. "You are the best principal in the whole district," and up goes the puff. Compliment after compliment and up goes the self-puff.

Then along comes an unexpected player. Someone in your space makes a point of truth. He or she exposes your weakness. True as it may be, an explosion and fireworks from you will be the result. The more self-pride and self-puff there is in you, the bigger the anger explosion.

Some people explode quickly with just a little irritation. Self-pride is built quickly and full anger comes often. Some people hold out for a major explosion. It may come every six months or yearly. Watch out for that anger bursting through. It's going to be thick, harsh, and God bless the soul it falls on.

The problem with anger is that the recipient of the windfall is not the reason for the rude behavior of the unhappy, angry person. The truth is that their pride has been taken down. The unhappy, angry, yelling person is exposed as equal to the rest of us. The pedestal of honor was not there after all. You don't know everything you thought you knew. And you are not everything you thought you were. When this is discovered by others, anger often results.

1 Corinthians 13:5 reminds us that love is never rude, love bears all things, and love endures all things. I know that is a tall order but that is Scripture. Jesus says, "I am the way, the truth and the life" (John 14:6). He is saying I will show you the way, you can learn to bear all things, endure all things and never be rude. That is why I am with you always. Ask me and I will help you.

The process of change can begin today in you, my friend. Did you see any pride in you today? I'm not talking about the one that makes you brush your teeth and comb your hair before you leave home. We all need some of that. I speak of the one that gives you entitlement to think you are better suited for living than any of your fellow men around you.

Did your pride show up in your evaluation mirror of self today? If he did, we will have to ask God to get him out. Pride cannot stay in the heart of a child of God for a second. Evict him now! Tell him to get out—now! And show the pride man the door. Just outside the door should be lots of lovely faces and people needing your love today. They may expose some weaknesses of yours, but you accept the criticism and make changes to improve your character. What a difference that exchange makes. The end result determines if our actions are from love or from self-pride.

Let's take a look at the author of selfish pride—Satan. Remember, pride is the reason he got kicked out of heaven (Ezekiel 28:17). Now let us look at the author of love. Yes, it is Jesus, our Savior. He wants us to be like Him. He wants to guard our hearts against pride moment by moment. We are but dust except that Jesus' breath, heartbeat, love, and salvation reside in us.

Anytime Jesus takes His breath back, our puffed up self becomes like a flat snowman. I saw a flat snowman on a neighbor's lawn one Christmas. In the morning when I left for work, it was full of air and had decorations on the snowman and all. The house was made very festive because of this snowman.

By evening when I came home, the wind or something had deflated the snowman. It looked like a wet pile of plastic for the trash. My friend, do not think of yourself more highly than you ought (Romans 12:3). Love and respect for our fellow men is what life should be all about. True love cannot fail. God backs you up when you love His people.

Let us ask God to give us power to give love. Let it not be said of you, "He or she did not have love." Let us pray for the consistent love that comes from the Lord. We will ask Him to change our selfish love into His love.

Dear Jesus of love,

Please come into our hearts today with a flashlight to seek out self-pride. Before our pride pockets can fill up, please destroy them. While You are in our hearts destroying our pride, please leave a map for us to follow true love.

I am sure You will give us a test today. You will put a person in our path that needs Your love. Give us spiritual eyesight to see and to obey and to love with a willing heart. Give us endurance so the change remains. We want to be like You. It will be hard but please be patient with us. May our daily growth reflect You.

Thank You for your grace and mercy that keep us in Your care as we grow. The last time we blew up and burst with all our anger, You did not cast us aside. We deserve to be cast aside. That snowman on the lawn was picked up and wind was put inside of him again. Please, Lord, try with us again also.

Thank You for fitting Yourself into our minds today so we can have more love for our fellow men. That is how we will show You that we accept Your love and that is how we will bless others.

In Jesus' loving name, Amen.

Day 27

STEPPING AWAY FROM PAIN

I'm alive! Thank God for another day to live for Him.

"...I will contend with those who contend with you, and your children
I will save" (Isaiah 49:25, NIV).

*S*ometimes our children stray from the Lord, as some of us may have
done. They choose a course of action that is not pleasing to God,
self, family, or others. We weep for them and they still do not change their
ways. We try to show by our actions, the more excellent way. We pray for
them. Parents have taken their children to church and taught them about
God. We encourage them to be students of the Bible. Some parents pay
to send their children to schools where they get religious and academic
instructions at great financial burdens to the family. Some parents surround
their children with good friends with families that have great role models.
All this is an attempt to encourage their sons and daughters to make good
life decisions when they grow up.

Painfully I write that my son, like many of your sons and daughters, does the exact opposite of what we had hoped for. The pain is heart
wrenching, and you feel it worse than anything explainable. We watch our
little boy or girl with such high hopes, but instead they choose the skids

of life and end up in the bottom drawers of society. They can often leave a parent feeling and asking, "Where did I go wrong?" Any parent out there today feeling like that? Today's Scripture verse should give you hope that God is on the case. In fact, read all of Isaiah 49 when you get a chance and see the hope God puts out there for parents He claims as His own.

I know many times when children reject parents and leave home and values behind, we are all turned around. We don't know what to do, but God does. He shows us a couple of parables that give direction at times like these. The first parable is about the prodigal son. We are to let them go, pray for them, and know that God will take care of them and help them come to their senses. Read about it in Luke 15. I am speaking of those who are of age. This does not apply to children running away from home. When an adult (above eighteen) decides he or she is not willing to follow the rules of your Christian home, they must leave. Your home is your sanctuary. You meet with God there, and you cannot tolerate sinfulness in your sanctuary. You cannot become like Eli in the Bible who was punished for not disciplining his sons. That story is found in 1 Samuel 2.

Take one step back and give God power in the lives of your sons and daughters. We must first believe God has all power. Once we are on the same page with who really has our children, we need to step out of the way. Stop worrying about your feelings of embarrassment or loss. Ask God to save your sons and daughters by any means necessary. Then ask God to help you fill your son's or daughter's need. You must pray to God for instructions on how to support your child. Do not go to the faraway place trying to drag them home. The prodigal's father did not do that. Oftentimes, consequences are the best teachers. I have heard it said that a picture is worth a thousand words.

I believe that God wants our children to be saved more than we do. He has the power to do the saving thing. All we can do is worry and fret and that is not what God wants us to do. Pray! Lord, You help my child. Take care of him or her. And you, parent, as hard as it is, step out of the triangle and let God save your child, while He fathers you. How is that for pain relief? I do know that sin is the cause of all of this. I know that Satan is trying to pull everyone down. But we cannot give in to defeat when we have a God Who in Matthew 11:28 says, "Come here mother/father, I will give you rest."

He will contend with them that contend with you and will save your children. He gave you His word. God is God! He is sovereign! He can handle everything perfectly. Give Him the reigns with your child and pray for healing within your own soul. This is a way for you to encourage yourself in the Lord today. Do not let your child's choices be the center of your life. Jesus should be the center of your life. Give Him the burden, and you go your way rejoicing.

We cannot see the pain our child has caused us and not see a correlation of how we hurt God by our rebellion and waywardness. If we don't see that, we can miss the point entirely. Sometimes it is when we see disappointment when our children make bad choices that we become aware of how we have hurt God, as His children.

He asks us to obey. He provides for us. He has been faithful to us. He takes care of our house, business, heart, mind, etc. Then comes the time for us to reach spiritual adulthood. We run away from Him in rebellion. We become disobedient to His Word because we think we're grown. Family values are abandoned and we go off seeking empty pleasures of the world. Not only is this a slap in God's face, it is an assault on humankind and our families.

It is time for us to stop blaming the youth of this society for the breakdown and grief of our society. Adults need to take ownership for some of the mess we cause. Much of the mess is caused by our awful examples of selfishness. I hope I am not offending you today, but someone needs to say stop! Look at what you are telling the boys and girls down the street to do. Maybe that boy or girl is in your house. It is time to stop the madness and the pain. Lord, give us the strength to spend time in prayer so that we can develop Your power to resist evil in all its forms.

Young people, you choose a more excellent way. You may be angry because of what you see. You may have been treated badly, but you too must go to God for healing so that your pain gets carried by God. Do not repeat the examples of wrong behavior that you see. God does have the right answer for you. Be obedient to God and be faithful. He can bring you through this time of searching without you choosing rebellion. Let us pray for power.

Lord,

Today, You are needed in families where there are crises going on. Children are leaving home and leaving their parents in pain. I need you to ease the turmoil in that parent's heart. They did what they could, Lord, You know that. They just want to have a peaceful day today. Please become the center of their joy. Show up with good cheer like only You know how to do. Cover their heart strings with musical notes so that the pain of the experience becomes dull with music. Send birds and flowers in their day to sing them happy songs. Give the disappointed parent hope that You are on the job.

If parents don't know where their children are or if they are in great danger, surround them with Your army, Lord. Please be the general leading the army to rescue their children. You know how to do these things per-fectly. Lord, there are numerous examples in Your Word as to how You deal with rebellion. Do a good thing with all of this for us today. You said in Romans 8:28, "And we know that all things work together for good to them that love God, to them who are the called according to [his] purpose."

Not *some* things, but *all* things. It is a promise. We love You, God, and we trust You to bring salvation to our children.

In Jesus' name, Amen.

Day 28

ROOSTER, ROOSTER

I'm alive. Thank You, God, for another day to live for You!

"And the second time the cock crew. And Peter called to mind the word that Jesus said unto him, Before the cock crow twice, thou shalt deny me thrice. And when he thought thereon, he wept" (Mark 14:72).

*I*n Mark 14:29, Peter told Jesus, "Although all shall be offended, yet I will not." In verse 30, Jesus informs Peter that during the night, before the cock crows twice, he would deny his Savior three times.

Today will probably be a very busy day for you. You had your prayer time and you are having your devotional with me. Then you will be off to the rat race. You have to pay bills, make arrangements for the family to get everywhere they have to be on time. You have to stop at the store. You have to be at work on time. On top of your regular responsibilities, today is a contract day or some other major event at your job. The big promotion you expected will be discussed and the beat goes on. You arrive at work dressed for the occasion. Unbeknownst to you, but clearly to God, you are about to be overturned, altered, changed, transformed, and reduced to a new level of trust in God.

Trials are often used to grow our trust in Him. Let me remind you of something in our verse today so that you will be strengthened by the time you get to your dilemma. God knows all about it already. He fixed it so that when you come to your dilemma today, you will find only enough pain in order for you to grow, if you accept His outcome. How do you know this, you ask?

The answer is in today's Scripture verse. Early in the morning, God told Peter to expect a rooster experience. He said, "Before the rooster makes two noises, you will deny me three times." That means to me that God is aware of all His created animals. He knows their sounds and the reason why they make their noises. He had to know all of this to tell Peter at what point he would have denied Him three times. Wow, did you get that? Then, exactly as Jesus had told Peter things would happen, they happened. The rooster went cock-a-doodle-dooooooo. Then Peter remembered the words of the Lord. Just what Peter said he would not do, he did. Denial happened the very night God said it would, and at the very time He said it would happen.

Peter caught on, though, that Jesus still loved him. He became so upset that he was not as strong in himself as he thought he was. He cursed and said, "I don't know Jesus," three times. Jesus knew that Peter was weak. So he had to go through a dilemma to grow. When Jesus' and Peter's eyes met, they both knew what had happened. Peter ran out to the garden and wept bitterly.

I don't know exactly what your dilemma will be today. But God knows all of it. He was in your today yesterday, and He laid out the victory for you. Your mission today is to respond in a trusting way to God. No cursing or swearing, like Peter did to cover his identity as one of Jesus' disciples. You must not deny Him in battle today.

Dear reader, there should be no changing of morals to suit any man or woman who knows nothing about when the rooster will crow. Please don't say, "I am on my own on this one." Don't say, "I don't need prayer or anyone to pray for me."

Life is tough and the rat race of life is real. The race is on to maintain our selfhood, but I caution you to remember that life still happens after you plan. That's when character and morals are fine tuned. God is busy building your character so that after the storm and rain He is there with joy and cheer for you.

After you come through your dilemma successfully (or not), He will bind you up. Should you come back for help and restoration, He is right there. God will use people, animals, cars, doctors, everything at His disposal—which is everything—to get you to see how much He loves you. He is in a battle for your life. He wants you to live with Him forever. Don't miss that as you go into your dilemma experience today. God was already there. If you don't get the promotion and you get laid off instead, remember that you represent Jesus. He is right there. No denying Him. God is God; it is God Who provides for you and your family, not you.

You may be planning to meet today with your child's teacher for a conference. Please do not blow up at the teacher. That would be denying the Lord. Instead, work together for the good of your child. If it seems hard to work with the teacher, keep in mind that God already has a plan for your child's life that can never be undone. Only your attitude will be tested.

Here is another situation to watch out for. You and your new spouse have your first really big blow-out argument today. You want to use the d-word—*divorce*. Close up those lips. In fact, *never* use the word divorce. It leads to insecurity. James 3:6 reminds us that the tongue can start an awful fire that is hard to put out. If you say anything other than kind words, you could be lying to yourself. You love this person or you would not have gone all the way to the altar. Start with "I love you," then go to, "Let us try to understand each other. I still want you to grow old with me because you are still the one."

I believe things will end differently if you use your words to remind your spouse that you want understanding and not anger. He or she will grow more special to you. It will help you both to learn to respond with kindness and affirmation. This will change things from an argument to a growing relationship.

You know what to do next. Say something in a time of crisis like, "Rooster, rooster, I need a crow." I'm sure that will bring smiles instead of separation. Remember, God is sure to come through for you if you obey His words. James 1:19 says, "Be swift to listen, slow to speak, and slow to anger," I guess James had not written in time for Peter. But Peter is still without excuse because Jesus had forewarned him. You are now getting your warning from me to help keep your home together in love.

Your dilemma may come in sickness. God can even use His animals to rescue you. I'm sure some of you have already experienced animals to the rescue. We are all God's creatures. If God needs to use a rooster in your life today, let Him talk and you listen, and don't deny Him. Let me say a prayer on your behalf.

Dearest Savior,

Maker of all creatures great and small, Who has compassion on all Your hands have made. I come today, bringing in prayer all my readers who want to be faithful to You today. Peter denied You, but we want to pass our test today. We don't want to fall into the same situation. We want to make a faithful leap at dilemma decision time. I want to thank You for being in our dilemma before we get there.

Lord, help us to share our victories with others so Your praises can go throughout the land, as Peter's later did. Help us know that if we fall down, Your mercies are new every morning and You are there for us. Give us peace because we don't need to worry about our dilemma or become frozen, expecting it.

May we just live life and know storms of life come to pass. You said it many times, "And it came to pass." I ask as You build up your kingdom of faithful victorious children, even if you need to use a rooster to lead us, please let us trust You. Thank You, Lord, for Your Word. It is truly our best guide through this world of dilemmas.

In Jesus' name, Amen.

Day 29

A CHANGE

I'm alive! Thank You, God, for another day to live for You!

"Then the King will say, 'I know you did not realize this because a
change took place in your life and kindness and compassion
became part of your nature'" (Matthew 25:40, CWV)

*T*oday will be an affirming day from me to you. So many times we
try to get things right. Yes, yes, yes, sometimes we get it right! All
because you counted on God to do this change in you. You saw you needed
to make a change in your life to be more like Christ. He showed you yourself—you know God knows how to do that. Then He shows you what to
do to change. You took this personal message from God and now more
compassion and kindness are blooming like flowers of beautiful colors in
your heart. You are making Jesus a very happy Savior.

Think about the last time you gave someone flowers. What did it do
for them? I'm sure it brought out smiles. Maybe it brought out happy tears.
Surely it brought out pleasant feelings. It made the person feel the same
feelings you felt when you received flowers.

Some places—I hear Hawaii is one of them—when a weary traveler
arrives at the island, he or she is greeted with flowered leis placed around

the neck. What a lovely thought. When you grow in kindness and compassion as you are now doing, you are like the fresh flowers around the necks of people you show compassion towards.

Please know that the kindness and compassion you have grown into did not just happen. Dear friend, I know you had to grow through pain in your own life to get to this place. You overcame hardships and disappointments. Someone was kind to you while you were down and out. You felt what the sweet flower of compassion and kindness means. Now you want to be able to do for someone else what was done for you. You did it! I affirm you again. Compassion and kindness have slowly emerged as your new nature.

Things learned must be practiced in order to become a part of your nature. You must continue to nourish and nurture those great traits. Isaiah 30:21 tells us that God whispers in people's ears, telling them how to live. You must obey that voice so that you can remain an effective, compassionate, and kind person. Do not omit saying thank you when someone goes the extra mile for you, putting your desires before their own. Say thank you.

Help clean someone's home that is sick and cannot reciprocate. When you hear of a death in a family, arrive with paper goods and extra food. They may have people in and out of their home and need extra supplies. When someone in your neighborhood gets married and moves in, make new neighbors, friends, by bringing cookies to them. It only takes a few minutes to make cookies from cookie dough and it will make kindness and compassion continually bloom in your own heart. It will be like fresh flowers delivered to your neighbor's soul as well.

If your neighbor has to be out of town, think of ways you can do a little extra for him. Get the mail, feed the cat, water the plants, and just take a number and say, "I will call you if I see any trouble." This lets others know that you care.

Another way to bloom compassion in your heart is to send birthday cards, and special situation cards can also go out when you know someone is going through a particularly hard time. This is compassion. This is kindness. When my little niece passed away, her mother got a note from someone who was just reading the obituary. She saw that a young child had died. Her compassion awakened. She wrote to the grief-stricken family that she was touched by their pain and would be praying for them. This brought such joy to the bereaved that people cared who had never met their daughter.

Wow, see how this thing blossoms? And to think that you are a part of this. It is happening in your heart through God's love to you. Go ahead, pat yourself on the back. You deserve affirmation today. Occasionally, you may meet someone who is suddenly out of work. That should say to you automatically, "They probably need help." Say to them, "Here is some money." This can help in many ways. It can mean formula or diapers for their baby. Your extra shoe money, and some have plenty of shoes already, could mean transportation for that unemployed person to find a job or get their car repaired. Do you get it?

We have to be the hands and feet of Jesus here. When we show compassion and kindness, we store up treasure in heaven. Let God lead you in how to give. You could spend a few dollars on lunch or lose it and never miss it. However, by sharing your money with someone who needs it, compassion and kindness is matured in you while you hang flowers around your brother's neck. Don't wait for him or her to ask you, "Please give me or lend me." Before this happens, you decide how much money you can give. Bear in mind, joblessness can mean major financial setbacks for a family, especially if it lasts a long time. Help if you can with something systematically.

Here is a caution about kindness and compassion. You do not give to receive. Let us not get it twisted. Compassion and kindness come from God. He offers unconditional love and we should do the same for others.

Another way to grow compassion and kindness is through words. Tell someone that their smile brightened your day. See what it does to their face and feel what it does to yours. Look for ways to give compliments. That will be the same as putting fresh flowers around their necks. We are talking about sincere compliments, not flattery. Other examples include, saying , " That was a well done presentation", to a presenter after a program or a class. You'll be putting flowers around the neck of the presenter. Compliments beautify the soul and nurture kindness and compassion in the giver.

Of course, an appropriate touch or hug can do the same thing. When someone seems heavy-laden and is crying or just weary, a rub on the back is often very soothing. Use judgment with touch as it can be misunderstood. If a clear message is sent that I care, it can bring some of the most rewarding moments in life. Take someone's hand and say, "Lean on me." May God grow you today in compassion and kindness, and I applaud you for your effort. Now let us pray.

Dear God of kindness and compassion,

I fall at Your feet today to ask You to show me how, in my busy walk today, I will find an opportunity to be kind and compassionate. Help me not to miss my opportunity when it comes. Help me to respond to You. If I need a nudge, God, please send me one. I want to nurture these qualities in me so that I can be more like You. I want to be a source of comfort to my family, friends, co-workers, neighbors, strangers, and all Your disciples around me.

Thank You, Lord, for hearing this prayer and being attentive to my request. At the end of the day, when I have passed out my flowers of compassion, I know You will smile because You are pleased. Then I will look down and see that I have a few flowers blooming in my heart also.

In Jesus' precious name, Amen.

Day 30

DOUBLE-MINDED

I'm alive! Thank God for another day to live for Him!

"A double minded man is unstable in all his ways" (James 1:8).

$\mathscr{A}$ lack of trust is often the root of many troubles. Think of all the problems that mistrust can cause in various relationships. Instability grows when one person says, "I will do this or that," and ends up not following through. Here are some examples. You stand at the altar and say, "I will love you forever" and "Until death do us part." You commit endless love, you say, "I will never have another intimacy with anyone." You say this with your mouth and you say it before God and man.

Then the double-minded man or woman, unstable in all ways, crashes the trust of another person; a third party is allowed to interfere in the sacred marriage relationship. What a travesty. Before you leave the beauty of working together selflessly, self-centeredness creeps in and tears apart what God had joined together. What happened to the covenant and the commitment? I think some double-mindedness went on.

At your job, you agreed to be the backup person for a shift. You say you will come to work if you are needed. The call comes to you and you can't even be found; you left town. You are a double minded-person. Now others who depended on you and expected you, should a need arise, have to stumble about to fill your place. How unfair you have been to your coworkers and supervisors.

Another situation could be an employer who says, "I will hire you for ten dollars an hour, and you work for me eight hours a day." You work your eight hours daily, and when you get your check, it reflects fewer hours or less money. Your employer is a double-minded man or woman.

What if the worker agrees to work eight hours a day and works only seven hours? The employee becomes a double-minded person, unstable in all his or her ways and not to be trusted. He has a lack of integrity.

Sons and daughters of God should be men and women of their word. That is what Jesus asks of His children. I hope I don't cause anyone too much offense, but we must build trust and not back down. Have you promised your spouse or ex-spouse that you would pick up the children after school and then never showed up? You left the children vulnerable. You eroded your spouse's trust in you. You were unstable in all your ways. No wonder the spouse you promised to do this for is disgruntled when left inconvenienced and scrambling about to secure the safety of the children. The situation may seem simple to you, but other people rely on what you say you will do. To do otherwise is double-minded.

Here is another situation. You say, "I will have the dorm room or house clean today" and he or she counted on it. Later they bring a study partner in, and find the room still untidy and smelling bad. You are unstable in all your ways and double minded. Your roommate depended on your word and when she brought in a study partner she expected a clean room. How can the roommate believe you the next time you say, "I will clean the room" when this time you did not?

In fact, how can anything you say be believable? In the mind of your roommate, you may have been put into the category of liar. "Just try me again," you say. No, that gives you entitlement to do as you please again. The roommate is embarrassed. You do as you please and that leads to insta-bility in all your pursuits.

Today is stop-the-double-mindedness-and-get-stable-in-all-your-ways day. Caution, the double minded person often seeks to blame or discredit the lack of trust he or she is creating in the other person. The person who did not follow through on his word believes it is all right not to accept responsibility. He thinks it is okay for others to forgive him because his change of mind is not that serious.

A lot of emotional pain goes around at work, home, school, and com-munities when people find out their leaders are double-minded. They prom-ised a whole lot of people one thing, and then everyone finds out that the promise was not kept. Think about how you would feel if a friend says, "If you will lend me one hundred dollars, I will pay you back by Friday." A Friday or two or three goes by and you don't see the hundred dollars. Then the friend starts avoiding you. You end up losing one hundred dollars and a friend. All this happens to you when you thought you were helping out in the first place.

That's how a double-minded friend, unstable in all his ways, erodes friendship. If we are trying to be ambassadors for Christ, we must try to keep our words and actions the same. This is the only way we can teach others to trust God. Others read our example. Now I am talking to God's people, who are fickle at best. We need to recognize God's Word. It is there to help us make changes in our actions and attitudes. God's Word makes it clear for us to see ourselves. That is how we become more like Jesus, right?

I don't want you to be unstable in your ways. Look inward and see the pain a double-minded mouth and action in an individual can cause a fellow disciple. Take ownership of your actions. Sincerely apologize when you recognize your double-mindedness. You can only fix the problem by apologizing sincerely and asking God to let your actions and your words be the same.

The Bible gives healing words for those who are unstable. But also for those who have felt double-crossed. God knows your pain. You may have been a double-minded person. Now you know how it feels to have the rug pulled out from under you. You thought you were standing firmly on a friend's promise. And now the rug is gone from under you. And you do not know where you belong anymore.

When I was a child, there was a cruel game that children would play on each other. Someone would go to sit on a chair, fully expecting the chair to be there. The child saw the chair, touched the chair, and went to sit in the chair, and went plop on the floor. Another child had pulled the chair out from behind and left the unsuspecting child to hit the ground, hurt and humiliated. Sometimes that can destroy trust for a long time.

Why do we do things like that to each other? We call it joking and laugh at the other person's expense. Let us leave the double-minded ways alone. If we keep on doing something when we know how awful and unlike Jesus it is, we become more and more unstable in every situation and in every relationship. We become more and more the enemy of Jesus and a friend of Satan.

Don't become a double crosser, which is another form of double mindedness. You will find that trust is your greatest need. You will not be able to find trust because you are not able to give it. I know you do not want that for yourself. So let us pray and ask God to give us strength to leave the double-minded life behind and help us build stable relationships, families, communities, businesses, and world by God's power. Let us pray.

Oh, Lord,

Not one of us can say we have never been double-minded. We apologize to You first for misrepresenting You. You have certainly kept Your word. We want to become more and more like You. I pray for all the people whose lives are in disarray because they trusted in double-minded people. They may have lost their families and their jobs.

Show up for them today, Lord, and let them know that You can supply all their needs according to Your riches in glory as stated in Philippians 4:19. For those who have become habitually double-minded and don't even know how to get off a hamster wheel show up in a powerful way today, Lord, and take down the strongholds.

As Your people, we make intercession for their strength to correct the mismatch between words and actions. I know this can be a strong yoke of bondage. You said You can do all things for a child who asks. So we are asking for Your strength as we make a change in our lives. We are finished with unstableness and entitlement. Help us to be strong for the sake of Jesus, Who did not double-cross us.

Amen.

Day 31

EVIL DEEDS

I'm alive! Thank God for another day to live for Him!

"...Men loved darkness rather than light because their deeds were evil"
(John 3:19).

*E*ver notice when the police are looking for a suspect from a helicopter they use bright lights? Wonder why that is? If the suspect has done some evil deed, he or she is hiding in darkness, hoping not to be discovered. They are also hoping the darkness will hide them.

Funny, we don't think about it, but evil deeds jeopardize everyone. The doer of the deed often has to face civil law, fractured family trust, financial loss, and a broken relationship with God. The recipient of this evil deed is also at a loss of property or maybe life. It is not difficult to become untrusting of people and even God after a personal violation. The result is a double loss. Nothing good for the perpetrator or the victim. Ever notice when people choose to do evil they hide? They won't take photographs. They usually will not disclose their address and will not tell anyone where they are.

I suppose if someone were exposed and the world saw their evil deeds, he or she would feel embarrassed. This would be exposed. But truth *never* hides. It is sometimes scorned and intimidated. But it is constant. Truth is not afraid of questions and remains open for anyone to examine. Truth doesn't mind being discovered. Truth always comes into the light.

Evildoers are the opposite. Let me give you an example of how I recently got caught up in an evil deed. I brought my non-working computer to a large retail store for the people there to fix. They charge a lot of money to do work there, more than I expected. They gave out a few perks as well. So I gave them my computer to explore the problems, fix them, and return it.

Ten days later—ten days without a computer is a long time—I got it back and it was still not working. The first time I was in the store, I met a worker at the counter. He was sharp and computer major at a local college. I could tell he was on a mission to fix my computer for me. I came back later to find out what he had found and he was gone for the day. His shift was up. I was left at the mercy of the remaining staff. I listened to them sell to most customers.

They charged a customer for checking out the computer before any work or diagnosis could be done. I heard many customers who complained about their unanswered phone calls. I could feel their anxiety; they wanted their computers back for school or business. Please don't get me wrong, I know the workers were trying their best. I focused on my problem. I started thinking, *This doesn't make any sense. There must be a small retail store somewhere where a young competent graduate in computer science hangs out.*

The thought grew. When I had to bring the computer back, whom should I see but the sharp young man who had started work on my computer the first time. He did not sell me with the "We'll look over computer" talk. He told me how he could fix the problem and what he planned to do to get it right. He told me he would start it before his shift was over. But before the job was done, he would have to leave at the end of his shift.

Again I said, "No way." Here is where my deeds start turning evil. I wanted this young man's expertise for my computer. After all, he could think things through for me in no time and I could be on my way, right? Wrong. He was an employee of the store and was not allowed to steal customers, I'm sure. Before he left, I started telling him how smart I thought he was. I told him that he must know a store around here where a friend of his from school worked so that he could give me information to keep my computer going.

He said, "The problem you are having I can fix. I have done something like that before."

I said, "I am sure you are very good."

The plot thickens.

I said, "I need some information," and pulled out my folder and told him to write some contact information on the back cover. See how evil deeds need to hide. I needed to get the phone number in a dark way. I caught myself, thank God.

I looked at him and he started getting nervous. He looked around to see who was listening. He began tapping his pencil fast and furiously. Notice how evil deeds affect everyone in a bad way. If everyone did what I was trying to do, the store loses. The store loses good workers, and it would soon have no service to provide for anyone. It gets even worse. Employers wouldn't be able to trust their employees not to steal their customers. Corruption and evil deeds would perpetuate. Everyone would think that they are getting over on everyone else.

The way of truth and honesty would be left by the roadside, waiting to be picked up in your heart or mind. When the Lord pointed out to me that I was acting as a tempter, I shuddered. I had tempted the young man to do an evil thing and I was asking him to do the evil deed.

The Lord rebuked me by saying, "I take care of all your needs, Dawn—your health, your wealth, your family, your salvation. Don't you think I can keep your little computer going and pay the bill also? Don't sell me out for a computer-fixing job that would save you a few dollars. You would encourage this man in the wrong direction and you would be caught in the middle of the evil deed."

Immediately, I said to the young man, "You don't have to give me any contact information. I am sorry that I even asked you such a thing."

He kindly said, "That's okay." He started working on my computer. He showed me what he was going to do and told me what the others needed to do to finish the task. I could see the relief in his lack of fidgeting when we were doing things right.

I had tempted the young man to do an evil deed. I am just thankful I did not become a devil that day in that situation. I listened to the rebuke from God and retraced my steps. When I returned two short hours—not ten days—later, my computer was working.

Thank God for the victory over evil deeds. Thank God for a working computer two hours later at no charge. When we obey God, He works things out for us. Evaluate yourself today. That is how the Word of God changes us from evildoers who love darkness to truthful deed doers who are living in the light of God's love.

Evaluate your actions today. Get rid of any evil deed activities you were scheming up for today. Turn them around before you embarrass the God you love so much. By His strength I did and so can you. God can supply you with much more than you are scheming for. No guilt from evil deeds and no hiding follow God's truth. Let us pray for transformation today.

Dearest Jesus, meek and mild,

Thank You for showing up today to point out our evil deeds. You are the light of the world. And we want to stay in that light. You are also our salvation. Please keep us in Your light. I pray for my readers who may be dealing with evil deeds they were about to do today. Let them not follow through with it. Let it be a victory.

Bless the people who may be coerced into doing an evil deed. Help them not to participate. Help them to be like the young man in our story, struggling for victory and overcoming. Give us patience with ourselves. We get weak along life's journey. Hold us to a high standard, Lord. We want to pass our evil deed test.

You have a crown awaiting those who choose light rather than darkness. Thank You for the victory You gave me today. I will forever lift my voice in praise and thanksgiving. It is because of Your victory on Calvary for me that I can be victorious today. Thank You for the soft yet pointed way You get us truthful and honest.

In Jesus' precious name, Amen.

Day 32

Songs of Love

I'm alive. Thank God for another day to live for Him!

"Thy statutes have been my songs…"
(Psalm 119:54).

oday's devotion is about songs that proclaim God's statutes. Their words glorify His love and His power in our lives. I hope that, as you reflect on the words of the songs I have chosen, you will grow deeper in love with your Creator. Whenever you sing a song of praise from a book, take time to lift the words off the page and hear what you are actually saying.

You are also saying to God through song, "I will make my heart more in line with Your truth." Songs help strengthen our resolve to trust God. Reflect on these:

I serve a risen savior; He is in the world today,

I know that He is living whatever men may say;

I see His hand of mercy,

I hear His voice of cheer,

and just the time I need Him He is always near.

He lives, He lives, and Christ Jesus lives today.

He walks with me and talks with me along life's narrow way.

He lives, He lives, salvation to impart.

You ask me how I know He lives, He lives within my heart.

"He Lives," Alfred H. Ackley

Wow! Here's another:

There are many troubles that will burst like bubbles,

There are many shadows that will disappear;

When you learn to meet them with a smile to greet them,

For a smile is better than a frown or a tear.

You can smile when you can't say a word,

you can smile when you cannot be heard,

You can smile when it's cloudy or fair,

You can smile any time anywhere.

"You Can Smile," Alfred H. Ackley

Another song is entitled, "Burdens Are Lifted at Calvary."

Days are filled with sorrow and care,

hearts are lonely and drear;

burdens are lifted at Calvary,

Jesus is very near.

Cast your care on Jesus today,

leave your worry and fear;

Burdens are lifted at Calvary,

Jesus is very near.

Troubled soul, the Savior can see,

every heartache and tear;

Burdens are lifted at Calvary,

Jesus is very near.

"Burdens Are Lifted at Calvary," John M. Moore

This one we used to sing at worship in the mornings before going to school.

Father, lead me day by day,

ever in Thy own sweet way;

teach me to be pure and true,

show me what I ought to do.

When in danger make me brave,

make me know that Thou can save;

Keep me safe by Thy dear side,

let me in Thy love abide.

When I'm tempted to do wrong,

make me steadfast, wise, and strong;

And when all alone I stand, shield

me with Thy mighty hand.

May I do the good I know,

be Thy loving child below,

and then at last go home to Thee

ever more Thy child to be.

"Father, Lead Me Day By Day," John Page Hopps

Imagine sending your child off to school with words from that song, which are powerful words against evil and wrong. Here is another powerful song.

O for a faith that will not shrink,

Though pressed by many a foe.

That will not tremble on the brink of poverty or woe.

That will not murmur or complain beneath the chastening rod.

But in the hour of grief or pain can lean upon its God.

A faith that shines in the bright and clear.

When tempests rage without.

That when in danger knows no fear.

In darkness feels no doubt.

Lord, give me such a faith as this,

and then, what er' may come,

I'll taste even here the hallowed bliss

of an eternal home.

    "O for a Faith That Will Not Shrink," William Hiley Bathurst

Now here is a catchy little tune that you can sing to get you right out temptation.

Victory is mine, victory is mine,

I told Satan to get thee behind,

victory today is mine.

                     "Victory is Mine," Dorothy Norwood

Praise and adoration must also be on our lips. You already know the heavenly hosts are praising Him. Remember, your lips must praise Him. My lips can't praise for you.

Praise God from Whom all blessings flow,

Praise Him all creature here below.

Praise Him above ye heavenly host

Praise Father, Son, and Holy Ghost.

    "Praise God from Whom All Blessing Flow," Thomas Ken

This next song sung in a group reminds everyone to pray for one another.

I need the prayers of those that I love
while traveling on life's rugged way,
that I may true and faithful be
and live for Jesus every day.

I need the prayers of those I love
to help me in each trying hour
to bear my tempted soul to Him
that He may keep me by His power.

I need my friends to pray for me
to hold me up on wings of faith
that I may walk the narrow way.
Kept by our Father's glorious grace.

I want my friends to pray for me,
to bear my tempted soul above
and intercede with God for me.
I need the prayers of those I love.

"I Need the Prayers," James D. Vaughn

Imagine your friends about you, singing and praising about your problem. What a unified strength.

This next song is titled, "My Faith Has Found a Resting Place."

My faith has found a resting place
Not in a manmade creed,
I trust the ever living one that He for me will lead.

Enough for me that Jesus saves,

this ends my fear and doubt,

a sinful soul I come to Him,

He will not cast me out.

I need no other evidence,

I need no other plea;

It is enough that Jesus died

and rose again for me.

My soul is resting on the Word,

The living Word of God:

Salvation in my Savior's name,

Salvation through His blood.

I need no other evidence,

I need no other plea;

It is enough that Jesus died

and rose again for me.

The great physician heals the sick,

The lost He came to save;

For me His precious blood He shed,

For me His life He gave.

"My Faith Has Found a Resting Place," Eliza Hewitt

I feel so sheltered, don't you?

'Tis so sweet to trust in Jesus,

just to take Him at His word;

Just to rest upon His promise,

Just to know, "Thus saith the Lord."

O how sweet to trust in Jesus,

Just to trust His cleansing blood;

Just in simple faith to plunge me,

'Neath the healing, cleansing flood.

Yes, 'tis sweet to trust in Jesus,

Just from sin and self to cease;

Just from Jesus simply taking

Life, and rest, and joy, and peace.

I'm so glad I learned to trust Thee,

Precious Jesus, Savior, Friend;

And I know that Thou art with me,

Wilt be with me till the end.

Jesus, Jesus, how I trust Him;

How I've proved Him o'er and o'er!

Jesus, Jesus, precious Jesus!

O for grace to trust Him more!

"Tis So Sweet to Trust in Jesus," Louisa Stead

When I'm in pain mentally or physically I usually sing this one.

Jesus, Jesus, Jesus,

there is just something about that name,

Master, Savior, Jesus,

like the fragrance after the rain.

Jesus, Jesus, Jesus,

let all heaven and earth proclaim,

There is just something about that name.

"There's Something About That Name," William J. and Gloria Gaither

May we carry the words to a song in our hearts as we go on God's business today. Let us pray.

Dear Jesus,

Thank You for music. Music lightened the load for Paul and Silas when they were cast into prison. Miriam broke into song after the successful crossing of the Red Sea. Music also cheered Saul's heart when David played and sang to him.

Now our hearts are gladdened because of the music You have given our souls. Thank You, Lord, for the gift of music. Thank You for the musicians You gave us to sing for our encouragement and enlightenment. Thank You for the instruments that add so much lightness to the words we sing.

We praise You for the skill of the musicians who play the instruments. Thank You for pretty voices that sing these songs to praise You. Thank You for our own voices. Thanks can come from our own throats with praise and adoration. Thank You for the song that the birds sing that is always very beautiful.

Lord, You thought about everything we need to bring joy to our souls. Today we just want to thank You for the gift of music. It has become a powerful blessing to use for You. Thank You, dearest Jesus.

Amen.

Day 33

THE LIVING GOD

I'm alive! Thank God for another day to live for Him.

"I beseech you therefore, brethren, by the mercies of God, that ye present your bodies a living sacrifice, holy, acceptable unto God, which is your reasonable service" (Romans 12:1).

*O*ur God is the Living God! This may be one of the most powerful concepts about the power God has in our world. When I recognize that God is alive, moving, arranging, and organizing things around us to make us more like Him, I get excited. The Scripture talks about our bodies being a living sacrifice. An easier way to grasp the living concept is to tell me what your 'alive' body will do today. It will shop, worship as you are doing now, exercise, sing, drive, cook, clean, walk, and more. All those activities and more describe what a living person does.

Some people take the text further and say, "We really have a responsibility to take care, special care of our bodies. They have to last for a while. Each person gets only one." To care for this body we get air, heartbeat, and functionality from God. He is the giver of life (Psalm 22:9). How can you give something you don't have? Impossible, right? We are clear about the fact that God is the giver of life. This confirms that God is alive in you right now. He is instructing you. Listen today to what He is telling you.

God is also providing for you right now. Have you ever been out of food, work, or money? Let me guess, you prayed and before you could start to wonder about your prayer, the answer was at the door or in the mail. Did you have a credit problem or apply for a loan that you felt would not go through, and then the loan was miraculously approved?

How about those court cases—remember how hopeless and impossible it seemed? You prayed to the living God, He showed up in the courtroom, and look at you now. God is a living God, active while you're driving your car. Who do you think took over the steering wheel when you fell asleep? It was the living God. Who do you think shut your mouth from cursing your boss? It was the living God. Who do you think protected your puppy from sudden death under the car? It was the living God.

Who do you think walked with your child into the classroom today? You guessed it. It was the living God. How can He be with my child and with me also? He can because He is an omnipresent living God. Who is it that formed the baby in your womb? Who do you think decided your loved one was ready to give their breath back to God? The living God. He gave the breath. He carefully measured it out, and when His purpose was completed He took His breath back. Everyone will get to that point someday. This is life and not a practice run.

While we have life from the living God, let us render a reasonable service. God said, "I made you in my image to look like me and to show the world how a child of mine living in my image represents me." God wants to be alive in you and promises you help along your journey. The living God said that, not Dawn. I have no power to change or to save you but the living God does.

Do you want to change the way you live? That is the living God working on your mind and giving you clearer thoughts. Clearer thoughts make more acceptable behavior that is patterned after Jesus' life. Ever wanted more wisdom and prayed for it? The living God showed up with His all-knowing self and he jumped into your mind with a sharpener. Then you said, "I got it."

The answers came from the living God. You just asked Him for a favor, and He granted it to you. God is alive and moving you towards holy character. He knows the imperfect nature of man. He knows the devil is out there as well trying to discourage God's masterpieces. You know that you and I are God's masterpieces, I'm sure.

God opened up His house in your heart and He is living there. If you ever get confused about what He is saying, He gave you the best reference book called the Bible. What you read there and understand are the many ways the living God is working on your behalf.

God is working mainly on our decision to accept the salvation He has to offer us. The living God knows if you accept Him you will live forever with Him. That is His greatest desire. He is also preparing a place for you so that you can be where He is (John 3:17).

You must develop faith through situations. He will show up in your life. Talk to your living God today; He is right there. Tell Him your true concerns. Tell Him about your boyfriend or girlfriend. Ask God if he or she is the right one. He should know, right? Then do what He tells you. Tell God about the recital today. The living God will be there, He will help you with the difficult sections.

God is also in your tomorrow because He is the living God. Ask God what to do about the new pain. Should I seek help today or not? Will it go away? Then listen for the answer from the living God. When He needs to move others around to get you through, He will do that too; He is the living

God. God can change, wonderfully change, the most hopeless situations in your favor, when you ask, believe, and faithfully obey. Let us pray today to God, our living God.

Oh, living, loving, Father,

Today we know that You gave us living bodies so that You can be alive in us. We just want to thank You that you didn't make us and then abandon us. You have already worked out our today.

Please don't give up on us if we act stubborn. Please keep pressing us to be obedient to Your Word. We know that if we follow You, we will live with You in paradise. Eternal paradise is where we want to be. We need Your help, living God. It surely is nice to have the living God sitting beside me in the car right now. I just want to turn to You and say thank You for being here.

In the worthy name of Jesus, dearest Jesus, I pray, Amen.

Day 34

BASKETS, BREAD, AND FISH

I'm alive. Thank You, God, for another day to live for You!

"Then the disciples said, 'How can we feed this huge crowd? All we have is five little loaves of bread and two small fish?' Jesus said, 'Let me have those five little loaves and two small fish.' When they brought Him the loaves and fish, He asked the crowd to 'find some grass and sit down.' He took five little loaves and the two small fish, looked up to heaven and asked a blessing, giving thanks for what He had. Then He broke the loaves in half and gave them to the disciples together with the two fish to pass out to the people. The huge crowd ate the bread and fish until everyone had enough to eat. When they were finished, the disciples picked up twelve baskets full of what was left (one basket of leftovers for each disciple). Five thousand men were in that crowd, not counting women and children." (Matthew 14:17-21, cwv).

We will focus on how Jesus answered the disciples' questions as He grew their faith. First, He invited the crowd to lunch. In Matthew 14:16 he said, "they didn't need to leave yet."

When Jesus invites you to lunch you'd better get ready to eat. Jesus is the One who invites us to eat. He created the meat for eating to sustain us.

He said, "We can feed them." Jesus wanted to feed the multitude. I know now Jesus wants to feed you and me as well. That is special. Jesus is hospitable. Jesus is our host today. Waitress/waiters are you listening?

The disciples said, "How can we feed this huge crowd?"

Jesus answered and said, "Let me have those loaves and fish."

The disciples obeyed.

Are you hungry today for physical food? It is your turn to give Jesus what you have. He says to find a comfortable spot to rest your feet. I notice the disciples said, "All we have is the loaves and fish." They did not remember that the "we" included Jesus, the Bread of Life from heaven.

They kept Him in their pocket as a teacher needing to hurry to the next meeting to avoid being late. They had Jesus in a category as one of the boys. They could not even think of the lunch of the size they needed that day to feed five thousand people with. The disciples, as we do today, forgot about God's ability to provide for His people. Yet He shows us how He provides in style for His people. This is because He and His Father work together for us.

In our Scripture passage, Jesus looked up, and giving thanks for what He already had, He asked for a blessing. Before you eat, do you ask a blessing on your food? If you do, keep doing it. If you don't, I encourage you to follow Christ's example. This is a great way to start. It shows that you know who provides. It makes you more thankful for your food. Blessed food is always more nourishing, I believe.

Another point is that Jesus gave thanks for what they *had*. It is easy to give thanks when there are fifty more meals in the refrigerator and money to buy milk and bread if you run out. The challenge comes when you have no means and the last bread has to be shared out many ways.

The storage cabinet is empty, so how do we just eat what we have and wait? The answer is coming. "He broke each loaf in half and placed the fish and loaves in baskets for the disciples to give to people." Jesus told His Father of the need: We need bread for these people. Please send some. God sent enough for everyone to be satisfied and extra so they would remember this moment. God knows how to feed His people. That is something the multitude would remember forever.

We have to ask God and pray for faith that He can provide. This is especially essential if we are often hungry. I am aware that there are people all around the world without enough food to eat. Where we can, we need to help to reduce world hunger.

Jesus knows all about real hunger as well. Remember that He had lived through forty days without food or water. That huge crowd had enough to eat. Here is a word we must remember—*enough*. Not more than enough, not less than enough, but enough. Find your enough and stop there. We should not make wasting food a habit.

After lunch, the Bible says, they stored twelve baskets of leftovers. You are one of His disciples today so you will get a basket. The first basket is filled with His power. The second one is filled with His hospitality. The third basket we will fill with His blessings. The next basket will have His thanksgiving. The next basket will be an invitation to eat with Him. The sixth is to be delivered to others. The seventh basket you are to pray over. The eighth basket is for you to share with those who do not have enough. The ninth basket is for you to eat, leisurely sitting on the grass. The tenth basket you get to clean up. The eleventh basket you get to keep and remind yourself of this day, and the last basket, you just take home.

God provides not only your necessary food. He also builds your faith and your thanksgiving and He then strengthens your soul. The next time you think you are the one providing for your daily bread, think again. Look up and give thanks and bless the food God has provided for you because it is enough.

God provides our daily food. Ask Him to show you how to get your daily bread. If you are not sure He will tell you. Just know that what He tells you to do, do it and He will provide for your needs. Remember, food is more than eating. One must realize it is an experience of receiving God's blessings, being thankful, and sharing your blessings with others.

You get to keep a basket to remind you of your food from God. Now let us pray.

Bread of heaven,

Thank You that You can and will provide our food for today. I ask You in a special way to be near the homeless. Please be with those who have no kitchens. Please be with those children around the world who do not have any food. Sustain them, I pray.

For people with an abundance of food, help them to stop eating at enough. Help them to share their food and resources with those in need. It may be a bag of fruit to the beggar on the street because it is not necessarily always money that is helpful. Give us ideas as to how we can be used by You to be bread for someone else. Maybe we can buy an extra sandwich at lunch and give it to the sign holder who says he is hungry. We will eat our enough today with thanksgiving and praise for our appetites. We will thank You for the ability to eat and digest and share food with others.

We will give You thanks for the growers and the reapers of the food we eat. We will praise You for the sunshine and the rain that kept our food coming from Your soil. Thank You for the long hours, untiring hours that the reapers worked to harvest the food. Thank You for those who prepared the grain.

Lord, we will not forget to thank You for the truckers who had to drive hard to deliver the food to the market. Thank You for the means to purchase the food. Thank You for leaving us this object lesson in Your holy Word that we can take and learn from. Let us eat the words so that we can grow in faith.

Remind us that You will provide for us as You provided for that multitude. Thank You, Bread of Life.

Amen.

Day 35

PEOPLE PEOPLE

I'm alive! Thank God for another day to live for Him.

"And the King shall answer and say unto them, Verily I say unto you,
Inasmuch as ye have done it unto one of the least of these my brethren,
ye have done it unto me" (Matthew 25:40).

I have visited some large cities, and I've been at large gatherings like ball games and conventions. I have often thought, *Wow, what a lot of people everywhere! Look at all these people. I can hardly get in and out of the parking lot from a game.* Sometimes it takes me over an hour to get out. People all around me are trying to do the same thing. Why are there so many people in the world? Why am I one of them?

What is all this about, Lord? I hear singers sing songs like, "People who need people are the luckiest people in the world." Is that why You made people so other people can be "lucky"?

Jesus said He loves us and wants us to be His disciples. Jesus can and will meet all our needs if we follow Him. I followed one day during His ministry on earth as it is recorded in Matthew 5. He spoke the beatitudes. He was surrounded by people.

Jesus is going to give you a lot of people to practice showing your love for Christ with. I will be in heaven working on your housing. I will be forgiving your sins and paying attention to your every need. This is what I want you to do for me. Love me by loving My people all around you. Your love is not to be based on another person's behavior. Your love is to be based on obedience to God. You must learn to love the people around you like I love them. That may sound easy but you cannot do it without My help. I am always available.

Ready for change? I hope so. How often do we group people together in a negative way and make fun of them with a group of people who are like us? As you are around groups of people, think of the true feelings you feel towards people in these groups. If they approached you, how would you react? "Fat people," "all people of a particular race," "all smokers and drinkers," "ugly people," "skinny people," "celebrities," "felons," "jackpot winners," "homeless people," "drug addicts and sellers," "rich and famous people," "homosexuals" . . . .

We characterize everyone in the group the same way. Our remarks can be very negative, and indicate we think people are below us. We elevate people in some categories to unrealistic expectations way over our heads. We categorize people according to our likes or dislikes. Few people hit our chord of love, sympathy, or compassion.

How many of these groups do you want to love gently to Jesus? How many of these people do you even care about? Jesus put people on earth, lots of people, so no one will be without excuse to practice His love on. "Oh, how I love Jesus," you sing.

Let us look at God's version of love. In 1 Corinthians 13 it says, "Everything we do spiritually is a waste of time for heaven if we do not have love for our fellow man." How do we love? Number one, love is patient. No yelling is allowed, at anyone, at any time. We have to grow into that, don't we? Wait your turn in line because there is no line-cutting allowed. Words like, "What's taking those people so long?" "Can't they learn English like the rest of us?"

A slow, older person should not receive sighs and gestures of impatience when he finally finishes doing his banking. Are we getting the picture of what patience means? Put yourself in the picture. How do you act when you are impatient with a child? Remember, love is patient.

Number two, love is never rude or disrespectful. Examples include words like, "Move out of my way. I am late for the airport." Other examples may be, "Don't tell me what to do" and "I'll tell you what the #!*$. Swear words with very harsh meanings, demoting mother and fatherhood—love doesn't do that. Love is never rude.

Number three, love is never puffed up with its own importance. Example, "I am the CEO, CFO, boss, chief of staff, top dog, get out of my way." This is puffy pride talk. Other examples could include, "I can't be bothered with those people, I have money to make, people to demote, derail, fire, etc.

When people are grouped negatively because of race, religion, or creed, as a lower, slower, unneeded group, love exits and pride busts in through the door.

Number four, love never keeps a record of wrong or holds grudges. Some hold on to hurt that was caused by a particular group. "See my story," they say, "I will never forget or love your kind of people." God is not pleased with that position.

Here is another example of keeping a record of wrong. "You told me off, up one side and down the other, you humiliated me in public, and I'll never forget that. I'll get you back." Revenge is of the devil. This cannot be the position of a follower of Christ.

"When we were kids you used to bully me." How long will you hold on to hurts of the past? Pick a past pain caused by the bully and let the bully be forgiven. I doubt he or she is even thinking about you. You become the prisoner to be set free. Love is never puffed up. Love is a more excellent way.

Let's turn to God for strength to be more patient and kind today. We must not think more highly of ourselves than we should. Let us not be rude or disorderly in our conduct. And let us not hold grudges. Disciples cannot behave like that. People are all around us to practice the love principle on. If everything you did or said about your fellow man bounced right back on you, would you speak or act as you do now? Would you carry out every action you have carried out to your fellow man today?

God's Word says, "If you do it unto one of the least of these people, it is as if you are doing it to me" (Matthew 25:40) When you recognize that you have hurt someone, you need to sincerely apologize and say, "I am sorry." Otherwise, you leave people hurting because you just don't care. Jesus cares; you should also.

You are His disciple, and you follow His example. Jesus had compassion for all around Him, no matter how many people there were. Dear friend, if you offend one of the precious children God has died for, you are wasting spiritual time and your service is not acceptable to God according to 1 Corinthians 13. It is only noise.

Look around at all the faces of people you will see today. Touch someone with a smile; give a tissue to wipe a tear. Compliment someone on something positive you observe. That is God's love in action. Move with friendship towards a group you previously avoided. Learn that differences are okay and everyone does not have to look and live like you. But all should be loved by you.

When I use the word *love* it is based on the four points of 1 Corinthians 13 that we just went over. Use God's Word as your clear standard. Any other man-made standards are flawed. Let love find lodging in your heart. When this happens, the world will be a better place for you and for me. People need the Lord. How can they find Him if you and I don't show them by our love?

Faith is good, hope is good, but the best is love. Let us pray together.

Father of love,

Pour on us vials and vials of love today. We want to pour it on our fellow men today, and we want You to be proud of our change today. We want to keep You real in somebody's day today. Take hate, grudges, self-ishness, and unforgiveness out of us today. Root it all up. Dig deep in our hearts and rip out envy and jealousy. Drag out self-importance.

These mean feelings come from the devil. We are tired of him and his games. Put it all in the trash can of life. Change us to live and to love like Jesus. We want to practice peace and holiness. We know the golden rule, do unto others as we want others to do unto us. Please, God, let that be what we seek after.

Let us show love to everyone where we have erred in the past. Lord, please forgive us. Thanks for not giving up on us with all of our self-im-portance attached. Extend Your saving grace and mercy toward us.

Lord, to be able to answer this prayer makes You some kind of God. Please, Lord, help us today to love people, our brothers and sisters. Help us to find someone to show the love of Jesus to each moment. Thank You for making so many people and all kinds of people so no one is without someone to practice Your love on.

In the loving name of Jesus, Amen.

Day 36

EARTHLY-MINDED VS. HEAVENLY-MINDED

I'm alive. Thank You, God, for another day to live for You!

"Obeying your sinful self brings death, but obeying the things of the spirit brings joy and peace" (Romans 8:6 CWV).

*L*et's make a damage assessment of what earthly sinful things have done. Because of sin, flowers, people, and pets die. Loved ones disown family members. There is widespread poverty. Thieves, crime, and violence incubate and escalate. Sin becomes the rule of the land. Earthquakes, tsunamis, and hurricanes are happening in record numbers.

Are you thinking of other evil as you read this? Can you name a few of the damages to people and our earth because of sin? This is painful and ugly. Evil paints a picture of starvation, injustice, homelessness, mistreatment of children, broken and dysfunctional families; all of this is a result of sin and evil.

Paternity issues, that plague us all, are due to selfishness and sinfulness. Rudeness, fighting, strife, and wars are all about sin—am I making it real? Sin is walking out on your family to obtain other sexual pleasures. It is based on selfishness. Just think of the hurt you are planning to do today.

I am only trying to keep it real. What has sin ruptured in you? What joy has sin taken away?

The next question, are you part of the sin problem or are you part of the solution? Is your life making the problem better or worse? First, know that all of us are born hopelessly sinful. Psalm 51:5 says we are born in sin and shaped in iniquity. We start out in life being selfish and self-centered. Think about it, parents. From the time your baby arrived, it has been all about them or else you hear about it loud and clear. The noise escalates from there to "I want, I want, I want." If the "I wants" are granted, everything is okay. But if the requests are not granted, the child screams in displeasure, and the parent is labeled selfish.

All of us are children of God. So lest you think I am only talking about your offspring, include yourself as a child of God. Most of us function from a selfish perspective; we think about ourselves before we think of anyone else. We must appear to our heavenly Father as a bunch of earthly-minded, needy individuals.

We come to Jesus for gifts like children do when Christmas comes. Many have grown into selfish individuals who do not fear God. Why would God even want to deal with us? How can we pull ourselves out of this quicksand? How can we get away from evil? I'm glad you asked.

These devotionals are about spiritual growth. They require change. How can we take a nugget from each day and grow a bit more like Christ? The nugget for today is in today's Scripture found in Romans 8:6. Obey the things of the Spirit. That requires us to think like Jesus; did you hear me? To think like Jesus. Let me say it again, to think like Jesus thinks. "Let this mind be in you which was also in Christ Jesus" (Philippians 2:5). This text focuses on our thoughts.

Thoughts come to us from many sources. They come from interactions with many people. Some thoughts come through the powerful media of television and radio. Books we read and study affect our thoughts. Some thoughts come from life lessons we have learned. Our everyday living and normal consequences cause us to ponder. Many thoughts come into our minds through our senses of touch, taste, smell, sight, and hearing. Those five senses capture what's going on around us and form our thoughts.

Our role is to recognize what causes sin, death, and pain. Then we must quickly weed out those things from our thoughts because now we know that they bring sin, death, and pain. Then we need to fill ourselves only with those things that we need for eternal life. Eternal life is still our ultimate goal, right?

Don't try to squeeze a little bit of self in with the change. It is not you who will change yourself. It does not happen when you say, "I'm going to stop lying today" or "I'm going to forgive" or "I'm going to give my used computer to the shelter today." That is not how it begins. Like David in Psalm 51:10, we must come to Jesus and ask Him to create in us a clean heart and renew a right spirit within us. When we pray that prayer, we get real backup power from heaven.

Bible reading increases and texts like Philippians 4:8 become your master guide: "Whatsoever things are true, honest, just, pure, lovely, whatsoever things are of a good report and full of virtue, think on these things." This principle will forever govern heavenly-minded people. They stop watching distasteful stories on television or reading distasteful stories in books. They choose the high road in squabbles and do not repay evil for evil.

Heavenly-minded people look for ways to make this world a better place by their selfless deeds. Long-suffering is a part of the fruit of the Spirit. Heavenly-minded people put the fruit of the Spirit on full display. The rest of the traits of the fruit of the Spirit can be found in Galatians 5:22: love, joy, peace, gentleness, goodness, and faith. Compare the difference between earthly-minded people and heavenly-minded people. Choose to stay away from the things that keep us evil to make more room in your mind to think about eternal things. Let the Lord begin your day with you.

We are leaving our earthly selfish thoughts for heavenly and eternal thoughts. Are you ready for the fight? I'm going to use an analogy of a boxing match. In the ring today is, "Earthly- Minded." He is wearing the off-color shorts to the left. In the right of the ring is the one with the brightly-colored shorts, and he is called "Heavenly-Minded."

In the early rounds it looks like off-color shorts is winning. That is because the fight is just starting. Don't get discouraged. You have not begun getting rid of the influences of negative people, fiction novels, and untruthful television shows. You have just started working on that.

Suddenly, you skip one distasteful television show a week. This happens due to your lack of desire to see evil. Next you stop reading that sinister novel full of lust. This book is no longer interesting to you. You find yourself interested in reading heavenly-minded literature and associate with heavenly-minded people.

You ask yourself, "When and how did this happen?" You even begin to notice the difference. You go to places to find heavenly-minded people. Some were around you already—you just had not noticed. When you become heavenly-minded, suddenly you realize how many other heavenly-minded people are around you.

I know that is why you are reading this devotional. Good job, God is pleased. Now how is the fight going? I think by halfway through the fight, the tables are turned, and Heavenly-Minded is winning.

Jesus stands and cheers and says, That's My loved one, Heavenly-Minded. Just call on Me, I'm here to help you. We're going to win this; we got this.

By the end of the fight, if you just stay in the race, Jesus says, "For your steadfastness I will give you a crown of life." We don't finish the fight as perfect people, but we are tied to Jesus and Revelation 2:10 promises us that Jesus is the rewarder; His grace is sufficient for our sins. Yes, we will die, but with the eternal in us. When we awaken, we will receive the crown of eternal life, and that is how the fight ends. Let us pray for that eternal goal.

Lord,

Today we come to you with one or two choices. Please help us to be aware that eternal destiny is in every choice we make. We know evil, we see evil, and we have had enough of evil. Let us remember at our office, while we are driving, while we are living to keep our minds and thoughts stayed on You.

Let us choose to listen to music that reminds us of the eternal choice. Let us choose friends with an eternal focus. We admit we are weak and sometimes cannot see evil coming. Sometimes we even participate in the evil. But please, God, at those times open our eternal eyesight so that we can move away from evil as soon as we recognize its form.

Help us not to focus for a moment on the lust of the flesh, eyes, or the pride of life (1 John 2:16). Close our senses down so that we won't think evil. We don't want to contaminate our minds today. Steer us away from our natural tendencies to evil.

Thank You for being in the ring with us today and helping us to win this round. Every round goes higher and higher until we get our crown of life. Thank You for You Word. It is truth and it is life.

In Jesus' precious name, Amen.

Day 37

LIVING CROWNS

I'm alive. Thank You, God, for another day to live for You!

"…Be thou faithful unto death, and I will give thee a crown of life" (Revelation 2:10).

*S*ome days I just like to sit and think about heaven. It will be a wonderful place for you and me when we get there. Do you mind if I review some of the vivid descriptions that Scripture tells us about heaven?

You may also dream about heaven. However, 1 Corinthians 2:9 says, "But as it is written, eye hath not seen, nor ear heard, neither have entered into the heart of man, the things which God hath prepared for them that love him."

So we have dreaming license. After all, heavenly thoughts are what we should dwell on anyway. Think of a home with twelve foundations, each of the foundations glow a different pretty color. Jasper is a clear green color. Sapphire is a blue green color. Chalcedony is a gray, grayish-blue or a shade of brown ranging from pale to nearly black. Emerald is bright green. Sardonyx is white or clear somewhat like a diamond. Sardius is an orange color. Crystallite is transparent and will be one of the colors in the foundation. Beryl could be blue, green, pink, yellow, or maybe it changes colors. Topaz is a yellow color. Chrysoprase is an apple-green. Jacinth is a red-orange color and amethyst is a violet.

So imagine living on top of a city with colors like that as your foundation. I cannot even imagine. We will be sitting on a rainbow of twelve colors with an opaque foundation in a huge city. That must be beautiful.

Now let's look at the walls of the city. They will be made of clear jasper, a transparent, clear green. You can look right through them. Those walls must be phenomenal! I have a friend who walked right into a window one day because it was clean and clear. To her it was completely transparent. She could not see it. She was okay, only having a bump on the lip. But she said, "I didn't even know glass was there."

I guess we will really see clearly in heaven. We will wonder where this wall ends, where does another one begin? We will live in a square city, and discovery will be fun. I will reach out and walk forward slowly until I touch the jasper wall. I will feel like a baby discovering his toes for the first time. Then I will marvel, "Wow." I will look down at my feet and be amazed to see what I am walking on.

In Revelation 21:21, John says the streets are also transparent gold as if it were glass. Can you imagine, transparent gold streets that allow me to see the foundations through them? This is why Jesus told us to lay up our treasures in heaven. I'm going to walk on transparent gold streets.

Then I will go to explore the gates of the city. There are twelve of them. Each side of this beautiful city has three gates. Each gate is made of one huge pearl. When Jesus says He is preparing a place in heaven for us, He is working on those big pearls to make each gate. Revelation 21:2 says, "I saw the Holy City, the new Jerusalem, coming down out of heaven from God, prepared as a bride beautifully dressed for her husband"(NIV). This tops the list. I cannot even imagine this beauty, yet there is more.

There is a river running through the middle of the streets with living water. I guess the water must sing or dance or something. Maybe it sings "God is love" or "Praise the Lord" or "Jesus is Lord" as it skips through the city.

Then there is the living tree that splits its trunk across the river. Half of the tree is on one side of the river and the other half of the tree is on the other side of the river. The river flows from the throne of God. The tree is laden with all our favorite fruit. Some of my favorite fruits are mangoes, peaches, cherries, and grapes, to name a few. You add your favorite fruits to make it tempting for you.

Now, imagine your favorite fruit, the best-tasting one you ever had. Top that by a million times and that will be the taste of the fruit of the Tree of Life. Imagine a tree with twelve varieties of fruit on one tree. This tree bears the tastiest fruit. The best part is that the tree bears every month. I wonder if it is twelve different fruits every month. We can always get a piece and there is always enough for everyone. We won't have to pay organic prices like we do in the supermarkets on earth. God put this fruit on the tree for our pleasure. We will be able to see the fruit growing since it comes monthly—what a tree. The leaves are for sustaining us also. I will visit the tree often—won't you?

Recently, I visited the redwood forest in California. We drove right through the trunk of one tree. The roots were on each side of the automobile, and the tree still grew and flourished, way up in the sky. I was awed and amazed.

Can you imagine what the tree in heaven must be like? In heaven there is no death, pain, sorrow, or crying. The problems of this world will all be passed away. We will have no nights, no darkness, no blackouts, and no more dark mental despair. In heaven, we will have only joy, unspeakable and heart-thrilling joy. Jesus will live there with us. So He will be the continuous light in our city. Everything will shine in His beauty.

There will be animals of all kinds and they will all get along. There will be no territorial fighting. There will be no food wars, and the animals will not have to worry about people eating them. They will get along with each other and with us. Lions and lambs will become associates—can you imagine that? I think for the first time I would rub a black leopard. Beauty and kindness will be everywhere among the fish and the fowl of the air.

The next best part about heaven—notice everything is the best part about heaven—is that people will be reunited. 1 Thessalonians 4:13-18 says, "Then we which are alive [and] remain shall be caught up together with them in the clouds, to meet the Lord in the air: and so shall we ever be with the Lord" (brackets added). So I will know you in heaven and you will know me there. Imagine when we meet in the new earth. We didn't know that we would even meet again in heaven. Won't that be fun? It will be ecstasy finding loved ones.

You will remember me, and you will remember how I helped you get here. I will say, "No, you helped me get here." Unselfishness will be the rule of the day. Love will be the character of everybody there. The whole place will be full of smiles and praises to God. Hello, hello, and never goodbye will be what we will say to our friends, loved ones, and family who will be all around us.

We will look around for things to do. I am sure I cannot do this one justice. The Bible says there are pleasures forevermore. Think of your most pleasurable activity or your most pleasurable time here on earth. Multiply that forevermore; you will just be happy endlessly. That is only on His right hand. The left hand has an evermore also, wow! (Psalm 16:11).

Children will be able to play safely and not worry about harm. I know for parents that will be such a relief, won't it? Zechariah 8:5 says, "The streets will be full of boys and girls." They will play together with no fighting. Moms and dads, they won't harm themselves, each other, or destroy property. They are God's darlings. They too love Him and want to be in heaven with Daddy and Mommy. Doesn't your heart yearn to go to heaven? Don't you want to take your children to that forever happy and beautiful place?

There will be flowers of all sorts. Think of the beauty of flowers that await us. Many flowers we will have never heard of or seen before. Here is a lively thought. When we pluck a flower it cannot die. It is living also and praises God also. I wonder if flowers will speak. If they do they will say, "God is love, God is love."

In heaven, there will be normal fairytale singing flowers. Imagine real flowers singing about God's love. We can even sing with them. Does someone out there have a voice you would like improved upon? Wait until you hear yourself sing in heaven. Maybe each of us will have four- part harmony in our voice boxes, wow. Sing on, friend, we are practicing for heaven.

When we all get to heaven, what a day of rejoicing that will be! We will also play musical instruments like the harp (Psalm 87:7). The harp is a hard instrument to master here. In heaven we will all play the harp. Jesus will give a harp to everyone.

The best part of heaven is that we will be with Jesus. He is the One who died for us. Jesus said to the thief on the cross before he died that He would take him to paradise to be with Him. Jesus called heaven paradise. He knows all about heaven and He called heaven paradise.

Let's get ready to go, are you ready? Psalm 87 tells us that Jesus will tell us where we were born as we enter the city. He really knows us, doesn't He? We will be no stranger to Him. He will be our loving heavenly daddy. He carried us when we were weak and He will have our living crowns already made and ready to place on our heads. Jesus will put living crowns on the head of each one of us as we enter the city. We shall receive the crown of life, which Christ, the righteous judge, shall give to us (2 Timothy 4:8).

I'm sure my living crown will say, "Welcome home, Dawn." Put your name where I put mine. The crown will further say, "Enter in; joy is prepared for you." I have been on the mind of God before He created me. I was on the mind of God before the earth was made. How the Lord must yearn to be with me in heaven. Wow, only a living God can do that.

We have to come back from our heavenly dreaming now. But we will get there if we accept God's grace. It will change us to be like Christ. We want to belong there. No vile person will make it who doesn't accept Jesus. You know what to do. Jesus is the way. Follow His path and it will lead you right to heaven. Now let us pray.

Lord,

Heaven is such a beautiful place. We don't want to miss out on our living crowns. Help us to practice faithful obedience and holiness that you outlined so clearly in Your Word. We cannot lose our way if we read Your Word, have faith, and treat our fellow men with love.

Thank You for making a plain path before our feet. Thank You that the path can be found in Your Word. We can read and find out more about You anytime of the day. Thank You for going ahead of us to prepare our mansions.

In Jesus' living name we pray, Amen.

Day 38

FORGIVE SELF DAY

I'm alive. Thank God for another day to live for Him!

"Forgive us our debts, as we forgive our debtors" (Matthew 6:12).

*T*oday's text reveals a very important process, one that I missed in the Lord's Prayer for a long time. One aspect of this prayer is it is often difficult to forgive others because we can't forgive ourselves. We often think there are some inadequacies within us that may be the cause of wrong that was done to us. Once we love ourselves enough to forgive ourselves, we can fully forgive others just as Christ has fully forgiven us. Welcome to Forgive Yourself Day! Let us start out our day forgiving ourselves.

Let me remind you how very special you are to God. God knows where you live (Revelation 2:13); He knows your name (Isaiah 49:1); He knows the number of the hairs on your head (Matthew 10:30); He knows what you are going to say before the words come out your mouth (Psalm 139:4). God has plans for you (Jeremiah 29:11). God knows what needs you have before you ask Him to meet them (Matthew 6:8); God loves you with an everlasting love (Jeremiah 31:3); the Lord gives us talents (Exodus 31:3); the Lord follows us around and orders our steps (Psalm 119:133); God knew you in your mother's womb and He put you together in there bone by bone (Psalm 139:16); He knows where you will be buried. God says not to talk back to Him. Shall what is formed say back to Him, "Why did you make me like this?" (Romans 9:19-20).

God is God and He made you unique. God has your statistics on the palms of His hands. When God made you He made a designer's original. Psalm 139 is a chapter of the Psalms that you should be aware of. It tells you that there is no one in this world that can walk or talk like you; no one can sing, kiss, or dance like you. Your smile is unique; the twinkle in your eyes is unique. No one can caress like you, speak or laugh like you.

Your shape is unique to you; your face is unique to you. Identical twins even have differences. You are one very special, one of a kind individual. Your emotions are unique to you. Your reactions to life situations are unique to you. Have I made it clear? You are God's special, unique, lovely, extraordinary creation.

Once you realize all this special beauty God gave you is for His glory, He can do some wonderful work through you only. Right now say in your soul, "Lord, I am giving myself to you." Say it again. Please say it as many times as you need to say it to believe it yourself. If you really mean it, He can free you now to forgive yourself. You are who you are because the Creator made you uniquely that way.

Are you ready for the next step? First let me share a story with you. I was in church when a woman shared with me that she cannot forgive another person. In fact, she hates and envies this person. While she was sharing her pain, I could sense hot tears of anger in her eyes. This other woman had broken up her marriage and married her husband. The lady speaking with me later went on to form a new union with a new man and she is in pain up until today.

Maybe you can sympathize or you perhaps you have been wronged. Someone has done the unthinkable to you. There is a wrongdoer out there who has personally done you wrong. I just took a few seconds to validate your pain. That is all the time it is worth. The wrongdoer has to go to God. God, who deals with sin, will deal with the actions of the wrongdoer.

If you are on the other end and have treated someone wrong, you also have a compassionate Savior who has plenty of grace and mercy for any person who accepts Him. This happens when you reject selfishness, put pride aside, and feel sorry about your sins. The action you did or that was done to you was wrong, but the individual is worthy of forgiveness, because of Christ sacrifice on the cross. We are all fallible humans, and we work according to our sinful nature when we do stupid things. We are subject to human frailties and at times fail. God does not hold grudges. He looks at the hearts of people ready to accept His more perfect way. When you make that decision to follow Him, redemption and reconciliation are all around you. This is God's mission for all of us.

I am sure the experience of pain the lady shared with me has been repeated daily somewhere. If you are in that group, please be a part of the release today. When unforgiveness is cultivated, you become a prisoner to the person you are unwilling to forgive.

This is a big key to opening the door and forgiving yourself. You are still the designer's original. You are still beautiful. You are exactly where God wants you to be. He knows the number of hairs on your head, remember? You are and always will be God's child. Even though you had a bad situation, you do not fall out grace with your Creator.

You are free to live and free to be uniquely you. You must walk away from the prison cell of failed marriage. Marriages break down, not because you are not a great person, not because you are not pretty or handsome. A broken marriage has little to do with who you are; it is a chain of circumstances that happen. Take yourself off the pain path and validate yourself in God's Word.

You can love yourself now, and you can love others, including the one now with your ex-spouse because now you love yourself. This is no easy task but doable with help with God's help. Take a deep breath, releasing yourself from the years of pain. The earlier you do this, the less sickness and worry you have to carry. Feeling better already, huh? I knew it.

God's Word is specific and always right. He is the giver of life and freedom. Now that you are free and happy, you must think happy thoughts about yourself. Now that you are out of your "self-prison," it will be easier to give those loving qualities you have gained to the person you thought you could not forgive.

He or she is even free to try to hurt you again because the hardest part was to forgive yourself. You are no longer a prisoner because of another person's painful action. You are free; you have moved on to love. You have a new love for self and more love for God. You can also love your fellow man that is God's original design, no matter who they are. Other people can now be loved by you, and you can smile at others without pain. You even begin to think about your former pain giver as God's creation, with feelings and emotions just like you. He or she may suffer just like you, may even cry just like you cry, and may even need a shoulder to lean on just like you did. Who knows, you might be that shoulder for your ex-spouse's new spouse. God has such a sense of humor.

I can tell you that the devil is angry now. He is mad at you—and me—so he may try to lock you up in your prison again. But be stubborn; you need to keep releasing yourself frequently. Think of all the people you have locked up through unforgiveness and hurt. Let them all out of your soul today. Feel freedom flying all around you. You have learned how to forgive yourself and now you have learned how to forgive others. Let us pray and thank the Lord for giving us such a sure path.

Lord, God,

We have done major work today by Your power alone. Thank You for understanding our need while looking beyond our fault. Thank You for making every one of us feel better. Thank You for your free pardon of our wrongdoing. Thank You that we are free indeed, because You made us free.

We now choose to accept this freedom. Thank You for always being there for us. Thank You for revealing to us that we can be free. Our lips can't keep from shouting your praises because of Your love. You are a wonderful Savior. Bless Your holy name. My lips will praise You as long as I live for the undeserved love You have given me.

In Jesus' forgiving name I pray, Amen.

Day 39

RESPECT

I'm alive! Thank God for another day to live for Him!

"Though the LORD be high, yet hath he respect unto the lowly:

but the proud he knoweth afar off"

(Psalm 138:6).

*R*espect is something people need to encourage them in their everyday lives. We ask, beg, or plead with our families to please respect us. We ask for it on our jobs. We need it while we are driving our cars. We ask for it when our relationships are being formed or being broken. Can I just get some respect from you, please? Some sing about it, just a little R.E.S.P.E.C.T.; you can finish the song. One can feel so good when given respect and so awful when disrespected. Yet we all often dish out disrespect and expect we will get respect in return. It doesn't work like that.

We are going to try to turn that tide around today. Galatians 6:7 says, "Be not deceived; God is not mocked: for whatsoever a man soweth, that shall he also reap." That means if you plant disrespect, disrespect will grow. "Whatever you give out to people it will be given to back to you." That means don't ask for or expect respect if you show disrespect.

In 2 Corinthians 9:6, we read, "But this I say, He which soweth sparingly shall reap also sparingly; and he which soweth bountifully shall reap also bountifully." In a home with disunity and dissention, respect is probably rarely practiced.

When you wake up in the morning and look up to the ceiling, do you respect God and thank Him for lending you His heartbeat again for a new day? Well, have you? That is the basis for respecting yourself and your fellow man. Do you show respect to God? Start your day by saying, "Thank You, God, for Your gift of life this day. Your mercies are new every morning." Start there now, respecting God if you have not done so already.

Second, think of your family, spouse, children, or roommate. What common courtesies do you generate? Do you smile at them? Do you ask how their sleep was? Do you give hugs and generate warm fuzzies with your spouse and family? You know all of this is part of respect. Some people live in homes where all they hear from a spouse or a family member is a grunt or a groan. But when that same person goes to work, everyone is greeted with a smile, hug, or a "How are you today?" They may even inquire about your time last evening. This conversation did not happen with the family they left at home today. They barely even got eye contact. Is that respect?

You may be stressed and frustrated because you can't meet the deadlines you have put on yourself. So you get overwhelmed, tight, with your feelings pent up and overloaded. A fellow co-worker comes by and says one thing to you that you don't feel like hearing, and an explosion of dynamite is heard coming from your mouth. Some are driving cars and frustrations are high and fingers start to fly when someone cuts them off in traffic. Sometimes we scream from our desks. When playing sports, it is not unusual to see fists flying. I ask you, is that respect? The emotions we give off are the responses we will get in return.

It is because of God's grace and mercy that He continues to respect us in spite of how we behave. We teach what we preach. You are saying loudly when you are upset with others, "This is how I want you to handle me when you are upset with me."

We scream, yell, point the finger, honk the horn, and fight. Do you do any of these things? Do you give disrespect to others? Others may be disrespectful back to you. Don't think that you can show favorites. You cannot disrespect your team but respect the boss. You can't disrespect the cleaning lady but respect the hotel manager. God doesn't honor playing favorites (Job 34:19). We are all His children and deserve respect.

Let us turn the tables and see how good respect can feel when we receive it. How do you feel when in traffic everyone waits their turn to merge, just like you waited for yours? Respected, right? When someone sees you struggling to change lanes to make an exit and the other driver slows up so that you can make your turn, you feel respected, right? How do you feel in a relationship with a girlfriend or boyfriend when they are upfront with you? How do you feel when the friend tells you that they like you or don't like you upfront or tell you where the relationship is going? You feel respected, right? Sometimes we are afraid of losing our respect and we become disrespectful to others. That is not the excellent way. Oh, how simple God's Word is when followed.

Respect comes in many other forms. I will just name a few. If you can find a way to make a change, the world will be more respectful to you. After all, that is what a child of God following Jesus will do. Please take care of the poor and those depending on you and validate them. The pets in our society, respect them. Don't kick the dog because you can't kick the boss. Don't kick the dog, instead talk to the boss. Loyal as pets are, they know they are being hurt and disrespected. You can see it in their eyes. The boss can also often read your disrespect in your treatment of others. He or she may also hear it from someone else.

How do you treat the wait staff, your garbage collectors, meter maids, TSA monitors, and airport traffic monitors? Do you assume your agenda is more important than others', park anywhere, and fuss and argue if your car is towed or moved along? Where is the respect shown by obeying the traffic lights? Do you tip your helpers? Many can afford to brighten someone's day by extending an extra dollar amount. It helps the provider of services feel respected. It also helps them to do their work better, brighter, and lighter. That's what respect does: it boosts energy and helps to overcome stress. It gives a sense of self-worth. It encourages the soul.

Give out compliments today to people you normally snarl at. Brighten someone's day. To me, that is all a part of respect. Remember, the measure given out to others is given back to you. My friend, that is biblical. God is not near the haughty and the proud, but the humble (Psalm 138:6).

I serve a God Who is able to back up His promises completely. Join me today in finding people to respect. Let us pray and ask God for power to be respectful today.

Dear God,

Today we want to be more respectful to all we meet, even those we will never see again. We know we can only do that by Your strength. When the loud, high-pitched scream wants to come out of our lips, help us to keep it down and do as James 1:19 says, "My dear brothers, take note of this: Everyone should be quick to listen, slow to speak and slow to become angry" (NIV). Help us to live in the more excellent way.

We want to be kind in word and deed to the poor and less fortunate in the world. Let us tip more freely because we can. Let us not throw out leftover food without thinking that it might be the only dinner a homeless person nearby has. Let us volunteer time to a group or organization and share the wisdom You gave us so that we can follow in Your footsteps.

Help us build respect in our communities because we, too, crave respect. Please help us take ourselves out of the picture. Let us not do something just to sit back and say, "I respected someone so now I expect the respect back." Let our actions today be out of a heart full of love for You. You did not ask us to do anything for You. You did it for us on Calvary before we were even born. We are Your disciples, and we must do things Your way. Thank You, Lord, for respecting us enough to keep our lungs filling with Your air right now. We love You, Lord. Amen.

Day 40

SCHEDULED FOR DISASTER

I'm alive! Thank You, God, for another day to live for You.

"But the day of the Lord will come as a thief in the night; in the which the heavens shall pass away with a great noise, and the elements shall melt with fervent heat, the earth also and the works that are therein shall be burned up" (2 Peter 3:10).

This subject starts out sounding terrible. It sounds like tearing down, destroying, pain, loss, loveless, mean, and negative. Combined, it makes for a scary end. I must admit it does sound scary.

I took a closer look at the world around me. I saw that things get old and run down. Cars wear out. Buildings break down and start falling apart themselves. Unattended bridges begin to shake. Bolts pop out and make it unsafe to travel on. The natural progression of things is death, decay, and wearing out. It happens all around us.

Our bodies eventually break down. Sometimes we get boils full of infection. Gall bladders, hernias, and appendixes get crazy on us. Crazy can cost our life if we don't get attention quickly.

Mother earth is not different; it also waxes old like a garment (Isaiah 51:6). Have you noticed how buildings or bridges are scheduled to be torn down? Demolition it's called. Demolition happens to old buildings and bridges that need to be removed. Engineers pick the spot to place the dynamite packs. They are carefully placed and timed to go off at a chosen moment. For the destruction to be complete, all the explosives go off together. When the desired moment comes, the timer goes off, the switch is pulled, the dynamite blasts, the building or large structure comes crashing down.

This demolition ends an era. Many times when demolition is announced, people come out to see the structure fall. Memories are blown away. Dust rises and falls. The end has come for that structure. It had its glamorous and useful days. But now time and use have left it unsafe or useless. What do you do with unsafe and useless old buildings or bridges? You destroy them, right?

In our bodies, sometimes boils come and send infection and pain throughout our bodies. When you go to the doctor, you get the boil opened up. The infection is drained. Dead skin and old tissue are cut away. Only then can healing begin and new skin grows.

In order to build a better, more useful and effective bridge or building, the old unsafe one must be done away with. This makes room for a new, safe, and useful structure. In the body, after the infection is gone, there is healing. No more pain and hopefully no more boils. I am sure you can think of other stories of breaking down to build up better.

This theme text that started out awful and cruel makes sense now, doesn't it? Let us put on our eternal focus now and see how we participate in the scheduled demolition of this earth. Yes, it is going to happen. The question is will you be ready for the demolition day at the demolition time?

The important things in life are not stuff. The main thing is not grabbing everything we think we need. It is not about owning this kind of car or house. The important thing is knowing that stuff gets old and becomes useless. When we die we will leave everything behind. Someone else will use it, waste it, or take it.

Eventually, the entire world will be destroyed and burned up. God will recreate the new earth. People often step over other people to get wealth. Some people are robbed to satisfy greed in others. Some even take by force what is not theirs to satisfy their wants. God is not pleased with the lack of love we show our fellow men for the sake of greed and selfishness. This is sinful, and the whole earth is affected by our sinfulness.

Tornadoes, destructive lightning, earthquakes, mud slides, and tsunamis tell the story. Friends, think about this. The earth is really waxing old like a garment. We can't really live here much longer in this dilapidated old world. We will all be at risk. We are tearing it up with our behavior. And it is tearing itself up because of the evil we as the human race are doing to it.

Trash is everywhere. We put contaminants in our water and air. The list of unsafe pesticides grows every day. Many of the things that damage our air come about because of greed at the expense of people. We are going to have to get out of here if we are going to survive.

I know we will all go the way of the earth someday, but there is something after that. John saw it in Revelation 21:1. He said, "I saw a new heaven and a new earth, for the first heaven and the first earth were passed away." God, our engineer, has everything timed.

You have this moment to decide, my friend, what will happen to you on earth demolition day. Do you want to be safe with Jesus? I'm sure you do. That is where I want to be. To be safe with Jesus, what manner of men or women are we to be? Micah 6:8 says, "He hath shewed thee, O man, what is good; and what doth the Lord require of thee, but to do justly, and to love mercy, and to walk humbly with thy God?" For emphasis, it says to do justly, love mercy, and walk humbly with our God.

Three things can get you ready to walk away with God on earth demolition day. I cannot give you any other formula than what the Word of God says. That gives me backup power to say what I'm saying because it comes from the Creator. You too must learn about earth demolition day and make changes in your own life.

You need to get ready now for that great and terrible day when everything in this old world will be destroyed. Check in with your Bible daily. Talk with your Lord regularly. Earth demolition day will be the end of sin, pain, and suffering. The ushering in of love peace and happiness forevermore will happen next. What a renewing day that will be. Be prepared. Let us pray.

Lord,

I thank You for the insight given us in the Scripture that the earth is one day going to be burned up. The stuff we collect will also be burned up. Money will be valueless and it will be burned up also. Things we fought for, stole for, stressed for, will be burned up like stubble on the ground.

Remind us that the character we develop now will go with us as we walk away from all this destruction because Jesus is our Savior. Teach us to love mercy, do justly, and walk humbly with You this and every day.

In Jesus' precious name, Amen.

Day 41

GRACE, GRACE

I'm alive! Thank God for another day to live for Him!

"Moreover the law entered, that the offence might abound.
But where sin abounded, grace did much more abound" (Romans 5:20).

We hear this word *grace* in songs. We read about grace covering our sins. We know grace comes from God. What is all this grace about? Do we really even need it? Can we get too much grace? I'm glad you asked.

Let us go to the only place that is all truth—God's Word—and learn all about grace today. We will focus on the spiritual definition of grace. It means undeserved love and favor granted by someone who can give it. That is it. You did something bad, you should be punished, and when punishment time comes you get correction, love, and favor instead. That is grace.

Why do we need grace? Where do we get grace from? When do we get grace from God and what are we to do with it when we get it? These three questions sum up our nugget thought for today.

The first question is why do we need grace? There are times when we are in need of grace, and we know it. One day I had a plane to catch. Several of my friends and I were heading to a vacation together. We decided to carpool to the airport. My husband and I went to pick up two other families. I underestimated the amount of time needed to pick them up and get to the airport on time. While driving to the airport above the speed limit, I was hoping I could make up some lost time. There was not much traffic on the road, so that gave me confidence that I would be safe as I pressed down the gas pedal.

It was not long before I saw red and blue lights flashing in my rear-view mirror. There were not many cars on the road. I knew I was speeding. *We would be really late now*, I thought. *How long will this officer hold us? Can we even make the flight now?* These are questions that were running through my mind. I knew I had to stop because I had broken the speed limit. *What kind of price will I have to pay for going so fast? I wondered. How long will he hold us up? Man, why was he out here this time of morning? He should be catching criminals.*

All these things had come to my mind by the time I finally stopped. The officer came to my window and asked me if I knew why he had stopped me. And I said, "Yes, officer, I do. I was speeding, right? I am sorry. I usually do not speed, but today we are trying to catch a plane."

The hour was late and I had broken the law. He said to me, "Show me your plane ticket" and we did. Everyone in the car pulled out their plane tickets. We felt grace coming on. He did not even take time to ask me for my driver's license and registration.

He said, "Okay, go ahead just not so fast."

Somehow, I felt that he had experienced a similar situation and could understand the reason for my haste. I could not thank him enough for his kindness, grace, and undeserved favor. On the vacation, we even commented that if the officer had held us up for any longer, we would have missed the plane for sure. Instead, he gave us grace and undeserved favor. He used his civil authority to determine our motive. I'm sure he figured our motive was not just speeding or joy riding. We were driving carefully fast to make our appointment. We should have left earlier and not sped, but grace covered us and removed our penalty.

It is because of God's grace that He adopted us as sons and daughters. God did not have to do this. He promised heaven to all His children who accept His invitation to become heirs. He did not have to do that either. To enter heaven we have to be sinless. God will not allow anyone in who is sinful. There will never be sin again when He gets rid of it finally. The Bible says sin will not rise up a second time (Nahum 1:9).

Tell me, then how will any of us get there when the Bible says all our righteousness is as filthy rags? (Isaiah 64:6). You got it, God's grace. How does God qualify to give grace? The police officer granted grace because he represented the civil law. God granted grace for all our sins by coming to earth, living a sinless life, and dying on a cross in our place. He could pay the penalty for our sins, which is death. When someone accepts Christ, He substitutes His perfect life for our imperfect life. We receive God's grace by becoming an heir. We are then sinless in His sight.

That is grace. The Bible says in 2 Corinthians 5:21 that He became sin for us, Who knew no sin; that we might be made the righteousness of God in Him. That is grace. God took the stripes for us. When we sin, He can, with authority, cancel our debt and save us. All we have to do is admit our sinfulness, submit to His directions, and accept God and His grace. We owe everything to God's free grace. It is only because of grace that we can be saved. Grace is a gift of God. We must accept it to be a disciple of God. On our own morals, we would be too sinful and wicked to make it into heaven.

We can never make it on our own; we need God every morning. We must confess our sinful ways for every sinful thing we do. When we receive God, not one moment will we be without grace. It is God's undeserved favor to us, day by day, when we are responsible children of God.

You got it? Regenerate it by showing grace to our fellow human beings today. Let God's grace in you be revealed in how you treat your brothers and sisters. When someone hurts you give him or her grace instead of what they deserve.

If someone has broken the traffic law and hits your car slightly, surprise them with grace. Tell them you are okay, and get each other's insurance information. Then go home and don't worry about it anymore. If it is slight damage, just tell him or her to forget the whole thing. You gave God's grace instead of the devil's anger. I think you see grace now. The car can be replaced, but injury to a precious child of God by your angry outburst would not represent any of the grace you have received from your heavenly Father.

As God's grace covers your sins, so you must cover others' and spread God's grace all around. It was the divine compassion of Christ for us that led Him to the cross. His love for us outweighed the painful death He endured. His desire to be our path back from sinfulness kept our beloved Jesus on the cross. What mercy, what love, and what grace! He gives His grace fairly and fully to us. He floods us with it in hopes that we accept it and pass it around. Here again, when we die after accepting God's grace, He can pardon our sins and fill in the defects of our character with His grace. When the Father looks at us, He will see Jesus' perfect life in us instead of our own filthiness.

Oh, for grace to trust Him more. Since grace is given to us freely, we do not sin just to test grace. Instead, we are truly thankful for grace. So we try not to do evil. That is the part that love for God plays. In fact, if we do sin we feel terrible. We feel like we kill Jesus all over again, and we really do. That is a revolting feeling.

Let us follow where He leads. We want to be obedient sons and daughters of God, walking in His footsteps, don't we? Let us pray and ask God for strength to walk in His footsteps.

Gracious God of the universe,

We are thankful that all over this world You have children and You have enough grace for all of us. We say thank You, thank You, thank You. Thank You for Your sacrifice on the cross and for wearing the crown of thorns for us. Thank You for taking the nails in Your raw flesh for us and for taking the spear in Your side for us. Thank You for taking the beatings, mockings, and humiliation for us.

If You had not done it for us, Lord, we would be hopelessly lost. I faint to think of this life without Your saving grace. Oh, Lord, we want to be like You. We want to be Your disciples today. No matter how much we give away, we still have more of Your grace remaining.

To whom can we extend grace today? We want to give Your grace away. Lead us. Help us to show patience and compassion to all we meet today, whether they deserve it or not. Thank You for Your help to see that person as you see them.

Fill us with tenderness. When all Your children follow Your example, we make the world a better place. Count us in, Lord, count us in. We want to be Your ambassadors of grace. Because of the precious name of Jesus we can pray this prayer.

Amen.

Day 42

OFFERS

I'm alive. Thank You, God, for another day to live for You!

"How much more shall the blood of Christ, who through the eternal Spirit
offered himself without blemish unto God, cleanse your conscience
[mind] from dead works to serve the living God?"
(Hebrews 9:14, ASV, brackets added)

Ever watch a game show that just gives prizes and money away? Some
require thinking and knowledge to win, while others have the participants guess without knowledge. Sometimes the guess is good, but most
of the time the guess is wrong. The participant just sits down and is told
he or she lost. The hype is there, and the occasional winner is used as hope
for the next participant to come on the show and win something as well.

These shows make big dollars. Advertisers who want to get their merchandise marketed purchase airtime. You get to be on television, sometimes
you get to give your friends a shout out. It all seems like fun. At the end of
the show, the winners have to settle with the IRS. Some have to give the
prizes back because they don't have the money to pay the taxes on what
they have won.

The offer sounded very good when it was made. Come play XYZ game show and win big. Come gamble at drag racing or animal racing, like dogs or horse races, and win big. Greed for winning drives the lottery, the stock market, etc. People keep trying to take an offer they feel will win them more and more money. Many dream about what offer they can accept that will put them in a better financial position. Now that is not all bad. In fact, careful financial planning is essential to being a good steward of God's money. A follower of Christ must evaluate, daily, what is being offered to gain more money.

Satan is the master deceiver. He is all about offering this world's goods wrapped in aluminum foil. If you put the aluminum foil in the sun you see a bright glow all around. You want to see what that is, shining so brightly. Upon closer inspection, you realize it is nothing of value just aluminum foil in the sun. Let's take a look at some of Satan the deceiver's offers.

Gamblers bet on horses, dogs, lotteries, cars, slots, etc. Winning does sometimes happen. You win money. Now think about where the money comes from that you win. The poor neighbor may be putting in his last dollars in hopes of winning big. Occasionally, the poor neighbor wins. But how much money did he spend before he won? Most of the time, the losses have outweighed the winning by a large margin, and still Satan has been able to convince people that gambling means they will win big.

Satan is not called the great deceiver for nothing. Read about how he deceived Eve in Genesis 3. Through the entire Bible, we see how effectively he deceived other Bible characters. He used jealously with Cain and Abel, which led to murder. With Ananias and Saphira, he used financial greed, buying and selling property and keeping money promised to God for themselves. He tricked David with immorality and lying. And I'm sure you can find the theme of deception throughout the Bible. They were given to us so that we can become aware of the deceiver's tricks.

Deception usually begins by offering money, power, and status in exchange for self-respect. When a disciple is suffering emotional pain, broken trust, loss, or despair, look out. Aluminum foil deception starts to glitter. The glitter points out all the reasons why you should be discontented about yourself, your finances, your body, your family, your job, your children, your friends, and your station or position in life.

This discontent shows up as worry, anxiety, and fretting. You become busy trying to make yourself successful in this world. When something you planned did not go the way you planned, it opens an opportunity for deception, depression, and fear. In an attempt to fix the situation, you are drawn to the aluminum foil glistening in the sun. What appears shiny in the sun is actually, Satan the deceiver's plan that plunges you further into woe. Clever, huh? Usually he lets you gain a little so that you will take the bait. After today, you have his game plan. You know his tricks. The final outcome of following him is pain and suffering. Satan's offers should remind us every day that this world is not a home for God's children. Let us take heed.

Now let us look at another offer. The world crowns success, but Jesus crowns faithfulness. Jesus allows pain and suffering as a challenge for His disciples to learn to trust Him. The difference between the child who trusts God and the child who trusts Satan is shown through the individual's life. When God allows trials, He sustains. He will never leave you floundering like a fish out of water. He brings joy and contentment through the promises in His Word. Your response must be according to His words. Read them! God's Word is true. He will see you through. He brings peace, self-forgiveness, and then forgiveness of others. Right away that lifts heaviness from the heart.

I recall a story in October 2006 when a gunman killed and wounded several Amish girls, then killed himself. I was moved by the Amish families as they forgave the killer. They made a verbal commitment that they would make life comfortable for the killer's family. The news reported that they had no anger or revenge whatsoever. It was so unbelievable to the media that the story quickly died down. Forgiveness was given to the killer before the shock of the crime could set in. In my mind, the Amish population taught the general population a real lesson on forgiveness. Their forgiving spirit freed the rest of us to feel compassion for the gunman and especially his family that he left behind. Thank God for their example. Jesus' name was magnified. The world learned a lesson in compassion.

God takes care of us in the pain and the loss of losing loved ones. The Amish people suffered in Lancaster, Pennsylvania, and their response to suffering has widened the hearts of many. Grief reveals the unknown depth of the soul.

Have you experienced grief while holding on to God's hand? Did you not find comfort from God and godly friends? Did you not find peace? Was it a nice resting place for your soul? God uses, to a large degree, broken, faithful people to be His bread for all nations of the world.

When we struggle for Jesus and remain faithful, our reward is not something that appears good from a distance, but heaven and eternity. That is not a deceiver's glow but a promise. We will get our questions answered about our trials, if we have any questions left, after we get to heaven. As we go through our trials, we must know that Jesus already walked the way for us. He left us a path. He showed us not only by His example how to suffer, but also how to overcome as He overcame.

He is up in heaven now. Following Him, we will be in heaven also. What a heavenly example, what a wonderful offer. There is no honor among thieves. Satan the deceiver has no honor for you, only pain, more pain, and all types of pain. Keep this thought on the billboard of your mind.

This world is not our home. A disobedient child, a needle stick, a car accident, or whatever your issue might be. Remember, this world is not our home. You have the offer on your plate today. Do you want to choose Satan's plans that appear brilliant, like aluminum foil that only folds down and blows away?

Will you choose Jesus, our sustainer and Savior? He has a real heaven to back up His promises. I know you can't see God's way clearly now, but He said, "Blessed are they that have not seen and yet believe" (John 20:29). Trust His Word and follow His example and you can't go wrong. Let us pray.

Lord,

Today we want to take You up on Your offer. Give us peace when we go through our storms of life. Remind us when the storms come that Jesus is the master of earth and sky. All storms obey the Creator. Let us keep that in our minds also. Our storms are included in your "to do list" today. In fact, they were taken care of a while back.

When our faith gets stronger, storms won't be our concern. We already know You have storms controlled. What we are asking for is that You would place within our hearts a desire to accept Your offer and Your offer only. Help us not to be deceived by Satan or any of this world's glitter and glory. We know the path it will take us down.

Jesus, we don't want to cause You any more pain. We are tired of bad outcomes to our bad choices. Today, Lord, we want to make a change and take You up on Your offer. Live in us so that we can be more like You. Do what You have to do in our hearts to clean us up so that holiness can live in clean hearts. Help us to represent you, the sinless Lamb of God.

Thank You for answering this prayer on our behalf.

In the wonderful name of Jesus I pray, Amen.

Day 43

GOD MY FATHER

I'm alive! Thank God for another day to live for Him.

"Don't worry about what you eat or drink or what to wear. These are the priorities of the world, remember your heavenly Father knows you need food and clothes" (Matthew 6:21-22, cwv).

A great dad is one who loves the Lord. His behavior reflects Jesus' love. He treats his family with tenderness and patience. He spends time with his family building memories, laughing, and playing with his children and his wife. He is accountable to her about his whereabouts. He is present in an emergency or when problems arise at home.

A great dad calls his family together for worship and teaches them about God. He takes time himself for meditation in God's Word so that he can provide God's nourishment for his family. He labors hard to provide for his family. He knows the dignity that comes from labor. He is just and plain ol' faithful to his covenant with his God as a husband and father. He has made a forever commitment to his wife and his children as well.

Please know that when God made man he was made in the image and likeness of God (Genesis 1:26). That means you men were made to be able to be all of those qualities I just mentioned. It is a God given ability.

I'm sure some of you reading are saying, "I really want to be all those things for my God, my family, and myself." Here is the question you must ask God: "How can I change my thoughts and my behavior so that I can be like You?"

In order for the good that you are already doing to become the better you want to achieve, a change must occur. That change must occur in your heart as you surrender yourself to Jesus. Ask Him to replace your heart for His. Since you are willing, transformation will begin immediately. You will be given opportunity after opportunity to be patient with your toddler or your wife. You can expect situations to arise where your response will be different now than it was before. The number one macho man will now begin to show tenderness and gentleness. You will find you look at your family through their eyes instead of your own eyes. What your buddies on the job have to say will not matter. You want to be the one who pleases God. In fact, check everything you do to see if it pleases God. Many times you cannot please God and man at the same time.

Dads, take time to hold the little ones on your lap. There is no more secure place for a little child than in the arms of Daddy. This behavior will grow your gentleness and compassion. Your affection towards your family will increase. I am sure that is what you really desire as a family man. You want love and respect from your wife, devotion and thankfulness from your children.

It is so rewarding to walk into your home after a long hard day of work and have your children run forward to you saying, "Daddy's home, Daddy's home!" There just is no greater joy. Your tenderness and compassion will release the love and devotion in your wife, and she will look out for your well-being. When her trust in you is affirmed by you, her sweetness grows.

We have just spoken about an earthly family. This family prays for God's power in the family members. God's presence is always invited into this home. Because of the connection with the heavenly Father, the earthly family can have a peaceful home.

Now let me remind you that we are God's earthly family. We are His children and the sheep of His pastures (Psalm 95:7). He is more willing to give good gifts to us than we are willing to give good gifts to our children (Matthew 7:11). We are evil and of this world. God is perfect and keeps His promises. I say, let us give God a try in our life, and let's see if He keeps His promises. Let's see if He is the living God Who can make changes in our hearts.

Some are wondering, *If I am a single mom or dad, will I get the same backup from God?*

Of course, we are all part of God's family. No matter what your birth father was like, God says, I am, and always was your real Father. Your father, your earthly father, cannot make life. I make life.

God formed you and put you together. He made you to have ears and eyes. Read all about it in Proverbs 20:12. What I create, I can sustain. God says, I wanted you here. I know all about you. I am the One Who watched over you while you slept. You were not aware of anything; you were out cold and vulnerable. I did not slumber or sleep while you slept (see Psalm 121:4). I keep My eyes on you (2 Chronicles 16:9). I touched your life this morning. I give you new mercies every day.

While reading today, remember that we all have a real daddy. Can't you feel the sense of belonging in your soul right now? If your earthly father was not there for you, remember he is earthly. Some men will act as God acts; others will not. Whatever your earthly father does will not take you one inch away from your heavenly Father's desire to grow you into a trusting, peaceful, happy child of God.

I know for some trust is easier because you had a trustworthy earthly father. For others it might require more praying, reading God's Word, and trials for you to learn of God's tapestry building in your life. He is recreating His trust in your heart. When a tapestry, needlepoint, or hook rug is viewed from behind, it looks like a bunch of tangled yarn. When the work is complete, it becomes a work of art. Just turn it over.

Turn your fatherlessness over to Jesus. He is up to the task. Keep in mind the fruit of the Spirit of God is love, joy, peace, long-suffering, kindness, goodness, faithfulness, gentleness, and self-control (Galatians 5:22). It will be made more obvious in your life, but you must be willing to endure hardship.

Fatherlessness may be just a trial for you to bear up under and through, in which you will learn long-suffering. Single parenting helps to teach faithfulness. A disabled child may be your test of gentleness. Whatever your test, know that your heavenly Father will do only what is good for you in His sight.

Settle your trust in your heavenly Father; He is also your Savior. Your friend in heaven loves you and wants you with Him forevermore. What happens to you in this life has His immediate attention. He says, "I am with you always, even until the end of the earth," (Matthew 28:20). Trust Him, my friend. Prove God to be true to His Word.

He is a trustworthy heavenly Father Who can turn an unfaithful earthly father into a father like Himself. I pray for all earthly fathers to receive the transforming power of God. It doesn't matter if they are good or bad in your sight. God still loves all fathers the same. He also wants to save them. He wants earthly fathers to display love in the same way He displays His love toward His earthly families.

God may use family's gentleness or long-suffering as the tool to bring about healing and joy for both mother and father. Focus on being like your heavenly Father. Watch for the good things He will bring into your life.

While He is working on you, joy and peace will bless you. God is in the blessing business.

My brother and my sister, remember that God is your Father. He will take care of you.

Our heavenly Father,

We need the fruit of the Spirit to explode in us today. Give us unrest until we become like You. Show us how to live and love. Take away false pretenses and pride from us. May our men realize there is no power in pride, but power in humility. Give them a teachable spirit as the rest of the family looks toward them for stability. Teach them that their own concept of fatherhood can never meet God's standard. Help them realize that God's transforming power brings satisfaction and joy.

God's power is always available. By studying God's Word we can become more like Him. Lord, keeps us all on the right track. Thank You, God, for stopping by here again today.

Thank You for giving us a word from Your Word that we can use to make the world a little better place for everyone today. Power us up to do Your will, and we will give You all the praise we get.

In God my Father's name and your Father's name we pray, Amen.

Day 44

RECYCLED BLESSINGS

I'm alive. Thank God for another day to live for Him!

"For it is God which worketh in you both to will and to do of
His good pleasure" (Philippians 2:13).

*H*ere me on this: it is God's pleasure to convince you to want to help others and actually do for others God's will.

I was away from home at a wedding. I was depending on my host and hostess, great friends of mine, to take me from place to place—they had to go to similar places as I did. They had to leave the reception early because their young teenage children were left home alone.

Parents, you know you have to keep very close checks on the gifts God gives you. They asked another one of our friends to give me a ride back to their home. This friend readily agreed to take my niece, who was with me, to her dormitory and then to take me to where I was staying.

While we were in the car, the driver expressed thankfulness to God for his wife, his daughter, his home, and his challenging circumstances. I inquired about the challenge. He told me he had been laid off from work for two weeks now. He said he was spread thin. I really felt for him. I know what it is like to want to work but no work is available. That means no income is available either.

Is there anyone out there who has ever been unwillingly unemployed? In spite of the circumstances, this man had reason to praise God. He said that he and his wife were really learning that God is their true provider and not the job. He was smiling and happy.

Then I thought, *He did not ask me for gas money. He did not hesitate to take my niece and me to our destinations. He just said, "My car is your car."* We felt comfortable and well appreciated. When I paused awhile to talk with my niece, he was patient and listened and lent his approval to the verbal encouragement I was giving her. When I got back to my hosts' home, the Lord spoke to me and told me to leave a monetary gift.

Later that week, I went to a store with a friend. We found a very nice outfit for me. It looked very, very nice. I could have bought it, but then this family came up in my mind. I thought, *Here I am buying clothes that will sit in my closet, while a family needs pampers, formula, and gas money to go back and forth looking for work.* I could not make that purchase. I went straight home, doubled the gift and mailed it to this couple. I felt I was doing what God asked me to do.

Isaiah 58:7 says, "Is it not to deal thy bread to the hungry, and that thou bring the poor that are cast out to thy house? When thou seest the naked, that thou cover him; and that thou hide not thyself from thine own flesh?" The rest of Isaiah 58 is pretty life-changing. Read it and ask the Lord to help you make those changes in your life. The Lord gives a promise of health and healing. This is how change that improves us happens. When you are more about Jesus, you act more like Jesus. He can keep His promises to you because you are obeying His directions and recycling His blessings. Isn't that glorious?

About a week later, I got a call from the wife of this couple I had sent the money to. She was weeping while she testified and thanked my husband and me for the financial blessings. Here is the note she wrote us to follow up on our phone call.

There are no words to adequately express our deepest and sincerest gratitude to you for your absolute generous and selfless gift of financial kindness to us. We were both completely shocked and surprised. Just that morning I had paid all the bills I could. Then I told the Lord, "I have no more money and can do no more. It is all up to You now."
That evening I got home and your check was in the mail. He used you to answer my prayer before I uttered it up. That's God. Pray for me as I learn not to worry for the future, but to focus on the present and remember He has led and provided for us in the past. I pray that one day we will be able to pass on the same gift to someone in need as you have helped and loved us.

I just sat there, crying. God used me at His right time. His daughter prayed for a financial blessing and He used us to answer her prayers. What is amazing is that her prayer and the blessing showed up at the same time! God is awesome, isn't He? Praising Him went from me to her and her family and back again. Bills got paid that may not have otherwise been paid had she not prayed.

You get to hear this story so that you can be a blessing when you hear it. I told her when we spoke on the phone that my husband and I had had the out-of-work-experience, and we know the kindness and generosity of those around us helped us make it until we got on our feet again.

Whenever I hear "I'm out of work," I automatically give money. The money I gave may be a dress or a pair of shoes for me, but for the family out of work it means diapers, formula, and bills paid on time. Then I get a verbal blessing from the recipient. "May you be blessed by the Lord with the same warmth and joy you have given."

Oh, what happiness I felt to have been a part of God's divine order. God used me, little ol' me, to help Him do His work. I was so, so, so happy. Isn't God awesome? Everyone is blessed and His name is glorified. Thank You, Lord, for that experience.

There are times you will not get to hear how you were a blessing in this life from the person you blessed, but God knows your gift and he says, "Lay up for yourself treasures in heaven where moths and rust cannot collect and thieves cannot steal" (Matthew 6:20).

I believe that is how one can lay up heavenly treasures. After all, you are obeying your heavenly Father. He is the One with the real blessings. He owns everything. The earth is the Lord's and the fullness thereof, and all that dwells therein (Psalms 24:1).

My friend, you cannot receive if your hands are closed. The more you give, the more God can use you to bless others. You can never run out of gifts. God directs you from self-centeredness to other-centeredness. God is glorified; you and others are blessed. We make disciples for God's kingdom by showing kindness, unsolicited kindness to God's children. Let us pray.

Dear Father in heaven,

Thank You for knowing our needs before we even ask. You said before we call You will answer and while we are yet speaking You will hear (Isaiah 65:24). That means You are beside us every day hearing our prayers, our call, and our voices. You were in our tomorrows yesterday and You came by today to take us through our moments. I say I will serve You until I die. You alone are worthy and can do all these marvelous things.

Thank You, Lord, for showing up in our lives, just when You do. Thank You for working in our finances when we are at our lowest point. Thank You for reviving us and renewing our faith. Thank You for preparing us for the time we will live with You. Take away all our selfishness. Help us to focus on the needs of others. We feel great now, Lord, knowing that You renew us every morning.

In Jesus' precious name, Amen.

Day 45

DONKEY DIRECTIONS

I'm alive! Thank You, God, for another day to live for You.

"And saith unto them, Go your way into the village over against you: and as soon as ye be entered into it, ye shall find a colt tied, whereon never man sat; loose him, and bring him" (Mark 11:2).

The verse comes in as a backdrop with Jesus about to make His triumphant entry into Jerusalem: He will ride in on a donkey that has never been ridden on before. The part of that text that builds my faith is that Jesus knew before He spoke to His disciples all about the situation. It was predicted in the Old Testament in Zechariah 9:9.

Jesus knew where the donkey was. He knew who owned the donkey. He even knew what the owners would say when the disciples went to borrow the donkey. Here is the real clincher: in the Old Testament, Zechariah foretold of the King coming into Jerusalem meek and lowly. That means without pride, riding upon a colt. Wow, is that powerful or what?

Jesus' actions verify the words of the Bible prophecy, fulfilling it. They also verify that God knows the future hundreds of years before it happens. What do I need to believe that God's words in the Bible are trustworthy?

When we obey God, the results are sure. When He says He will do something, He will do it.

Suppose the disciples chose not to follow Jesus' directions. Suppose they invented their own plan. Suppose they went to another town of their own choosing to find a donkey. Oh, my, the outcome would have been different. They would have messed up Zechariah's prophecy. They very well may have messed up the triumphant entry of Jesus into Jerusalem. I'm just glad they obeyed.

When we look at Scripture we have a hindsight view. We can see twenty-twenty and see how things happened. Often we don't think about obedience and disobedience as we read. We just read. The disciples did as Jesus asked and He rode the donkey into Jerusalem. Obedience had to play a part in the disciples' choice. We read about obedient and fruitful results.

Now let us put some of that donkey business in ourselves today. The Lord has given us instructions in His Word about living morally, loving our enemies, forgiveness, and living humble lives, has He not? Where are you today in your life? Are you going for the donkey so that He can have His purpose fulfilled in you? Or are you on a wild goose chase in some other town, looking for the donkey in a place of your own choosing? My guess is that you will never find it there. You will not find the one that God has for you. You will have to come back and ask Him His way again.

When we obey, we will find pleasure forevermore. Jesus does not ask too much of us. What He asks of us is intended to clean us up. He wants to vacuum up the stubbornness. He wants us to cooperate with Him in saving others for the kingdom. How can we be a good influence if we don't obey God's directions?

When we witness to our neighbors and tell them Jesus is love, we are following God's directions. A few days later the neighbor hears us cursing someone out. That neighbor may rightfully question God's love in us. If

God can't change His disciples, I better stay where I am. That is an example of not following donkey directions. Satan will try to get you not to follow the Lord's Word today. Remember, a lot more preaching is done through living obediently than through speeches.

Follow the donkey directions God is giving you through His Word. If it is in the Bible, then it is truth. It will lead you to complete God's plans for your life and give Him glory. Familiarize yourself with God's rules and then obey them. Start with the Ten Commandments in Exodus 20:3-11. They can only clean up your life. They can lead you to Jesus, Who will give you peace, joy, and trust.

Donkey directions can be trusted to take you into the New Jerusalem, which is heaven. God bless you as you make the transition from disobedience to obedience. Let us pray and ask God for His power to make the necessary changes.

Dear Jesus,

Thank You for personally taking an interest in our lives. Thank You for knowing about the animals around us. You know how they will interact in Your created world. You are all knowing. I just want to thank You for being a living God like that. Thank You for the faith that is built up in us as we discover daily how dependable and trustworthy You are.

Lord, You have never failed us. You rode that donkey You sent the disciples to fetch. That was Your last hoorah before Your crucifixion. You knew your biggest test was coming. Yet calmly You rode the colt into Jerusalem. You are to be praised. Let praises ring from our lips today and every day. They cried, "Hosanna." May we cry, "Hallelujah." May we really learn every day to trust You more and more. May we see from this Scripture passage that You do know our business even before we do. You are the only One Who does.

You are the only wise God. Help us to follow You gladly. Give us the willpower to be obedient, Lord. Fail not to grant us our request. We want to be good examples of Your disciples today and every day.

Please be patient with us. We are just learning how disobedience can mess up what You planned for us centuries ago. We want no part of that. Your way is the best way. Please, please Jesus, we know it may be hard work, but we want to be obedient to You. Help us, help us, keep us in Your Word so that we can be strengthened and knowledgeable of your commands.

In Jesus' precious name we pray, Amen.

Day 46

COMPLACENT

I'm alive! Thank You, God, for another day to live for You!

"Be sober, be vigilant; because your adversary the devil, as a roaring lion, walketh about, seeking whom he may devour" (1 Peter 5:8).

*T*have watched nature shows on television, and a hungry lion is an angry lion. He doesn't stop hunting until he kills something to eat. He will terrorize all animals until he finds food. He especially goes after easy prey. This includes the young, the old, the infirm, or the slow animals. He captures the weakest animal, then takes it out and has it for supper.

There is a warning here for our real life situation. That is why Jesus, through Peter, tells us to be sober and vigilant. To be sober means to be mentally and emotionally balanced. Be serious enough not to be misled by worldly excitement. Vigilant means watchful and awake, always on the lookout for danger or trouble. It means not to let your guard down.

Those two words, *sober* and *vigilant*, alert you that Satan the lion is out there wanting to hunt you down. He wants to take you from your heavenly Father and into his kingdom of wickedness. Once he has you there, he can fill you with evil thoughts. He can have you behaving in a disobedient way.

He can get you to lie. You may even find yourself killing others with your words, looks, and actions.

The next step is to get you involved in immoral acts of all sorts. What happened to the praise and thanksgiving you used to give to God? These no longer come out of your lips. In Satan's sorry kingdom, it will be luck and self-exaltation. "I am just like this or I am like that," "I raised the money," "I am, I am, I did, and I did." This will be your recurring theme.

What a scary, selfish kingdom to be in. There is no honor among thieves so watch your back. You are going to be preyed upon again and again. What a mess you have accepted by joining Satan's kingdom. Count on misery. Once Satan has you, if you want to rejoin God's kingdom, know it will not be a cake walk. It will be like trying to escape an alligator struggling to get its prey.

I heard a story once about a young boy who went swimming in a lake. He was having fun, but his father saw an alligator swimming towards his son. He knew his son did not see the alligator. He called out loudly, "Son, swim to shore, swim to shore—fast!"

Immediately, the son obeyed. In the meantime, the father ran to shore to retrieve his son and hopefully get away from the alligator. This was not the case. Just when the dad grabbed the son's arms, the alligator grabbed the son's legs and a tug of war followed.

The alligator put up a fight. He started turning over and over to try to wrench the boy from his father's arms. The father was just as persistent, hanging on to his son. He dug his nails into his son's arms to tighten the grip through the struggle. There were screams of pain and determination. The more the alligator pulled, the more the father hung on. How much longer would Daddy be able to hold on? Would the alligator give up his would be prey?

Just then a neighbor passing by in a truck heard the noise and saw the dilemma. He had a shotgun in his truck, took aim at the alligator, and fired a deadly bullet in the alligator's head. The father was able to pull his son to safety while the neighbor called for medical help. The boy was bloody and wounded.

The local news heard about his amazing story. They interviewed all parties to hear firsthand what had happened. They followed the young man through his recovery. When they asked to see his scars, he showed them the ones on his legs. When he was asked why he did not show the scars on his arms he replied, "These are the ones that saved me. These are the ones from my father who wanted me to live and not die."

We are not to be complacent, swimming around in the cesspool of this world. Be sure that the enemy is waiting to get you in an unexpected situation. He loves it when we feel confident in our own strength. He wants us to turn a deaf ear to the calls to come home. The calls from the Father who brings us back to safety.

Friend, listen to your heavenly Father. Jesus died to save you from death by the predator. Satan is that lion, after you to get you to disobey God's commandments. He wants you to be one of his victims.

What can you and I do to get away from the predator? I am glad you asked. Begin by reading the Bible for yourself. Mark the verses that reveal God to you in a special way. Pray for God to send you His Holy Spirit. He will change your heart.

When you have been healed or are starting to heal, share your story about Jesus' rescue mission in your life. Oh, the end of the story is so marvelous. We are saved, but we bear our scars from the struggle. We once were lost but now we are saved. We were complacent but now we are vigilant. We no longer see freedom as swimming in the cesspool of worldliness. We see freedom in the arms of a loving Father. We reject any part of lying, cheating, stealing, cursing, taking God's name in vain, or damning Him. We want to be out of the cesspool.

We look forward to the life the Father really intended for us. We begin looking for joy, peace, and God's presence continually in our lives. We want to always be in His watchful eye. The alligator did not care whom he got for supper. So remember, you are never safe away from God. The lion gets the weakest and the slowest prey. Our weakest and slowest disciples are the ones who do not read the Word daily and pray. The handicapped rebellious ones are the disciples who dilute their faith by rebutting God's Word. They question whether predators are really out there to destroy them.

Please note that the Bible, our guidebook, says in Ephesians 6:12, "For we wrestle not against flesh and blood, but against principalities, against powers, against the rulers of the darkness of this world, against spiritual wickedness in high places." What a fight we have on our hands! The next verse in Ephesians 6:13 shows the way to escape: "Wherefore take unto you the whole armour of God, that ye may be able to withstand in the evil day, and having done all, to stand." Just stand in God and He will do the rest. No complacency allowed. Be ever watchful and pray. Now let us pray for divine eyesight.

Lord,

Today is a new day that You have given us. We want to thank You. Thank You for the reminders You give us in nature to let us know You are all around us. You have never left us. You promised You will never leave us. We are Your chosen people, and for this we give You praise. We are aware of the war going on over our souls. You dug Your life in for us, as the dad did for his son in the alligator fight, while You were on the cross. You have scars to prove that You fought an enemy because of us.

For this, Lord, You are worthy to be our redeemer and Savior. We love You, we thank You, and we praise You. We can never repay You for what You have done for us. All You want us to do is to reject sin in the world and obey You and Your commandments. You even promised us Your power to do that. Keep us faithful and keep us praising.

May all we do today bring You glory. We are sorry that we have not been watchful. Many of us are even caught still swimming in the cesspools of sinfulness.

Today, Lord, we want to make a break from that—please help us. We want You to keep on pulling and tugging on our hearts until we make a change. Thank You, Father, for not giving up on us while we were in danger and not watching. It was then that You rescued us so that we would not die.

Praise Your name. We rejoice that You still want us. Lead our hearts towards You always. May the distractions of this earth grow strangely dim.

In Jesus' caring name I pray, Amen.

Day 47

PRAY, PRAY, PRAY

I'm alive. Thank God for another day to live for Him!

"But thou, when thou prayest, enter into thy closet, and when thou hast shut thy door, pray to thy Father which is in secret; and thy Father which seeth in secret shall reward thee openly" (Matthew 6:6).

The next time you pray, it would be a good idea to record your prayer and play it back to yourself. Think about the prayer you prayed this morning. It will reveal to you the way you speak to God. Was the prayer the heart of a friend talking to someone who can make a difference in a situation? Was it just a garble of words and praises that ended with "In Jesus' name, amen"?

Many people cannot remember the twenty-second prayer they spoke this morning. It came out fast and without much thought. I would like to encourage you to change the way you pray from this day forward. Talk to God in real time. Thank Him for His blessings, then name a few of them, including your breath and heartbeat. Thank Him for the ability to move about on your own. Thank Him for making you special. Thank Him for all the talents He gave to you.

This will help remind you not to take any of God's blessings for granted. Here is a specific prayer I prayed for a friend. She seemed depressed to me. In fact, I wrote and told her that I had talked to God about her and this is what I said to Him.

I started with the words from the "Black National Anthem":

"God of our weary years, God of our silent tears, God who has brought us thus far on our way, thou who has by thy might led us into the light, keep us forever in thy path we pray."

Today my sister is very sad. You know all the circumstances that generated the tears. I am talking to the only person Who can do something about her sadness. Lord, please keep her focused on You and not on her plight. Help her to see that her tears are making water for the blooming flowers coming her way. Take away the pain as quickly as You can, after the repairing work is done. Replace it with unspeakable joy.

Lord, help my sister to know that You are right beside her in her trial, at her desk, and even in the bathroom stall. Help her to know You are her joy and her salvation. Help her to see and feel Your presence all the time. You promised in Your Word in Psalms that You are close to the brokenhearted and those with a crushed spirit. You also promised that You would never leave us or forsake us and that You would be with us to the very end.

Thank You for the exceedingly great and precious promises for my sister. Thank You for putting her in my life. I am proud of her spirit, in spite of all she has had to overcome. Help me to reach her heart and do my part in giving her Your smile or Your hug through me. Just help me to love her for You. Thank You for the privilege of lifting my sister as I climb the hill also. Help us to be faithful to You so that when You come again, we both will be able to receive Your reward and be in heaven with You. In Jesus' name, Amen.

When you pray in a public gathering, do not use cliché after cliché. God likes prayers to Him from your heart. He wants to hear your prayer for changes that you want made in your journey towards the kingdom. He wants you to say the names of those you wish to pray for and ask God's blessings upon them.

Here is a prayer I prayed as I was going up in an airplane. I never want to take for granted takeoff and landing. I want to especially note the expanse of the sky and praise God for making the beautiful clouds and awesome landforms.

Dear God of this beautiful day, today I will fly in an airplane. Please, Lord, please, You pilot the plane. Use men and women to fly whom You trust with the life of Your child. You be the engine and please be sure that everything is working. Whatever the outcome, I thank You already.

While I was flying through the clouds, another prayer burst out of me.

Lord, I see the beautiful puffy, white clouds You have made for me. Thank You. They are inspiring. I know that no one else can make them. Only You can make these clouds. You put water in them and then You send them somewhere in Your earth to deliver buckets of water. Who but You, God, can do that? Not only are these clouds beautiful, but they are also useful.

Thank You for that rainbow I saw in the cloud over the airplane. I feel protected by my Father. You sent the Holy Spirit to stay with me and let me know that You have this airplane in Your hands. Thank You, Lord, I do feel Your presence.

When I saw the coastline, I felt another praise coming out. You put enjoyment in nature. People can relax at the beaches and remove themselves from the struggles of life for a while. Thank You for the mountains that are so large and majestic, yet you are larger than the mountains. You must be a mighty big guy. I know You can answer my prayers. Finally, bless all the passengers on this plane with me. Keep them in Your care and bless their families. Thank You for providing the dollars so that I could be on this flight.

In Jesus' name, Amen.

This is just a prayer I prayed from the heart while flying. Talk with the Lord talk in your closet, and keep it real—He loves that. When you go to visit a sick person, pray for them. Petition God on behalf of their families. Save the other kinds of prayers for when you are not praying specifically for someone sick and in need.

Kind Father in heaven, my dear brother has come down with a dreadful disease. His initial response to his disease was fear. He was concerned about what would happen to himself and his family if this disease should take him out. There is a lot of soul searching going on in my brother. He wants to know if there is something that he may have done that would have caused this infirmity. Keep my brother focused on You and not on his problem. You are the center of his joy, not his disease or infirmity.

Help him to know that he will never find all the answers as to the cause, but he will find strength to make it through the challenges. You said in Deuteronomy 33:25, "And as thy days so shall thy strength be." When in pain, be the pain bearer. When uncomfortable, remind him that you are the God of comfort.

When He is wondering when a happy day will come, please have someone send some flowers or a card to remind him of Your love. Show up and encourage my brother. May this sick time be a time when he can spend more time with You, reading Your exceeding great and precious promises.

Lord, please bless his family. They are very concerned about his well-being. Be close to each family member. Talk to them in the night and let them know Your plans for the health of your servant.

May the rest of us intercede in our prayers for him continually until God's work—God's marvelous work—is completed in my brother. Remind him that You do not allow anything to happen to us until You are sure that we can take the trial. Thank You for being in his today yesterday. Thank You for sprinkling flowers along the path that he has to travel. May each petal be a reminder of Your love for him.

Give him strength to bear the trial that he must face with You. Remind him that he is never alone. When he awakens in the darkness of the night, remind him that darkness cannot hide the face of God from His chosen people. We pray for strength, endurance, courage, and faith for my brother today. Let these blessings fall from heaven like snowflakes on a snowy wintry day.

In Jesus' worthy name I pray, Amen.

Here is a prayer that you may pray for yourself.

Dear Jesus,

I want to learn to pray about myself. Mentally, please keep my mind sane, and physically keep me in working order. I know You took time to create this body, and You did a very good job. Please help me to do my part in caring for it. Remind me that for the choices I make, I have to give an account to You, for how I cared for the body You loaned me.

Help me not to take my body, Your sanctuary, to places where You ask me not to go. This makes You unhappy. Thank You for knowing my thoughts afar off. Bring them in line with Your thoughts for me. I have nothing but praises and adoration for You. You are the master of the ocean, earth, sea, and sky. I can never be away from Your presence. Thank You for loving me dear God.

In Jesus' living name, Amen.

Day 48

BEAUTY AND BRAINS

I'm alive! Thank God for another day to live for Him!

"Thou wast perfect in thy ways from the day that thou wast created, till iniquity was found in thee. By the multitude of thy merchandise they have filled the midst of thee with violence, and thou hast sinned: therefore I will cast thee as profane out of the mountain of God: and I will destroy thee, O covering cherub, from the midst of the stones of fire. Thine heart was lifted up because of thy beauty, thou hast corrupted thy wisdom by reason of thy brightness: I will cast thee to the ground" (Ezekiel 28:15-17).

In this passage, God explains how Satan lost his place in heaven. Whenever I read a Scripture passage like the one in Ezekiel, I stop and pay special attention. God is giving me some important information. The devil was made perfect; he had everything he would ever need. He was the brightest and most beautiful. The Bible says sin was found in him. Where did this sin come from? This is the mystery that only God has the answer to. But once a seed of sin starts in the heart and is fed by self- importance, it soon gets out of hand. Sin had Satan thinking he was better and brighter than God, his Father and Creator.

We'd better watch out because there are several cases of people who were given a little extra beauty and brains at birth. For example, we read in the book of Esther that Queen Vashti was fairer than many women, and king Ahasuerus called her forth so that others could gaze on her beauty (see Esther chapter one). The beautiful have people lingering and looking at them. Many people confirm their beauty verbally. That can either be good or not so good, depending on how the compliment is received. How the extra attention is dealt with will determine if it was good or not good.

If an extra-beautiful person sees himself as God's creation he will do His will. He will stay focused on others and be about blessing others using the beauty and the brains God gave him. If the very beautiful person becomes full of self and thinks more highly of himself than he should, there can be very different outcomes.

Beauty can be wasted, and it can be used to bribe. Samson's story in Judges 13-16 speaks of Samson's betrayal of his promise to God. Delilah, a beautiful woman, bribed Samson into telling her where his strength was. She accepted a bribe to share the information with the Philistines. Samson was so taken up by Delilah's beauty that he betrayed his God and himself. He ended up blind, working for his enemies, and finally dead. What a price to pay just to spend a little time with a very beautiful woman. I am sure if I asked Samson if it was worth it, he would say no!

A beautiful person can create fear in the heart of the man or woman they choose as a spouse. Abraham had that fear. Genesis 12:11-16 speaks of Abraham telling Sarah that whenever the king saw her and wanted to take her, she should tell them she is Abraham's sister so that he would not be killed.

There is often the fear of some other person trying to take the beautiful person's heart away from his or her commitment. Some intruders can be very ruthless about this. What the eye of evil sees, the eye of evil wants.

Very beautiful people have to avoid evil diligently. Pride can so elevate them by the affirmations of society that they forget that they are humans just like the rest of us. They (beautiful people) can in fact be more easily drawn into pride. Pride goes before a fall (Proverbs 16:18).

When Esther was chosen to be a king's wife (Esther 2:15-17), it was because of her beauty. She used her beauty to enter into the king's presence and save her people. The book of Esther is a short one. Read about Esther, the brave and very beautiful woman.

In 2 Samuel 14:25-26, Absalom, one of David's sons, was very handsome. He had people wanting him to be king because he was handsome and had a lot of beautiful hair. He became very boastful and felt he should be king. Pride caused him to disrespect his dad the king. He even attempted to dethrone his dad. This story ends sorrowfully as Absalom was hung by his own hair and then killed. David was very sad about the death of his son. David loved Absalom. Read that story in 2 Samuel 13-19.

Beauty can become a curse. If you are very beautiful, stay close to the Lord. Remember, Satan lived in heaven when pride grew in his heart. You ask me where pride came from since he was created perfect? Then that is the mystery of sinfulness. Saul was chosen king by the people because of his height and beauty. But his self-pride and his self-elevation cost him his life in a battle. Any life without God is a loss, a great loss.

Another pit of quicksand to look out for is high intelligence. Many people affirm the brilliant as they do the beautiful. Many say, "He or she is brilliant and is going places" or "He or she is a certified genius." Many of these compliments may be true; however, we know that all intellect and brilliance without God leads to ruin.

Satan felt that he just knew everything. When he discovered that Jesus knew more than he did, it upset him and he became angry. Read about this in Ezekiel 8:14-17 and Isaiah 14:12-14. Count how many times he used the

"I" word. Isaiah records five times. Be careful when everything is all about you. "I will do this," "I will do that," or "When she does this I will do that."

Were it not for God's grace you could not do anything. If someone is in a car accident, scars on the face can end beauty in a flash. A stroke can end brilliance just as fast. If the almighty hand of God was not lovingly giving you His sustenance every day, the beauty and the brains would not matter.

Many intelligent people became failures with their families as they fail to develop other parts of their lives besides their intelligence. Ask God to keep you, my highly intelligent and beautiful friend, and recognize that all wisdom comes from God.

Solomon was given a lot of wisdom. He is called the wisest man who ever lived. Yet when he left God, he had to declare in Ecclesiastes 12:13, "Let us hear the conclusion of the whole matter: Fear God and keep His commandments for this is the whole duty of man."

When you were in your mother's womb, God had a purpose for your life (Psalm 139:16) and that is why He gave you extra beauty or extra intelligence. Make God proud that He created you. Use yourself in honorable service to make mankind more faithful to God. He will bless you and your end will be better than your beginning.

Don't give in to the temptation of pride, but ask the Lord every day to empty you of yourself. He will answer your prayers. As you reflect on the qualities of inner beauty—love, kindness, and peacefulness—you will be brighter and more beautiful, inside and out. The brains and beauty playing field is even. When I show up with God in me, I, too, become a bright and beautiful child. He will judge me on the qualities I use for Him here on earth.

He will look for the people I help make beautiful and bright by the encouraging words of Jesus. You will be surprised how your words can encourage someone to be what they never would have become had you not encouraged and motivated them. Some crushed soul will find faith because of you. That is bright and beautiful. Since we are all created by God, we are all beautiful and brilliant. God said He made everything beautiful in Ecclesiastes 3:11.

Lord,

Today we have all seen ourselves through Your eyes. We are all Your beautiful and brilliant children. Some among us have been given an extra amount of beauty and brains. For those people, we ask that You remind them of self-pride. Keep them walking humbly before You. You blessed them more so that they will be more of a blessing for You.

When the pain of the extra gift gets tough, bear them up as You heal their pride. Let them know You are the giver of talents. You expect them to have increased their blessings (talents) when You return for them. Help us to stay away from deadly pride. It is Satan's weakness and he wants it to be ours.

God, You are the Creator of heaven and earth. From our lips and by the life we live, we lead others to you. We will only serve one God and live for one Father. Help us never to make self our God. Give us staying power to love You and remain faithful.

May our words not be full of self, may they not be flattering to tempt the bright and beautiful. But may we always give You praise and thank You for being bright, brilliant, and beautiful. Thank You for not giving up on us.

In Jesus' beautiful name, Amen.

Day 49

A BIG, BIG GOD

I'm alive! Thank You, God, for another day to live for You.

"For as the heavens are higher than the earth, so are my ways higher than your ways, and my thoughts than your thoughts" (Isaiah 55:9).

"Heaven is my throne, and earth is my footstool: what house will ye build me? saith the Lord: or what is the place of my rest?" (Acts 7:49).

*W*hen my children were toddlers, we watched a television show that tried to teach them size. Big and small, tall and short, fat and thin, and so on, was the concept they were to learn. The learning method used was contrast. An elephant and a mouse would be put side by side to show big and small. A giraffe next to a child to show tall versus short, a hippopotamus would contrast with a slender gecko to contrast fat and thin.

However, I have tried to find a contrast for God and isn't one. Job 11:7 asks, if a man, by searching, can find out God, or can man find out the Almighty. Job 37-39 is what I consider required reading or homework for today. I can never do God justice in contrast because He is God. Job 37-39 fills you with the awesomeness and the scope of God. God is in charge of lightning and thunder. What man can harness that power? Can you speak to the lightning or thunder and tell it what to do? I can't. God's voice is majestic like the thunder. He commands snow and rain and tells them when, where, and for how long. What man can control snow? None that I know of. He has a chamber where He keeps the wind. He declares how much wind will blow, when it will blow, and where it will blow. Can man declare that? In the last hurricane I saw captured on television, the reporter had to wait until the storm was over or else he would have been blown away with the wind.

God controls the ice caps. Their freezing and melting times are under His command. He directs the clouds as to where they can bring moisture and rain. It is God Who dispatches light. What man can make morning?

He controls the temperatures of the regions of the earth. God is consistent. Down by the equator it is hot, and contrarily, by the poles it is consistently cold. God spreads out the sky over all the earth. That is a lot of sky. When everyone looks up at night they all see the same moon and stars. When it is day and you look up, it is the same sun, sunrise, and sunset we see. God oversees all of that consistently.

God is perfect in power, judgment, and justice. He does not oppress; He lets the just and the unjust enjoy His nature, and He shows no partiality. God determined the measurements of the earth before any man was born. What man can change that? What man can tell the waves of the sea how high to go and where to stop? God asks us in Job 38:12, "Have you commanded the morning since the day began or caused the dawn to know its place?" My friend, only God can do that. We rely on His reliability.

God asks, "Can you name or number the stars?" "Can you feed the lion by hunting his prey or satisfy the hunger of her cubs?" Yes, all these questions Gods ask us in Job. Do you know the gestation months of all the animals? Can you bring them forth at due time and feed them? What man can? All this caretaking work is done by our big God daily. God asks us if we can even make an animal or a bird. Can you teach an eagle how to find its nest?

These are questions God has for us when we ask Him why He does what He does. If you cannot fill His shoes, and no human can, we must accept that God is sovereign. We can hardly get the pets we have to obey us, and we are not their creator. How much more should we obey God.

The eyes of the Lord are always upon us. Psalm 139:1-2 confirms that we cannot hide from God. The night is as bright as the day for Him. He sees all you do; He knows where you are at all times; and He knows what you plan to do before you do it. God is God. There is no hiding place down here for the ungodly.

Jeremiah 23:24 continues to declare the bigness of God: "The Lord fills up heaven and earth." God is eternal (Revelation 1:8). That means the same God Who was with Daniel in 605 B.C. will usher us into heaven. It means the Creator in Genesis 1:1 will be the God Who lives with us through eternity.

Wow, we do have a lot to learn and a lot to look forward to! God is immortal (1 Timothy 6:16). He was first; He is last; He is everything in between. God always is and always will be. Our text for today shows us that we cannot search out God. He is too much for our limited understanding. God is omnipresent—He is everywhere at the same time. He lives in heaven and in our hearts doing always what God does.

God is unchangeable(Malachi 3:6). What He says cannot be changed. That means His commandments that He gave to us cannot be changed. In the words of Scripture, He says, "Don't you, man, try to change My words or you will get hell and the plagues (Revelation 22:18-19).

These are some strong warnings from God. He is serious about His words. Do not try to change them. God is all powerful and omnipotent (Isaiah 40:26-31) and what God says, He has the power to do.

We read in Job about the arsenal of hailstones God reserved for battle and war with His enemies. The Lord can use the winds and the waves, and they obey His will. He can use mud slides and drowning in the Red Sea to stop the enemies of His people. God can have a confused military killing each other instead of God's people. This is the weapon God used in one of the fights in Bible times.

God can back up His Word with power to ward off the enemies of His children. Have no fear; the God we serve is a big God. God is also omniscient or all-knowing. 1 John 3:20 says that God is greater than our hearts and knows all things. It is time to start yielding to God. It is time to start yielding to God's call in our lives. We now know we can never outdo God. If we cooperate with Him, we can experience His peace. He wants us away from His enemy, Satan. He wants to keep us safe until He can get us and take us home.

Ever play the game "Sorry"? As long as you are not in the home zone, you can get knocked back to start. Don't be stuck on the sorry road of sin. Get in the safety zone and stay until Jesus comes and takes us all to receive our reward in heaven where we will live with Jesus forevermore. (See 1 Thessalonians 4:16-17.)

When we review how big God is, it makes us feel very small, doesn't it? However, I also feel cared for. I feel uniquely special and I feel loved by a daddy Who wins for me if I allow Him to. I know He knows all the right answers for my test in and out of the classroom. He can open up His vast warehouse of knowledge and pull them into me if I only ask Him. I feel protected. I also find freedom to make bad choices and not be abandoned. If you haven't already, why not choose our Father, Who is willing to live in our hearts if we let Him in.

Let us pray about this.

Dear really big heavenly Father,

I come to You today, thanking You that You are such a complete God. I don't have to plant You or bring You to where I am or make You—You are already with me. You stay with me and You keep Your promises. Thank You, God, for that.

Lord, whenever we have questions, may we be reminded to come to You first to get answers to our questions. Send us to Your Word when we are in doubt or despair. When we read Your Word, it gives us unspeakable joy and happiness.

We realize we serve a God who is able. Please, Lord, stay with us as our faith grows. We don't want to be cut off ever from Your presence because of our unbelief. Give us Your power to fight back when temptations try to overpower us.

Give us peace in this world of turmoil and poverty. Let us be mindful that You own everything and that You can take care of our needs and even our wants. You set up kingdoms and take them down. Let us not live in despair because You've got this.

We love You and respect Your ways, God. They are not our ways. Show us how to move out of Your way so that You can lead us in this life down here on the best path. Then show us eternity. Life eternal with You, our eternal God.

In Jesus' all-knowing name I pray, Amen.

Day 50

THREE DAYS LATER

I'm alive! Thank You, God, for another day to live for You.

"When you pass through the waters, I will be with you; and when you
pass through the rivers, they will not sweep over you"
(Isaiah 43:2).

*I*t was a miraculous, unforgettable day. It was the kind of narrow
escape day when you ask yourself, "Did that just actually happen?
Did I come out of there alive?" I have heard of some terrible automobile accidents that involve fatalities and yet from the same accident others
walked away without a scratch. It is on days like that that you really recognize God's providence in sparing your life. That is the way God's children,
the Israelites, who had a crossing of the Red Sea experience, felt.

God had miraculously opened a dry path for them through the Red
Sea. I am sure some felt a bit fearful as they traveled the river path. They
might have wondered if the waterbed would be their grave. They wondered
if God's hand was leading them or if they were doomed. Some may have
wanted to stay behind but Moses said, "God has made a way of escape for
His people."

As they walked through the water they could see the mountains of water on both sides of them. They would have been caught and brought back as slaves if they had not been given this awesome escape route from God. The animals went through, and the aged and the infirm followed.

I'm sure some of the children went back and forth to experience this moment completely. When the last duck quacked its way to the dry ground on the other side safely, the Lord removed Himself from the back position of protection to the front position of leadership. Now that the pursuing army could see their slaves in front of them, they jumped in the path to pursue them.

However, the Lord protected His people and led them through and then the natural flow of the river took over again. Everyone intending harm towards God's people was swallowed up by the sea.

When God told the water to do your natural thing, the enemy was overcome by the waters. Those who obeyed God were safely on the other side of the Red Sea by then. They began to praise God for their miraculous escape. They danced and sang. Exodus 15:1-21 tells of the celebration they had.

What a jubilant service of praise that was. Miriam, Moses' sister, took out her tambourine and the ladies and children danced. They had a merry celebration. Four hundred years these people were slaves and yet that day they were free and their oppressors were dead. What a story.

The story was recorded for future generations. The people were sure that in years to come people might not think the deliverance through the Red Sea was a miracle. So they praised God and prayed and they wrote of God's miraculous delivery. They rested and reflected. What an awesome event. They were, as some would say, pumped.

We know God can do anything. Have any bills you need to get paid? No problem. God can make a way out of no way. Do you have a marriage that is failing? Take courage. God can do anything. Somehow the tuition gets paid for college. God opened a Red Sea for you.

The doctor said you will probably be dead in three months, but somehow God gave you a Red Sea experience. He parted the water for you and now it has been three years or more and you are still here. Some have been told that they will never walk again and now they're walking without crutches or a cane—they had a Red Sea experience.

I'm sure many of you have had a Red Sea experience. I am sure you can tell me story after story. Review in your mind right now a miraculous blessing God has given You, and then thank Him and praise Him right for it now.

As the Israelites began their travel through the desert, not even three verses and three days after the Red Sea experience, the travelers got thirsty and grumbling began. The complainers told Moses that he had brought them into the wilderness to die of thirst. They said they would have rather died in slavery. The water they found was very bitter. They could not drink it. Their response to Moses was harsh, thoughtless words. Moses went to God and asked Him what to do to fix the situation. God told him to put a stick in the water and the bitterness would clear up. God worked a miracle on behalf of His people. Here Moses risked his own life for these people. They knew it was God leading them, yet they complained so sorely. That was only three days ago and yet here they are complaining.

Another experience of the unknown brought the children to their knees in doubt and despair. They had completely forgotten the miracle God had performed three days ago. If they had faith in God, could they not depend on God to bring them through this also? Should they not have developed that sustaining faith? They did not get it. Off they went, grumbling and complaining.

Are we like that sometimes? God gives us a house, even with bad credit. We are in the house giving thanks and praise to Him. A few weeks later, the car acts up. God says, "Wait on that one." And we get to grumbling and complaining, "Why won't God give me a car? I'm faithful, I go to church, I am a good person." The miracle of the house is forgotten, and the present problem has robbed us of our praise. How sad. How short-sighted.

Don't we get it that God can provide all we need? He said He will always be there with us. Sometimes we have to have hard times to develop our faith and our strong trust in God. The times when you cannot see a way that is when your faith grows. Life has changed you from a young and strong to an old and weak, and still you must keep the faith.

Know that God is still alive. He is the same God yesterday, today, and forever (Hebrews 13:8). Have we not learned that God rescues His faithful children and His not-so-faithful ones as well? Jail cells are not for God's people. Sometimes we do land up in there for our bad behavior. But even then, God is on a rescue mission to save our souls. Please be reminded, dear friend, that salvation is what is on God's mind for us.

Waters of sorrows and mountains of impossibilities are not jail cells for God's people. They are opportunities to develop a deeper relationship with God. They help the true disciple know that God is always there. If you have lost sight of the miracles and jubilant days of your life, rehearse them. Go back over the way the Lord has led you. Stop complaining and grumbling and give God praise.

Psalms 50:15 says," And call upon me in the day of trouble...." The trouble is only Satan in another form. God is used to him. So God is the only One to call upon. Often we go to other men, or some go to friends and family for advice, but God is the One who is always true. He is the only One who can really do something about our problems.

God quenched the thirst of the travelers by putting Himself in the water and making it sweet for them to drink. Only God can use a stick to sweeten your life and mind. Let us learn something from these weary travelers. Let us learn that God is always with us. God can take care of us. He makes our impossible situations possible. We must trust God and call upon Him in our difficult moments. Hasn't He always come through? Well, He will do it again. Let us pray.

Dearest dependable God,

You have been a strong tower in my life. You have passed me through some Red Seas. I know without You I would have drowned. My faith has grown because of Your consistent rescue mission in my life. I want to praise You. Many faithful disciples reading today want to be reminded that they can depend on You. Remind them of miraculous days when You showed up for them in the past. May praise come out of their lips. May they know you are still God and in the wonderworking business. All we need to do is follow Your lead.

Keep us on the path to heaven. If we have slipped off into our own way, gentle Shepherd, lead us back, away from temptation. Help us fix our eyes on You, not on our desires or things of this world. Help us to know You are not frightened by our troubles. You know the way we need to take.

We love You, Lord, and thank You for the Red Sea experiences and the bitter waters we have in our lives. We also want to thank You for the Red Sea experience recorded in the Bible. It is an awesome reminder that You are a big, big God. Help us today to stop complaining and grumbling and start trusting in You.

In Jesus' name I pray, Amen.

CPSIA information can be obtained at www.ICGtesting.com
Printed in the USA
BVOW05s1650190914

367455BV00002B/3/P

TO MARY PHELAN AND SIMON TAUB

Sustaining members of the
Plotnikov Literary Society

THE ELEMENTS OF AUTHORSHIP

UNABASHED ADVICE,

UNDILUTED EXPERIENCE, AND

UNADULTERATED INSPIRATION FOR

WRITERS AND WRITERS-TO-BE

Arthur Plotnik

toExcel

San Jose New York Lincoln Shanghai

The Elements of Authorship

Unabashed Advice, Undiluted Experience, and
Unadulterated Inspiration for Writers and Writers-to-be

Published by toExcel Press,
an imprint of iUniverse.com, Inc.

For information address:
iUniverse.com, Inc.
620 North 48th Street
Suite 201
Lincoln, NE 68504-3467
www.iuniverse.com

ISBN: 0-595- 00119-X

Formerly HONK IF YOU'RE A WRITER
A Fireside Book, published by Simon & Schuster, 1992.

ACKNOWLEDGMENTS

WITH heartfelt thanks to editors Phil Turner and Edward Walters; agents Adele and Ralph Leone; and writers Billy Collins, Ian Morris, James McCormick, Andrew Kaplan, and Carol Felsenthal. Also Ed McLarin, Sean and Wilma Morris, Edith McCormick, Bruc Frausto, Tom Gaughan, the American Library Association, and family boosters Mary, Annabelle, Julia, Katya, Simon, Barbara, and Tommy; with memories of the late Marilyn Litvin; and belated thanks to Jane Cullen, editor of an earlier book and a friend in need.

"The incurable itch of writing possesses many."
—JUVENAL, *SATIRES*, SAT. 7

"Do you really need to write . . . ?"
—MOLIÈRE, *THE MISANTHROPE*

"Literature is achieved anxiety."
—HAROLD BLOOM

" . . . I never called myself a writer—in some ways I think it's a curse to claim the title!"
—LE ANNE SCHREIBER

CONTENTS

Overture

BEING AND NUTTINESS

THE TRUTH IS THIS: Writing is a bumper-to-bumper crawl through hell with an occasional jolt to the next level of anguish. To be a writer means hitching one's self-esteem to the slimy tail of success. Slip loose, and it's into the wreckage of failed artists.

If there are cheerier routes to the blessed state of author-dom, few take them. Like a nation of exiles, millions of tortured souls go forth in search of a byline and a word of approval. Only a three-chain flagellant is assured more misery. Yet being a writer remains the dream of any romantic who ever watched the seasons change or fell in love or counted the zeros in some lucky idiot's book advance.

The reality behind the dream is kept from view. Too many interests thrive on the mystification of writing. Schools for would-be authors proclaim, "There's a writer inside you," as if some secret pearl resided in your oystery innards. Established authors and other literati become cabalistic on the subject of writing. The normally lucid Susan Sontag: "Writing is a very mysterious mix of being highly conscious and self-conscious and just following something that you seem to feel."

A certain hysteria fills the air, now that all living creatures have decided they are or will be something called *writer*. What *does* it mean? they clamor. What does it take? Can anyone be one? Is one chosen? Born with The Gift? Can you learn it? What do you write and how much? How do you act? Do you have to be *published?* What's the payoff? The price? Can they take it away from you? Where does it hurt? Are you better off as a writer than as a happy person? Are you special? Do you go to Martha's Vineyard when you die?

A CERTAIN mystique has long shrouded the process of being and becoming a writer, but surely it wasn't always so. From what we can tell about earlier times, the mantle of writer was attained by groveling for the patronage of a duke or wielding a hot quill in a cold garret. For grovelers, the trick was the mewling dedication: "My Lord—All wit, all youth, all hopes of mine have spent themselves for thee in these poor epic lines, unworthy dung beside the least blemish upon thy nether cheeks . . ." ("Yo," a duke would say, and a writer would be pensioned.)

As for wretches without a duke, eyes burning beneath frosted brows, being a writer meant somehow maneuvering a quill as one's blood turned to slush in a wintry hovel.

Simpler times. Today the mystery of being a writer is compounded by overload: too many writers, too many images of writers, too much advice on how to write, not to mention the verbal big bang—the explosion of communications technology. Everyone is outputting words. Few are reading them. Many are looking at pictures. Many are shuffling screens of data and chunks of text. But who *writes* for whom? Where is the power of the pen, the sustained individual voice, in this cataclysm of unstable electrons?

Even as the writer's voice somehow transcends the electronic static, it is muffled by a Neo-Puritanism—from left as well as right. In the name of family values, fundamentalists have unleashed a new crusade against the erotic, the titillating, and the funny. The liberal thought police have their own truncheons poised for insults to oppressed species. Today, by the time a sentence is morally, politically, and environmentally correct, it has the buoyancy of a Mississippi chain gang.

WITH all this in mind, I offer a sustained and unabashed honking through the hell of the literary pursuit. As one who has long traveled the convoy en route to being a writer, I offer both cautionary blasts and rallying toots to fellow travelers.

To benefit those new to the journey I share my own travel journal, an honest primer for would-be writers. A primer is a small teaching book, originally a prayer book. And in my own manner I do pray for writers, because they are clearly up against unnatural forces. They are not a joyous lot overall. Despite such self-deifying writers' organizations as P.E.N., they are not the chosen. Many are the cursed, the afflicted—at the very least, the ill-prepared. They need a friendly talking to. They need a laugh. They need to understand themselves as writers; they need someone who understands and speaks the language and who is willing to feed a lifetime's experience into a prose compacter.

Some of my honking is an anguished outcry on behalf of all writers, because writing is an anguish better shared than borne in solitude to the grave. And the better shared, the better such anguish (including my own) is channeled into writing that makes the whole world sorry it didn't discover you sooner.

AND so this wee tome speaks to aspiring writers, writers in crisis, and writers metamorphosing from unpublished larvae to pupae-in-print. It speaks to gentle dabblers and muscled pros.

It speaks to lovers and spouses who lie with writers and to editors and publishers who lie to them. It speaks to writers who lie to themselves.

It speaks to never-say-die writers holding out in Arizona behind Remington typewriters, and to kids in headsets sulking at blank monitors. It speaks to parents who fear (with reason) the writer's glint in a child's eye. It recounts the excruciating episodes along the way to evolving as a writer, and it speaks to writers skewered on the stakes of failure.

All such people need a book that speaks nakedly and not mysteriously, not delicately, on the subject dearest to their hearts.

NAKED TRUTHS

I come before you naked. Here I expose myself as a writer with all the whining complaints of the struggling author, all the ignoble motives of the lowliest hack, all the devious means of gaining attention and turning nothing into something, and the usual murderous dependencies on success or approbation.

The difference between me and most other writers: I have also been an editor for long years, have demystified the editor's role in an earlier book, and now as a hands-on publisher continue to beat bad habits out of decent writers. Throughout, I have trained a careful eye on the whole burlesque of being a writer. The editor within me, the skeptic, has stripped the writer-self of certain illusions many other writers hold sacred.

At times in the chapters that follow, I offer truths illuminated by my own experiences—for what kind of writing haven't I done? My modest triumphs and thumping failures link me to most of the world's working writers, if not the most celebrated. And after all, what *can* celebrity authors tell us relevant to our smaller struggles? Such writers become publicity industries who babble on about agents, package deals, guest shots, and author tours; or they seek refuge in the literary high temple, refusing to deal with the mundane world—a world that once provided the stuff of their art.

Even such a genial author as the late Walker Percy, who probably understood writing better than most, decided to go mum on the subject. In an "interview" with himself not long before his death, he "refused" to comment on his own writing, said he couldn't stand to think about it, and that he had nothing to say about the vocation of writing in general. The best he would offer, sly devil, is that a serious writer is an ex-suicide, a zero, with a "knack" for writing "as little understood as chicken fighting or entrail reading."*

If the high priests write at length about writing, they usually do so to impress one another in journals of benumbing intellectuality. Should I, too, attain the priesthood, I will probably do the same. Such is the inevitable winter of the writer's life cycle.

PLOTNIKOV'S PRIMER

But now, in the midsummer of my journey, I am eager to share some hard-won insights and practical lessons. I have decided to share them not in the first person—the "I" voice that oppresses us day in and day out. Instead, beginning next chapter, I will veil myself thinly as a character named Plotnikov and speak of him in the third person. All his experiences, however, are mine, and are nonfictional.

Plotnik itself isn't a bad name; in Russian it means "carpenter," an apt metaphor for a hewer of prose. But Plotnikov, with its tragi-comic Russian ring, allows me some literary distance and the challenge of creating a character from autobiographical fact. Through characterization I can put a human face on the abstractions of the literary pursuit. Plotnikov, then, is me, stripped of all baggage except that which carries forth the writer's quest; Plotnikov is you, progressing from first literary cry to the "achieved anxiety" of success.

ALTHOUGH the first chapter starts at the beginning of the writer's journey, Plotnikov's primer could as well begin in the mid-sixties, when he sat forlornly in a session with Dr. Boris Anolik, an Albany, New York, psychiatrist.

* Walker Percy, "Questions They Never Asked Me." *Humanities,* 10:3 (May/June 1989) pp. 9–12.

Plotnikov had recently quit his job as a reporter for the Albany *Times-Union* and was pounding out one trashy paperback novel per month for the voracious Nightstand Books of Chicago. He was a writer, with dreams of greater works; yet he had lately returned from a visit to his New York agent with bowels on fire and voice box frozen. In sign language, he had begged his wife to call a shrink.

Now, in a black vinyl chaise in Dr. Anolik's dim consulting room, Plotnikov worked through his thirtieth or fortieth session, watching the Freudian's face for a flicker of compassion.

"I'm still lost," Plotnikov croaked after one long silence. "Is it crazy to keep writing?"

Dr. Anolik paused the usual ten beats before the inevitable, "What do *you* think?"

Here, twenty-five years and mountains of manuscripts later, are the thoughts of Plotnikov.

1

THE WRITER'S FIRST CRIES

"The tongue ever turns to the aching tooth."
—PROVERB

LIKE normal people, writers enter the world screaming. But normal people subdue the incessant cries; writers keep them up. Societies without official keeners need writers. Someone has to blubber over the human condition in a way that stirs hearts or sells newspapers.

Words are a writer's tears. Writing itself might be defined as edited crying. Even a child's whimpering contains the elements of a literary voice. After all, why do children cry? Out of agony, terror, impotence, rage, and nastiness—the very arsenal of mature authors. To succeed as a writer, the sniveling brat needs only discipline and a good agent. When children begin to polish their whining—"She has *infinitely* more chocolate than I"— they may be uttering their first cries as authors.

Writing begins as crying, and being a writer means endlessly scavenging through one's hurts for new scraps of saleable material. This is not a happy business.

Consider Philip Roth, author of that ultimate lament, *Portnoy's Complaint.* Was Roth ever happy? Yes. Plotnikov* observed Roth in a singular moment of bliss in 1961. This exultation came not from Roth's National Book Award for *Goodbye, Columbus* or from the adulation of graduate students at the Iowa Writers Workshop, where he taught. Roth's happy face snapped into view during a weekend softball game in Iowa, when he punched a single between a poet (Donald Justice) and a student novelist (John Yount).

Plotnikov, a Workshop student himself, watched from his position at third base as a heavy-thighed Roth chugged along and took his turn toward second, as near to euphoria as he would ever appear. Why? Because for one golden moment Roth was both away from his writing *and* not feeling guilty about it. Roth was not at his typewriter lamenting the human condition; he was at *play,* lighthearted as a guppie, doing what children do when they are not crying.

For years afterward, Plotnikov watched Roth's countenance darken in magazine mug shots. The eyebrows thickened like storm clouds; the five-o'clock shadow lengthened into late evening. Plotnikov studied each of Roth's new books and listened to the cosmic wail of his fictional protagonists—Zuckerman's ululations among them. Roth had been a kind and patient teacher at Iowa, and Plotnikov worried: Would the man cry himself out? Or would the cycle of misery and its regurgitation know no end?

Roth himself answered in *The Anatomy Lesson:* "If you get out of yourself you can't be a writer because the personal ingredient is what gets you going, and if you hang on to the personal ingredient any longer you'll disappear right up your asshole."

Not happy talk. It is more pleasant to think of Philip Roth on first base under the prairie skies—but not as instructive.

* A.k.a. the author, Arthur Plotnik; see Overture.

Writers do become their hemorrhoids, finding relief only in artful cries of distress.

The distress is more explicit in some writers than in others. One commentary on Joyce Carol Oates's *You Must Remember This* catalogs the novel's first fifty pages: two rapes, three attempted suicides, the smells of an outhouse, portraits of two concentration camps, and a boy run over by a coal truck, "blood spilling out of his mouth, ears, like you'd squeeze paint out of a tube." (*Fessenden Review, No. 10*).

Oates cries long and loud; others vent in horrific bursts. V. S. Naipaul's repressed male characters—Jimmy of *Guerillas*, Salim of *A Bend in the River*—spit in women's orifices for relief. Why are such wretched outcries attended by millions and awarded literary prizes? Because these criers have met the great challenge of writing: To package human distress as *cathartic diversion*.

CATHARSIS MADE SIMPLE

Every beginning writer must acknowledge Aristotle's principle of "catharsis," or purgation, as formulated in his *Poetics*. Good drama (tragedy) arouses pity and fear, but in doing so cleanses the audience of these distressing emotions, giving a sense of relief and even elation.

The cries of the child-writer begin as self-catharsis. By calling attention to newly awakened fears, the child seeks to purge them, or even better to make the nearest grown-up feel lousy. Composition teachers know this form of expression as "My *God* the Pain!" writing. It fills student anthologies:

> My head is exploding, man.
> My heart's gonna burst.
> Nobody knows how it's killin' me.
> The world.
> Hey, I can kill, too.
> Like myself?

Although the authors may feel purged, such outcries fail to cleanse anyone else or to give, hey, like a little elation? Cathartic diversion is writing that goes beyond primal whimpering to bring elation and relief to an audience. That reaching out is the craft of writing and editing.

The lessons come over a lifetime. One's own mother can launch the learning process when she advises, "You have such talent, but why always the morbid stuff? *Why don't you write something nice?*" What she means is what Aristotle said: "Fear and pity may be aroused by spectacular means; but they may also result from the inner structure of the piece, which is the better way."

LIKE most teenagers, Plotnikov failed to read Aristotle into his mother's admonitions. His first cries on paper were self-indulgent whimpers that aroused no one. Only in school journalism did he begin to transform whimpering into diversion, through the medium of humor. Plotnikov was a shy sort, but a closet comedian who would do anything for a laugh if the laughter was guaranteed. A jelly bean up the nostril was typical. In a weekly feature, "The Tongue of the Tiger," Plotnikov aroused the puerile agonies of his classmates at White Plains High School, and during the next few years he pressed his wit on the upstate innocents of Albany State College for Teachers. There he developed a farcical column called "The Open Mind," whose broad readership gave him the illusion of being a writer.

Soon came overtures from campus literati, including a kind word from Yale-bred Townsend Rich, professor of English. Plotnikov promptly bolted the Mathematics Department to join the ranks of brooding English majors on the cusp of the Beat Generation.

Now the comic journalism wouldn't cut it. Plotnikov went literary. He plunged into Dostoevsky, Camus, Joyce, making up for lost time. He drank vodka, smoked imported cigarettes. He grew a moustache and goatee. A city newspaper would soon describe him as "a thin, pale young man whose 'round-the-mouth beard and haunted look are reminiscent of D. H. Lawrence as a youth." Perfect!

Having established his new self-image, he attended to the

necessary business of putting words to paper. In a basement apartment his junior year, he fashioned a garret by wedging a drawing table and stool into the pitched alcove beneath a stairway. Here, in ragged jeans and sweater, he could connect with the cosmic stream of threadbare garret geniuses.

Little can be said about his first "serious" efforts beyond the comments offered by an early mentor. Having written some verses in the style of Keats, young (Arthur) Plotnikov offered them to an English instructor whose first name—Arthur—gave hope for compassion. Weeks later Plotnikov dared to pause at the instructor's doorway. Arthur Collins looked up, smiled as if with some pain, and waited. The trauma of first judgment, such as every writer can recall, was at hand. Plotnikov smelled the oak of the doorframe, radiators steaming over winter drafts, his own sweat oozing from every pit and crevice. He made Collins so nervous the poor man had to wet his lips to speak. Plotnikov could hear the words already: *I'll be generous, young man. Your scribblings are to writing as canine feces are to new snow. Go back to the Math Department. Lock yourself in an isosceles triangle and remain there.*

"I liked your verses," Collins said. "Let's see . . ." He rummaged through papers and found the three or four pages Plotnikov had left. "They capture the, uh, Keatsian. . . . But, uh, perhaps you should try something in your own voice?"

"Mine? Me?" Was Collins talking to *him?* Plotnikov extended the moment, tested it: "I don't have. I just. Fool around with writing. I."

Collins raised a finger and a brow. "Ah, we never fool with writing. It cannot be fooled with. It is not a pastime. We do it completely. Or we don't do it."

That year, Plotnikov lingered wherever Collins taught and was not disappointed. The disappointment—enough of it to yield a truer state of writerdom—came from taking Collins's advice.

2

GOOSING THE MUSE

WHAT TRIGGERS WRITING

"This sickness, to express oneself. What is it?"
—JEAN COCTEAU

SOMETHING, perhaps the kindness of misguided mentors, turns a thousand young fools a day into aspiring writers. Educator Jacques Barzun rails against the coddling of young artists, who, he says, are sent by the thousands into high-tech, postindustrial society armed only with palette and brush. There they become a glut of youthful energy that might have been applied in more socially useful capacities.

In the case of writers, the kindest mentors might better seize the Plotnikovs by the ear and march them directly back to Mathematics. But they rarely do, because being a writer, like being an artist, is viewed by frustrated romantics as a higher calling and one that must not be denied—until the world squashes it.

Almost every semiliterate youth gets the writing bug at some time and fools with words; but certain vulnerable young souls experience a crossover, when the need to be a writer becomes entrenched like an African guinea worm under the skin. What feeds that need? What drives the first serious cries of a writer?

Ancient Greeks blamed the divine Muses, because little else could account for the obsessive-compulsive behaviour of epic poets and dramatists. Calliope and Erato (poetry), Thalia (comedy), and Melpomene (tragedy) were the sacred quartet, and writers continued to invoke them for more than a millennium. Oh Muse! Into my quill infuse thy spirit that I may tell of wondrous . . . and so on. Few writers feel divinely inspired these days, and those who do usually write badly. Perhaps the Muses lost interest when writing machines replaced quills.

Often the writer's first cries are driven by the natural rebellion of youth against an impersonal universe. The writing bug takes hold about the time a youth leaves protected childhood and lands powerless in a callous, even hostile, world. Angry, aggressive, the first writings cry out: "Whether you care or not, *I am here.* I didn't ask to be here, so don't ask me to conform! In spite of you, I will be heard; *I will be someone.*" The youth believes that being a writer somehow vaults one beyond insignificance, conformity, and all the world's insufferable crap. The myth is sustained by the few writers, the Henry Millers, who seem to have triumphed by giving the world the finger. But rebel writers succeed only when, in spite of trying to screw the readers, they end up courting them.

ENVY AND LOVE AS INSPIRATION

First cries may derive from simple envy: wanting what other young people have achieved through writing. The glamour. The bucks. Every publishing season brings a tormenting new "phenom" under thirty. Imagine the waves of envy sweeping the nation's campuses in, say, 1989, when twenty-five-year-old Marty Leimbach's first novel (*Dying Young*) sold for some $500,000 up front, including rights in nine foreign nations and a motion-picture deal with 20th Century-Fox. How many lifelong fantasies were launched by this precocious triumph? When a newsmagazine described the novel as an "unsentimental account of a young woman's coming of age amidst a complicated involvement with two men," one could hear the bleating of ten thousand envious minds—"Who can't write one of *those*?"—and a stampede of would-be writers striving to be rich and famous. Yes, they, too, would sit in their agent's sunny Manhattan backyard, chatting easily with *Publishers Weekly* or *The New Yorker,* saying that success would not change their lifestyle and that they would go on living with a dog and a cat in a little house on the Massachusetts shore, driving a used Volvo.

Envy may prod a daydreamer into writing, but it doesn't enhance the writing itself. Love is another force behind the writer's first cries, and may actually elevate the laments into something resembling literature. Through love, some authors at least become other-directed in their outcries, striving to bring cathartic diversion to the loved one—and hot feedback to themselves. If all goes right, one's oh-so-beauteous passions are unfurled and the depth of one's sensitivity overwhelms the love object. ("Oh, Arthur—and I'd thought you were such a nerd!")

But as every sophomore knows, love is an emotion writers must recollect in tranquility before tackling a sonnet or a novel of amorous anguish such as Scott Spencer's *Endless Love.* First cries written in love's mad fervor yield a sort of canine howl—ahooooo!—or a jumble of inept sentiments. Student love poems call to mind the etymology of the word *writer:* from Old Saxon *writan* plus *ere*—one who tears, scratches, writes.

Before he abandoned poetry, young Plotnikov fell in love simultaneously with a city (Montreal) and a woman he met there. Naturally he was moved to weave these passions into an ambitious set of cantos. Still in love's vertigo, he meandered through the city's Old Quarter, gathering images, stopping at sidewalk cafés to tear and scratch at his verses. *Canto the First: The City Awakens.* He was very much the writer, pencil to mouth between sips of café au lait. But *The City Awakens* put his loved one to sleep.

Kindly words, envied writers, love objects—all are powerful external stimuli to writing. But some early cries spring from within, driven by an irrepressible verbosity in one's makeup. Perhaps a genetic strain makes grandpa a storyteller, mother a yakker, and daughter a writer. One can almost spot those children with a swollen right brain ready to explode words like seeds from a thistle: the big-eyed Eudora Weltys, silent as wisteria as they take in the chatter of a summer night; the Woody Allens, bantam contenders in the family shouting matches; the Jimmy Baldwins, overflowing from a pulpit taller than themselves. Sooner or later these children will cry out as writers and there is no stopping them.

For certain unlucky souls, first cries bespeak the world's torments: famine, disease, human savagery. The inept writer will scream and rant, putting readers to flight and achieving self-catharsis at best. Successful literature of suffering reaches out by artful restraint, as in *The Diary of Anne Frank,* or by integration with other monumental themes, as in the works of Solzhenitsyn.

With an artist's self-control, fifteen-year-old Frank rewrote an original version of her diary, softening certain outbursts and polishing the style. Aleksandr Solzhenitsyn did his suffering at the front lines in World War II and then for eight years in the gulag, where he underwent primitive butchery for cancer. Not until age thirty-five, after Stalin's death, did he deliver his first cries as a writer; then the dam broke. Words gushed forth and thirty-five years later were still pouring out. In 1990 he was working on an epic to run more than six thousand pages.

(DON'T) HAVE A NICE DAY

The forces that turn young people into serious writers echo the great themes of literature: unrequited love, physical suffering, fear, envy, revenge, injustice—themes that cry. Why isn't having a nice day a great literary theme? It doesn't cry enough. In Joyce's *Ulysses,* Leopold Bloom tries to have a nice day, but only in failing does he cry his way into literary immortality.

Like their protagonists, serious writers *never* have a nice day. What happens is this: The moment one takes writing seriously, something goes *whompff, screech,* and *boing,* and life is never the same. Life-lived-for-itself takes a powder, and now all experience becomes grist for the grinder. Life as a journey? Live as adventure? Forget it. The writer chooses *life as material,* and oh, what a drag that can be.

Material. Fodder. Everything that should be savored is instead sucked in and stockpiled. Friends, lovers, relatives, pets, scenery, sounds, thoughts, phrases, murmurs—*whompff*—sucked into the notebook.

The journalist ambles through heaven's own landscape of heather and gorse, thatched cottage and country pub, until—*screech!* Pull over, you, for an hour of mood-killing recapitulation. Get those spellings, directions, and prices, and be sure to translate ambience into adjectives until the feeling lives for the world and dies for you. The novelist encounters a lover, savors the magic of those grey eyes, whispered words, until—*boing!* Time to start grinding up the experience into setting, plot, dialogue, characterization. . . .

"Stopping to smell the roses" has become the stock metaphor for noticing life as one passes through it. The nonwriter inhales the fragrance and says, "This is good. Thank you, life." The writer takes a whiff and agonizes, "Lousy metaphor. Used up. What the hell can I do with it? And why am I smelling roses when I should be writing?"

In turning serious, the writer makes a Faustian wager, offering life-lived-for-itself against the rewards of being a writer. Some of those rewards are genuine; others are trick rewards worthy of the Devil's imagination: Ten free author's copies of your published book; an invitation to address the Little Pee Dee Literary Society; and a $30 tax deduction for paper supplies. Who wouldn't gamble life's sweet nectar for these payoffs?

RAGING AND PUKING FOR ORIGINALITY

Young Plotnikov took the gamble, as cavalier about the odds as any sucker who lines up for a lottery.

He tried his first short story, a piece of science fiction. It cried. Its characters raged and puked. Its grammar writhed in agony.

. . . He bit his hand with a vehemence inconceivable to the human mind until it bled. He spat and hissed with fear . . .

. . . She looked at his blackened eyes, the filth under him, his horrible water-starved body, and his ghoul-like face, and screamed a red scream . . .

"What have you done, you lousy fool?"

She picked up a large metal pipe.

"God save me!" She smashed the controls.

"God save me!" She smashed again.

"God save me! God save me!"

God saved the reader; the story was never published. For all its pity and fear, this first cry (and others like it) failed to divert, lacking such elements as wit, grace, majesty, or simple originality. Plotnikov had put aside his wit in turning serious and "not fooling with writing." The grace, majesty, and other literary virtues were decades beyond his present talents. What remained to him, if he were to burst upon the world as a writer, was originality.

But how do young writers achieve originality? What they imagine to be fresh perceptions mimic those of a billion young souls before them. Their voices parody the masters. Their experiences, with few exceptions, are as common as first teeth.

Plotnikov ransacked his own life for some unique experience. Growing up near New York? Nah. Working-class Jewish parents? Nah. This? Nah. That? Nah. But he did have an uncle in Beverly Hills who had broken with family tradition in two ways: He had money and he had flair. Not everyone could write about an Uncle Simon or of Uncle Simon's recent and classy confrontation with an ulcer. Plotnikov gave it a try, and the result impressed the editor of *Primer,* the school literary magazine.

The published piece boosted Plotnikov's standing as an author and fed his self-image. "I'm kind of passing through State College, but I'm really a writer," he told denizens of the forbidden downtown taverns. He spent late nights in small apartments with the school's literati, sharing jug wine and offering sly opinions. One night it was decreed that he would be next year's *Primer* editor. His switch was flipped.

Riding on positive feedback, Plotnikov determined that he would bring a new level of originality to the *Primer,* beginning with his own stories. Now, "not fooling with writing" meant testing the limits of tolerance at a college for future teachers. What one lacked in experience and technique, one could offer in *daring.* In *shock.* And thus was born the short story, "Degeneration," a morbid, scatological outcry that aroused considerable fear and pity in the school administration, but failed to purge these emotions through any sort of golden catharsis. In fact, the only purge was of Arthur Plotnikov, clear out of the college, by decree from the dean of the state university system.

Plotnikov's expulsion became a local cause célèbre. The city's afternoon daily, the Albany *Knickerbocker News,* shouted:

SCT STUDENT BARRED;
WRITINGS STIRRED ROW

Features, editorials, and letters to the editor speculated on the limits of student expression. Plotnikov, at first swept up in the celebrity, soon found it a nightmare. Yes, he'd been a nonconformist, but, golly, only in the tradition of decent young writers seeking to transcend the ordinary and crying to be heard in an indifferent world! But now he learned how quickly the writer and his writings become one, and how the world strikes back when its indifference is shattered by offense. This was the first disappointment and the great lesson of "not fooling with writing." Cry out for recognition—and risk a beating.

Plotnikov took a few good blows. The English Department chairperson disassociated himself from the "mistake." Student officers called the story "plain dirty, written by a poseur, without conventions." The college dean, in his Scottish brogue, cried, "Ooot of all bounds of decency!" Newspaper accounts pointed to an "unhappy and distasteful tale" by a bohemian author with "little belief in the dignity of the individual." A letter writer characterized Plotnikov as "an unfortunate person more to be pitied than censored." Plotnikov's mother wept. His father shook his head.

Plotnikov kept to his basement apartment a while. He watched the Albany light turn grey as November approached, and he handled his humiliation as young outcasts usually do: by wallowing in self-pity.

FROM the lessons of his first outcries, Plotnikov began to understand the "why" of being a writer: in part to uncork the world's and one's own distress. But botching the job only added to the strain, like breaking a wine cork and leaving a stump. To achieve that certain *pop,* that felicity, that cathartic diversion, one had to cry like an angel. Plotnikov's early trials and errors had been instructive, but what he needed now was instruction—in the "how" of writing.

3

FISHTRAPS AND CORNFIELDS

STUDYING TO WRITE

"Fine writers should split hairs together, and
sit side by side, like friendly apes, to pick the
fleas from each other's fur."
—LOGAN PEARSALL SMITH

OH, to be a writing student forever! Not in the sense of lifelong learning, the burden of every high achiever; but in the sense of perpetual stimulation among, say, the Green Mountains of Bennington, Vermont, where writing is taught.

A brochure promoting the Bennington Writing Workshops shows a gaggle of students in an outdoor session. One of the participants seizes the air with curled fingers, as if to say, "You gotta grab that reader by the short hairs." Oh, to languish evermore amidst such verities!

But writers do not live on verities alone, and the cost of two weeks at Bennington comes to about a decade's worth of pizza. For that price, workshops must offer more than mountain scenery and a barrel of clichés.

The best writing instruction forces students to write at some length, suffer brutal feedback from faculty and fellow students, then write again, suffer another pounding, and repeat the cycle until self-indulgence is beaten out like dust from a rug. In this process, something will be learned about writing for others.

The best feedback comes from other aspiring writers in a workshop. Where else would it come from? Friends are too kind, editors too tired. Reviewers don't tell writers how to write. Publishers give instruction in avoiding risk—"Change 'pimp' to 'pastor' "—not in shaping sentences.

Readers do sometimes write letters to authors, but most such reader feedback goes like this: "I loved your book. Will you find me an agent?" or "I think I'll kill you and your family."

So if a writing course offers theory and practice plus exposure to a critical mob, it's not a bad investment. If on top of these virtues the setting is romantic, it might be worth the vacation savings. There are enough dreamily situated workshops to house every literary wanderer. At the dawn of the 1990s, the sun rose over some 850 annual writers conferences, including those at thirty-two colonies and retreats.* If Bennington isn't beachy enough, one can polish one's prose at Coral Gables, Florida, or Kalani Honua, Hawaii. An overseas retreat, the Tyrone Guthrie Center, beckons from Annaghmakerrig, Ireland, where many a pint has been raised in tribute to the muse.

The Fishtrap Gathering in Wallowa Lake, Oregon, is probably as good a conference for writers as the next; but its name suggests a certain lure-and-hook aspect of all literary workshops. Combining the advertising hype of just three reputable programs produces this blurb:

> . . . develop an individual voice encouraged by individually designed projects in a rigorous, supportive, noncompetitive structure; benefit from detailed manuscript criticism by and sustained dialogue with accomplished writers who are also committed teachers; and enjoy the unique opportunity to meet and talk with

---

* *The Guide to Writers Conferences* (Coral Gables, Florida: Shaw Associates, 1989).

some of the best American writers, editors, and agents focusing on writing for publication during five intensive days in a stimulating, literary environment. [Adjectives theirs.]

And so the fish swim in by the thousands, pay their money, and take the hook. Some are eaten alive by staff and other predators of meager talent. Most are quickly measured and thrown back; agents have bigger fish to fry. And a few swim away with the bait: Their writing improves; they make a contact. Every so often in a good program, a writer snaps the tug of despair and soars Marlinlike into the platinum light.

IOWA: WRITING IN THE FOOTSTEPS OF THE GODS

As a writing student, young Plotnikov raised no pints in Annaghmakerrig, walked no coconut groves. The year that John F. Kennedy took office, Plotnikov arrived in Iowa City and entered the University of Iowa's hallowed Writers Workshop, then situated in barracks buildings below the university's hilltop quadrangle. Among these military huts had marched legendary heroes: Flannery O'Connor, Robert Lowell, Wallace Stegner, and Robert Penn Warren, among others; and here one sat at Round Table with instructors Philip Roth, Vance Bourjaily, and poets Paul Engle and Donald Justice. (Among the luminaries who later passed through were John Irving, Gail Godwin, Kurt Vonnegut, John Cheever, Anthony Burgess, Richard Yates, W. P. Kinsella, Raymond Carver, Frank Conroy, John Casey, and Bharati Mukherjee.)

Most of Plotnikov's classmates had enjoyed some glory as writers, if only as local heroes. They came believing they were writers of destiny. Acceptance into Iowa's elite program had confirmed their speciality, and a welcoming embrace from director Paul Engle topped it off. ("Dear Mr. Plotnikov . . . I am determined to have you here and get some sort of fellowship. . . . [Your writings] are lively, interesting and in need of shaping and pruning. Sincerely, Paul Engle")

For most new students, Plotnikov among them, the first

days of the fall session were heaven descended. The high September skies put the glow of Mecca on the Iowa campus and surrounding town. The neighboring cornfields yellowed and sweetened the air. In one of Iowa City's little white houses, Plotnikov and his brand new wife made a cozy two-room nest.

Workshop students fell into two large groups—poets and fiction writers—each with its own instructors. As classes progressed, a further division emerged: about half the students were city-oriented and wrote of street action, whacked-out hippies, and anomic terror in the urban hives. The other half were country-oriented and treated their classmates to heartland virtues and prairie imagery: fly-fishing with Uncle Ray, hounds and pickups, struggles in a storm, Grandma's funeral. Somewhat outside these two cultures were the foreign students. Jolly Bienvenido Santos was billed as the leading writer of the Philippines, and who knew any different? Eun-Kook Kim, lately a Korean lieutenant, was considered a pain in the ass by some for asking endless questions in minimal English; he would soon astonish his classmates with *The Martyred,* a best-seller.

Ostensibly, students got along. Plotnikov witnessed only one overt clash, early in the semester. At an apartment party jammed with Workshop students, a husky poetry student from Chicago appeared leather-clad and menacing, trailed by cronies. He swaggered samurai-like through the rooms until a wheat-haired young man confronted him over some unknown matter—perhaps the number of lines in a rondeau. The samurai abruptly pummeled the poor fellow's face—loud cracks, fleeing bodies, broken glasses, bloody shirt. *Hey,* a dozen or more writing students thrilled, *this is awful—but this is life!*

GOODBYE COLUMBUS, HELLO PHILIP ROTH

Paradise was complete when the writing gods materialized in the first Workshop sessions. In the Fiction Workshop, a tall, intense twenty-six-year-old snapped the creases of his chinos, settled himself on the front edge of the instructor's desk, and announced softly, "I'm Philip Roth. . . ."

Philip Roth? Oh, is that all? Plotnikov mused. *Hottest new writer in America? Author of* Goodbye, Columbus *and the greatest stories I've ever read?* But Roth was unassuming, comfortable in his role as teacher. One would not have guessed from his dutiful classwork that here was the winner, in a two-year period, of the National Book Award and the Agha Khan, Daroff, and O. Henry Awards—not to mention his string of fancy fellowships, including a Guggenheim.

Roth could have hawked and farted away the semester and gladly would his students have paid the tithe. Instead, he was teacher and taskmaster, with a stern classroom manner punctured now and then by his icepick wit. He showed patience in the fiction workshops but little passion; that emotion he reserved for his lectures in "Contemporary Literature," where he demanded appreciation of the European writers he favored. Kafka was his hero, the writer's writer awash in anguish. But there were others: Svevo, Gascar, Verga . . . lesser-known masters representing the nongeneric writer; the writer self-defined; the writer self-purified; the writer self-crucified; the writer impaled on his own writings. Tales of the crippled heart. Cosmic horrors distilled into dark comedy. These were the paths Roth laid open, drawing the student writers away, away from the banalities of their own lives and works, away from the tinsel of the marketplace.

Roth's passions manifested themselves in a deepening of the mighty clefts that split his chin and forehead. To get a rise out of him was the dream of every student and no mean achievement. He was polite, encouraging; but nothing less than Gregor Samsa's cockroach act was likely to stagger him. Students tried mimicking the Europeans, but fell short of that artful melancholy and got nowhere with the master. Although the Workshop frowned on "derivative" writing—pale rip-offs of Salinger, Faulkner, Parker, and other originals—it tolerated imitations of faculty writing. Mimicking one's mentor, after all, was a natural tendency and a way for students to break from their first cries.

And so Plotnikov, with *Goodbye, Columbus* dancing in his brain, wrote a Rothian novella for Roth's workshop. Decades later, a page from that novella remained enshrined among Plotnikov's papers. In the margin Roth had penciled the words *very good,* which at the time thrilled Plotnikov like a banner strung across Iowa: WELCOME TO THE COMMUNITY OF WRITERS. YOUR PAL, PHIL.

VANCE Bourjaily was an easier touch. Of all America's unrecognized writers, he was the most recognized for being unrecognized. Like Norman Mailer, at age twenty-five he had published a critically acclaimed World War II novel (*The End of My Life*) and had been dubbed one of the "After the Lost Generation" writers; but unlike Mailer, he had never quite received the popular recognition and big bucks for his war novel and later works. Such a fate could have made him mean spirited; instead, he compensated with an outpouring of kindness to all student writers and lavish recognition to any who achieved even a personal best.

Bourjaily had already taught three years at Iowa, but hadn't hardened to the cries of young authors. Slight, dark, crew-cut, he sat forward listening to student readings and squirmed and rocked in empathy with the writers. If a student sweated visibly, Bourjaily's forehead beaded. When a nervous writer reached for a laugh, Bourjaily's generous crooked-toothed smile signaled that it was okay: humor appreciated.

"I laughed all night," Bourjaily told Plotnikov on one occasion, handing back a short story assignment. "I had tears in my eyes." Plotnikov reread the story four or five times to make sure it was that funny. He approached Bourjaily's own works fearing some disappointment. But the power commanded by this slightly built and gentle author was a lesson in itself: A mortal shape could indeed conceal a literary god.

Plotnikov's heaven on earth continued into late fall, when Bourjaily put on a succession of revels at his farmhouse in bucolic North Liberty. Oh, this was *it* for the normally withdrawn graduate grinds—out in the smoky air among the husks and leaves, those evenings of rare fellowship under a Halloween moon. In the basement rec rooms, brew gushed from kegs and roast beef landed kerplop on paper plates like fallen game.

Bourjaily orchestrated the gay abandon and took part. Later

he led staggering revelers through the house—this perfect writer's house, past grinning family members, trailed by writer's hounds—to a perfect book-lined writer's study. In drunkenness there was revelation: Perhaps the world hadn't recognized Bourjaily, *but he had recognized himself as a writer.* He was doing it, living it, *being* it, as much as any writer on the planet, and who needed more?

Oh, perfect setting! Perfect mood! Perfect days!

And then the skies darkened into winter, and down the icy slopes of gloom came one student writer on top of another.

4

LITTLE DEATHS AND FIRST PRINCIPLES

SECRETS OF TWO WRITERS WORKSHOPS

"The beginning is easy; what happens next is much harder."
—MAVIS GALLANT

WRITERS must die before they are born again. Not only is that a cute opening line, but there's some truth to it. Like French lovers, writers are always dying little deaths, from the death of innocence to the (temporary) death of talent. Usually they recover and write about it, unless they go the route of Sylvia Plath or Hart Crane or Ernest Hemingway, who had their fill of *petites morts.* "It won't come any more, George," Hemingway said to a friend shortly before he put gun to mouth.

But certain normal stages of development come as little deaths: the death of self-obsession, the death of singularity—of the notion that one is unique. And always, at some early stage, comes a death of confidence.

For Plotnikov and fellow students at the Iowa Writers Workshop it came at mid-winter, when an epidemic loss of confidence swept through the barracks classrooms like a yellow fog.

Anyone in the market for death metaphors will find Iowa's winter horizon a swell offering—that world's-end emptiness stretched across frozen fields. Workshop students used to prairie spaces could handle it; but the metropolitan set grew nervous and took drives to Cedar Rapids, where the Quaker Oats silos were the closest thing to an urban landscape.

Early exhilaration gave way to fear of exposure. In class, one had to bare one's literary buns by reading selections from works-in-progress. Most students managed to choose their worst passages, the least representative of their strengths, the most confusing and embarrassing. *What madness possessed me to read this piece of crap?* one thought with horror when it was too late and wolf-eyed peers were frothing for the kill.

A few students thrived in these sessions, notably the Southern writers who could animate some magnolia-mouthed missy well enough to delight the most sullen Easterners. *"Well, Ah nevah!" declared Miss Coleen. "A growed woman got no bidness bein' poo-wushed through tay-yown in a buybee prayam!"*

Eun-Kook Kim, the Korean war officer, escaped criticism because he took so long to read an English sentence that no one could remember what was wrong with it. Kim was already unpopular for his favorite question, "But what is *meaning* of that?" which he would ask when class had ended and students were packing off. No answer would satisfy him until at least another fifteen minutes passed.

A number of students considered Kim a mediocre talent whose scant English vocabulary gave his writing a false simplicity. These were the students who lost their breakfast on a February morning some three years later, when they picked up *The New York Times Book Review* to see Kim's novel, *The Martyred,* heralded on page one as "a magnificent achievement . . . written in the great moral and psychological tradition of Job, Dostoevsky, and Camus. . . ." It was the book of the season.

Students who achieved publishing success while in the Workshop were publicly cheered by their classmates and, in most cases, privately loathed as traitors to the student struggle.

Soon the writers divided into two castes: the published elite, and the unpublished untouchables. Envy and spleen entered paradise. When a student's work found its way into the local bookstores, the untouchables would stand before it and hiss as if to curse it back to obscurity. Eventually most would outgrow such infantile malice, a natural stage of becoming a writer; those who became fixated in it can still be found hissing in bookstores.

The entire Workshop seemed to hit the doldrums in February. Cold, wet students shuffled into the barracks and cocooned themselves in their coats and scarves. On darkening afternoons, the young writers showed all the enthusiasm of rainy-day campers. Roth snuffled. Even Bourjaily's blue eyes hazed over. Students continued to read from their works; but now passages meant to elicit a soft "ahh" at their conclusion drew only a "huh?" or a killing silence from the sourpussed classmates. The stage fright of some of the most withdrawn students was almost unbearable; and yet the nastiest student critics, smelling blood, swooped in to pick the writer clean:

"The dialogue rings false!"

"Her actions were unjustified!"

"Cows can't fly!"

"Author intrusion!"

"Derivative style!"

And, as the writer tried to flee, Eun-Kook Kim's *"What is meaning of that?"* went off like a burglar alarm.

But the dark days passed; and for all the agony of the criticism, all the little deaths, students found their work getting better. Spring came, and while in the outside world Kennedy failed at the Bay of Pigs, students advanced in the more important matters of building irony and handling dialogue. Learning absorbed them.

TEN LESSONS OF THE WORKSHOP

And what was learned? For the most part, the lessons of the Iowa Writers Workshop differed only in intensity from those of less celebrated programs. The big ten principles went something like this:

- *Understate.* Excessiveness kills. Show, don't tell. The best writing is completed in the reader's mind. Don't stretch metaphors into conceits. Zap modifiers. Let context do its work. "She said," not "she enthused."
- *Surprise.* Predictability is death. Declare war on the generic and the cliché. Pop in the unexpected word. Take characters out of character—but within their character. Fake in one direction, go the other.
- *Reward.* Delight. Writing must divert. Keenness of eye, melodious cadence, freshness of phrase, and wit lightly applied. Let style establish itself. Mix it up: long, short; upbeat, downbeat; cosmic, microscopic. Give the gifts of enlightenment, substance, catharsis. Challenge, do not punish the reader. Say goodbye to self-indulgent, inaccessible, and anal-retentive writing.
- *Focus.* Kim's question must be answered—what *is* the meaning of all this? Meaning trickles from every element into a mighty flow.
- *Believe.* Get inside the subject. Insincerity begets boredom. Irreverence from the chronically irreverent is tiresome.
- *Be accurate.* Cow's can't fly, at least not in a rigid zeppelin after 1937. Readers care about truth in detail; slipups hurt credibility.
- *Particularize.* Not "bird," but "red-breasted nuthatch." Exploit the delights of nomenclature, the power of association, and clarity of the senses. Use all the senses, but not all at once in every description.
- *Justify.* People act, things happen, for good reason, even if that reason is perverse antireason. Logic rules the reader. The quirkiest turns of plot and character must add up in the end.
- *Dramatize.* Set the stage and get out of the way; keep the author's hand out of the action. Let motivation arise from characterization, and action from motivation. Intensify: Create conflict and tension—someone fights someone or something; someone strives against the odds; something awful is happening and must be stopped.
- *Get attention.* Leap above the ordinary. Somehow, shake the audience from its television-induced torpor. Close in, seize the

most immediate, most intimate yearnings; probe the least touched, most sensitive territories of heart, soul, and flesh—or, put another way: You gotta grab those readers by the short hairs.

One doesn't need a workshop to encounter these principles; they appear in every other instructional medium for writers and probably on the bathroom walls at *The New Yorker*. But Iowa students absorbed them well as they struggled to beat the classroom critics, appease the faculty gods, and meet their own rising standards.

The lessons stuck—and left one to be learned: how to stand out in a universe swarming with talented writers. In a workshop of Iowa's stature, mere excellence distinguished no one. Most writers left the workshop with a healthy sense of their insignificance to the world's agents and editors.

SCREEN FEARS

This is not to say that most left the workshop healthy. Creative writing students are notoriously neurotic, and, in fact, a study confirming the correlation between creative writing and mental illness—including suicidal leanings—was to focus some years later on the Iowa Workshop.*

Into the second semester, Plotnikov thought he saw madness in the gaze of certain students, but his own perceptions were skewed by an onset of death anxiety. This icy fear had begun during an assigned reading of Tolstoy's *Death of Ivan Ilych,* in which the antagonist bewails his imminent death at excruciating length. For weeks after, Plotnikov seemed a character out of Ingmar Bergman's films. He saw death in snow, death in clouds, death in his old Ford, death in dirty dishes, and death in sex—which pleased his wife no end.

"Screen fears," concluded the pleasant, bull-necked psychiatrist at the university clinic. "You fear final exams, you fear

---

* Andreasen, Nancy C. "Creativity and Mental Illness: Prevalence Rates in Writers and Their First-Degree Relatives." *American Journal of Psychiatry,* 144:10 (October 1987), pp. 1288–92.

domestic responsibility, you fear failure as a writer. But a high achiever can't admit such fears, and so he puts up the most convenient screen: the fear of death."

"Isn't death to be feared?"

"Not so greatly. We adjust. It's always something else."

Plotnikov asked some of his classmates if they feared death. They jerked their heads as if to duck a wasp and frowned at him, and he knew they had the terror. Only one student, a De Niro–faced Richard Lyons, brushed the question off lightly and suggested they engage themselves in something less morbid: ice skating on a local pond. They found ice skates. The pond was empty, the ice pristine and surrounded by frosted reeds. They floundered, they flopped on their butts, and it felt fine. The setting sun was just a sun that evening. There would be more anxieties and a hundred little deaths, but also hope: There would be life, even writing, after Iowa.

ARKANSAS: A WORKSHOP IN THE NINETIES

Some three decades later, Plotnikov asked a graduate writing student named Ian Morris about hopes and fears circa 1990. Morris, a tree-tall young man Plotnikov had known since acorn-hood, was midway through a two-year program at the University of Arkansas Writers Workshop, one of the best. In a deep voice broken by a few amused arfs, Morris described life among writers preparing for the twenty-first century.

Like Iowa's program, the Arkansas workshop divides itself into poetry and fiction sections. The program accepts some forty students each class out of the two hundred to four hundred applicants who send manuscripts. Novelist and Iowa Workshop graduate William Harrison has run the show for twenty-five years (as of 1990) and takes part in the fiction section. Author of the story filmed as *Rollerball,* Harrison has several Hollywood deals behind him or in the works, and the students enjoy this whiff of the fast lane. A kindly mentor, Harrison can also shoot a caustic warning to writers short on talent; "You know, they're hiring at Taco Bell," is one of his favorites.

As Morris passed through the four-semester workshop, regular faculty included Michael Heffernan, head of the poetry group, and Jim Whitehead (*Joiner*), a jolly giant at six-six. Though certain names keep popping up throughout the nation's writing programs, the workshops are not entirely inbred; each manages to achieve its own identity. Morris chose Arkansas as an alternative to such celebrated meccas as Iowa and Stanford. Even to a youth raised in the Midwest, "Arkansas sounded sort of like the Peace Corps," Morris said.

Fayetteville, Arkansas, turned out to be a civilized town of some thirty-five thousand whose locals took Workshop writers and other hotshots in stride. "In Wisconsin, you said you were a writer only if you wanted to be left alone. In Fayetteville, I could say it and pull up a stool in a town bar," Morris noted.

Among the student writers themselves, Morris saw little of the general anxiety that Plotnikov had observed in Iowa, though students still anguished over how they would find an individual voice in a world roaring with literary talent. The competition was friendly, the critical exchanges welcomed. In each session, students discussed from one to three of their classmates' stories, which were received in advance.

"You sat at two long tables pushed together, about eight students on a side," Morris said. "There were legends about students leaping across the table with a knife—I never saw anything close to that. Usually the author shut up. In general the comments were polite, but you learned how to interpret them: Twenty minutes of perfunctory praise was the kiss of death; an hour-and-a-half of torturous criticism meant you had said something worth discussing.

"The critical motifs seemed to vary from semester to semester. When I arrived, experimental prose was out; the party line said, 'You just *tell the story.*' So my first story was soundly shredded because my approach had been, 'How am I going to manipulate this manuscript?'

"Students could submit more than one piece to the class, and eventually I worked my way up to the local standard of storytelling. But sometimes I think that everything I've learned at Arkansas I learned in the first half hour of getting critiqued.

One of the graduating poets told me he'd have learned all the same things on his own—but not as fast as in the workshops.

"Some of the criticism became predictable after a few weeks. At one point, someone was always saying, 'Name one great author who does that!' Even the faculty authors had their clichés. Here's one about writers taking on grand themes: 'Either you blow a tuba well or you blow it badly.'

"I'm not saying we didn't grow. Most of us did. Just to get any negative criticism was healthy—having been coddled as undergraduate geniuses because we could write a sentence. And faculty comments weren't limited to clichés. Usually, student authors conferred with the instructor after class critiques. There the tone was constructive, encouraging."

Morris valued the sense of community the writers shared in and out of the classroom.

"We felt like writers without having to dress in L. L. Bean sweaters. We were eager for each other's views, as long as they were given to our face. There were plenty of parties and everyone came—poets, fiction writers, spouses, friends, faculty. The faculty hung in for the evening and drank and kidded with us. Writers would also meet in the local joints, places along Dickson Street with names like George's Majestic Lounge. Often we'd talk about writing in general, but not our own writings; that would have been tacky.

"If a student got published, we didn't froth with envy. I went out of my way to congratulate Dale Ray Phillips when he got in *The Atlantic Monthly*. It didn't mean my seat had been taken at *The Atlantic*. It was good for the program, and it motivated the rest of us.

"But we haven't seen a lot of instant success. Arkansas is more isolated from publishers, editors, and agents than some other programs. At least that forces a certain aloofness to commercial trends."

Asked to name some of the memorable principles he would carry away from the workshop, Morris listed these:

- Just tell the story.
- Eliminate and condense.

- Take responsibility for what you say and mean.
- Write what you know.

To a Midwesterner, the Southern-regional flavor of Fayetteville was new and seductive, and every other drawling hog farmer seemed ripe for characterization. But Morris was advised not to write Arkansas regional fiction his first few weeks in town. "Close to half the workshop students were Southern," he said. "Regionalism wasn't discouraged, but you had to stake out some territory of your own. I discovered that I actually had a region. Central Wisconsin may not be as alluring on the surface as the South; but I knew it well, I could work something fresh out of it. The point is not to tackle a subject you can't control."

What, Plotnikov asked, was the bottom line of being a writing student late in the twentieth century? Did one feel like a writer? Was that feeling worth having? How did one approach the future? "It's been a humbling experience," Morris said. "And it should be, if it's done right. And yet for me it hasn't been discouraging. I feel less discouraged now than when I began. As you go along the numbers winnow, the less determined writers seem to drop away. Some of the students concede that they'll never be great writers, but they'll be happy to get a few things published. You have to find what will do it for you, and what won't. We had a successful Harlequin Romance writer in class who was desperate to get out of that genre. She's still trying.

"No one at the Arkansas Workshop had a real bleak sense about being a writer. I still feel that if I write something worthwhile, it will find its publisher. But I think we all face some separation anxieties up ahead. For two to four years we've been in an accommodating environment for writers. Suddenly, we'll be thrown into the world without a support system.

"I still haven't figured out why I'm a writer," said Morris, who was then supporting himself as a teaching assistant in the university's English Department. "All I know is that whatever happens, I'm going to write."

5

SHARP EYES, HARD NOSE

THE WRITER AS JOURNALIST

"A news sense is really a sense of what is important, what is vital, what has color and life—what people are interested in. That's journalism."
—BURTON ROSCOE

"When journalists speak, truth takes a leak."
—ANONYMOUS

SOONER or later every creative writer entertains the notion of being a journalist. Journalism offers a way to publish within one's lifetime. Journalism offers a breather from the tiresome pursuit of large truths.

A journalist is someone who writes about current affairs, as opposed to affairs between sixteenth-century hellions and renegades. Topics of current interest—so-called "news"—range from the breakup of the Soviet Union to the annual cherry-pit spit in Mesa, Arizona. Journalism is an end in itself, a special kind of popular literature; it can also be a stepping-stone toward snootier forms.

Legions of creative writers have worked as journalists; some have lead dual lives, interweaving literary and journalistic writing. Tom Wolfe may be the ultimate meld; with a Ph.D. from Yale, he served a lowly general-assignment apprenticeship with the Springfield (Massachusetts) *Union,* then moved on to the Washington *Post* and New York *Herald Tribune,* eventually creating the "new journalism" that crossed into the realm of literature. The hard-nosed and gonzo techniques he perfected as a journalist drive his blockbuster novel, *Bonfire of the Vanities.* The journalist's job of reporting, said Wolfe, is "the most valuable and least understood resource available to any writer with exalted ambitions." A half-dozen examples underscore the point:

- Ernest Hemingway began his writing career as a cub reporter for the *Kansas City Star* and later wrote journalistic accounts of four wars for various newspapers.
- Nora Ephron wrote news and sports for the *Los Angeles Times* and earned her wings as a general assignment reporter for the *New York Post.*
- Gabriel García Márquez took up journalism at age twenty. He scratched out a living as a columnist for *El Heraldo* of Barranquilla, Colombia, served as European correspondent for *El Espectador* of Bogotá, worked for several magazines in South America, and landed in New York as assistant chief of Fidel Castro's official press agency.
- Alex Haley retired from the Coast Guard as its first chief journalist, then developed the interviews and other magazine journalism that led to his renowned works of nonfiction.
- V. S. Naipaul learned "a way of looking, an example of labor" from his father, a reporter for the *Trinidad Guardian.* He worked in radio journalism for the BBC before publishing his first magazine essays.
- Ishmael Reed wrote a newspaper column for the Buffalo *Empire State Weekly* at age fourteen. Later, he served the *Weekly* as a staff correspondent. During his early years as a poet he supported himself writing for New York–area newspapers, including the Newark *Advance.* In 1965 he became editor of the *Advance* and cofounded *The East Village Other.*

The full list of great authors who prostrated themselves before a city editor reads like an all-star masthead: Walt Whitman, Mark Twain, Willa Cather, Stephen Crane, Carl Sandburg, and so on. True, many literary lions were never newsroom cubs; but creative writers with a journalistic background enjoy a certain advantage, even as they find themselves tormented by conflicts in style and approach. For example, while creative writers languish over a sentence—

Journalists get the point. Pronto.

Journalists seize the reader. They write punchy words that rip, blast, nab, and oust. They have a weapon called the "lead," which packs the who-what-where-and-when of life into one short opener. If James Joyce had been a reporter, he would have disposed of *Ulysses* in three lines:

> DUBLIN—Advertising solicitor Leopold Bloom garnered spiritual fatherhood early this morning after marathon talks with Stephen Daedalus and other denizens of Night Town. . . .

Journalists spew out words. Words are only "copy," something to slap on a blank page, and not art, not literature. Copy is to pound out. Copy is disposable.

Journalists keep control of tone and rhythm. News sounds like news, not like Proust writing a press release.

Journalists have sharp eyes that inform their writing. They see movement, change, and patterns where others draw a blank; they grasp the big picture. They see the sharp angles. "Journalism helps fiction," says Anna Quindlen, who crossed over successfully. "You learn to observe the telling detail."

Journalists have their ears to the ground. They hear what isn't said.

Journalists have hard noses. They practice detachment from their subjects even as they burrow into them. They shun meditative asides and compassionate browbeating; they go for the facts, the truth—though they rarely achieve it.

WHERE JOURNALISTS FALL SHORT

What counts in journalism is the *look* of truth—those bold heads, those chunky paragraphs, those shotgun sentences. Readers tend to believe the short and punchy locution. "In the beginning God created the heaven and earth"—a credible lead.

When it comes to grabbing attention in a world of information overload, journalists are the pros. It falls to literary artists, however, to be the truth tellers—the reporters of news that stays news and describes the human condition. Literature would be out of business if journalists could tell the truth of the heart.

Journalists fail as truth tellers not for want of trying, but because their reach exceeds their grasp. Their codes aim far beyond the loose objectives of literary writers. For example:

> We believe in public enlightenment as the forerunner of justice, and in our constitutional role to seek the truth as part of the public's right to know the truth.

But what qualifies journalists to know the truth when they see it? Are they philosophers? Judges? Theologians? Do they have the leisure to reflect upon events and their meaning? Rarely. According to media critics such as Janet Malcolm writing in *The New Yorker,* journalists are manipulative devils who see truth mainly where it suits their stories and careers. In defense of their shortcomings, journalists point to the pressure of deadlines, the callousness of media owners, and lust of mass audiences for an endless stream of novelty, sensationalism, and pseudo-events.

Only in the aggregate does journalism manage to achieve a surface-level truth. When everything under the sun is poured into thousands of parched news holes each day, some truth will bubble over—enough, at least, to keep politicians, generals, and racketeers on their toes.

JOURNALISM is a mixture of virtues and sins, and a writer must choose carefully when reaching into it: Journalism is the chronicle of human activity; a crock of insignificant crap; "the first rough draft of history"; news that gets old; objective observation; warped perception; the arsenal of truth; the stronghold of arrogance; the voice of the people; a self-serving tool of the power brokers.

Whatever its failings, journalism teaches the writer certain skills that would otherwise come slowly, if ever. Writers who have never practiced journalism must sharpen their powers of observation in other ways: Walker Percy spent a few decades in medicine, rummaging through cadavers. To master what a journalism student learns on day one about getting to the point, writers must undergo years of rejection and editorial abuse. And for simple outpouring of words, the only better training than journalism is forced confession by thumbscrew.

EDUCATION FOR JOURNALISM

Where does one acquire journalism skills? Should writers attend schools of journalism, or J-schools, as they are called? These are the graduate and undergraduate programs, hundreds of them,* that teach the history of mass communications, sociological-measuring techniques, basic nonprint journalism, media ethics, a little news writing beyond what was learned on the high school paper, and a hundred newsroom clichés (e.g., "There are no good stories; only good reporters making them so.") Journalism is also taught in two-year institutions† that tend toward remedial writing instruction with a media slant.

Upper-level J-schools have been criticized for emphasizing theory over practice, making them no different from other professional programs taught by burned-out practitioners who are naturally more stimulated by theory. Students graduate with a muscular grasp of libel law and an atrophied command of language.

Improvements are underway, however, and writers who want the option of news-media careers should pursue the master's in journalism. Other writers might better attend creative writing programs and somehow acquire journalism fundamentals outside J-school. They can pick up a handbook (*The Asso-*

---

* Listed in *Journalism & Mass Communications Directory,* published annually by the Association for Education in Journalism and Mass Communication, University of South Carolina, Columbia.

† Information is available from the Community College Journalism Association, County College of Morris, Randolph, New Jersey.

ciated Press Guide to News Writing from Arco is lively and concise) or a basic course here and there, or plod through a journalism text and workbook.

One approach to self-instruction is simply to start reading good newspapers with an eye toward style and pace. When doing so, the novice might focus on these ten characteristics:

- The inverted-pyramid approach to narrative: most important events first, thinning down to the least important.
- Attention to concrete, factual detail.
- Economy of expression, particularly in headlines and leads; the means of signaling in so few words what is new, different, and important in the story that follows.
- The "second-day story," which invents new importance for yesterday's news. (First day: "Lawyer Slain"; second day: "Slain Lawyer Had Few Friends.")
- Quick delivery of background information.
- Organization of a narrative into accessible chunks. (A long report on poor neighborhoods appears under these subheads: History, Violence, Community Organizing, Apathy, and Revitalization.)
- Directness of style: a minimum of subordinate clauses.
- "Slanting" of a story to the interests of the audience.
- Circling of a subject, viewing it from the perspective of more than one observer, giving the impression of wholeness and balance. (In its first three paragraphs, a story on breast implants presents three different case histories: one successful, one disastrous, and one mixed.)
- And the purposeful manufacture of *tension*.

HOW TENSION WORKS IN WRITING

Tension is the journalistic version of literary conflict, foreboding, and other devices to worry the reader. Literature applies them selectively; in journalism tension is applied to every trivial event, the better to stress the living bejesus out of every reader from morning to night—and to gain attention. If a beagle appears in sunglasses on Rodeo Drive, an element of tension must somehow be contrived: Traffic disrupted! Shopkeepers concerned! Animal rights violated!

Not long ago, when rights to the Dewey Decimal System had been sold, Plotnikov won an assignment from *The New York Times* business section to do a story. The *Times* editor insisted, however, that the story have tension. What tension? That the Dewey numbers would run amok and take over the world?

Freelance journalists must be aware that tension sells stories. Calloused editors, with thousands of readers to be distressed in a hurry, seek the ominous and malignant; yet most freelancers keep pumping out the benign. Media editors don't care about autumnal splendor in the Berkshires unless ticks bearing Lyme disease lurk behind every leaf. When a miracle drug is introduced, what sells the story is its outrageous price, imminent shortage, and terrifying side effects.

The freelance journalist must test each draft of an article against three major criteria: Is it edifying? Is it electric? Is it *distressing?*

Writing for tension is an important part of every literary pursuit, because humans are so crazily attuned to stress and fear and conflict. In literature, as in Henry James, the tension might be an intellectual turmoil admired for its "disturbing" quality; but in journalism the tension is visceral, and when worked into a thousand stories eventually fuses with the journalist's personality. Reality becomes rooted in crises. News hounds develop into high-strung terriers.

When Plotnikov entered the kennel of journalism midway through the Kennedy administration, he had barely been paper-trained. He would soon learn to bark and bite—well, yip and nip—his way through a story.

6

BETWEEN JOHN F. AND WILLIAM KENNEDY

Lessons of the Newsroom

*"I loved the . . . illusion of being at the center
of things when you were really at what approxi-
mated the inner lining of the orange peel."*
—William Kennedy

*"The city room is an outhouse. You can get
black lung just by working on the rewrite
desk. . . ."*
—Jimmy Breslin

At the Albany *Times-Union* in New York's capital city, the
newsroom characters ran in circles, grabbed phones, rushed out
on assignment, and returned smelling of action and Seagram's.
They sparred for lineage allotments from a hulking bald bowser
of a city editor who looked like a Barney Fowler and was named
just that.

The *Times-Union* was a thriving daily, then owned by
Hearst, but it operated out of a warehouselike building in a
seedy neighborhood. The executive offices looked like toll-
booths. When a top editor squeezed a rug into his booth, the
union shop steward set off like a wasp. "I don't see a carpet
in *your* office," he buzzed in every rank-and-file ear. Rank-
and-file had no offices, of course, but shared a large room

whose green and black linoleum tiles seemed to suck in the light.

Unlike today's bright, carpeted, computer-beige newsrooms, well secured against irate citizens, the *Times-Union* city room was bus-terminal grungy and open to the public. Any rummie could stagger in and raise hell, and, since a few such unfortunates were staff editors, no one objected.

Drunk or sober, reporters performed a time-honored ritual when they returned from a beat. They threw trenchcoat at typewriter along a row of filthy desks, swept away the morning's debris, and snapped a sheet of copy paper into place. Then, out came the cigarette.

Reporters hacked and cried rivers as they dangled Camels or Pall Malls from their lips. Smoke hung in feathery clouds and ashes greyed every surface that wasn't already battleship drab. Butts piled up like termite mounds.

One feature writer named Bill Kennedy had a merry friar's countenance—youthful, freckled, with busy brow and impish grin—into the middle of which he would stick a fat dark stinking cigar as he wrote his stories. Who would have guessed that from this noxious fog would emerge the Pulitzer Prize–winning novelist William Kennedy?

For Plotnikov, trying to moderate his smoking, the only escape from the stench of tobacco was the men's room; there a puck of raspberry-ammonia urinal soap overpowered everything else—and in years to come remained his dominant image of newspaper work.

Into this atmosphere were mixed the noises of communication circa 1962. News flowed not in silent electrons, but in the relentless hammering of typewriters and teletype machines. The machines of the Associated Press bureau were some twenty feet from Plotnikov's desk and competed with the newspaper's own clattering monsters. To be heard above the racket an editor developed industrial-strength vocal chords, which, when the machines hit a lull, sounded like Jehovah's wrath.

"PLOTNIKOV!" Fowler the city editor roared in such a moment one afternoon. The newsroom chatter stopped cold.

Cub-reporter Plotnikov sat directly across from Fowler at the city desk.

"Where the *hell*," Fowler said slowly, "did you get this spelling?" He held up a length of copy paper containing Plotnikov's morning work. "Charles L-I-T-T-L-E!"

"I assumed Little is spelled little."

Fowler had him cold. "YOU ASSUMED!" he bellowed, waving the copy sheet. "YOU *ASSUMED?*"

Some of the reporters went back to their work. It was the old "you-assumed" tirade, and the rest was well-known. It should have been familiar to Plotnikov: During a half-year tour of Army duty a few months earlier, a Brando-voiced drill sergeant had lectured, "Don't *ever* lemmee hear yous droopy dicks *assume* nothing. Remember: ASS U ME. You assume, you get *my* ass killed, not to mention your own stinking butts." But the sergeant had been talking about weapon safety, night patrols, that sort of thing; he'd never said it applied to journalism.

So the lesson from Fowler was well taken. The correct spelling had been Liddle—Charles Liddle III of 104 Chestnut Street. The only little was Plotnikov, as little as a chewed-up pencil stub under Fowler's glare.

"When you get it wrong in print," Fowler said, "you get it wrong one hundred forty thousand times. You mislead one hundred forty thousand good people. You tell one hundred forty thousand lies that Charles Liddle has to live with through no fault of his own . . ."

PLOTNIKOV switched a few gears that day. He would do his assuming in fiction—where assumed behavior is the writer's stock in trade—and not in journalism. Without accuracy, journalism was nothing, a tale told by a schmuck. On the other hand, if one mistake equalled one hundred forty thousand blows to the Albany populace, then one good piece of journalism was like a Hail-Mary pass in the Rose Bowl. A stunningly accurate account would reverberate in every household from Climax to Coxsackie—the two towns by which *Times-Union* wags defined their boundaries.

Plotnikov became a zealot of accuracy and of other journalistic principles reinforced at the city desk. He began to *feel* like a journalist and revel in the power of the press. But there were times when the power seemed more than he had earned. Like many young writers, he suffered the imposter complex, the sense of being a know-nothing fraud who will soon be discovered, mocked, and punished. And true enough, most writers have little that is new or magical to offer the world. Yet, such shortcomings have not muzzled the tens of thousands of young writers thrown upon the stage of a metropolitan news medium and told to write. Plotnikov, too, overcame the complex. He played the journalist, pounding out copy and launching it into eternity. And, lo, there was no mockery, no exposure. No one was gunning for fraudulent writers.

The Cuban missile crisis of October 1962 gave Plotnikov another perspective on writing. During the week of the ultimate showdown, when the U.S. blockade of Cuba threatened to unleash World War III, the *Times-Union* writers sat as quietly as ever they had, waiting with the rest of humanity for a hopeful news bulletin—or the blinding light and mushroom cloud. That stony doomsday silence was the great leveler. Writer, nonwriter, fraud, hero, putz—it would all seem pretty much the same and all insignificant near the end.

From that week and others in journalism, Plotnikov learned —or at least sensed—that writing provides the *manageable* truths and *controlled* distress that readers crave, perhaps to prepare themselves for the dire truths and catastrophes. He learned that in a democracy a writer is either accepted or ignored, rarely skinned alive. With these principles accepted, he understood that it is safe to write one's heart out and let the chips fall where they may. Just get the spelling right.

Plotnikov found he could write *something* on any topic, from cockroach extermination to nuclear disarmament. As an interviewer of celebrities, he fell short in his own estimation: He asked Jimmy Durante nothing more original than, "How's the schnoz?" and face-to-bosom with tall Jayne Mansfield he could manage little more than, "Like the city?" But no one noticed. Nothing terrible happened. Readers looked at the accompanying photos, scanned a sentence or two of text, and got the idea.

And at the end of a work day, Plotnikov could drive home feeling the pleasant bump of Western Avenue's cobblestones and the thrill of being a writer.

LEARNING TO ACT DUMB

In his writing career, Plotnikov would keep a hand in journalism of one sort or another and continue to learn from it. Some years after leaving the *Times-Union,* he worked as a press officer for the Library of Congress serving a boss with the initials H.A.H.

H.A.H. was a journalist herself, weaned in the city rooms of Ohio's best dailies, and a stickler for detail. To cope with the relentless paper flow, Plotnikov would arrive early in the morning when he thought he might write in peace. But there was no peace: His work from the previous day would be spread over every available surface with a note taped to each item and signed *H.A.H.:*

> Congressman uppercase.—H.A.H.
> legislative lowercase.—H.A.H.
> book end two words.—H.A.H.
> Conn., not Ct.—H.A.H.
> Doesn't tally.—H.A.H.
> Did you check?—H.A.H.
> Too florid.—H.A.H.
> Too flip.—H.A.H.

It was like being greeted by the Joker. By the fiftieth HAH! each week, Plotnikov was ready to tear down the Library's pillars. But he learned what H.A.H. knew* and he learned that the learning never stopped, neither small nor mighty lessons. From H.A.H. he learned the wisdom of Midwest journalism, that "the smarter they are, the dumber you act, or they'll never tell you what you need to know," and he stopped trying to

---

* Including the U.S. Government Printing Office *Style Manual,* the authority for H.A.H.'s corrections.

impress his news sources. He even learned to imitate H.A.H.'s famous Ohio *"Huhhhh?"* when speaking to some of Washington's chief eggheads.

PLOTNIKOV might have stayed with the *Times-Union* and in newspaper work but for two factors: He noticed that reporters who had been there forty years were pounding out the same old stories he'd been writing as a cub and making just a few dollars more; second, an opportunity came along for writing *novels* full-time—one a month, at three times his current earnings, payment guaranteed!

What kind of novels? Well, sex novels. But so what? It meant writing at home, writing for a living, Being a *creative* writer, like that freckled friar behind the cigar, Bill Kennedy.

Kennedy, who had recently studied under Saul Bellow in Puerto Rico, was laconic and offhanded about his own writing, which made him all the more intriguing. Seven years Plotnikov's senior, he was amused by, if not quite sympathetic to, the younger writer's plan to leap from the city room to the sex parlors of the imagination.

More amusing was Plotnikov's notion that the leap would be upward. . . .

7

FREE TO WRITE FULL-TIME

THE KILLER DREAM

*"All you need to do anything is time to do it,
being let alone long enough to do it, and a
center to do it from."*
—WALKER PERCY

*"Many writers do little else but sit in small
rooms recalling the real world."*
—ANNIE DILLARD

IN a sobering cartoon that appeared some years ago, a beggar
works a street corner with tin cup and a sign that reads:

SOLD ONE STORY, QUIT MY JOB.

Who, with a gift for words, has not dreamed of independence from the workaday world and the freedom to write in one's own nest, at one's own pace, according to one's own passions? Yes, it's a stupid unrealistic fantasy, and most people know better—including those who seem to have achieved writer's nirvana. But fantasies are by definition stupid and unrealistic; the question is, are they lovely fantasies that perfume one's imagination even as they wilt away? If so, they have a place in this vale of tears.

Why is the dream of writing full-time so alluring? Why would anyone rather trade jobs with, say, a Cynthia Ozick than a Sandra Day O'Connor? Ozick's independence came only after some five decades, enabling her to hole up and wrestle with moral issues most of the time. That, and having tea now and then with friends in Manhattan, constitutes her personal paradise. Thousands envy it.

Other writers have achieved independence much sooner—and in such abundance it didn't fit in one place. John Irving was in his mid-thirties when the success of *The World According to Garp* won him the freedom to write full-time. Within a dozen years he had set himself up in Vermont, in Toronto, and in the Hamptons on Long Island. The posh Hamptons lacked only a wood-frame Vermont house to satisfy Irving's whims: so he had one pulled apart in Vermont and reassembled on the Island.

Aleksandr Solzhenitsyn left his Vermont buildings where they were, on a fifty-acre, high-security mountain retreat. Such independence enabled him to work eighty hours a week in a three-story sweatshop containing his workplace, library, and a typesetting and proofreading facility.

Though appealing in their ways, these aren't the situations that ordinarily tempt people to quit forty-hour-a-week jobs and write for a living. Here, in detail, is the standard fantasy of being a full-time writer:

THE OFFICIAL WRITER'S FANTASY

The sun will flood my bedroom at six A.M., and Zelda the calico cat will leap to my pillow, pressing a black-patched nose to my cheek. I will rise and feed her, then grind fresh beans and steam some milk for a caffelatte on the little terrace. On these late-summer mornings the ocean undulates softly, like vast swells of lamé, and some of my best thoughts will billow up from the mind at peace.

After oat bread and fresh berries, I will half-jog, half-walk about a mile on the wet sand along the cove, as far as the highway. There, lizard-faced commuters will be slithering through the lanes to reach their city cages. I will shudder to remember that I was one of these monsters, and I will head back to the cottage, gathering my thoughts for today's five pages.

My study is one of just three rooms, along with the bedroom and dining-living area. It faces the rocky cove, which is quiet even in the tourist season. The scenery is breathtaking, but the water is cold and the swimming hazardous. By September the summer people will be gone, though while they linger I will enjoy them and their fascination with a full-time writer who braves winters in the cottage. But winters will be undaunting. Warmed by a stone fireplace and woodburning stoves, I will treasure the change of seasons and the pageant of snow, wind, and waves.

When I can get them, I will fill the study with fresh-cut flowers. Willa Cather surrounded herself with orange blossoms and camellias in the winter, jonquils and lilacs in the spring, creating a spice-heavy garden environment that nourished her imagination. In my small front patch along the picket fence, hollyhocks will alternate each year with morning glories, signaling a soaring of the spirit, an overflow of creativity.

I will write every weekday from eight until noon, and from two to five, or until my five-page daily average is achieved. My self-discipline will be unshakeable, for that is the professional approach to writing. Fortressed by floor-to-ceiling shelves of books, I will work at my word-processor—no Luddite, I—breaking only for coffee and to reassure Zelda that she is not forgotten.

For lunch, in good weather, I will bicycle into the village and enjoy contact with droll acquaintances over a croissant and chicken salad and mineral water. They will inquire about my writing, and I will say: "An author never tells a book; she writes it." Into my bicycle basket for the return trip will go: a newspaper, a library book, a crusty bread, a wine for evening. . . .

In the afternoon I will polish some of the morning's work and try to reach a logical stopping point by five.

For my good discipline, I will reward myself with an hour or two of reading and wine-sipping on the terrace as the shadows lengthen around the cove. Sometimes good acquaintances will stroll past and I will invite them to join me. Often our lively conversations will run to sunset and continue over dinner. Known as a writer with a unique and stimulating point of view, I will receive many invitations to dine with intensely perceptive individuals, and during the week I will accept them gladly, reciprocating when I can. I will reserve weekday evenings as well for such students and interviewers who care to make the pilgrimage to my workplace and comprehend the writer in her setting.

On weekends, however, I will accept only the hospitality of my agent, editor, or other friends in the city, so as not to lose touch with the vibrancy of urban life. On occasion certain business concerns will be discussed, such as film options, translation rights, and multiple-book contracts. I will trust the advice of my agent in these matters, but I will exercise my own judgment in choosing among media opportunities and promotional tours. Publicity has its place, of course, but neither writing time nor my forthcoming year in southern France must be compromised . . .

This, then, is the standard fantasy that every part-time writer has a right to enjoy. The male-only version is similar, but usually substitutes a nubile groupie for the cat.

Oddly enough, these fantasies do reflect the reality of full-time writing, except for a few minor details:

- A beach cottage would impoverish most authors—a kitchen table in the city is more like it.
- Intensely perceptive people—if there were any in an American beach community—would intensely avoid writers.
- Lunch in the village would become a four-hour avoidance tactic, ending the day's output.
- Writers in solitude become less Thoreau-like every week and

more like the monstrous Jack Nicholson in *The Shining* ("Heeeere's *Johnny!*").
- Nubile groupies prefer rock musicians.
- Agents and publishers have better things to do with their weekends than noodle with authors.

Some writers squander more imagination on the question of *where* to write than on what to write, which makes sense, because where is easier to imagine and seems terribly important. If a dog can sniff for eight blocks before raising a leg, why shouldn't writers scour the world for creative relief?

Henry Miller had a simple answer to the "where" question: "All you need is a place to put your ass." But Henry put his cheeks in some extraordinary settings—Paris, Greece, and Big Sur, not to mention Brooklyn, New York.

Every writer deserves a shot at writing full-time in a setting conducive to great works. But what is that setting? Many contemporary works are produced in Connecticut, where half the writing establishment lives with aging pets and sullen kids. Connecticut is a lovely place, but it isn't yielding many great works these days. Like Martha's Vineyard and Key West and other writer-infested locales, Connecticut has been stripped clean as a source of inspiration. That fact suggests the first of ten considerations in sniffing out one's ultimate writing place. . . .

WHERE TO WRITE: SOME CONSIDERATIONS

1. *Not infested with writers*. If writers have crowded in, the setting will be exhausted; one starts writing about other writers, which gets sickening. At the publishing houses, manuscripts originating from writers' colonies may be greeted with such cries as "Not another cockamamie from the Keys!"

2. *Not too remote*. Bangor, Maine, where Stephen King writes, is probably about as remote as a writer should get. One needs communications. One needs a library. One needs greater diversion than watching the algae and fungi get it on. "A place to put one's ass" may have been okay in Miller's time, but now the word processor and printer need a place for

their little butts as well, a good circuit, a town that sells disks and print ribbons.

3. *Stimulating but not overwhelming.* Anne Tyler writes out of Baltimore, which is alive and colorful and feeds the senses, but doesn't overwhelm one's subject matter. No one is overwhelmed by Baltimore, or by James Michener's two habitats, Austin, Texas, and Coral Gables, Florida. Anne Rice creates her vampire world from New Orleans, which—like Chicago, Boston, and San Francisco—is powerfully stimulating but still can be subjugated to the writer's imagination.

Places like New York, Los Angeles, and Washington, D.C., however, overwhelm and confound the intellect. That's fine for local journalism; but if you write a book in New York, then New York is in your book like a kosher deli pickle in a lunch bag. When Joan Didion writes from L.A., the madness of La-La Land touches all. And no one who writes out of the nation's capital can escape Potomac fever—that breathless fascination with some of the world's dullest power brokers.

4. *Not near the beach.* What you don't need, for concentrating on great works, are blasters shattering the eardrums, sand in the disk drives, or tropical rays scorching the brain cells. Anyway, what's so stimulating about oily gulls fighting over garbage and hypodermics washing up in the surf? Worst of all, the watery grave is always there to tempt you when chapters go bad or the tenth rejection arrives in the mail.

5. *Not in the woods.* Ah, the cabin in the woods. But woods are best recollected in the tranquility of a civilized abode. Woods mean bugs. Bugs never leave writers alone. Mosquitos suck the juices as springtails boogie on the CRT. Woods are okay for such lyrical entomologists as Howard Ensign Evans (*WASP Farm*), who sees bugs as protagonists; for most writers, bugs are just antagonizing as hell.

6. *The academic groves.* If one vows never to write about love triangles in the English Department, the campus community can be a suitable base. The libraries are good, the folks congenial, the bugs trapped in petri dishes. And Joyce Carol Oates, writing out of Princeton, proves that campus civility needn't pretty up one's world view.

7. *Regional writing.* William Styron, Eudora Welty, and dozens more are so sick of being called Southern writers they wish they'd been raised in Greenland. Authors from certain other areas are also branded regionalists, a hated limitation that eventually insinuates itself into a writer's self-image and writing style. Which regions are regional? Any area the New York literary establishment views as a region with literary traditions: the Southwest, the Prairie, and sometimes New England. The publishing world puts quotas on regional writers: "Great piece of writing, but, sorry—we did a Prairie book this decade."

Library Journal surveyed ninety writers whose first published novels were appearing in 1990 and asked them to comment on how regional roots had affected their writing. Usually the home regions were embraced as subjects, but cast off as places to be from. Young writers are learning quickly not to be regionalized. "I don't think of myself as a Chicago writer or a New York writer," said David Breskin, who stayed his longest in those cities. "I think of myself as an American writer in the American grain." To prove it he wrote *The Real Life Diary of a Boomtown Girl,* a first-person saga of a female coal miner in Wyoming.

In the survey, the greatest number of authors (eighteen) were from California; not all wrote paeans to the Golden State. "Southern California," said Mary Pjerrou (*Coz*), "is a place that makes you wish time could go backward and everything could be undone and sent back to where it came from."

Will Aitken (*Terre Haute*) feared that his heartland Indiana origins—"drab, provincial, reactionary, hypocritical"—might recapture him when he novelized them. "I was wrong," he concluded.

8. *Writing abroad.* That most delicious of all fantasies is usually a bad idea. Prodigiously talented writers like Gore Vidal—living part-time in Rome while he tossed off American historical fiction—can handle the distraction. But lesser souls find themselves swept up in the "foreign" atmosphere, writing gushy mood pieces that later seem as moronic as travel videos. Americans lose touch with their idiom and start writing clipped British dialogue or indecipherable Australian "jumbuck"s and "hard yukka"s. Narrative is streaked with foreign phrases in

italics. Ultimately the expatriate writers find themselves physically undone, dreaming of reclining chairs and New York pizza. Time to go home.

9. *The well-tempered study.* The fantasy of a cozy writing study crammed with books and other beloved *objets* can be taken too far. Writers who festoon the workplace with a lifetime's mementos may never write again. They will daydream and pace the study like a high-brow television host, fondling books and glass paperweights and murmuring poignant opening lines such as, "How swiftly passed the days . . ."

Many a writer has dissipated the creative force in fashioning bookshelves, sanding furniture, and equipping the perfect study—which then sits idle. But now, at least, house guests can be shown a refinished rolltop desk with polished brass fittings and a pigeon hole for every thought, and it *seems* that a writer lives here. That may be enough for some.

The longing for a charming study comes in part from visits to reconstructed homes of famous writers. Leaning over a velvet rope, tourists gape at the ceiling-high cases of leatherbound tomes, a garden view through lace curtains, and the child-sized writing desk in a slant of light. Throughout the room are ships in bottles, silver quill holders, vellum notebooks, and other paraphernalia of an intellectual life well lived. "Hey, I could write here!" one thinks. But did the original resident write here? The small print on a placard reads, "reconstructed with contemporary furnishing," meaning no one knew what the writer had in the room, nor does it matter; for it turns out—as with Washington Irving's much-visited "Sunnyside" estate near New York—that most of the time the writer lived elsewhere and wrote little of significance on this romanticized stage.

10. *Away from the study.* The best writing room may be the most mundane, not a study at all, but a small office with ample desk and work tools suggesting a day's labor. Legends abound of writers who shunned the study desk for some more theatrical prop—Voltaire, supposedly, used the back of a lover, Capote wrote lying prone on a couch, Rostand and others composed while soaking in the tub. Word-processing in the bath makes less sense, but whatever works works. For some, the best writ-

ing is done in transit, when the sense of change and movement stirs the muse. Paul Theroux, who lives in Cape Cod and London, claims to be one such writer, inspired to write even on Chinese trains with nagging loudspeakers, foul toilets, bad food, and sub-40-degree temperatures—as long as he is left to himself. In *The Old Patagonian Express,* describing his train odyssey through South America, he notes, "What is required is the lucidity of loneliness to capture that vision which, however banal, seems in my private mood to be special and worthy of interest. There is something in feeling abject that quickens my mind and makes it intensely receptive to fugitive impressions."

WHERE to write, then? For the best odds, seek an uncluttered office free of bugs in a civilized town (not a writers' mecca) in one's own country. Jane Smiley triumphed in 1989 (front-page rave, *The New York Times Book Review,* for *Ordinary Love & Good Will*) because she lived and wrote in just the right community: Ames, Iowa, population forty-six thousand, home of Iowa State University. Good libraries. No beach. American English spoken. Bugs under control.

Naturally the most defiant writers will buck the odds—as if the chances against success weren't already astronomical. They will hit the beaches, woodlands, and foreign shores in pursuit of the dream setting. It's their right. Most will never be heard from in print. A few will end up like Andrew Kaplan.

WRITING ON THE RIVIERA

Andrew Kaplan likes to play out his fantasies. Striving since puberty to make it as a writer, he lived and wrote in New York and Los Angeles, he ran around South American jungles, he fought in Israel, he pestered agents, he did all the writerly things and grew older while yuppies just out of school scored the big best-sellers. He kept trying.

By 1984 he finally had to his credit a pair of thrillers—well reviewed and low-earning. Beyond that he had an agent in England, an outline for a new book, a wife, Annie, a baby, Justin, and a mortgage on a house in L.A. The prudent thing would have been to hole up and get the new thriller on paper.

But ever since childhood, Kaplan had dreamed of the literary pursuit in its most romantic version—the expatriate flings of Hemingway and Fitzgerald, the villas and haunts along the French Riviera, the lost weekends and the Lost Generation. He decided it was now or never to play it out and do his book abroad. Sharing her husband's view, Annie took leave from her career as a school psychologist. The furniture was stored, and the Kaplans, with baby Justin and seventeen pieces of luggage, set off in October for the ultimate writer's fantasy in southern France.

In a recent interview with Plotnikov, Kaplan described what ensued and offered advice for other dreamers.

"We figured we could last a year. We'd worked it out to the last penny, trying to tell ourselves it was rational. But if it wasn't—what the hell? This was our guiding philosophy.

"First stop was London and a scheduled meeting with my agent. She'd been holding the outline and first chapters for *Dragonfire,* my proposed new book, and I hadn't heard a word. But when we entered our hotel room, there it was—a spread of flowers to say that British rights had been sold for about $25,000 up front. Not so crazy after all!

"Our euphoria lasted until we hit France, where the dollar chose this particular year to plunge 40 percent against the franc. Okay, so pretend half our money had been stolen or the $25,000 bonus wiped out. Still, winter was approaching, and our notion of finding a cheap off-season villa turned out to be folly; most of the villas were locked up tight against rip-offs. Those still open wanted to rip *us* off. So we found ourselves in hotel rooms, some so small we had to book a second room for the luggage."

As the Kaplans hauled themselves and the luggage from place to place, they decided they needed a station wagon. A wagon turned out to be a "luxury" item taxed an extra 33 percent and costing some $1,000 a week with all the hidden charges. What the hell; it was part of the fantasy.

"We were thinking of ditching France for Italy when we spotted a giant villa in Cap d'Antibes, overlooking the beach community where Hemingway wrote *A Farewell to Arms* and Fitzgerald *The Great Gatsby*. It was just what a humble writer needed: Entering by a stately wooden gate, one drove through the huge private grounds to a two-story house with six bedrooms and six baths. Roman Polanski was the most recent tenant. We took it.

"Maybe it was Polanski's curse, but the place was forever cold and damp. We closed off half the rooms, and still it cost some $750 a month to heat—on top of the bargain winter rental of about $2,000 a month.

"Living the ultimate fantasy cost ultimate bucks at every turn. We had come for the Riviera's night action—but local baby-sitters went for about $50 a shot.

"Along the Riviera it cost some $400 to photocopy a novel-length manuscript. Second-rate computers were so expensive they were out of the question. I ended up hand-writing a draft—if Voltaire could do it, why not Kaplan?—and later I borrowed a computer.

"Winter was surprisingly cold, and we all got sick at some point. I had been told our Blue Cross policy would be good here; but nobody had told the French. The doctors took cash only—thousands in cash.

"One of our little pleasures was driving over to Italy for lunch. We also had to go there to get a French-residence visa—unavailable in France! When we registered this visa locally, as required, we naturally gave our villa address to the gendarmerie. One day our landlord all but attacked us: 'You imbeciles—you have exposed me! Get out! Get out!' Guess who hadn't been reporting his rental income? Rather than devote creative energy to tackling the French legal system, we moved.

"We found an available villa near the beach in Eze-sur-Mer, between Nice and Monte Carlo. It was smaller and warmer than Villa Polanski, and cheaper—about $1,000 a month. On the beach side we could watch the February gales whipping the Mediterranean, and from my writing room I could see a mountain, woods, and a little path on which Friedrich Nietzsche took his constitutionals. I finished the draft of *Dragonfire* here."

Kaplan reflected on the experience as a whole.

"We had our season," he told Plotnikov. "We found a literary society and friends from all strata. We drank good wine into the mornings and carried on as if it were the twenties. Even baby Justin was a star of the beach crowd.

"Writers are still special on the Continent, and even someone of modest achievement was welcomed into circles where writing mattered. Back home in the Hollywood community the phrase 'I'm a writer' is always ambiguous; it could mean you're a screenwriter or just a crazy. You stop saying it. Abroad it seems to stimulate people, and your own juices get going.

"The challenge is, how do you resist the endless call to pleasure? Somehow I managed. Even on days when writing was like digging granite with my fingernails, I worked from 7:30 A.M. to about 1:30 P.M. without a break, five or six days a week. Then we could live a little—as long as the dough held out."

The money held out only until spring; but the book was done, and so the Kaplans returned to the States to face their debts. Then something special happened. Usually, the Fates would have punished a writer for living out his fantasy abroad instead of hunkering down in Iowa. But they rewarded Kaplan. Warner Books smiled upon *Dragonfire* and gave him a multi-book contract for $250,000. (Ultimately Simon & Schuster published the second book, *War of the Raven*.) Hollywood kicked in with a contract for a James Bond screenplay.

Kaplan summed up. "Did I write better because I was living the fantasy? Yes, I was turned on—and the book picked up the atmosphere of France, which was appropriate for the setting and characters. But I'm not sure I'd push my luck and uproot the family again. Writing itself is a gamble. For those who want to live the big fantasy, giving up their regular income to write full-time in a romantic setting, I've got this piece of advice:

"Friend, you'd better be a high-stakes roller."

8

SEXUAL SOLITUDE IN A FOOL'S PARADISE

A TALE OF WRITING AT HOME

"Freedom is like a blanket which, pulled up to the chin, uncovers the feet."
—JOHN UPDIKE

WHEN Plotnikov quit his job as a reporter to write sex novels full-time, his domicile was already true to the Henry Miller standard—merely a place to put one's ass. With his first wife, he lived in a $50-a-month basement hovel in Albany, New York. Their block, elegantly named Elberon Place, was also home to white-trash zombies sucking on pint bottles and spitting end-over-enders from their stoops. Plotnikov fashioned a writing den from a closet-sized room looking out on back-alley rubble.

As a cub reporter he had earned a then-respectable $96 a week; but soon, as a member of the Nightstand Books stable, he could expect $900 for each two-hundred-page novel—and he believed he could whip off a carnal saga in about three weeks.

the main risk was not a financial one. By leaving the cheery society of the newsroom for a solitary tryst with his libido, he knew he was putting his mental health on the line. And a cheap enough wager it was, for the prize of *publishing novels.*

How had Plotnikov come to this, er, literary opportunity? He came to it first because the opportunity existed. In the sixties, before videos were available for every naughty appetite, "potboiler" paperbacks offered sexual fantasies couched in so-called contemporary fiction: adventure, psychological drama, social commentary. Posing as literature, potboilers skirted the obscenity laws and could be sold on newsstands and drugstore racks as well as in shops specializing in "one-handed magazines." Titles often sold in the 100,000-copy range.

No one has to write sex novels; virtuous writers can always starve or sell Tupperware. But since the opportunity was there, many good fiction writers turned to potboilers to make ends meet. One such writer was Hal Dresner, a skinny clever New York kid who took advantage of a stint with the Scott Meredith Literary Agency to grab a sex-novel contract for himself. After cranking out a number of such titles, he decided to base a legitimate comic novel on his own experience. So he subcontracted some of his sex novels to a writing acquaintance named Bill Coons in upstate New York.

But Coons, who also ghost-wrote sex novels for a noted mystery writer, soon found he was good enough to have his own contract. He proposed that Dresner's books be written by an amusing little college pal named Arthur Plotnikov, now kicking around Albany waiting for military duty. Dresner was apprehensive. Three weeks before Plotnikov was due at Fort Dix, Dresner called him. Come to Brooklyn. We'll talk sex-novels. We'll see what you know.

Plotnikov went. In a dark basement apartment that seemed half a mile long, Dresner showed him how to write metaphorical sex scenes and how to take up space with orgasmic dialogue:

"Ohh!"
"Yes!"

"Baby . . ."
"Ahhh—"

Plotnikov yakked about the Iowa Writers Workshop. Dresner gave him a try anyway.

Plotnikov returned to Albany and wrote *The Girl Takers* in two weeks; the rest is history. . . . What? You never heard of *The Girl Takers?* Written under Dresner's pseudonym of Don Holliday? Surely the cover blurb stopped you in your tracks: *They were students of sin—and the big city was their classroom . . .*

No matter; Dresner liked the book and promised Plotnikov he would use him again, after the six-month Army tour.

Dresner was true to his word. Soon after Plotnikov returned from Fort Dix and joined the *Times-Union* staff, he was offered a second subcontract: $600 to write Dresner's next $900 assignment. Plotnikov treated the offer like a Nobel Prize. Writing nights and weekends as his wife studied toward an undergraduate degree, he banged out another title in about two months.

Plotnikov had based *The Girl Takers* on a cross-country fling taken six years earlier; in the new book he recalled some college episodes. His experience was running low. Still, he felt he could churn out more pages by using the "serious" themes he had stashed away and by padding out chapters with punchy journalistic paragraphs and the orgasmic one-liners. In fact, pulp writing didn't seem very different from journalism except that you didn't have to verify details. *You could make it all up and get paid!*

The next assignment was slow in coming. Plotnikov put his heart into the reporter's role and the months passed quickly. Then one day he got the word: Dresner's career had taken off. Not only had Simon & Schuster signed for Dresner's novel, *The Man Who Wrote Dirty Books,* but a Broadway producer had optioned the story for a five-figure sum. Dresner popped up in Hollywood soon after, riding high on a four-picture screenwriting contract with Jack Lemmon. "Up here is great fun and much anxiety," he wrote Plotnikov. "I hope you find out for yourself soon."

But down below, Plotnikov was just discovering the fun and

anxiety of writing full-time at home. Dresner had arranged for Plotnikov to work directly through the Scott Meredith agency, which at the time handled a stable of pulp fiction writers along with such name authors as Norman Mailer. Plotnikov's assignment: one sex-novel every two months under Dresner's pseudonym, Don Holliday.

THE WRITER'S GLANDS

Like every hack before him, Plotnikov resolved that only half his work hours would be devoted to bread-and-butter writing, leaving half for the good and true literary pursuit. He figured that if he wrote two pages an hour on weekdays he would complete each sex novel in a month, allowing an entire month for truth and beauty before beginning the next assignment.

The day he quit reporting it seemed he had achieved writer's freedom: no pit bull terrier of a boss breathing down your neck, no time wasted commuting, no set hours of work, and no trivial responsibilities keeping you from the one thing you were put on earth to do: write your butt off.

Plotnikov had it all figured except for two factors: (1) The ineluctable law of writing at home: *Time It Takes = Time Available;* and (2) the little-known hypothalia gland (after Thalia, muse of comedy) that monitors the law.

Normally dormant, the hypothalia is located at the tip of the coccyx and is activated by vigorous squirming motions of those who sit before a blank page or computer screen. Once stimulated, the hypothalia retrieves the true deadline of a project from the brain and parcels out the creative juices accordingly. The writer might try to override the hypothalia by setting early deadlines—but they won't work. The gland knows, and the right juices won't flow. Worse, if the writer somehow gets a jump on the true deadline, the hypothalia spurts virulent fluids leading to depression, avoidance, and a writer's block the size of Gibraltar.

Just how the hypothalia evolved has been a subject of arcane debate; but all experts agree: It acts to prevent a dangerous overpopulation of great works and contented writers.

If on a good day Plotnikov exceeded his fourteen-page

quota, the gland would kick in and the next day he would stare at an empty page for seven hours, smoking his allotted five Pall Mall cigarettes (cut into fifteen mini-smokes) and whining at his wife when she returned from classes. Or, if he still felt energetic after a productive hour, the gland would send him hopping off on important chores and errands: hunting for a missing sock, returning three Pepsi bottles for deposit.

The initial Don Holliday novel ate up the full two months available; but Plotnikov brushed off the lapse in self-discipline and allowed himself a measure of self-esteem. So the book had taken some effort; but, by God, he had breathed life into a set of characters who would live and love until the pages that sustained them crumbled into dust (which on pulp paper wouldn't be long). He hoped the next books would come easier; but if not, he would devote night and weekend hours to literary endeavors.

Meanwhile, he could savor the sweet reality of being a bona fide, published *novelist.* The first mail had arrived from the literary agency—notes typed on heavy chain-laid paper with agents' names in an elegant typeface: Scott Meredith himself, and soon-to-be-superagents Henry Morrison, Richard Curtis, and Joseph Elder. Now Plotnikov could say, "my agent," and "my publisher," and "my contract."

His two earlier Nightstand Books were out on the racks. He placed his own copies on a new shelf of personal works, which he imagined would one day stretch across a room and hold dozens of renowned titles in multiple editions and translations. (Years later he would see a photograph of just such a dream shelf, belonging to John Updike, who remarked on how much time it took just to "shepherd" the various editions of his works.)

As Plotnikov began his next book, he thrilled to the idea that each page completed was money earned—$4.28 to be exact—and that when he pumped out two pages of orgasmic cries in thirty minutes, he had earned the then-dizzying equivalent of $17.12 an hour or $684.80 a week!

Being a full-time writer in this early stage gave him a certain gait on the street—hands in pockets, head cocked perceptively—and panache at social gatherings, where he would discourse on the sex-novel industry to any who seemed enthralled.

And, after all, the industry did make for one of the more bizarre tales around. About a dozen years later, the editors of Gale's *Contemporary Authors* asked Plotnikov to recount some of the juicy details for his biographical entry. What he wrote for them was a pale version of the following account, which, in the Nightstand Books tradition, might be titled:

LITERARY LUST BUMS
*"With naked talent and twisted prose,
they hungered for the fleshpots of fiction . . ."*

IN the third quarter of the twentieth century, dozens of authors writing under pseudonyms spilled their guts into hundreds of lurid paperback novels. None of these works will be found on the Great Books list. Neither can it be said that they harmed anyone, except the authors themselves.

The sex novels, or "potboilers," were contemporary tales revolving around superstuds or vampish lesbians. Although the major publishers required a sex scene in every chapter, obscene language was forbidden—yes, forbidden!—by the nervous entrepreneurs. Thus, sexual descriptions tended to be subtly metaphorical: "His rock-hard desire erupted in her sea of blazing passion." When the writers had exhausted the classical images of fire, oceans, and volcanoes, they turned to new-world metaphors—exotic matings of steam engines, oil wells, wrecking balls, and Bessemer furnaces.

One of the novelists, Arthur Plotnikov, developed an elaborate grid of images from which he could randomly select new combinations. *Choose one from each group:* "He stroked her (Group A: rosy, ripe, mellow, rotund, smooth, taut, tender, supple, pliant, firm, globular) (Group B: moons, planets, melons, orbs, loaves, wineskins, cannons)." The publishers, who provided the titles and jacket copy, had their own grid: sin, lust, twisted, carnal, flesh, vixen, harlot, and so many "wanton"'s one could only think of soup—"He dipped his wonton noodle in a broth of lust . . ."

The king of potboiler publishers was a gentleman named William Hamling, who later went to jail after a court decision as absurd as the book that got him there: an illustrated version of the government-sponsored *Report of the Committee on Obscenity and Pornography.* But his potboilers were successful enough to sustain a stable of writers for years and support an editorial office in San Diego.

Hamling published his titles under such quaint imprints as Nightstand, Bedside, Pleasure, Midnight, Sundown, and Late-Hour Library. All Hamling books had the same look: A hot yellow or pink spine and an airbrushed cover illustration that seemed quickly executed and thus clandestine.

"Flip appeal" was another mark of Hamling editions, meaning that the browser flipping through was sure to find some alluring word—such as "naked"—on every page. The writers supplied the "flip" words, but they could work them into any context: "He washed his naked socks." In some novels, panties and bras hung like Spanish moss from every paragraph.

Because Hamling feared conviction under the obscenity rulings of the time, his editors regularly issued bizarre directives for toning down the prose: no obscenity, no bestiality, and so on. A directive dated April 22, 1965, hit Plotnikov particularly hard: "In amorous situations, one never makes any reference to 'heat' in any of its forms. Similarly, one never uses food imagery: eat, taste, devour, hungry."

Plotnikov, who had recently nested two lovers in a vat of warm chop suey, had to delete half the terms from his grid and reset the sexual thermostat. Thenceforth, it was love between reptiles.

When the phrase "socially redeeming value" began entering obscenity judgments, Hamling editors decided that each book must have a brief introduction documenting its value to society. The writers had to prepare it, quoting from at least one authority in the social sciences. Here is how Plotnikov validated *The Reluctant Stud:*

> Dr. Kenneth Chapman, a noted authority on drug addiction, writes: "Many persons become addicted because they fear their erotic drives and seek to suppress them with drugs." (From *Problems in Addiction,* W. C.

Bier, Fordham University Press, 1962.) Dover's love for
the luscious young junkie drew him deeper and deeper
into her wanton world of needles and dreams . . .

Although the potboiler authors might have felt like writers,
no form of authorship could have been more anonymous and
isolated. The publishers changed the imprints, pseudonyms, and
titles at will, and never sent published copies to the authors. To
find his books Plotnikov had to first find the shops that carried
them and then flip through the new titles hoping to recognize a
familiar character. By that time the shop clerk would be hol-
lering "This ain't no library!" which was obvious enough.

It became a bleak and lonely business. Except for a few
New York writers who played poker together, the authors had
no community, no support group. Perhaps if they could have
gathered to tell one another, "Since my third or fourth book,
I've felt like a pustule on an amoeba's tush," they might have
allayed the crushing sense of worthlessness that befell most writers in the genre.

The agents at Scott Meredith were polite to their lowest-
level drones, but somewhat wary of them. Every potboiler hack
had the same story—"I've got a serious book on the back
burner"—and the agents had a stock response: "We'll be glad
to have a look when it's done." Very rarely did they have to
bother. (Some twenty years later, one agent wrote to Plotnikov,
"Remind me to tell you about one of our circle who drank
himself to death because he couldn't stop writing dirty books.")

Plotnikov worked his way up to one book a month. For a
while he had his own pseudonym, A. P. Williams, until the
publishers pulled another switch. Now and then the agents
would offer an assignment other than sex novels. Plotnikov
outlined a waterfront thriller, which a publisher accepted; the
publisher went bust. Another assignment came along, to write a
pseudomedical text on fetishism under the pseudonym Dr. Mur-
ray Stevenson (Ph.D.). "What do I know about fetishism?"
Plotnikov asked the agent. "Go to the library," the agent told
him. Plotnikov went; he read about men in love with a cousin's
shoe, an aunt's handkerchief, and he produced *Fetishism in*

Modern Man for the Monarch Human Behavior Series, which to this day no one has ever reported seeing.

But the $1,500 paycheck came anyway, right on schedule, as did all the others through the agency. It wasn't a hopeless life for those who could overcome the hypothalia gland and free themselves now and then from the grind of hack writing. Some, like Dresner, did so by subcontracting. David Case, a roguish associate of Plotnikov's, established himself with Nightstand, moved to London, and subcontracted up to two books a month to the most literate souses he could find in the pubs. Given the strength of the dollar at that time, Case lived like a lord on half the Nightstand check. In his liberated hours, when not carousing, he wrote his "better" books—several well-received gothics and westerns under his own name.

But for Plotnikov the sparkle of being a published hack soon faded and he felt trapped. His own literary output for two years amounted to little more than three poems, published in a book of lithographs done by an acquaintance. He had come to despise the demands of the sex novel: one torrid sex scene every fifteen pages or so, which meant at least one during every fifteen hours of writing. By his twentieth potboiler, he had raided all the best plots and characterizations he'd hoped to use in his Great American Novels. Sometimes these plots and characters took on a life of their own, pulling in literary directions that had nothing to do with lurid sex. But then came the fifteenth page, like a tsunami wave, and Plotnikov had to drench the whole works in oceanic orgasms.

There was no way out of it: To write hot sex, one had to think about hot sex—ever new and different versions of it. And so much sex on the mind led either to a lonely turn-on or a turn-off. Often, when too many fictional sex scenes shut the libido down, it seemed the end of marital harmony, self-esteem, and the ability ever to write another word.

DESCENT TO NEW YORK

It was in such a mood that Plotnikov took a bus from Albany to Manhattan one grey March day for his first visit to the Scott

Meredith Literary Agency. All prior contact had been by letter or phone. Plotnikov had a sex novel to deliver and a few odds and ends of business to discuss; but mainly he needed to touch some base of reality in a world that had become unreal in his isolation. Was there really an agency, with people who would talk to him? Did he himself exist outside the dreariness of his writing cell?

In a dark corridor of 580 Fifth Avenue, approaching the Meredith suite, he experienced an attack of cold sweat and nausea. Where oh where was that fearless brio he had developed as a reporter? It was gone . . . dissipated in a thousand heaving haunches and quivering loins.

Within the Meredith suite a wall-to-wall counter with a small gate protected the agents from crazed authors. Plotnikov was early. He announced himself to the receptionist and asked for a men's room key. Inside the mustard-walled lavatory he sensed an ancient miasma of tormented literary souls.

He waited by the counter past his appointment time. He drew not even a glance from the busybodies behind the counter, and why should he have? Measured by his contribution to the Meredith coffers—some $100 a month in commissions—he was nothing. Measured by the junk he was writing from some basement hole in upstate Nowhere, he was less than nothing: slime.

It was no illusion; Plotnikov was only absorbing lesson one of the publishing industry: Enslimation of Authors. Trade publishing recognizes two categories of writers: bankable and slime. The one is coddled reluctantly; the other—perceived as unsaleable ick—is treated accordingly. For an unknown to call a publisher and announce "I'm a writer" is like saying, "Hello, I am risen from the fetid slime of the Black Lagoon. May I ooze upon you this morning?" Escape from the lagoon is by stealth, miracle, or a process as long as evolution.

The dichotomy between slime and bankables is a matter of survival for understaffed publishers and for agents who help filter out the most relentless muck. The Great Sewer of the Unpublished may hold a bankable writer or two; but opening the trap brings such an inundation of attention-starved creatures that no major publisher will take the risk. Agents, too, must protect themselves by maintaining low profiles or charging high reader fees and by putting up gates.

The gate finally buzzed open for Plotnikov, but the outer-office staff kept their distance as they nodded him toward Henry Morrison's doorway. Morrison, a pale, indoors man with a scant dark moustache kept to his seat as they shook hands. Throughout the meeting, he maintained a single neutral expression, as if it were painted on. Increasingly rattled, Plotnikov stumbled through his questions; Morrison answered not unkindly, but quickly. And then the worst thing happened: Norman Mailer phoned.

It was only a brief call, but it had to do with a $250,000 partial advance from Dial Press for *American Dream*. Morrison's expression never changed, but he seemed slightly more animated as he summed up the conversation for Plotnikov. And then, abruptly, it was back to Plotnikov's $100-commissionable masterpieces and the meeting was over.

Plotnikov took the next bus back to Albany. He felt so small, so devalued, if he could have wedged himself like gum into a Trailways ashtray he would have done so. He puzzled over why the trip had plunged him into despair instead of boosting his spirits. Couldn't he now say he had "visited his agent in New York"? Couldn't he say, "Mailer called while my agent and I were talking"?

As a matter of fact, Plotnikov couldn't say anything, barely a word, when he got home. That was the evening he directed his wife, with sign language, to call a psychiatrist.

"THIS golden-haired boy you really vant to be," Dr. Boris Anolik told him some forty sessions later, "maybe he needs a haircut." It was one of the doctor's most explicit offerings and didn't mean much to the patient at the time. If, however, it was to direct Plotnikov toward a less glamorous way of making a living, it worked. He decided to give up the monthly sex novels and pursue a graduate degree in library service—a humanistic field that would not sap his literary energy, he reasoned.

With that decision made, he perked up in his last days as a

full-time writer. He kept to his schedule and put more energy into his marriage, which cheered his wife almost as much as the prospect of getting rid of him during his graduate studies. Then one day in mid-February, as if to herald the anniversary of his breakdown, a small notice appeared in the *New York Post,* quoting from a collection of stories published by Doubleday: "Among the most interesting writers of the decade so far we suggest you note such now generally unfamiliar names as . . . Arthur Plotnik[ov]. . . ."

The praise came from Whit and Hallie Burnett, who had published one of his Iowa Workshop pieces in their revived *Story* magazine. It hardly catapulted Plotnikov from the Black Lagoon of the unknown; but with that small validation of his existence outside sex novels and the likelihood of a clean well-lighted career ahead, he felt what every writer must who emerges from the independence of full-time writing at home:

He felt free.

9

WORD MAVEN

How to Support the Literary Habit
as a Hack of All Trades

Maven *(from Yiddish* meyvn*): An expert or connoisseur*

Se tu segui tua stella, non puoi
fallire al glorioso porto
—Dante

"If you follow your star," wrote Dante, "you can't miss that glorious port." Easy enough for Dante to say in the fourteenth century, when twenty million writers weren't hankering for literary fame. Today every daydreamer who can hold a pencil aspires to—nay, demands—a place in the Port of Glory.

People with writing talent have a hangup about destiny; either they will make it big as literary artistes or forever hold the world in contempt. Mention some less glorious option such as writing annual reports, and starry-eyed writers blanch as if you'd broken wind.

Great expectations are fed by schlock about artists who refused to "compromise" their talents. Who hasn't watched *Lust for Life* and said, "Yes, I'll grit my teeth like Kirk Douglas and do it my way!" Even some godawful miniseries on Hemingway has writers swaggering off to meet their destinies in Paris. Such portrayals only reinforce the astrological delusion: that a star burns for each writer, lighting the way to brilliant works and panting publishers. Just keep watching the firmament and steer clear of earthly compromise. Compromise is death.

The truth, O self-destructive writers, is that compromise is *life*. Writers can wait—eternally—for romantic destinies to happen, or they can view themselves as tradespeople with a practical skill. Purveyors of words, willing to apply the trade where needed, can make a living and a life without abandoning the literary pursuit.

WHAT is a writer but a word maven, a connoisseur of fine and fancy word goods? The word maven fashions words to order, or whips up an original creation. What the world needs, the maven provides—and maybe earns a little something for the trouble. Most aspiring writers don't see themselves that way. Writing is hardly a trade, but a holy quest guided by a star of destiny. They would follow the path of authors who dedicated their lives to literary ideals and purity of purpose, starving, begging, and dumping on loved ones rather than prostitute the word.

Yet for every celebrated author who followed a star and somehow survived, dozens simply applied themselves as word mavens, letting destiny fall where it might. Even Dante produced functional works both before and after the immortal *La divina commedia*. He traded on word power for political achievement. He engaged himself in the practical world, and he achieved his immortality through just one aspect of a multifaceted life. Dante followed many stars.

Writers say they want to serve society; why do they shudder at the thought of applied writing? Is it so bad to help the world express its business? Too many writers, it seems, want only to express themselves. They want to cry and relieve the pain. They want fast bucks and French villas just for making up stories in their heads. They want to unveil the beauty within and be adulated without. They fear that writing for the Potato Institute will not satisfy these longings.

Perhaps the occupational nomenclature turns them off. Writers are romantics by nature, and what romantic wants to be a *communicator,* applying *verbal skills* to press releases and corporate reports? Who worships the "writer" in *technical writer?* Who goes weak in the knees on meeting a *trade journalist?* These are the terms describing word mavens who have chosen to live by the pen rather than impale themselves on it. They are writing specialists who may or may not call themselves writers for what they do at work; but their writings make the world a better place than if nonwriters sat at their desks.

Is applied writing a sellout of the literary gift? On the contrary, it is a gift to the arid commercial world—an irrigation from the springs of creativity. Those who write press releases or taxpayer instructions or white-sale catalogs will write them better because they care about words and their uses; and if they truly have the urge for literary expression, they will find an outlet.

The compleat writer writes about everything and anything, as opportunity allows. The literary pursuit can begin here, as one develops the muscle, range, and worldly knowledge for the long journey to the Glorious Port.

FAMOUS HACKS

Outside literature and news journalism, most writing falls into these categories: advertising, public relations, public information, business communications, technical writing, science writing, and professional and trade journalism. Every day some word maven steps from these fields into literature, often with potent material gathered along the way.

Joseph Heller wrote advertising copy for *Time* and *Life;* John Jakes did it for Abbott Labs. Kurt Vonnegut banged out press releases for General Electric. Richard Yates wrote publicity for Remington Rand. Elmore Leonard scripted educational films.

C. P. Snow—who considered science a more imaginative art than literature—wrote about infrared investigation of molecular structures when he wasn't spewing out novels. Poet Wallace Stevens wrote business memos in his lifelong career as an insurance executive. "It gives a man character as a poet to have this daily contact with a job," he noted.

In preparing for her literary career, Edna O'Brien learned to write prescriptions—she was licensed as a pharmacist. "I think a degree in arts might have been slightly ruinous for me," she said, "because it's a handicap for a writer to be in a literary, aesthetic, mandarin environment."

Cynthia Ozick's first job after graduate school was as an advertising copywriter. Amy Tan worked as a technical writer and also cranked out horoscopes for a telephone service. Both Danielle Steel and Judith Krantz did their early writing in public relations. Krantz also produced such nonfiction as "The Myth of the Multiple Orgasm."

These are some of the better-known word mavens who got what they needed from applied writing—if only confidence or grocery money—and went on to build literary careers. They proved that every writer needn't start off in publishing or teaching or survive by mooching off friends. Some literary mavens never leave applied writing, finding themselves reasonably satisfied. What does one need after all? Work with words? Creativity? A living wage? Feedback from readers? Respect from peers? A touch of notoriety? Safe romance? All can be realized in the nonliterary writing trades.

THIS is not to say that the special-interest writer leads the literary life. While applied writers shepherd their words along the paths of commerce, literary hunters stalk the night, to kill or be killed. Who is better off? If applied writers suffer less—or at least kill themselves less—they are also less likely to experience the ecstasies of the successful literary writer. As word maven for the meat packing industry, a writer may not realize the ego-rocketing joys of a book sale, the leap from obscurity to literary darling of the week. But neither will she face public humiliation as a "minimal talent" or stone-cold rejection after years of slavery and debt.

In applied writing there are trade-offs, as in all areas of life. One puts aside literary self-expression, the songs of the heart, to sing someone else's tune. One trades the novelist's giddy dreams of renown for such modest recognition as Footwear Writer of the Year. The supposedly stimulating society of literati is fore-gone; one's colleagues talk about soybean commodities or sand and gravel. But one finds kindred souls, one has bright and shining moments, one is called a writer, and one gets paid.

SOMETHING TO WRITE ABOUT

Most important, perhaps, one has an ever-present *subject*. A writer for *The Garlic Times* or *Bottled Water Reporter* never staggers around crying, "What shall I write about?" One trades the nebulous byways of the literary pursuit for the well-lit special-interest track.

Dante's most quoted passage is probably these opening lines of *La divina commedia*—"*Nel mezzo del cammin di nostra vita . . . ,*" etc., which usually translate into something like: "In the middle of life's journey, I found myself in a dark wood, and the clear path was lost to me." To be sure, this is everyone's mid-life crisis; but to many a writer the words say, "After turning half my life into literature, I've been chasing my ass in circles for a new subject."

Poor writers. They only have to run on empty a few months to appreciate the blessing of guaranteed subject matter. "When I have nothing to write, I feel only half alive," said Elizabeth Bowen. Most writers have subject enough for a first inspired work, but the "second-book syndrome" is a killer. It usually afflicts writers who explode on the literary scene with a por-trayal of some special world they inhabited or imagined—a war, a pig farm, a hospital, a slice of prehistory. They've exhausted that topic, as far as they're concerned, and now what? Write about—yawn—how fame corrupts a writer?

But now with agents calling *them,* they must write more books: So the writers go generic, imitating themselves and writ-ing more tales about cave clans or homicidal anaesthesiologists. Or they riffle through newspapers for inspiration, since the news no longer comes from within. Often they seize on some true crime story for literary treatment. In 1990, the case of Charles Stuart—who survived a supposed double-murder attempt in Boston only to emerge as the apparent killer of his pregnant wife—drew scores of frenzied writers smelling best-seller. Agent Morton Janklow remarked, "I've never seen such a shark attack."

But one musn't blame the writers, who, like sharks, have no choice but to attack a fresh subject. Otherwise, it's back to chewing on old standbys: coming of age, finding love, facing death—subjects shared by thousands of competing writers. An astonishing number of cancer-death books were written in the late 1980s—books by Le Anne Schreiber, Susan Kenny, Kate Braverman, and Bobbie Ann Mason, to name a few. Literary romantics may not aspire to disease writing, but, hey, it's a *subject,* it can be individualized, and it's mass marketable.

SPECIAL-INTEREST NICHE WRITING

Because writers are many and mass-market subjects are limited, the last decades have seen a rise in niche writing: specialization in narrow areas. Niche writing has entered the literary world as well as the trade media; even fiction writers are specializing in subniches within such larger genres as children's books, science fiction, crime, horror, and romance. Somewhere, believe it, a writer is specializing in complete-your-own-story Civil War romances for young black Christians.

Nonfiction writers have burrowed deepest into niches. Gone are the Lucretiuses discoursing *On the Nature of Things.* Recently a reviewing journal praised two books of typical breadth: *Great Gift Wrapping,* and the 210-page *Rust: How to Keep It from Destroying Your Car.* Amazingly, such niche writing can bring all the rewards of publishing a book—except, perhaps, literary adulation. Things can get awkward at cocktail parties:

"And what do you do?"

"I'm a writer."

"Ah, I should have known. And you write . . . ?"

"Rust books."

The seeker of "authentic" authors will be hard put to avoid niche-niks, who comprise the majority of people writing for a living. Where does the literary generalist find a market? Book publishers mainly want topical nonfiction. Literary media pay nothing and tend to lose one's manuscript. Large, general-interest media are practically nonexistent. Those that do publish are amalgams of specialized departments, written by specialized staff and freelancers. What newspaper is without its niche-writers in auto care, computers, and lonely hearts babble?

Most publications today are special-interest media serving niches about as wide as a coffin. *Casket and Sunnyside,* for example, serves the world of funeral directors and calls for writers who can describe the reconstruction of mangled stiffs. Such writers exist and sell their prose to *C&S, Mortuary Management, The Director,* and several more journals in the funeral industry. Often they write books and video scripts in the field and secret poetry at home.

Niche writing may seem crushingly dull and limited; it can be, but no more so than writing the fifth draft of a disease novel. In fact, no literary milieu can match the overall variety and intensity of the special-interest environment. Odd, that the *Paris Review* never interviews writers for *Pig Journal* or *Female Mud Wrestling;* for here are authors whose readers devour every word they write—sometimes literally, as in the case of the short-lived, edible *Chocolate Journal.* Special-interest writing means just that; it is based on an interest that is special to certain readers, and sometimes passionately special.

PUBLISHERS divide special interests into "horizontal" and "vertical" markets: a horizontal interest—such as a passion for chocolate—is scattered across the general population. A vertical interest runs up and down the strata of one group, usually an occupational group such as morticians.

Because vertical markets are represented by organized groups, publishers find them easier to reach than diffuse horizontal populations. As a result, more and more publishers cater to narrow trade and professional segments, and more authors than ever make their livelihood writing for northeast truckers, southwest beer distributors, Hoosier bankers, and Golden State urologists.

Some thirty thousand vertical-interest media—commonly known as "trade rags"—employ writers in the United States alone. It is the great invisible market because trade rags rarely appear in public. A large newsstand carries perhaps 150 specialized media from baby-care to gun-fighting, each seeking out passionate interests within the general population. But the hidden vertical market addresses thirty thousand additional American interests—if not all passionate, at least important to the specialized reader.

Special-interest writers face the challenge of staying interested in the subject that feeds them. Sometimes it's easy; writing for *Cat Fancier* and *Dog World* might coincide with personal affinities; but the owner of *Dog World* also publishes *Rock Products*. Sustaining interest in gravel can be daunting, unless one somehow gets inside the industry.

Plotnikov got to see writers inside the telecommunications industry one spring when he consulted at Northern Telecom's headquarters in North Carolina. The technical writers, working alongside engineers amid wire jungles and robotic controls, seemed happy composing this type of prose:

> The technician also has the capability of injecting errors into the data stream by way of the BERT INJECT command in order to verify IBERT is working properly.

But writers for the firm's public relations magazine, mainly humanities majors, looked rather wistful as they churned out articles on the Meridian Digital Centrex from Michigan Bell. One writer confessed he was working on a novel and dreamed of creating more exciting dialogue than, "We have been most pleased with the DMS-10-based network."

"AUT inveniam viam aut faciam," reads the motto on C. P. Snow's coat of arms. "I shall either find a way or make one."

And that is how special-interest writers maintain their sanity. They think of themselves as word mavens and hold on to their self-esteem, even at literary soirées. They immerse themselves in the specialized environment, identifying with the dreams and heartaches of fast-food equipment manufacturers. They bring literary flair to technical subjects, realizing that technical readers are humans who respond to the human touch:

> . . . In four or five hours of driving that day, we passed only two cars—and one of those was the mailman's. . . . Hills of red shale and sandstone roll across the plains into the distance. Roadside markers trace the fateful path that George Armstong Custer's Seventh U.S. Cavalry traveled on its date with destiny and several hundred Sioux warriors more than a century ago. . . .

The beginning of a novel? No, the lead-in to a Northern Telecom report on a fourteen-exchange digital network in Big Sky country. Whatever the subject—machine tools, computer chips, wood pulp—there are human elements, and the good writers find them.

For a while such literary challenges are sustaining, as are the paychecks and perks of an occupational field. But the subjects cannot be kept at arm's length; eventually, one must internalize some of the most intrinsically unexciting activities of humankind. One must spend eight hours a day *thinking* about dental management or boxboard packaging.

These, then, are the questions for the creative writer seeking a means of support: Shall I earn a Ph.D. and teach freshman composition as an underpaid adjunct instructor, or apply my writing talents to the commercial world? If the latter, then which nonliterary topics can I bear to internalize? And what will a day of thinking about gasoline distributors do to my literary sensibilities?

Writing in *Independent Scholar* (Spring 1989), Lila Freedman argues that a dull but demanding job—such as special-interest educational writing—can actually stimulate creative writing during off-hours:

... the mind is like a boiler or steam engine: pressure begets ideas ... thinking begets more thinking. ... Or mental energy is like the form of the wave: once it is in motion it goes from subject to subject shaping the elements within it. ... The often boring, exhausting, demanding work at my job does not seem to preclude other private work, whether it is done despite or because of, or perhaps both, I don't know. ...

REGENERATION

In his years as a special-interest writer, Arthur Plotnikov would find just such energy exchange between daily job and private writing. On the job, creative juices thrashed against the limits of a single subject; after hours, they would break loose and sweep him into a maelstrom of unsaleable prose. Mornings, he would find comfort in the clear beacon of a specialized subject. Was it for nothing, symbolically speaking, that for six years he worked beneath the dummy lighthouse of the H. W. Wilson Publishing Company in New York?

But that was only after he had found a subject to liberate him from sex-fiction slavery.

As a sex novelist, Plotnikov had freed his time for writing but had chained himself to a degenerative specialty. What he needed now was a *profession*—not a shamanism like writing, with its mock body of knowledge, but a well-lighted, learned discipline embraced by the real world.

It was spring, the season of regeneration, when an article in *Esquire* magazine suggested, "Young Man, Be a Librarian." The nature of library work had changed, said the article. Males were being recruited to relieve a shortage of workers in the field. Bun hairdos and sensible shoes were out. Computers and pinstripes were in. The field was modern, it was socially oriented, it was cool.

And so Plotnikov trotted off to graduate library school and within a year was a word maven who knew the inner workings of the library world. When he published his first professional paper, he was thrilled to see himself in print as an expert on something besides sex with shoes. Suddenly he was a writer again, only this time with a subject that would never run dry and with readers who kept their pants on.

Word mavens catch fire in specialized fields, once they master the fundamentals of the specialty. Soon Plotnikov was a press officer for the Library of Congress and writer of its weekly newsletter. He could not have been more fulfilled. The massive Italian Renaissance library on Capitol Hill was his oyster. As a privileged member of the Librarian's staff and gatherer of news, he moved freely among the institution's five thousand staff members, its 55 million volumes, its secret warrens and off-limits stacks. In the rarefied rooms of the Manuscript Division, he could examine the personal papers of the world's most exalted authors—rummage in Hemingway's letters with their spirals of crazed scribblings.

Wandering through the endless rows of books, Plotnikov came to accept that all things had been written a thousand times over, and that the stacks awaited a thousand more volumes on each minute subject from a million more word mavens in the wings.

As a word maven in his own field, Plotnikov would gather most of the rewards sought by literary authors and rarely attained: his name in print in bylines and bibliographies, attention, fan mail, the power to shape opinion and even events, national awards, world travel, proximity to renowned leaders— the Hubert Humphreys, Daniel Boorstins, Jesse Jacksons, Jimmy Carters, Ted Kennedys, Gloria Steinems, and others he revered. At conferences he would gather groupies under his wing. He appeared on television and in the press for his views. His parents, shamed by his expulsion from college and silent on his sex-novel career, could say once again with pride, "Our son, the writer."

But nothing was to be more rewarding than those first years of being *needed* as a writer, a feeling unknown in the literary world. Washington was grateful to word mavens who came and stayed to tell the government's story. It paid them well and gave them security, enough to sustain a literary habit on the side.

Yet Washington is no writer's paradise. Suffocated by the

summer humidity and Potomac fever, one lives a predictable existence linked to government cycles. Plotnikov left after three years. He could never get the congressional names straight anyway. He took a happy wife and eighteen-month-old daughter to the Bronx, where marital life would sink, but a new post would illuminate his path as a writer. In New York, he would be an EDITOR, and simply follow the subway signs to the *glorioso porto*.

10

PLEASING THE EDITORIAL GODS

And the LORD had respect unto Abel and to his offering; but unto Cain and to his offering He had not respect.
—GENESIS 4:4–5

As the gatekeepers of publishing, editors seem as gods to mere writers. A manuscript is offered, and the writer waits for a sign. And waits. And waits. *Give me a sign, O Editor!* And finally the Word comes down: "THOU HAST PLEASED US. CONTRACT TO FOLLOW." Or, "WE CANNOT USE THINE OFFERING AT THE PRESENT TIME."

Aspiring authors rarely meet editors, and so they imagine a race of deities in the misty heights of the publishing empyrean. Wrathful and capricious, these higher beings decree which writerlings shall be raised from obscurity and which consigned to the hell of the unpublished.

Higher beings? *Au contraire!* Most book and magazine editors serve as minions to the real gods: the publishers. The only mist that enshrouds them is their cold sweat as they run to killer meetings. They labor in suburban office plazas or in midtown warrens with flimsy partitions and locked bathrooms. Surely no deities ever needed keys just to relieve themselves—or worked sixty hours a week for chump change. Ergo, editors are not gods at all, but mere godlets at best.

The godlets appear in many forms, depending on the size and nature of their publications. In small operations, a few editors do it all: plan the program, acquire manuscripts, copy-edit the text, abuse authors, and oversee production, marketing, and distribution.

Magazine editors tend to be the most wrathful and capricious godlets, and any one of them can seal a writer's fate. The assistant editor says, "Yeah, let's see the thing," when an article is offered; the associate editor reads it, votes yes; the managing editor concurs; the copy editor tightens the prose; the senior editor tears it apart; the chief editor postpones publication; the production editor saves the file; the editorial assistant loses it.

Short deadlines make magazine editors shrill and subject to mood swings. Because they can transform a publication so quickly, some actually view themselves as gods—especially the chief editors. They play the role, thundering "DO IT OR YOU'RE HISTORY!" to staff, squashing writers underfoot. They can be puckish as well: One New York editor likes to show off his private manuscript collection—most of the articles sent to him over the last two or three years, unacknowledged and jammed into a case behind his desk. "Something for a rainy day," he says.

Book editors, those who acquire manuscripts and review proposals, are generally less wroth. Children's-book editors seem almost perky; the others look tired, more oppressed than angered by their countless deadlines and assignments. They spend half their time on proposals that go nowhere; the other half on projects they may never see to fruition. Occasionally a good sales report or the literary environment itself produces a buzz; then it's back to the gloom of overload.

Literary agents, who are gatekeeping godlets themselves, help reduce the number of hopeless manuscripts. Still, most editors face armloads of paper to lug home and read far into the night, when real gods should be out cavorting as bulls or showers of gold.

Book editors are decent humanists who probably *would* be merciful to writers if there were time and they got paid for it. They would read unsolicited manuscripts; they would answer calls and letters from writers; they would offer advice, criticism, and consolation, what the hell. But book editors are not hired to answer the wailing from the multitudes; they are paid to turn words into net profits and please the Number Gods who run the show.

If editors are less than gods, why should writers quake before them? Because editors, lowly though they may be, still guard the gates of Paradise and wield a few thunderbolts. Editors can cut a writer off cold, or support a writer throughout the publishing decision, or help make a writer a star, or, in rare instances, make a writer a *better* writer. Editors can bring writers to orgasm with a word ("*Loved* your book . . .") or to dementia with another (" . . . got a *problem*").

Until writers achieve their own godhead as bankable brand names—or at least land a powerful agent—they must learn to please the editorial godlets. Knowing that editors are in fact quasi-mortals who can be swayed and even fooled gives one some courage; but courage alone will not win the day, any more than a stupendous manuscript will find its own way into an editor's heart. One must learn how to beg for editorial favor.

THE ART OF SUPPLICATION

Arthur Plotnikov knelt before many an editorial godlet in his career as a writer, even as he toyed with writers from three of his own editorial perches. From these perspectives he observed the art of supplication: how writers can please the powers that be. As a minor godlet, then, as well as an author with a butt full of thunderbolts, Plotnikov offers these tidbits of advice:

An editor bases her (or his) first evaluation of a proposal more on instinct than divine justice. Like a clam sorting tidal microbes, the editor performs a food-nonfood dichotomy on incoming materials. To an editor, food is something that readers will eat up. Fresh, bite-size and pungent—the editor knows it when she sees it.

Nonfood reveals itself in a number of ways: too big, too small, wrong look, funny smell. *Never* must a writer offer anything that signals nonfood:

> manual typing on yellowed paper
> misspellings in the cover letter
> the wrong publisher in the address
> military service number
> shaky handwriting
> cartooned happy faces
> a list of school publications
> snapshots of the grandchildren
> home-brewed (amateur-looking) graphics
> an account of how friends adored the manuscript
> quote marks around "slangy" words
> signs of paranoia and rage

Just *what,* you protest, do any of these signals have to do with literary merit? Intrinsically nothing; but an editor, unable even to skim every submission, has to play the odds. The odds say that most people who can't spell haven't undergone the discipline that makes for saleable writing; they say that writers who include such extraneous items as service numbers and snapshots are rank amateurs who just don't get it. Editors are conditioned to clam up at amateurism, just as they close themselves off to the pathetic:

> Dear Editor,
>   Maybe this isn't the best novel you'll ever read; but it's a novel that has stolen thirty-five years of my life, destroyed a marriage, and brought me nothing but rejection and emphysema. . . .

Pathos is nonfood. Editors can't handle writers' pathos any more than doctors can sympathize with anguish; the sheer abundance would destroy them in a day.

Editors look for the easily rejectable. Imagine yourself with geological layers of reading matter on desks, chair, sills, and floor. Phones ring. Faxes click. Mail arrives. Meetings call. This is an editor's environment, and somehow she must dig herself out. So she sifts through the piles and looks for quick ways to reduce them. Newly arriving materials meet a natural resistance against taking on more work. This is not callousness; this is survival. And callousness, too.

The writer's challenge: *Don't help the editor resist you.*

New writers defeat themselves so many ways. Not only with happy faces after their signatures, but with woeful presentations, apologies, and demands.

In an age when form is content, presentation is everything. Let's get mundane a moment: The writing pro presents a crisp, flawless electronic printout on fresh 8½ × 11 white stock. The type is letter-quality or a simple laser typefont. Margins are generous. Cover letters are single spaced; manuscripts double spaced. Pages are usually sent loose, not stapled. Understated binders are used when binders are necessary, not ring binders or cardboard cut from a pizza carton. One copy of each item will do. Computer disks are not sent until called for; one merely identifies the word-processing software used, shunning pathetic out-of-date systems such as CP/M (see chapter 20).

Proposals begin with a lean and lively cover letter. The writer's impulse is to tell all—all the dreams and heartaches behind the organism in the editor's hands; but editors appreciate restraint. The essentials, for nonfiction proposals, are:

- An opening grabber
- What it is you're sending: a brief description of it and a "high concept"—the essence of the work in one phrase
- Why it (not you) should be published
- Who would read (or buy) the proposed item
- What audience-related factors distinguish it from similar items
- Your expertise and reputation in the field; your connections to the target audience, the market
- Your most important previous publications
- When you could complete the project (be realistic)

- Software data, if any
- A closing grabber, showing a touch of writing flair

An outline and one or two sample chapters complete the nonfiction package. The hotter the topic, the less literary talent need be demonstrated. As long as the facts are authoritative and the prose editable, an editor can see the potential.

In cover letters for fiction, minimalism is the key: A paragraph on your literary achievements, a few sentences on what you think distinguishes the submission. Don't try to charm fiction editors (or agents) in the cover letter; people who read fiction for a living know all the sneaky lowdown posturing of characters in search of favor.

Send the whole fiction manuscript if it's a short story. For longer pieces send a synopsis and two sample chapters with the cover letter—which now becomes a query letter asking if the editor wants to see the rest of the manuscript. (Most editors don't want to see unfinished fiction.)

The chapters sent are usually the opener and another showing your best stuff. Synopses run from one to five pages, depending on the length of the book. They try to sell the book, not recreate it. In narrative form (usually present tense) move through the plot quickly, showing major twists and turning points, a hint of setting and atmosphere if important, and the characters with their strengths, weaknesses, goals, and conflicts. So as not to weigh down the synopsis, some writers also send an outline detailing the structure of the whole story.

OBSTACLES WRITERS CREATE

Editors often work on impulse: Something hits them at just the right time and they decide to pursue it—until they encounter the first obstacle. Writers create obstacles with crummy presentation packages. For example, they often fail to provide telephone numbers, which belong on cover letter, outline, and first manuscript page. As editor, a harried Plotnikov had little patience with authors too coy to be dialed. Writers with cute letterheads were the worst—Old Ink Well Road, Weasel Run,

Pa.—and no numbers. Others withheld phone numbers as if they might *die* if ever an editor called. In fact editors favor the telephone because it's fast and doesn't require the careful wording of a letter or fax—just as long as they, the editors and not the authors, do the calling.

One way to clam up an editor is to phone in proposals. "You got a few minutes? We were sittin' around watchin' *Jeopardy* and I got this terrific idea for a book. . . ." Editors receive a great many such calls, some of them spitefully transferred from another editor. Phoned-in proposals offend the godlets. They lack organization, they can't be passed around for evaluation, they demand attention in the middle of other obligations. Half the breathless proposals by phone never make it to paper. "Send a query," most editors will say and cut the conversation there. Plotnikov, one of the softer touches in the business, would frequently pretend to listen while cleaning his ears with Q-tips. The authors were no better off than if he'd hung up.

Writers may safely telephone editors to ask which staff member should receive their proposal. Editors don't mind a call they can handle with three or four words, such as "try Suzie Doaks" or "send it to me." You don't have to give your own name; no one will ask.

It is better to address a specific individual than to write "Dear Editor," and a good bet to use the editor's first name: "Dear Philip" (not "Phil"). It gets a sliver more attention and won't hurt. If on the phone the editor said "send it to me," then write: "Thanks for agreeing to review my query [or proposal or manuscript]." Maybe the editor didn't quite agree; but he won't remember and he'll feel obligated to read one more paragraph. And that paragraph, the grabber, should wake the dead. Say just about anything that will get attention, if it's not too sick. All rules for breaking into publication boil down to one: *Get attention.*

> Dear Philip,
> Thanks for agreeing to review my proposal.
> I lost my virginity at age eight. . . .

Later you can explain that you meant figuratively, or according to some cult you intend to expose. If you've got one hell of an idea and can deliver, editors will accept the opening hype. Don't squeeze out your cards; show your ace as quickly and as clearly as possible. You can't ask an overloaded editor to read a complicated proposal for no obvious reason, or to deduce, guess, or extrapolate what is special about your offering.

How many writers put these and far stranger demands upon the busy godlets! By the end of a rough day, what editors would most appreciate from authors is a note that says, "Please find nothing enclosed, nothing to read or do. I ask nothing." Instead, in comes a mean-looking megascript with this cover letter (a composite of letters received by Plotnikov over the years):

> Dear Editor,
>
> Herewith is the manuscript I described, in part, in my queries of June 23 and October 27, to which one of your staff responded, though I have misplaced that correspondence. Perhaps you could check your files.
>
> You'll note that parts 1 and 3 of the mss are in typescript; part 2 is on the enclosed disk in a CP/M Wordstar format that needs a simple conversion to the DOS system via an ASCII output. I trust you have that capacity in-house.
>
> Several footnotes were added after part 1 was typed, so please add three digits to each superior number after footnote 5, and one digit to the total after the original footnote 9, so that superior numbers match with the list of footnotes.
>
> Actually, part 1 is more or less a rough draft. Perhaps you'd look it over with an eye toward what should be dropped and what developed and how.
>
> Should you need some author background, you'll find it in *Who's Who in the Fort Wayne Business Community* (Fort Wayne Chamber of Commerce, 1953). Please see that 25% of my fee goes to the Hoosier Horticultural Preservation Society. . . .

Each day editors face such demanding little critters, whom they zap faster than gnats in a bug light. As well as being annoying, such demands signal that the accompanying manuscript will ask all and give little. The presentation package should make one demand only and an implicit one at that: *Begin reading.* The rest should follow naturally.

THE LIMITS OF HUMILITY

Scores of writers' guides (and the appendix of this book) give detailed instructions for manuscript submission. Writers must review and observe these fundamental rules, even as they master the subtleties in dealing with editors. Can the basic rules be broken? Yes, if your name is, say, Iris Murdoch and you've published two dozen successful novels. Murdoch writes her manuscripts in longhand, and, without making copies, delivers them personally to her publisher. How many authors could walk in with a paper sack of deeply philosophical fiction and demand it be published as written, without a change? Approximately one.

Most other writers must be proper supplicants and follow the rules. Supplication is begging, let's face it—*please* read my manuscript, *please* see its merits! But kneeling before editors does not mean self-effacement. Editors are already negatively poised when apologetic writers start mewling and puking about their inadequacies. Such cover letters echo the ritual of humility once attributed to Japanese hosts: "Please enter my disgraceful house and meet my ugly family and accept our putrid refreshments." In writers' terms it usually goes like this:

Dear Philip,

Forgive my using your first name; I was advised to do so, but I probably shouldn't listen to all those tips. I'm so sorry to trouble you with this manuscript, which is overly long and probably gushier than the kind of thing you usually want. Blame it on my total ignorance of publishing. I set my story in Des Moines, the only big city I know. It was probably dumb of me not to use New York just because I've never been there. I could change the setting as well as the main character, who was based on myself. Telling my story seemed like a good idea; but when I finished I realized, who'd want to read about me?

"Right," says the editor. "Next!" Somehow this rebuff surprises the apologist, who was only fishing for kindly reassurance and expecting this response: "Trouble? You little minx, are you kidding? Your work is what publishing is all about! Overlong? Gushy? An otherworldly collision between Thomas Mann, Luigi Pirandello, and Iris Murdoch is what we're calling it along Publishers Row! We not only lived to read each page, but we want you *here, now,* signing *contracts!*"

Funny, that letter never comes.

11

CRASHING THE GATES

MORE TRADE SECRETS

If you wish in this world to advance
Your merits you're bound to enhance;
You must stir it and stump it,
And blow your own trumpet.
Or, trust me, you haven't a chance.
—W. S. Gilbert, *Ruddigore*, Act 1

THE urge to be published may be tops among human vanities.
Small wonder that a thousand manuscripts wriggle through the
lowliest publisher's transom for each one that will penetrate an
editor's skull. Just to get a good reading requires talent, persistence, timing, and often a little boost from an insider. But one
must never despair: Certain tricks of the trade can improve
one's odds from Hopeless to Who Knows. And Who Knows, at
least, is a start.

One trade practice is the "multiple submission" or "simultaneous submission," which sounds like some kind of perver-
sion but means submitting a manuscript to more than one
publisher at a time. Trade book editors, realizing they can take
as long as six months to report on manuscripts, have come to

accept this once-forbidden practice. Now a writer can shotgun one novel to twelve publishers simultaneously, gathering twelve rejections in only six months instead of six years—or maybe, just maybe, hitting the right editor at the right time, before the manuscript turns to fungus.

Some care should be taken when submitting to different publishers under one conglomerate roof—say, Knopf, Random House, and Pantheon; they might compare notes on a hot manuscript. To see who is allied to whom, check *Literary Market Place* (*LMP*), available in most libraries. Use *LMP* as well to see which houses publish which type of books, and to look up agents and other writers' services and groups.

Should no-name writers tell each editor about the multiple submissions, as agents do when they seek an offer from several houses? Editors say they are used to such notification and that it doesn't bias them. On a terrific book, the competition might even drive up the initial purchase offer to perceived "market" price. If trying to develop a personal relationship with one editor, however, a writer might offer an exclusive look. Should one publisher offer a contract, writers must by all means notify any "losing" houses with a matter-of-fact note. Don't apologize. And don't say, "Blind fools!"

When submitting manuscripts to agents, you're safer going to one agency at a time and pushing a little if necessary. If the item is sizzling, break the rule; but let each agency know what's going on. Agents won't actually handle a property until assured they're the only one on the case.

Magazine editors who sit on manuscripts for half a year don't deserve exclusive submissions, but that's what the buggers expect. The frantic publishing cycle often prompts them to throw a manuscript into production as soon as they've decided to use it, before the author has even been notified. Acceptance of their offer is assumed, and woe to the author who later replies, "I forgot to tell you I'd sent it to six other magazines, two of which are publishing it next month." Blacklist City.

If your article is hot enough and time-dated, go for the multiple submission and let the editors know they're in competition. Otherwise, send to one magazine at a time, but politely limit the reviewing period. Show compassion: "May I ask for a report within six weeks? I know how manuscripts pile up, but I do need to place this material while it is current." You'll be ignored as usual, but you've covered yourself for submitting elsewhere after eight weeks or so.

Why do editors take so long to report? They have the best intentions and are forever holding meetings to improve the reviewing process. But in a given day a score of matters arise that must be taken care of immediately: production deadlines, personnel crises, advertising problems, a sale at Bloomingdale's. Manuscript reading is the one obligation that can be put off till tomorrow . . . and tomorrow, and tomorrow.

Often, especially with magazines, sheer force of presentation can explode the system and get a manuscript read before it hits the deadly backlog. After the opening grabber in a cover letter or as part of it, a "high concept" should set editorial ears ringing.

The high concept is the ultimate distillation of your offering, a nugget that only a fool could resist. It's a selling handle, such as Hollywood hustlers drop on producers in the few seconds allotted to them. "Little alien with big eyes gets help from cute kids—do you love it?" In book publishing, editors like a quick concept they can sell to superiors. Later, the same handle can help sales representatives pitch the book to booksellers.

The selling handle should relate to audience rather than writer: not "a collection of my favorite anecdotes from kindergarten," but "inspiration for lost grown-ups from the lessons of childhood." The editor is teased and decides to peek at the opening pages instead of putting the manuscript in its queue.

Few can imagine what rides on those opening pages. If they look putrid, no one will hunt down the literary miracles in later pages. If they're average, the script goes in the queue and eventually gets an adversarial reading—okay, *show* me something. But if the opening goes for the jugular, sings and dances, stands up and takes a bow—bored editors come to life and miracles can happen. The script is passed around like a juicy new rumor. Editors read it in an advocacy mode: Come on, baby—keep it up, don't let me down, gimmee something I can sell!

Many a literary masterpiece has opened slowly, and sometimes the nature of the work demands some holding back, some mystery and confusion. Name authors can indulge in this luxury; others take a gamble by doing so. The average writer should apply the best tricks of journalism to any opening, literary or not. In her long essay on the treachery of journalism itself, Janet Malcolm didn't hold back a thing:

> Every journalist who is not too stupid or too full of himself to notice what is going on knows that what he does is morally indefensible. He is a kind of confidence man, preying on people's vanity, ignorance, or loneliness, gaining their trust and betraying them without remorse.

Editorial godlets can be fooled. A good opener preys on an editor's weakness for the forthright and pugnacious. If it's fresh and feisty, substance be damned. Except in the highest literary latitudes, an acquisition editor buys a piece on its overall feeling and marketability; line editors can worry about filling in the holes.

THINK LIKE AN EDITOR . . .

To please an editor, think like an editor. Authors think of writing as self-expression: if it feels right coming out, it should feel right going in—to a reader's mind; so let it all hang out, baby. But editors don't give a damn about anyone's need for self-expression. They let nothing hang out that's better tucked in.

In the editor's view, writing belongs to the reader. It is selected, shaped, and presented for the reader's stimulation, not the writer's. Stimulation takes many forms, of course. To Yugoslavian author Milorad Pavic, "the reader is like a circus horse which has to be taught that it will be rewarded with a lump of sugar every time it acquits itself well." For Franz Kafka, books must "wound and stab us." Whatever works, as long as readers are lured, jolted, or hacked out of their natural resistance to a stranger's blather.

Think like an editor. With a clear sense of reader resistance, an editor at the old *The New Yorker* used to snicker "This'll cut like butter" before hacking off belabored opening paragraphs. An editor protects readers from boredom; a writer can beat her to it. "I leave out the parts people skip," said Elmore Leonard when pressed to explain the power of his fiction. But Leonard calls on good instincts plus years of reader feedback; most writers would leave out the wrong parts. Think like an advocate of the reader's pleasure, not like some minimalist moron.

Trim fat, leave substance. Frank Feather's *G-Forces: The Thirty-Five Global Forces Restructuring Our Future* came in to William Morrow Publishers the equivalent of twelve hundred typeset pages. His editors trimmed it to four hundred, "without losing a thought or a piece of evidence," said Feather himself.

Trim fat, leave style. You may not always know the difference, nor do many editors; but if you have a rationale, go with it. When Beatrix Potter used "small little" she meant it to stand and told her editors that piled-up adjectives were part of her style, period.

Can editors be told anything? One hopes so. Editors will never understand writing if they don't learn from writers and readers. No editorial academy prepares editors for the million judgments they must make in their careers. Most editorial godlets get their wings long before they know how to fly. Appeasing such air cadets is easy:

Simply take them aloft with words that soar and ideas that orbit the universe.

. . . OR BE AN EDITOR

One sure way to crash the publishing gates is to become an editor and publish one's own works. Who gets to be editors? Often, writers who can handle specialized subjects. The editorial wings get pinned on the first day.

Arthur Plotnikov was thirty-two, a little older than the flower children, when he got his wings. It took him some twenty more years to know how to edit, at which point he shifted into publishing. Along the way, at least, he became a wiser author.

When he left Washington for the Bronx to help edit a magazine in the library field, Martin Luther King was dead,

Nixon was in power, protests were shaking the nation. Plotnikov gave lip service to the causes, but essentially he was apolitical. He would march against the war and wear the peace symbol, but the strident rhetoric of the era gave him indigestion. He pursued his literary identity as wordsmith and wit. Everyone else seemed to be writing sermons.

The magazine offices looked out on the East River. The surrounding neighborhood was just scruffy enough to strike a young writer's fancy. After Washington's scrubbed monuments, these mean streets were the stuff of life. Down the hill from his company stood Yankee Stadium amid tenements, warehouses, playgrounds, and the howl of elevated trains and aroma of corned beef and pickles. A block west loomed the Bronx Courthouse, as hellishly grim as depicted in Tom Wolfe's *Bonfire of the Vanities*. Plotnikov was no Wolfe, unfortunately, but into his writer's bank went the same image: The hulking grey monolith sucking in and belching out its miscreants and parasites.

Plotnikov made his home in a quieter neighborhood. With his wife and young daughter he settled in a plain apartment in the leafy northern Bronx. He painted his writer's desk yellow and squeezed it into the bedroom, facing a mauve Indian tablecloth tacked to the wall. Plotnikov spent long hours gazing over his typewriter at the cloth; but no greater triumph accrued to the yellow desk than a holding letter from *The Paris Review:* "We are holding your story, 'The Decision,' for re-reading . . ."

Plotnikov's literary pursuit entered its *re* period: rewriting, revision, the one rereading, much rejection, and several brief reviews for *Library Journal*. Editing for a living made him a merciless reviser of his own work. With other writers he exercised some restraint; something had to be left to publish. But as he learned the fundamentals of editing, he fell upon his literary works in a fury. His credo: *Attack your writing as if you hated the writer. No holds barred.* The credo is a valid one that eventually works; but in the beginning Plotnikov merely lopped off his *cojónes*.

Sparring with book reviews was perhaps the best training, pound for pound, for a writer and editor at Plotnikov's stage. His assignments forced him to read first novelists and muse about the pitfalls of those early efforts; *Library Journal*'s stingy word limit helped trim a style fattened by two years of governmentspeak. He said goodbye to ". . . utilization of programmatic priorities to optimize the feasibility of interagency nodes," and hello to the pinched prose of one-paragraph critiques.

As a reviewer bedeviling first novelists, Plotnikov enjoyed a small measure of power at the yellow desk; but from his office above the East River he could actually shape the fortunes of writers like himself. In the volatile sixties, his trade journal had evolved into something of a "little" magazine. The gates were thrown open to liberal commentary related to books, intellectual freedom, and the world's oppressed. Articles appeared with such titles as "The Right to Receive and Possess Pornography," and "Finding People Who Feel Alienated and Alone in their Best Impulses and Most Honest Perceptions and Telling Them They're Not Crazy." The manuscripts poured in as fast as other liberal journals could reject them.

Fresh manuscripts came as well, many riding on the hope that competition would be sparse at this pimple among periodicals. But—writers be advised—there exists no publishing pustule on earth without its stacks of unsolicited manuscripts.

Feeling guilty about his power to crush authors, Plotnikov wrote openhearted rejection letters. " . . . your manuscript promised so much, and yet failed to come to life. . . ." The rejected writers phoned right back to vent their spleen or sent spiteful replies and more unuseable manuscripts. If he suggested cuts they cried "emasculation!" If revision, "butchery!" Soon Plotnikov limited himself to stock editors' phrases—"I regret" this and "I'm delighted" that—though magazine editors rarely feel regret or delight over a manuscript decision. They feel the piece stunk, or that they could have done better themselves for the money.

DREAMS OF BIGGER PONDS

For an addicted writer, editorial work is a living, not a cry from the artist within. Magazine editors get attention from all the wrong people—the people promoting this or grousing about that. No one sings your name; no one knows how you feel about things except for what you've written in editorials—which express only how you think you should feel about some ephemeral matter of the month. Plotnikov needed to honk as a bylined writer, and soon he began to publish himself.

Magazine writing was new and stimulating. Livening up an ordinarily dull field made it all the more challenging. He covered professional meetings like a front-line correspondent—bush jacket and all—lacing his reports with analytic sidebars, interviews, and layouts of his own photos. In the spirit of the New Journalists, he ditched objectivity and sometimes reality for the sake of what he considered truth; but readers cheered and honors rolled in. A series became a book. Other triumphs followed. In his small pond, Plotnikov became a big frog.

He should have been content—but writers are frogs yearning to be kissed by fate. Incorrigible dreamers and malcontents, they roll their eyes to the larger kingdom, where princes and princesses publish best-sellers to the admiration of all. One whistle, and hop, hop they go, off in pursuit of literary castles. . . .

Plotnikov hopped from one publisher's reception to the next, enjoying entrée as editor and reviewer. It wasn't exactly gate crashing; his magazine had long been on invitation lists of publicists who needed bodies. No one asked humiliating questions, and Plotnikov could melt into the background to watch the heavy hitters of the New York literary scene. A few celebrated writers in their splendor were enough to turn his head, and he saw scores of them. Here, then, were the real gods, who made the minor editorial godlets crumble into insignificance.

On a December evening Plotnikov attended a small Park Avenue reception and watched Jorge Luis Borges, blind and frail, sandwich himself on a love seat between two young female admirers. Cocking his head, tapping a massive cane to emphasize each high-voiced observation, Borges could still command a chorus of aahs and oohs. Other writers had come to honor his latest publication, *Imaginary Beings*. Across the elegant drawing room, George Plimpton, with the bearing of Peter the Great, held court before a fireplace.

With a sad glance at Plotnikov's identification tag, a publicist introduced him to Borges; and what could Plotnikov do but touch hands and move away to allow Borges the happiness of the warm young haunches? Borges himself, Plimpton, and all celebrated authors seemed like imaginary beings, deities, to whom a mortal could not utter banalities. The old question always haunted these occasions: What does one say to a majwoot (major writer of our time)? Perhaps, "I like your shoes," or, "I have always considered your work a frontal attack on the emotional fatuity of our times." Nothing seems right.

Writers themselves don't know what they want said to them. Most are put off by praise from strangers, small talk, or repartee. At receptions, they are animated mainly by booze or flirtation with attractive members of the opposite sex; otherwise they seem to fall into a catatonic state like animals in the jaws of predators. At best, they offer a pale imitation of themselves to appease the handshakers.

Plotnikov brushed the fingertips of a hundred such imaginary beings in New York's imaginary castles—gilded consulate chambers, oak-paneled clubs, penthouse gardens. At the American Academy and Institute of Arts and Letters, Norman Mailer delivered a wretched talk and struck boxer's poses in the crush of the reception that followed; nonetheless did Plotnikov know the power of a god as they touched hands for an instant.

Almost always there were godly emanations, whatever else Plotnikov could recall from close encounters with the great ones: Tom Wolfe, chatty and perspiring in his ice cream outfit; W. H. Auden, blasted and in his bedroom slippers to receive a National Medal for Literature; I. B. Singer, Yiddishly charming, especially to himself; John Cheever, soft-spoken and unwell; John Irving, a wrestler's neck and needing a shave; Eudora Welty, defiantly pleasant; John Updike, a loveable caricature with huge whinnying head above tweed jacket; Joyce Carol Oates, snapping at a young man in a lobby.

Only a few seemed approachable—Jean Auel, more the backyard neighbor than the millionaire to be; James Dickey, strumming a guitar and haw-hawing; Ray Bradbury, raucously friendly, blunt, sometimes fired up by sauce. Bradbury was among the handful of deities who dealt with Plotnikov once or twice on editorial matters, and he did so with characteristic verve: "It'll cost you three thousand bucks, Bud!" On one occasion he wrote Plotnikov: "Am overwhelmed with work and underwhelmed with energy. Busy finishing a novel, a book of poems, a book of plays, plus a screenplay. . . ."

OH to be so overwhelmed, Plotnikov mused, as his discontent mounted. All that seemed to overwhelm him now were literary longings and a ten-year itch to take advantage of the post-Woodstock (pre-AIDS) Free Love movement. The sirens called. Bare navels puckered up between tie-dyed halters and low-rise jeans. Marijuana and patchouli oil perfumed the air. Potential lovers were everywhere: at the literary receptions, professional meetings, in every park and pub. No writer could let the Age of Aquarius pass by without the dawning of a new love or two. . . .

12

HEARTS AT RISK

THE STRUGGLE TO WRITE, LOVE, AND BE LOVED

"[Love is] the main generator of all good writing. . . . Love, passion, compassion, are all welded together."
—CARSON MCCULLERS

"There's almost nothing worse to live with than a struggling artist."
—JOHN UPDIKE

"I wake my wife up at 3 A.M. and say, 'Listen to this!' "
—BARRY HANNAH

LOVING and writing form a double helix, coiled together like strands of DNA. Sometimes the bond is perfect, yielding happy and productive little Barretts of Wimpole Street. More often, messed-up chemistry creates monsters in monstrous situations. The writing doesn't always suffer, but the writers do and they make sure their love companions suffer double.

Writers, remember, are children who never stopped crying. That doesn't make them bad people. Collectively they lighten the human condition; individually, they can sink themselves and everyone near them in their creative misery. "When my work is going well, I am usually sort of sick," says William Gass. Such pleasant company.

Everyone and everything can go piss off while writers piddle with words; yet they have an extraordinary need to love and be loved. Rarely can they face the literary pursuit alone. They must draw people in, and, as clever talkers, usually have no trouble doing so. They seem easy enough to love, so sensitive in their writings, so bubbly in public appearances. No writer will stand before an audience and scream, "You don't know shit about me!" as they will to their devoted spouse of thirty years. Instead, writers are usually seen at their most effervescent, when they have just published a book and are walking around in that euphoric promotional froth. Writers' intimates loathe such behavior, but in media bites it looks good: "Well, Bryant—hah, hah—the book could have been based on my own life or *yours* for that matter, hah, hah, hah—but [intensely] here's the *real* message of the book. . . ."

The real message! Haven't the writers' loved ones been hearing that one for the last five years—hearing it, reading it, living it, talking about it, not talking about it, all according to the writer's daily needs? Writers must believe they have a real message to lay upon the universe, or what's the point? But since the universe isn't sitting across the dinner table, bleary eyed and defenseless, guess who gets to hear and respond to the real messages each evening?

Writers both demand and resent feedback from loved ones. Most workers come home and unload the day's frustrations on their beloved, and the beloved grunts in sympathy, and that's that. The day's work is history and can't be changed. Turn on the tube, go to bed. *Not so with writers.*

All the work a writer does in a day *can* be changed, and much of it *should* be changed. There is no peace at day's end. A sympathetic grunt won't do. The writer must draw out loved ones to share the agony of the decisions, though the writer knows full well the risk of talking about the day's writing and of dealing with the feedback. In fact, a writer knows that you never force the role of literary critic on loved ones. If there's easy, honest rapport on all matters, then an opinion might be solicited. Forget the idea if sparks fly. When Nadine Gordimer won the 1991 Nobel Prize in Literature, a news photo showed her surrounded by husband, son, daughter-in-law, and granddaugh-

ter. "It's very nice," she told *The New York Times,* "but nobody
in that group ever sees a word that I write before it's printed. I
never discuss it."

But most writers—full-timers in particular—have exhausted
all self-discipline just in nailing themselves to their desks for a
day. When someone asks, "How did it go?" they fall apart and
unload. Writers are criers.

SCENE: An evening after work. She's an attorney; he writes.
   HE: So how did it go today?
  SHE: Well, we got a conviction.
   HE: Hmmph.
  SHE: You should have seen my cross-examinations.
   HE: Hmmph.
  SHE: How about you? How'd it go?
   HE: I don't *talk* my books, I write them.
  SHE: Come on, tell me.
   HE: All right. Since you insist.
  SHE: Well?
   HE: I threw out yesterday's sentence and wrote a new
      one.
  SHE: That's it?
   HE: That and nine hours of considering other options.
  SHE: Why did you toss yesterday's sentence? I liked
      it.
   HE: Yes. Well. I didn't.
  SHE: Why not?
   HE: What's the difference?
  SHE: Answer the question.
   HE: Don't cross-examine me.
  SHE: We spent an hour talking about that sentence last
      night in the middle of my trial. I have a stake in it.
   HE: Well, I'm sorry. It rang false.
  SHE: False? That was the truest passage in the book!
   HE: You think so?
  SHE: I know so.
   HE: That, my dear, is why you're a lawyer and I'm a
      writer.

SHE: *Is* it? Well I'm too tired to argue. I'm going up for
a bath.

HE: Before you go . . .

SHE: Yes?

HE: Would you just read the new sentence?

Poor writers' spouses—but pity the poor writers, too. The
devil made them into closeted scribblers who must somehow
answer to those who throw their shoulders into real toil.
"Writing is very easy," goes Red Smith's famous quip, "all you
do is sit in front of a typewriter keyboard until little drops of
blood appear on your forehead." The trouble is, only other
writers appreciate the brutality of a day's work that may produce no more than a dangling participle. Loved ones soon begin to wonder how much real exertion goes on behind that
knitted brow and what it's worth to anyone. Unpublished
writers, especially, wear out the patience of those who sustain
them.

Published or not, writers must never expect loved ones to
equate sedentary word-crunching with the rat race of job,
business, or household. It just won't fly. Relationships sink
when writers not only insist on their recognition, but claim
superiority or privilege by virtue of their calling. "Damn it, I
don't *care* if the baby's sick and you've got a sales meeting
tomorrow—*I'm* trying to rhyme a couplet!" It may be true, as
David Rieff says, that you need "a messianic view of your calling just to get up in the morning," but it's still the writer's
own absurd choice to labor with words instead of mortar or
meatloaf. For all its romance, is writing any more essential to
human equilibrium than selling insurance or planning a birthday party? The writer who respects the preoccupations of
loved ones, who listens to their stories, will probably be a better writer for it.

THE WRITER'S UNBEARABLE PHASES

Writers' long-term companions, on their part, must somehow
accommodate the three inevitable phases of the writing life:
l'enfant terrible, euphoria, and crisis of confidence.

Young writers are self-confident brats ready to take the world by storm. They play the angry young artist, with wild hair, sullen glances, defiant fashion touches, and mockery of everyone's views. They feel the juice of genius running through their fingers, and they thrust their rough drafts into the mugs of loved ones as graciously as Cagney served grapefruit to his gal. "Writing is all!" is the credo, not "Writing and cleaning the toilet bowl is all!" and not "Writing and picking up my dirty socks," but just writing. Loved ones may be doing the other stuff, but there's no time to notice. The young artist has made the "total commitment" to writing, risking all, sacrificing all.

But who bears the brunt of the risk and sacrifice? Usually the beloved. Hettie Jones, devoted wife of Beat Generation poet LeRoi Jones, says she put her own poetry aside to work wretched jobs, clean up after Jones's wild parties, bear and raise their children, and deal with his womanizing. Her reward: reduced to an abstraction as Jones's ethnic consciousness took form; dumped in 1964.

The angry-young-artist phase at least livens up a household. But phase two, euphoria, is simply obnoxious. The writer has published that first outcry and for a split second has the undivided attention of the literary world. What a trick that attention plays on the ego, creating the not-immodest notion that you and your writings are everything that ever mattered and ever will matter to anyone and everyone who ever lived.

Most writers lack the sane perspective of a Margaret Atwood, the Canadian novelist who says she enjoys the brief flair of celebrity accompanying a new best-seller or its movie. "It's fun if you understand it's not serious, not real life. It's interesting to experience and observe. But if you start seeing the billboards and believing you're Cinderella, then you're in very serious trouble creatively."

For the average writer in euphoria, the eyes spin like wheels of fire while the lips churn out megalomaniacal ravings—
"*. . . me-my-agent me-my-publisher me-my-major book chains me-my-miniseries me-my-subrightsrollingin . . .*"

The loved ones will hear it at dinner and in bed and out with friends: the manic litany of triumph and self-promotion, as if the wonderful warming spotlight will go dark the second the writer shuts up. And it probably will.

Eventually the light dims even for the most triumphant books, and the next phase—the writer's crisis of confidence—comes along to torment any loved ones who have hung in thus far. The crisis may manifest itself as "the second-book syndrome" that so many writers suffer after a first success. What to do for an encore? The early inspiration is gone. Those who thought the first book a fluke may be right. *Am I a one-book author? A fraud?* One faces the options of (1) imitating the first success without the first-time inspiration, (2) treading unfamiliar and slippery ground, or (3) giving up while ahead. *The American Literary Almanac* cites "baffling" cases of authors who virtually quit after one big book, among them Harper Lee (*To Kill a Mockingbird*) and Ralph Ellison (*Invisible Man*). But what's so baffling? What law says writers have to keep beating their brains out for the masses if they can find other diversions?

Every writer faces a crisis of confidence, especially those who have yet to be published. The love companion suffers with them as the writer cries, "What should I do now? Don't tell me!" Panicked, the writer makes a few false starts and then—*plop!*—loses the whole momentum of the literary pursuit.

A few writers—those with iron genes—know they will find it again. They stay calm. They vacate their writing prison for a few weeks and go somewhere new and different with loved ones, opening the senses and letting life happen again. Eventually, they hit their stride and live happily and lovingly until the next inevitable crisis. But the more familiar pattern is of shattered egos and desperate attempts to transfer one's shame. The stinking world can go bugger itself! *And you, too, Honey!* Honey, who just wants to help, can do no right. Somehow Honey's at fault, and if Honey doesn't like the way I the writer am carrying on, Honey can take a walk and *just get off my back.*

Writers who have tied up all their self-esteem in the literary pursuit find no comfort in the lover's continuing devotion. They look for solace in booze, in affairs, even death—when the only true remedy is a reordering of life's priorities.

*   *   *

A LOVE relationship is the miracle that any clearheaded organism would cherish above all else; writing and the literary pursuit are cockeyed lotteries to be played with a gambler's stoicism. Writers who put art before people ought to live alone, or at least, like author Allan Gurganus, aim their literary neuroses at something less vulnerable than living things. Garganus collects masks, which he nails to the wall of his New York apartment. "They're enormously good company," he says. "They don't talk back. They smile. I read my work aloud repeatedly, and it's always nice to have an audience. . . ."

Some writers seek living masks as lovers, ever-smiling faces capable of appreciative discourse at the snap of a finger. Unfortunately such faces tend to twist into devil masks as they come to revile what once they worshipped. What might suit writers better would be no-nonsense, independent mates who neither disdain nor revere writing and help keep it in its place. These are the mates who would drag a whining writer by the ear to the word processor and declare, "Here's where you do your crying. Away from here, your business is loving."

WHY WRITERS FAIL AT LOVE

Why do writers find loving so difficult? Writers—those minstrels of love? Why did Mary McCarthy, who made a religion of friendship, go through four marriages? Why did Norman Mailer log six wives? Why did Sylvia Plath turn so bitterly on her husband Ted Hughes? Perhaps writers are no more inept at love than the rest of the population; but writers have documented their failed loves by the thousands, and so we look for answers in that rubble of letters, autobiographies, and telling fiction. The usual dilemma seems to be that writers cannot succeed at love until they succeed at self-love, and they cannot succeed at self-love until they succeed as writers, but when they succeed as writers they fall in love with success and fear any love that threatens it.

But there are hundreds more obstacles to love. Almost everything about writing seems to get in the way. Writing is crying out about one's self and the world—Whitman's barbaric yawp. Can anyone yawp and love at the same time?

Writing is dissection of experience, and no love can be scrutinized like the innards of a pickled frog. Writing is the hunt for material, preying on everything in sight—loved ones, loved ones in bed, even loved ones as they lay dying. The death agonies of one's beloved was a fashionable topic circa 1990. In a nonfiction work, Molly Haskell chronicled the hideous encephalitic virus suffered by husband Andrew Sarris and dissected their entire emotional relationship. Somehow Sarris survived, as did, according to Haskell, the unlikely love between these two professional critics. A miracle.

The very obsessiveness of the writing act spills over to kill the spontaneity of love. Psychiatrist Donald W. Goodwin (*Alcohol and the Writer*) characterizes careful writing as "an endless chain of small decisions—choosing the best word, excluding this, including that—and the good writer, while writing, is an obsessional. Restricting obsessions to a nine-to-five workday is difficult; the wheels keep turning. . . ."

Writers are always writing their lives as they go along. They fashion their speech as if writing dialogue, trying to meet their own expectations as writers and hating themselves for such clichés as, "I love you." If fiction writers, they practice their narrative skills even in bed, thinking of themselves in the third-person past. Colette said "You don't write about love while making love"; but at the most intimate moment a writer will launch a thought balloon: *"He entered her"* or *"She received him."*

Writers examine a loved one's every word and gesture under the obsessional microscope, wincing when the pattern doesn't fit their aesthetic. In these relentless close-ups they start to see loved ones as grotesques: *Look at his mouth . . . I never realized how ugly it is, his lower lip like a bloated leech . . .*

If there were no other obstacles to love, writers would simply tangle themselves up in the business of self-identity. How they twist and squirm as they try to interpret themselves as art—i.e., figure out what they've got to say that makes them different and that matters to anyone.

Vaclav Havel, who would later wrestle with his identity as president of Czechoslovakia, wrestled with the theme of writer-as-inventor-of-himself in his 1984 play *Largo Desolato*. Leopold Nettles, Havel's comic and pathetic protagonist, struggles to reinvent the self who was once a dissident writer and hero to the oppressed. But Leo is empty, so empty he almost longs for the arrest and imprisonment he feels is imminent. To friends and former lovers who would help redefine him, he claims himself incapable of love; he incorporates their clichés in his own bab-ble of self-definition. Reduced to a self-parodying buffoon, he greets his arresters eager to go—but they tell him he is no longer under arrest. Why? Because he no longer matters. His identity is gone.

DIFFICULT as they may be, writers are not always the villains of love turned sour. Often they are the victims. Did Edith Whar-ton force her banker husband to embezzle from her? Did Eliz-abeth Bishop's devotion to Lota de Macedo Soares cause the woman's suicide? Writers tend to pick mates who, like them-selves, have what Leslie Fiedler calls a "charismatic weakness." These engaging flaws may become festering wounds; but even so, love can prevail. As far as anyone can tell, thousands of authors live in peace with loved ones, having made the neces-sary adjustments in temperament or fitted their neuroses to their companion's. For every writer tormented and debilitated in the quest for long-term love, no doubt another has found inspira-tion in it, even some happiness, or at least the rage that stimu-lates writing.

TURNING LOVE AND ANGER OUTWARD

On his thirty-fifth birthday, Arthur Plotnikov found anger—and explosive writing energy—when a marriage gone sour forced him into unwanted bachelorhood, apart from young daughters and the comforts of home. Blame the Age of Aquarius, blame Plotnikov, blame a book he'd reviewed called *Open Marriage,* with its permissive view of extramarital adventure—but he'd pushed things too far even for a writer at war with conventionality (as he sometimes saw himself).

Knowing the end was near, he'd rented a studio apartment nearby but couldn't quite get himself to move. He'd made a last-ditch effort to reform. It was too late. As if by structuring the hurt he'd be able to deal with it, he'd plotted his grand departure to take place on his "mid-life" birthday. The day arrived, and never had he felt emptier and angrier. Never had he cared less about writing. Yet that week he began the most driven writing of his life.

Nothing spurs word people like a feeling of injustice. Wherever the blame actually lay, Plotnikov felt unjustly stripped of hearth and kin. An unjust electric bill turns ordinary citizens into writers of epics; when wordsmiths suffer love's injustices they rack the heavens. Their prose, though sizzling, tends to be profane, libelous, and unpublishable.

Plotnikov began what would be a two-hundred-page tirade the week he moved out. Blocked for years from writing any living prose beyond journalism and book reviews, he now wrote as fast as he could type, hours at a stretch, words hitting paper like oil on a hot pan.

No excerpts need be offered; Aristotle made it clear that purgation can produce hot stuff. The question is whether love's anger can stimulate *good* writing.

After a year, when the anger had run its course, the journal sputtered to a halt. But Plotnikov looked it over, liked its force, and decided to take a shot at publication. He polished the rough edges, called it *35* and sent it to the publisher of *Open Marriage,* the book that had launched a thousand separations. Immediately he had misgivings. Why air his dirty laundry? Why embarrass wife, children, and lovers, who were only thinly disguised? Why push a successful act of purgation into literary gain?

The rejection note, from an editor named Pamela Veley, resolved the questions for him:

Dear Mr. Plotnik[ov],

35 is a very moving and very personal story. A number of us here [at M. Evans] read it and were impressed by the writing—by the sense of immediacy the book creates. We felt too, though, that the story the book tells is almost too personal—that it doesn't really generalize outward enough. It evokes empathy, but empathy directed at a very special person, under very special circumstances. . . .

Love and writing. How to project the love experience outward? That, perhaps, was a craft Plotnikov had not yet mastered if ever he would, and he had sense enough to put the journal away. Eight years later, however, he would find himself writing in the charged atmosphere of a love affair on the rocks, and the book that emerged would sell tens and tens of thousands.

His secret: The book had nothing to do with love.

13

THE PIT AND THE PINNACLE

CHILLS OF GETTING PUBLISHED

*"When I'm writing I enjoy it and I enjoy
reading my proofs. But the minute it comes out
I detest it; . . . I'm vexed and sick at heart
about it."*
—THE WRITER TRIGORIN IN CHEKOV'S *The Seagull*

*"It was the greatest feeling I'd ever had in my
life. . . . I remember hearing Sammy Davis Jr.
on the radio singing 'I Gotta Be Me' and
thinking to myself, 'Yeah, that's it—I gotta be me.' "*
—CHESTER KARRASS ON FIRST GETTING PUBLISHED

TO be published! To sign a contract with a bona fide publishing house! To see one's name in gold-foil type! To appear on a dust-jacket, hand to cheek in self-love!

Except perhaps for the birth of a child with a halo, no thrill in life can match the galactic explosion of ego when a mainstream publisher says *yes* to one's work—particularly to a book. Writers recall that moment of acceptance more vividly than what they were doing when Kennedy was assassinated or when the city power failed or an earthquake struck. And why not? An established business enterprise is telling you how smart you were to spend seven years earning nothing and driving everyone insane. They are telling you that you exist, that you have value, that they will edit, typeset, print, market, and distribute *your thoughts* to the general public and give you a shot at immortality. Why shouldn't your head swim?

When Macmillan publishers told Arthur Plotnikov they would publish his book, he recalls, he stood at a phone booth at 10:02 A.M. at the Jean Stratton Porter Plaza on the Indiana Turnpike. It was a fleecy day in late May, about 80 degrees. Plotnikov was headed east from Chicago for a holiday. He had phoned editor Jane Cullen at 10 o'clock, as she had instructed, to hear the result of the publishing committee meeting that would sanctify or torpedo the rest of his life.

"Of course we're publishing your book," Cullen told him. "Did you have any doubts, ha ha?"

Did Plotnikov's head swim? Only like this: It greased itself up and leapt into Lake Erie at Sandusky, bolted Niagara Falls, shot through the St. Lawrence River and out to sea, dropped down the Atlantic to the Strait of Magellan, ran with the dolphins up the coasts of two continents, rolled in with the fog under Golden Gate Bridge, and skipped like a stone through every lake, pond, and pool from San Francisco Bay back to Sandusky. The trip took about an hour, and left Plotnikov's head treading water for the next four weeks.

That's the first feeling of getting published. Every year it happens to some forty-five thousand book writers in the United States alone. That turbulence out at sea, all those whitecaps— those are forty-five thousand writers' heads swimming.

PUBLISHED! How does it happen? What mystery surrounds that sacred passage into print at someone else's expense?

The process seems straightforward enough: an author writes a decent book or proposal and sends it to a few agents listed in literary directories. An alert agent recognizes a good thing and presents the project to the right editors at the right "houses." At one house, an editor embraces the project and shares copies with colleagues, who consider it in a "publishing committee" meeting. Marketing likes it. Sales likes it. Production sees no problems. The decision is to acquire. Some terms are proposed, editor and agent negotiate, and agent phones author with the magic words: "I've got some good news."

No one can knock that particular good news, for ultimately it is better to be published than not published. But did anyone think publication was the *end* of a writer's agonies? MOOWA-HA-HA-HA-HA!!!

The gloomiest pessimist cannot imagine the torments that may follow upon a book contract: cancelations, hysterical deadlines, excruciating delays, hateful revisions, editorial abandonment, publisher hostility, squalid covers, unreadable typeface, small press run, zero marketing, murderous reviews, fouled distribution, returns from bookstores, negative earnings, early remaindering, law suits, assorted unique horror stories, and a black mark on Publishers Row for the author who writes a "mid-list" book—a book that had its chance and sold only middling well.

Ambitious writing projects, those that require years of dedication, are especially subject to the vagaries of the publishing industry, where vagary is rampant. While an author sweats out the two or three years between contract and publication, *everything* wanders and goes eccentric in the publishing house. Trends shift; enthusiasms wane; editors leave; new owners take over; lists are cut back; corporate debts suck away the budget for your book.

A recent example: According to a *Publishers Weekly* report, Andrew Malcolm spent ten years writing a modern Platonic dialogue of colossal size, then revised it with the understanding that Oxford University Press would publish the work. But the editor with whom he had an understanding was overruled by an executive who later left the company, and the publisher's editorial board decided there was no binding contract. What to do next? Malcolm went to court, suing for publication, still dreaming that perhaps one day he would be signing books instead.

After years of struggle a writer may be published "at last"— and still wind up being last in line for the rewards of the literary pursuit. All but the hottest published writers gripe that they are last to get any attention from the publishing house, last to hear how their book is doing, last to have book shipped to reviewers and retailers, last to be paid except for the initial advance, and last to be considered for the next book.

IN 1990, at the American Booksellers Association convention in Las Vegas, authors were last on anyone's minds as publishers hawked new titles and foreign rights from more than two thousand exhibit booths. Celebrity appearances and book signings took place off to the side of the bazaar. One of the few writers actually working the crowd was Arthur Ginolfi, unknown author of a tiny book from a tiny publisher. Ginolfi stood mostly ignored at the entrance to the cavernous exhibit hall, handing out photocopied promotional flyers and announcing, "Hi, I'm the author of *The Tiny Star* . . ." Here was a writer in the full glory of publication.

In the Las Vegas setting, one was reminded that the author-publisher alliance isn't about love, but about gambling, with publisher as high roller and author as rube with one chip. When luck is running high, the sweet nothings fly and the romantic notions of the relationship are perpetuated: "Our authors are our lifeblood; without them, there is no product, no publishing." Or, "My publisher believes in the book and is already talking sequels." But when luck takes a powder, as it inevitably does, the partners revert to a more normal state of mutual contempt.

In the view of most authors who have been through the mill, a publishing firm is a commercial whorehouse run by literary boobs and corporate Neanderthals who make all the wrong decisions and publish a book only to destroy it. To hardened publishing staff, an author is a paranoid misfit and megalomaniac whose ignorance of publishing is so profound that dealing with an intermediary agent at twice the cost is preferable to facing the whining overgrown brat.

TALENT + X = PUBLICATION

The basic route to getting published may seem straightforward, but each writer takes an individual journey of hair-raising twists and turns. The only rule of the road is that getting there requires a *combination* of factors—usually writing talent plus something else, at least one other element. That element may be technical expertise, a well-placed connection in publishing, a close association with a celebrity, a background that rouses lurid interest, or such personal qualities as blind persistence and eagle-eyed opportunism.

Although such combinations underlie most entries into publishing, none of them guarantees publication. *Nothing* guarantees publication, not even intimate relations with a film star. One of tough-guy Charles Bronson's later wives tried to sell her story recently, but there were two problems: Charlie never smacked her around with those lethal fists, and another wife published a more intimate story.

Talent plus sensationalism may sell a book, if one can find the narrow zone between shock and offensiveness. Stories must exceed the latest frontiers of gore yet cause no editor to lose her lunch. In his nonfiction best-seller about Andean plane-crash survivors, Piers Paul Read introduced middle-class munching on human limbs. In 1990 Piers Anthony (what is it with these Piers's?) raised the ante in fictional horror. His shocker *Firefly* featured a thing that lured human victims by excreting irresistible pheromones—then sucked away all soft tissue, leaving only bones.

Another ideal combo is talent plus a literary connection. Sponsorship by an established author, for example, would surely sling one into a publisher's lap; but when it comes to giving new authors a boost, most established authors are about as friendly as union thugs to scabs.

Even so, a number of writers have been helped by literary hotshots who were one-time lovers, or friends of the family, or kindly mentors. One such mentor helped a little-known William Kennedy publish his novel *Ironweed,* which later won the Pulitzer Prize and catapulted Kennedy into the stratosphere.

Talk about fate—the paths of William Kennedy and novelist Saul Bellow crossed in San Juan, Puerto Rico, of all places, where upstate New Yorker Kennedy was working as a journalist and Chicagoan Bellow happened to be teaching a university creative writing course. More than twenty years later, after *Iron-weed* had been rejected by thirteen houses including Kennedy's prior publisher, Viking Press, Saul Bellow read the manuscript and wrote Viking: ". . . that the author of *Billy Phelan* should have a manuscript kicking around looking for a publisher is disgraceful." Thickening the strands of fate was the return to Viking of a powerful editor partial to Kennedy's work. Viking published *Ironweed* and reissued Kennedy's earlier Albany novels.

See how easy it is? Another Kennedy—John Kennedy Toole—achieved publication by a mere combination of comic brilliance, his own suicide, a persistent mother, and a sympathetic author. Toole wrote *A Confederacy of Dunces* in the early sixties, and, failing to get it published, killed himself in 1969. His mother tried eight more publishers, then pleaded with the nearest great novelist, Walker Percy, to help out. Percy agreed grumblingly, but soon marveled at the work and recommended it to Louisiana State University Press. The book became a classic and Toole, one hopes, sits among the happy published authors in the sky.

Novelist Valery Martin, who scored with *Mary Reilly,* also found persistence and literary connections to be a winning combo, even if being a "mid-list" author weighed her down. Martin published her first two novels to good reviews, but over the next eight years wrote four novels that her agent sent to at least twenty editors, with no takers. Martin, who teaches writing, remarked in a later interview, "I tell my students if you want to tell whether you're a writer or not, just see if you can stop. It's the basic test. I never thought that I should quit because I couldn't publish."

But neither did Martin quit *trying* to publish, exploiting any opportunity that came along. Moving to the University of Alabama, she met writers Margaret Atwood, whom she befriended, and Craig Nova, who took her earlier books to a new agent; but the new agent wasn't eager to market rejected manuscripts. Martin told Atwood the sad story, and Atwood said, "Give me the books." Atwood took the manuscripts to her own editor, Nan Talese, who bought them.

To be published! There are some who would kill for it. Just murder someone, go to prison, write something angry, and get a name author to see it. That sequence worked for Jack Henry Abbott, one of the thousands of jailhouse writers seeking a publisher. At the close of the seventies, Norman Mailer helped Abbott gain parole and publish a collection of visceral letters, *In the Belly of the Beast,* which earned some $100,000. Abbott must have thought this was the way to go; shortly after his release, he murdered a young waiter and was returned to prison —and he got another book and film rights out of his story. About ten years later, however, a jury awarded the waiter's wife $7.57 million in damages—every penny Abbott ever earned or could ever possibly earn. Mailer had no comment, but for many an established author the message must have been clear: Don't help.

AT first it's easy for most writers to believe they don't need help, that they have the talent and the perseverance that ultimately will win publication. The trick is to maintain that belief when manuscripts limp back from the fortieth rejection looking like someone beat them with a mace. "If I knew how many years it would take to publish a book, I might not have kept going," said Mississippi firefighter-turned-novelist Larry Brown. Rejections piled up for ten years, but Brown persevered, meanwhile reading everything he could about the craft of writing and taking a course to help him along. Perhaps after fighting flames, smoke, and collapsing walls, Brown could handle a wall of rejection slips. By 1991, with his second hit (*Joe*), he was red-hot himself.

Another hot fiction writer, James Ellroy, made it on sheer strength of manuscript. He wrote his first book (*Brown's Requiem*) in longhand, had it typed, and sent copies to four agents listed in *Writer's Market 1980* who were willing to read manuscripts over the transom. All four wanted to represent him. He chose one, and got a sale to Avon. Simple—but what made the writing so strong? Perhaps everything Ellroy had to overcome just to reach the point of writing: his mother's murder when he was ten; his father's death seven years later; twelve years on the worst streets of Los Angeles as an indigent, drug user, and alcoholic; twelve convictions for theft and burglary and eight months in jail; a lung abscess and alcoholic brain syndrome; and years of meager income as a humble—though sober—caddy. The dream of being a published writer had been with him for a long time, however, sustained by hundreds of crime novels he'd shoplifted. With a plot in mind, he paused one day on the golf course and prayed, "God, would you please let me start this fucking book tonight?" Chances are, Ellroy made it on his own.

AFTER all such rocky ascents, writers who thought they had reached the pinnacle by being published might yet find themselves at the edge of a bottomless pit—or deep within it. A thousand stories issue from this sad bedlam. Best known among recent tales it the saga of Salman Rushdie. *The Satanic Verses,* a novel that elevated Rushdie from an English mid-list symbolist to world-renowned intellectual, did so by offending the Islamic world and especially Iran's Ayatollah Khomeini, who condemned Rushdie to death and offered a reward of up to $3 million to whoever performed the execution. While the book earned a fortune in sales, Rushdie had to go deep underground in 1989 and stay there in fear of murder. His reports from hiding indicated he was not having a good time.

Less known was the fallout suffered by Rushdie's American wife, Marianne Wiggins. Wiggins had published a few deft novels, but now—just before the *Satanic Verses* outcry—Harper & Row was ready to bring out her most accomplished work, *John Dollar,* with fifty thousand copies and a seven-city tour. It was to be her "breakout" book, as the jargon goes; but the Rushdie furor was the only thing to break out, and *John Dollar* as well as Wiggins's identity as an individual writer were lost in the shouting and hiding. Wiggins couldn't do much about it except leave Rushdie, which she later did.

Developments in the Rushdie affair caused cancelations of at least two other books dealing with Islam, whose authors had signed contracts and jumped up and down and bragged to friends and felt their heads go leaping with the sailfish. Now they will wander the world like the Ancient Mariner, seizing strangers to tell their publishing horror stories.

MINI-THRILLS OF PUBLICATION

Horror stories, horror stories—are there no tales of bliss among those forty-five thousand authors who see print each year? Of course there are; along with the frustrations and disappointments of each publishing experience comes a procession of joys, large and small, that may be the nearest thing to prolonged orgasm in the creative arts.

Every literary dreamer knows the list of great thrills: the agent's call, fat advance, movie sale, media raves, peer admiration, and the agony of one's detractors. The average published writer settles for only one or two of these macro-thrills, but enjoys a sequence of mini-titillations that in the aggregate can be just as keen.

One such titillation is simply seeing one's words in crisp black type and neat page layouts. Some time after the contract is signed and the manuscript completed, the author receives a set of galley proofs—the manuscript set in type and ready to be viewed for corrections. "Proofs" is an apt name because they prove that publication is actually going to happen, that the contract wasn't another of Cousin Shecky's practical jokes.

Soon after the author sees them, these proofs, sometimes in a simple binding, are sent to notables who might offer a kindly comment for publicity, such as: *"Brilliant and riveting from start to finish! Iris Murdoch, move over!"* In seeking these blurbs, the publisher asks the author to provide a few well-placed names, and now the author cashes in every chip ever held with friends in high places. The ambitious author sends out some thirty or forty requests for comments, hoping to catch three or four raves. As each blurb comes in, the thrills mount.

The merest acquaintances will sometimes act with astonishing generosity, either to keep their own names in print or because they are astonishingly generous people. For his editing book, Plotnikov hooked man of letters Clifton Fadiman, whom he had never met. "Plotnikov comes to the rescue," wrote Fadiman. "Every writer, journalist, publisher, literary agent and editor should shelve it [this book] next to his Strunk and White." Plotnikov's eyes watered.

Soon, in the usual course of mini-thrills, comes the author's preview of dustjacket design: front and back covers, one spine, and two flaps of pure ego gratification. It seems a miracle just to see one's name as big as life on the front cover and not hidden under the flap like some shameful tattoo; but now the author's mug peers out as well, one happy toad beaming from the literary pond. It's always amusing to see first authors trying to look blase in these photos, when what they're feeling is *"Naa, nah, nah, naa, nah! I'm published and you're not!"* Beneath the photo, choice biographical notes skim the cream from the writer's vita. For the newly published it's off to the copying machine to print a small edition of dustjackets for family and friends.

Holding the complete manufactured book in one's hands a few weeks later is a titillation that borders on the erotic, for it represents the corporeal climax to a five-year seduction of agents, editors, publishers, and anyone else who could help make this moment happen. Something may temper one's joy as the binding and soft pages are fondled: a typo no one caught on page two; or a dedication to one's "beloved," who has now moved out and is owed a year of child support. But unlike all those dozens of books published and handled in one's dreams, the books that evaporated at dawn, this one is real. You are a published writer.

The physical book may provide a sensual experience; but seeing that sacred object on the shelves of a bookstore sends a religious tremor through the soul. For new writers, the appearance of one's book on the altar of the marketplace is the epiphany of being published. Established writers are not immune to the thrill; Richard Brautigan is said to have frequented Doubleday's in San Francisco to stare at his titles for an hour. As a young clerk in Greenwich Village's Paperbook Gallery, Plotnikov observed some of the flakiest writers of the Beat generation in solemn communion with their works. To this day, Plotnikov performs the ritual of all authors who come upon their books wedged in with others on a retail shelf: He squeezes competing books into a tight row, displays his own titles face-out, and steps back to worship.

On the other side of this epiphany lies the experience of *not* finding one's newly published book in the stores. This black hole might be the fault of the publisher's bad timing or bad selling, a distribution snafu, or of the book itself, which for some reason has left retailers cold. Whatever the cause, the effect is devastating. One gawks at the shelves and knows the horror of *Firefly,* in which all soft tissue has been sucked away.

SIX-POINT CELEBRITY

Yet, even the writer whose books have vanished can enjoy a share of "six-point celebrity"—one's name in six-point type in scores of reference books. Like publication itself, six-point celebrity confirms the writer's existence, as one becomes part of a vast and permanent international bibliographic record. Even before publication, one appears in *Forthcoming Books* and other advance listings perused by booksellers and librarians. Name and book are registered forevermore in the U.S. Government's *Catalog of Copyright Entries.* The Library of Congress prepares or approves an official bibliographical record that will appear throughout the world on catalog cards or in computer catalogs linked in networks. When the book appears, listings and mentions sprout like dandelions throughout the literary community, in *Books in Print* and *Cumulative Book Record* and bookseller catalogs and industry databases. Is there anything so documented as a book?

Historian and political analyst Walter Laqueur has some thirty distinguished books to his credit—even his agent has lost count; but for all the great thrills of publication over five decades, he cites the six-point record as evidence of success: "It's not elegant to blow one's horn," he told an interviewer, "but . . . if I look at *Books in Print* or at this giant new paperback, *Reader's Catalog,* I think I have more entries than anyone else in my field."

Unaware of bibliographies, many new writers miss the six-point satisfactions and suffer a protracted silence until publication day. Plotnikov, with his library connections, savored every last bibliographic notation on his Macmillan book. He couldn't pass a library without dragging friends in to share his bliss. During visitations with his daughters—now about twelve and fourteen—he called their attention to the family name in six-point type as they stared at their fingernails in rapture.

REVIEWS, which often start appearing before publication day, may be less than titillating for most writers. Reviewers distinguish themselves by swipes of the rapier, not handfuls of posies. The first reviews usually appear in trade publications for libraries and booksellers—if there are any reviews at all. Some books remain chillingly ignored. Media raves are as rare as magic rainbows. The average writer must thrill to modest reviews in small or specialized journals; but thrilling they are when charitable, and often their praises are picked up in press releases, specialized lists of books, book-review digests, and certain electronic catalogs that include review extracts.

Virtually all authors enter an electronic record. The world's largest electronic inventory of books is the catalog maintained by the Online Computer Library Center (OCLC) based in Ohio. This database, which grows by thirty-five thousand records each week, not only indicates the title, author, publisher, and certain contents of more than twenty million books, but tells which of thousands of U.S. and foreign libraries have reported the title to be in their collections. Practically every legitimate book published in North America is acquired by at least one of the OCLC libraries and entered in the OCLC catalog, a database used more than 2.5 million times daily by librarians and others working at some ten thousand terminals.

One little-known titillation available to authors is to have a librarian search the OCLC catalog under their name or book titles. Quickly, one's records pop up on the screen, followed by fields of information identifying the works in detail, and then a state-by-state list of OCLC-network libraries reporting one's works among their holdings. Here, in each abbreviated library symbol, is assurance that the life of one's mind is in safekeeping. This partial OCLC record shows the format:

```
ASYNC1    PRISM     BLK
Search  Edit  View  Actions  Options  SID: 13645          OL
Beginning of holdings displayed.

OLUC da plot,ele                              Record 3 of 8
All locations
Plotnik, Arthur. The elements of editing: a modern guide for
editors and journalists / by Arthur Plotnik. New York :
Macmillan : London : Collier Macmillan, c1982. DLC In IEH
OCLC: 8590243

STATE     LOCATIONS
IL        CGP IAA IAC IAD IAF IAG IAI IAL IAN IAO IAQ IAR
          IAS IAZ IBB IBF IBI IBK IBP IBQ IBZ ICD ICK ICM
          ICS ICV IEH IEV IFG IFK IHD IHE IHG IHO IHT IHW
          IHZ ILM INO ITA IUO IVY IWE JAE JAG JAM JAS JBE
          JBI JBL JBR JBW JDB JDX JFD JNA SOI SPI UIU
AK        UEM
AL        AAA AAU ABJ ACM ADA AJB ALM AMP ANO ASL MWR TSR
          TTR TTW
AR        AFU AKE AKH AKU AMK
AZ        APF AZD AZN AZS AZT AZU AZY MSA PNX YCC
CA        ALD ALH APO BHP BUR CBA CBC CBL CCH CCO CCP CCT
          CDH CDS CDU CEB CFI CFL CFS CFU CGF CGL CHU CIY
          CLA CLB CLO CLU CMK CNO CNP CNS CPA CPC CPE CPO
          CPP CPS CPT CPU CRH CRP CRU CSA CSF CSJ CSL CSO
          CSP CTU CUF CUI CUN CUR CUS CUT CUY CUZ CVL CVP
          CZA DAC DOC FBS HBL HCK HVD IVX JQD JQF JQH JQI
          JQQ JQR JQW JRB JRS JRI JRK JRL JRP JRQ JRT JRU
          JRW JRX JRY JRZ JTA JTD JTH JTO JTP JTW LIV LOD
          LPU MCF MEY MIR MLV NEV NPR ONT ORK ORO PFO PVL
          SAD SAR SFR SJP SLO SMP SMX SNR SPA SSJ STA SXP
          TCB TSL UCS UPL WRP YOL
CO        ACF CDF COA COB COD COG COH COS COV COX DAD DAJ
          DMP DNH DPL DVA DVN DVP DVR
CT        BPT CGA CTD CTL FAU FEM GRN HPL LEO LIC NHP SSA
          UBM UCH UCW WES WHP
DC        ABA ACT ACY AGD ARL BNA DBI DGU DGW DHU DJD DLC
          DWP EAU GWM HOU LCJ LIS LRB MPG NAR NDU SCH SEN
          SMI UCA USI USP
```

For the writer seeking meaning in the publishing experience, these six-point tidbits should not be dismissed; they help mitigate the apathy of one's publisher and the fickle tastes of the reading public. They indicate that, like brains in cryogenic preservation, one's words have indeed entered the vault of humankind, where someday they can be retrieved when the world is ready for so powerful a dose of genius.

14

SOUNDING LIKE A WRITER

A WAY WITH WORDS

*"Writers are the servants of language.
Language is the common property of society,
and writers are the guardians of language."*
—OCTAVIO PAZ

*". . . words, . . . I think I can influence them
slightly and have even learned to beat them
now and then, which they appear to enjoy."*
—DYLAN THOMAS

"IF I can't write, at least let me *sound* like a writer," Plotnikov prays whenever he confronts a blank page or a sensitive face. Sounding like a writer means more than lifting sesquipedalian phases from the borborygmic innards of a fustian tome, like so. It means living up to one's reputation as a word person. That reputation begins early in life, maybe with a precocious thank-you note to Aunt Flo. Later, as spokespeople for the human race, writers are expected to roll out the golden tongue as naturally as bees lap nectar. The truth is that for each honeyed word, writers drone from sunup to the antelucan hours.

In pursuit of literary panache, word people *compel* themselves to sound like writers. Where others blow air, writers speak in quotable quotes. They can't send a postcard without huffing for the right words. Around the house they are walking thesauri: "Darling, I am dry, drouthy, parched, anhydrous—run, dash, scud, fetch me a drink!" Every utterance must transcend the mundane. "I felt a happiness so deep it was solemn," remarked the author of a 1990 novel on seeing the first copies off the press. Even answering machines must sound like Oscar Wilde. "I can't come to the phone right now—I'm in the gutter looking up at the stars."

From adolescents scrawling love notes to corpses moldering under self-composed epitaphs, writers are determined to be the word people, distinguished by their way with words.

And what is a way with words? The gift of literate parents? The *Oxford English Dictionary* dropped in one's playpen? A richness of neurological synapse? Is it a proclivity, or a drawn-out process? Anyone who has watched Aegean fishermen tenderizing squid—whacking it for hours on concrete—can appreciate how writers beat a word or two into shape. It's not fast and not pretty.

A way with words means *having* one's way with words—forcing them to do one's bidding, no more, no less. In this effort the writer struggles against two deadly tendencies of language: to retreat to the commonplace or leap to the baffling and bizarre. A way with words comes only with agony, agonizingly, in the sense of the Greek *agonizesthai:* to contend, to struggle, for a prize.

ONE struggles not only with language, but with material, something to say—usually wrung from long and arduous experience. Adlai Stevenson, who had a way with words, defined experience as ". . . a knowledge not gained by words but by touch, sight, sound, victories, failures, sleeplessness, devotion, love . . . the emotions of this earth and of oneself . . . and perhaps, too, a little faith, and a little reverence for things you cannot see." How to convert that mess into language?

The first obstacle to writing is the limitation of words themselves. In his sixth book (*Lifetide*), scientist Lyall Watson confesses that "words, with their weight, have a tendency to fall like birds of prey on delicate ideas, carrying them away before they have a chance to reach fruition." If words constrain even the poetic Dr. Watson, awash in the language and subject matter of six scientific disciplines, how intimidated is the average writer, say a Plotnikov?

A Plotnikov is no Nabokov—that prolific word master who enjoyed every advantage of heredity and environment. Born to aristocratic intellectuals in St. Petersburg, Nabokov was tutored in Russian, French, and English and as a teen devoured the classics of those languages as modern youths gulp Whoppers. Later he polished his skills at Cambridge and in Europe's literary capitals. Plotnikov, raised on working-class platitudes, came late to literature and landed in the library profession, whose jargon is to writing as urine is to camp fires. Never could he write to the level even of those first Nabokovian words he read with a swoon in 1955: "Lolita, light of my life, fire of my loins. My sin, my soul. Lo-lee-ta: the tip of the tongue taking a trip of three steps down the palate to tap, at three, on the teeth. Lo. Lee. Ta." But he wrote anyway, as have tens of thousands of writers whose verbal heritage was, so to speak, unspeakable.

Beginning writers may lack confidence in their language skills but must never hesitate to fail forward. Some lose heart when they discover the community of word watchers, the linguistic fiends who write letters to William Safire, work the *Times* crosswords, and read *Verbatim*. Word watchers may intrigue one another, but they are little more equipped for literary expression than the plodding latecomer. Soon enough all writers suffer gut-shriveling inadequacy, as if challenged to ply the galactic seas on a surfboard. Contemporary English offers some three hundred thousand living words and billions of possible word combinations; relatively few of these combinations have the power to find an audience and make it listen, quake, delight, understand, and remember. The rest—the overwhelming mass of verbal communications—will fail in these aims, even for an audience of one.

WHAT READERS WANT

Writers can succeed on less ambitious levels, however, as they build literary power. Not all readers want to quake full-time. What readers generally ask is more basic:

1. Tell me something I don't know.
2. Tell me something I do know in a way that moves me.
3. Refresh me from everyday drivel.

The first task is easiest, at least in nonfiction. Even with language as worn as hand-me-down underwear, mass-media journalists still command an audience by passing along new information. The trick is to use no more words than the information is worth.

Making old information dance requires more imagination, but not always ten-dollar words. "The heart is the third ball," says a García Márquez character in *Autumn of the Patriarch*. Douglas Adams writes in *The Long Dark Tea-Time of the Soul,* "There are some people you like immediately, some whom you think you might learn to like in the fullness of time, and some that you simply want to push away from you with a sharp stick." We knew all that, but it tickles us again.

Some authors can make a living sounding like a writer, stringing lively sentences into information and entertainment. But those who refresh humankind from drivel are the true literary artists and heroes.

Every so often a newspaper reports on the "fecal dust" that blows through certain cities from the open latrines of shanty-towns. The imagery sticks in one's mind, with that piercing word *fecal* and the unsettling notion of airborne waste. We thank heaven we don't breathe it, yet day and night we are assailed by toxic drivel from office, media, and motor-mouthed acquaintances. Choked on this fecal verbiage, people turn to the literary word for refreshment.

RISING ABOVE DRIVEL

Good writing differs from drivel in how much the writer has agonized over words and how little the agonizing shows. The jumpy listener who gets the *shpilkes* after three sentences of talk can pass the night with a book, never knowing how long the writer chewed each word. Communication scientists have determined—though God knows how—that in conversation eighty percent of the message is carried by body language and intonation: by wiggles and whining. Since the words count so little they are coughed up mainly as noise to fill a silence. No agonizing. If speakers *were* to struggle over each word, listeners would have to wait like psychiatrists, without the fee.

But for writers, the listener's time is always suspended until the words can gather force. One attraction of writing is this magical opportunity to rummage for the *bon mot* or perfect squelch or ultimate love call while the world stands frozen. And so the writer struggles with words, chooses them with care, arranges them to refresh the listener's mind and ear, then heaves them out and shops for better words and rearranges them for hours, days, months, until nothing can be added, excluded, or shifted to make them more refreshing, more stimulating. But when the words are uncorked in print, the effect is instantaneous: "By God, that's what *I* would have said if I'd had a year to think about it!"

That goal—a year's worth of sweat for an instant of reader refreshment—guides writers in their struggle with words and also drives them up the wall. Writers always dream of finding stories that will write themselves; they soon discover that *not one #!*@ word* has ever written itself.

TO appreciate writing as refreshment from drivel, it helps to review the nature of drivel, especially as practiced in the United States. Americans have many worthy preoccupations, but elegance in casual expression is not one of them. In mainstream America at least, the eighteenth-century art of conversation has long given way to generic expression.

"When you've heard what a Yank has to say in the first five minutes, you've heard everything he'll say the rest of his life," observes a character in Robert Stone's *A Flag for Sunrise*. Why should that be true, when Yanks enjoy unparalleled cultural diversity and freedom of speech? Because in their preoccupation with other matters, most Americans have disdained the enormous riches of a three-hundred-thousand-word language and settled on a few generic grunts in which to wrap their thoughts.

Generic words come without agonizing. They are the brand-less black-and-white packs of toilet tissue raked into the shopping basket. Chief among such words are: great, really, like, lots, neat, and unbelievable, the half-dozen that dominate our drivel.

Here is how drivelers describe a party at a friend's house: "Unbelievable, like a really great time with lots of neat people?"

Here is how drivelers describe the Renaissance: "Unbelievable, like a really great time with lots of neat people?"

As a decent word that became a generic monster, great is of special interest. From the Great White Way to the Great Divide, in every Great American Dream and on the Great Seal of the United States, the word has become the national adjective—and one drained of all force.

In use at least eight hundred years before it arrived in America, great has been hammered, twisted, and stretched to suit the Great Society's ambition and hyperbole. Its prevailing sense in Old English was "coarse, thick, stout, big." In 1839 a British traveler reported the odd Yankee usage of great as fine or splendid, as in "She's the greatest gal in the whole Union." For the last fifteen decades Americans have applied that meaning indiscriminately and obsessively. No politician can live without "the great people of this great city of the great state of . . ." Sportscasters are so free with the adjective that any athlete, fan, or marching band not labeled great must be something less than antimatter. In media coverage of Rose Bowl events, a day-long barrage of greats begins with the first parade float and ends with the last cliché of a losing coach.

Rampant use of great has deprived listeners of the freshness and varying shades of meaning available in a hundred alternatives such as astronomical, surpassing, transcendent, and thumping. One waits for listeners to rebel, even demand a moratorium on great until a richer mix of adjectives fills the air. But like other generic words, great has been so imbedded in American speech that only a writer can pry it loose. An American Heritage word-frequency analysis in 1971 showed that U.S. students were being exposed to some 4,269 *greats* in the course of their early schooling. Those students are now on the loose as managers, politicians, parents, and broadcasters, most of them spreading the word, *that* word. A few, one hopes, are dedicated writers who will struggle against the force of 4,269 repetitions to give readers some relief.

WORD BOOKS AND STYLE GUIDES

To rise above generic drivel, writers need help finding words to enrich and distinguish their work. Naturally, their base vocabulary comes from reading, study, and general experience. To find the *special* word, or simply to revel in the joy of words, they turn to a genre of reference tools loosely known as "word books."

The term often refers to collections of interesting, unusual, or problem words (Richard Lederer is one of several gifted collectors); but it can also refer to vocabulary builders, usage guides, thesauruses, word histories, and special dictionaries. Writers not only haunt the word-book sections of libraries and bookstores, but fill their own shelves with plump compendia of word and phrase. Like creatures of the night, they suck at the verbal juices to restore their anemic prose.

Here, for, example, are a few rich specimens from Plotnikov's desk collection: Roy Copperud's *American Usage and Style: The Consensus,* a summary of expert opinion on how thousands of words and phrases are best used; *Roget's Thesaurus,* not a dictionary of synonyms, but words grouped by concept; B. A. Phythian's *A Concise Dictionary of Foreign Expressions,* for *jusquauboutistes* and others; *The New York Times Everyday Reader's Dictionary of Misunderstood, Misused, and Mispronounced Words,* edited by Laurence Urdang ("this is not a succedaneum for satisfying the nympholepsy of nullifidians"); *The Book of Jargon* by Don Ethan Miller, an informed slang dictionary of twenty-five modern subcultures; Samuel Rosenbaum's *A Yiddish Word Book for English-Speaking People; Lis-*

tening to America, an upbeat word history from Stuart Berg Flexner; *The Queens' Vernacular; A Gay Lexicon* by Bruce Rodgers, one of the liveliest, funniest, and cruelest subcultural vocabularies; and *Concise Science Dictionary,* filled with the lush and whimsical words hogged by scientists—the gluons, podzols, purple-headed sneezeweeds, and nictitating membranes.

DULL words are only one element of drivel. Writers must struggle as well against clichés, circumlocutions, redundancies, euphemisms, inept metaphor, and vogue words. These Beelzebubs forever torment one's writing. How to rout them? Through daily readings in style-and-usage bibles and immersion in good writing.

Style guides are as common as Gideon Bibles, and most offer abundant examples of each problem and suggest remedies. They can be wearing unless taken a little at a time, like sermons lived with for a week. Some guides are so proscriptive they put the writer into catatonia, unable to write a word without hearing the shriek of *DON'T.* Other guides are better teachers. Strunk and White's *The Elements of Style* may be turning prissy as it ages, but ounce for ounce remains a good primer on common problems. The oft-reprinted *Words into Type* includes a compact section on "Use of Words" culled from some twenty style classics.

As to immersion in good writing—aspiring writers don't need a hellfire sermon to tell them to read. How else did they fall into this cockamamie literary pursuit except by reading? By age thirty their spines curl forward and their eyes look like pinto beans. They read classic and contemporary works: journalism and literature; mainstream and alternative writing; authors of all colors and cultures; the sacred and the profane. "Reading was the real life," says poet-playwright Ntozake Shange of her childhood. "I read all the Russians in English and the French in French and the Spaniards with the aid of dictionaries."

Writers read while others put in their daily five hours at the tube (and they watch enough tube themselves to keep up with media cant and clichés). They read to see what's already been written, and as students of writing to see how the pros flesh out rules of standard English or stretch or break them.

As writers read, they highlight words and passages they like and copy them into notebooks. They mimic the sounds. Writing begins as an outcry in the voices of others. All organisms, even viruses, learn by mimicking; why not writers? At age thirteen Joan Didion typed passages from Conrad and Hemingway to see "how sentences worked." Eventually the composite literary voice—the *sound* of writing—fills the mind like songs of angels. Beelzebubs loosen their grip.

Here, from Plotnikov's notebook, is just one small sound of writing—by Wallace Stegner in *The Spectator Bird,* as the protagonist comments on his son's "life style":

> Curt lived with his silly surfboard and his dreary girl in his raffish community of streak-haired mind-blown demigods and demigoddesses, disciples of sun and kicks. Intent upon what? Rebellions? Repudiations? Apathies? Boredoms? Fears? Panics? Terrors? Or just on Now, on the galvanic twitches of the eternal pointless present? What is that life style . . . except a substitute for life?

Stegner, who also teaches writing, notes in an interview that the work of other writers is "the only place you can learn how language is used plasticly to make new things. I don't think you can learn it as rules or anything of the kind."

Yet the so-called "rules" of grammar, style, and usage do provide the plaster for casting new forms. The rules describe how respected writers usually pattern units of expression: The sentence has a subject and a verb; the verb agrees with the subject in number; a comma separates compound sentences. This is style in its dry sense. To move from style to *a* style, as in a distinctive style, a writer adds blood, tears, and adrenalin and starts mixing. That sounds like a disgusting mess and usually is at first; but watch what happens. . . .

15

SOUNDING LIKE A WRITER

A WAY WITH STYLE

". . . we approach style in its broader meaning:
style in the sense of what is distinguished and
distinguishing."
—E. B. WHITE, "An Approach to Style," in
The Elements of Style

OH God it's the S-word, *style,* with its two literary meanings: wee style, the patterns of grammar and usage preferred by established writers, and high style, a *distinctive* way with words.

High style is a mix of wee style, self-expression, show business, and selected ambient sounds of the universe. Shooting for high style, a writer agonizes over words, then phrases, then passages to somehow imbue the whole with a show-stopping personality. Ah, but that stylish personality cannot be forced, everyone says. Forced style leads to mannerism, phony and transparent, like preppies talking jive.

Style "is the total of all the choices a writer makes concerning words and their arrangements," says Thomas Kane in *The New Oxford Guide to Writing*. Writers live in a swirl of choices, yet in agonizing over style some beginners seem trapped in a vacuum; the breath grows short, the eyes bulge. These are writers hung up on the elusive self: Who am I? What should I sound like? Rather than seek a distinctive voice from within, it may be easier to harvest the voices and sounds of one's particular environment and see how they can be shaped into pleasing forms. Individuality will come by itself.

In mastering wee style, writers can take advantage of certain stylish mentors. William Zinsser's *On Writing Well* is calm and elegant, John Simon's *Paradigm's Lost* impassioned. E. B. White's Chapter V in *The Elements of Style,* cited above, approaches the seamless prose to which all stylists aspire.

Other works are engaging if not inspiring. William Safire's *Fumblerules* teaches standard grammar and style by puckishly exaggerating their violations—"Don't use no double negatives." He stretches the gag, but manages some perky advice along the way. Karen Elizabeth Gordon has built a following with nonsensical, gothic melodrama to illustrate points of style: Use of the hyphen—"The starry-eyed sycophant prowled about the antechamber in her underwear, her catlike movements foreshadowing the self-conscious grace of her imminent and all-out attack."* In *Strictly Speaking* and *A Civil Tongue,* Edwin Newman crusades against redundancies—words and phrases added to self-sufficient expressions: *alleged* suspect: green *in color; new* innovations, *basic* fundamentals.

AUDIENCE

If high style is to stop the show, it behooves one to consider the audience. There they sit in the shadows beyond the footlights, the ultimate arbiters of style, the unknowable readers. How each reader receives a piece of writing depends on individual temperament, background, and situation. For a daunting thought, consider that some 400 million people of staggering diversity read English, and that each individual is a composite of

---

* From *The Well-Tempered Sentence; A Punctuation Handbook for the Innocent, the Eager and the Doomed.* For more instructive nonsense see Gordon's *The Transitive Vampire.*

tastes, a protean organism in evershifting environments. Writers themselves change enough in twenty-four hours to loathe everything they wrote the previous day.

Whom should one write for? (Any who simply answer "Yerself!" go back to chapter 1.) Most English style guides presuppose an audience of Western-educated Anglos who prefer their language *simple and direct*. This is a crucial audience, because it includes most English-language editors and critics. But S&D, like S&M, can get out of hand. As a reaction to Victorian excess and modern subterfuge, S&D makes sense; it guides the writer toward unencumbered and honest expression—but not to language that pleases all the people all the time.

Simple & Direct is the mantra of writing education in the United States, as well as the title of Jacques Barzun's small volume of rhetoric for writers and a score of other treatises. The theology of Simple & Direct parallels that of the Plain English campaign in the U.S., one of whose proponents (J. Y. Dayananda) offers this familiar litany:

- Prefer the shorter word to the longer one. Use simple, everyday words rather than fancy ones. Prefer verbs over nouns and adjectives. Prefer the specific word to the general.
- Write short sentences. . . . Use the active voice rather than the passive. Be a miser with compound and complex sentences and a spendthrift with simple sentences.

And so on. Simple & Direct is one style that refreshes an audience from drivel, because drivel goes all over the place and gets nowhere; but drivel also fails to satisfy because it lacks texture, ornament, and complexity, which S&D can't always provide. Peruvian author Mario Vargas Llosa told *The New York Times,* "Usually my language is restrained and invisible, but this story [*In Praise of the Stepmother*] about obsessions and rituals required a visible and sensual language that . . . conveyed music and sensations."

Good writers (and editors) know that Florid & Serpentine might be just as refreshing as Simple & Direct—even more so to audiences who enjoy Umberto Eco, John Fowles, Lawrence

Durrell, or T. Coraghessan Boyle. In Durrell's love dervishes, how enchanting is the music of his *etiolated, tenebrous,* and *ambuscades,* just as Boyle's *algolagniacs* and *cicatrices* draw one through his mazes. Such authors touch the roots of tribal storytelling—an art of spellbinding and intricately woven word pictures, not minimalism. For all the critical praise heaped on minimalists like Raymond Carver, few would linger round a storyteller's fire for such Carverisms as, "This friend of mine from work, Bud, he asked Fran and me to supper."

WHICH STYLE?

Lean & Mean, or Full & Florid? Either style can refresh, and some of the master stylists mix it up. First page, James Joyce's *A Portrait of the Artist as a Young Man:* "When you wet the bed, first it is warm, then it gets cold. His mother put on the oilsheet. That had the queer smell." Last page: "Welcome, O life! I go to encounter for the millionth time the reality of experience and to forge in the smithy of my soul the uncreated consciousness of my race."

Only the best writers can work the lean or florid styles to their extremes. Joan Didion's finger exercises, mimicking Hemingway, appear to have paid off in how she handles the muffled sounds of emotions exploding underground. Readers of *A Book of Common Prayer* will remember this chapter opening:

> In fact she had.
> Told Leonard what she was going to do.
> She was going to stay.
> Not "stay" precisely.
> "Not leave" is more like it.
> "I walked away from places all my life and I'm not going to walk away from here," is exactly what she told him.
> . . . "You have to pick the places you don't walk away from," Leonard had said that night at the airport. . . . "This isn't one of those places. It's the wrong place, Charlotte."

And was it ever. But the words—grim, fatalistic, agonized—were on target.

Like Didion, National Book Award Winner John Casey practices "an extraordinary respect for and complete control of individual words, so that every word in a sentence or paragraph carries its maximum resonance and weight." Thus praising Casey's novel *Spartina,* his Knopf editor Carol B. Janeway adds, "He has what I would call a 'Japanese' style, which is to say one in which everything extraneous or decorative is pared away to leave the beauty of maximum simplicity" (per Edwin McDowell in *The New York Times*).

Because it is simpler to pare than to build, the lean style always looks easier than it is—a misperception that has launched a thousand works of derivative and minimalist drivel. Creators of editing software consider lean style a matter of zapping enemy prose with search-and-destroy programming. But never, never are a few well-chosen words a simple matter. If the words come easily they are facile; as facile as the extended metaphors of romances and alliteration of news headlines; as facile as jokes about vice presidents; as facile as drivel. Throw them the hell out. While some style guides and software aid the paring process, *the right words have to be there first*. And what makes a word the right one—the one that lends style?

"Something that plays a part for me in every phrase and sentence is the sound," says Shirley Hazzard. "The weight of sound, the kinds of syllables that are there—these influence the way something is read." Hazzard warns against obsession with sound, citing one writer who can't bear to repeat a preposition within a paragraph. But all authors struggle to get some volume into a medium that is in fact silent and that lacks the gestures and mugging and squeals of live communications. One could view high style as language that acquires voice when it hits the reader's brain. It does so with words and patterns that trigger the strongest associations.

Jesse Jackson, at his best one of the world's most stylish and forceful communicators, can write passages that sing out on their own and others that die without his voice behind them. His address at the 1988 Democratic National Convention had some of both. A dead passage: "Common good is finding commitment to new priorities to expansion and inclusion. A commitment to a shared national campaign strategy and involvement at every level." Drivel! But listen to this one:

> Wherever you are tonight, you can make it. Hold your head high. Stick your chest out. You can make it. It gets dark sometimes, but the morning comes. Don't you surrender. Suffering breeds character, character breeds faith, in the end faith will not disappoint. . . . Keep hope alive. Keep hope alive. Keep hope alive. Keep hope alive for tomorrow night and beyond. Keep hope alive. . . .

ELEMENTS OF FORCE

High style comes in as many shades between plain and florid as there are good writers. What such writers share is the element of *force*—the ability to break through the limitations of soundless, odorless, colorless words on paper and refresh the human spirit. The best writers have something to say, of course; but they also command the literary devices that bring force to words—enough force to stimulate a motley, drivel-deadened audience of resistant readers. Here, partly in recapitulation, are some of those devices (italics mine):

Exactness—Words that pinpoint the meaning. Not "she laughed a lot in a really unbelievable way," but "she *howled*." *Howled* triggers the association. One word, and you can hear the character and see her.

Aptness or *felicity*—Words so perfectly matched to the situation they raise goose bumps. Pulitzer Prize–winner Oscar Hijuelos describes the longings of melancholy Nestor Castillo in an ill-fated affair: "By evening they were sitting out on a pier by the sea necking, the head of his penis *weeping* semen tears."

Freshness—New expressions not quite vogue, not yet tired, just in from the lingo of a subculture. Readers perked up at the first exposure to *schmoozing, rapping, jawboning, segue, campy*. Also, old words used in new combinations, such as "botanic silence" (Scott Spencer) or "primordial soup," and energetic words such as *hectored* called up to relieve fatigued terms such as nagged or bullied.

Originality—A new idiom, a new way of sounding like a writer. "A Rose is a rose is a rose is a rose" is original is original was original. Those who could create a forceful new style and sustain it are few indeed—among modern Western writers maybe Whitman, Joyce, Beckett, Hemingway, Gertrude Stein, Jack Kerouac, Gwendolyn Brooks, and a handful more. The first hazard of originality is that it baffles editors; the second, that original stylists must imitate themselves in subsequent works, competing with parodists and better imitators. A dazzling original, Kurt Vonnegut has finally worn down the critics by remaining himself. "And so it goes."

Storm, stress, and violence—Words associated with mighty forces: *tornadic, magma, maelstrom.*

Surprise—Unexpected words and loopy images that catch listeners off guard. In *Riding the Iron Rooster* Paul Theroux describes the Chinese yak as "a lovely long-haired animal, *like a cow on its way to the opera.*"

Juxtaposition—Words of different character linked for effect: "He's the pinnacle of swell" (an example also of *understatement,* with its reverse force).

Spleen—Bitchy words, like *bitchy* itself, that satisfy the human taste for vengeance and vituperation. Old curses show the way: "May your head grow in the ground like a beet." Originality helps. Yale literary critic Harold Bloom calls Marxist, feminist, deconstructionist, and new historicist critics "a rabblement of lemmings." Profanity is best used in the service of the spleen, but polite vituperation is just as nasty: "Sir, you have performed, in the most reckless and appalling manner, a grave national disservice to the hard-working people of the Free World. Your bankrupt, outrageous, and malignant actions constitute an irreversible victory for human degradation."

Concrete images—Words (you've heard it before) that readers can see, hear, taste, touch, smell. All readers are creatures of the senses and quicken to this stimuli. Feed them. Even a spread of food is an act of literary force. Bharati Mukherjee serves up this imagery to readers:

The coffee table is already laid with platters of mutton croquettes, fish chops, onion pakoras, ghugni with puris, samosas, chutneys. . . . Maya counts four kinds of sweetmeats in Corning casseroles on an end table. She looks into a see-through lid; spongy, white dumplings float in rosewater syrup. Planets contained, mysteries made visible (*The Middleman and Other Stories*).

Isabel Allende makes visible the mystery of the dying:

The smell of medicine and decay hit him in the face, a sweetish odor of sweat, dampness, confinement. . . . His mother . . . was a block of solid flesh, a monstrous pyramid of fat and rags that came to a point in a tiny bald head with a pair of eyes that were . . . blue, innocent, and surprisingly alive (*The House of the Spirits*).

And T. C. Boyle pours the horrors of Okefenokee on the reader's lap:

. . . bastion of cottonmouth, rattlesnake and leech, mother of vegetation, father of mosquito, soul of slit, the Okefenokee is the swamp archetypal, . . . fanning out over 430,000 leaf-choked acres, every last one sodden as a sponge, . . . acres of stinging, biting and boring insects, of maiden cane and gum and cypress, of palmetto, slash pine, and peat, of muck, mud, slime, and ooze . . . (*East is East*).

Muscular verbs—Verbs of action and power. Drivel relies on such limp abstractions as "to be" and "to have" in their various forms. When too many such verbs appear in writing, authors must substitute some kinetic verbs—if they can do so without spending an hour restructuring each sentence or overloading it. Sports journalists would perish without action verbs. Not "Hrbek had a home run," but "Hrbek *jerked* it out of the ball park"; not "Central was the big winner," but "Central *skewered* the competition." A writer he is not, but football announcer John Madden knows how to invent action verbs when old ones no longer cut it: "Looks like Perry *doinked* him from behind and he's not getting up!" or, "When a guy's *loadin' up* on you, you gotta *load up* on him."

Music, rhythm, and soul—Words that touch the inner ear and biological roots. Drivel is vernacular or "native speech" with the music, rhythm, and soul removed. Put those elements back, select the best, time it well—and, Honey, you got literature that *boogies down,* whether the beat is African, Caribbean, Mongol, Irish, or whatever.

From V. S. Naipaul comes these Trinidad Indian rhythms as a chap named Moti discourses on the bully Mungroo:

> He don't rob the rude and crude shopkeepers, people like himself. He frighten they give him a good dose of licks. No, he does look for nice people with nice soft heart and is them he does rob. Mungroo see you, he think you look nice, and *next* day his wife come round for two cents this and three cents that, and she forget that she ain't got no money, and if you could wait till next pay day (*A House for Mr. Biswas*).

Alice Walker creates a soulful narrator in the character of Celie:

> He beat me like he beat the children. Cept he don't never hardly beat them. He say, Celie, git the belt. The children be outside the room peeking through the cracks. It all I can do not to cry. I make myself wood. I say to myself, Celie, you a tree (*The Color Purple*).

And the music of Mary Flynn, nagging mother, animates Patrick Kavanagh's novel of dreary Irish country life:

> He'd pull a ha'penny out of cow dung with his teeth. . . . Never had a day's comfort in me whole life. Never a day that I hadn't some misfortune to contend with. . . . You be to have some curse-o'-God carry-on with her. . . . And another thing, don't be always going down the road or yous'll get a bad name (*Tarry Flynn*).

Onomatopoeia—Words whose sounds resemble what they describe. *Buzz. Rumble. Vrooom. Splat. Clang.* In modern prose,

CHRISTIAN HERALD ASSOCIATION AND ITS MINISTRIES

CHRISTIAN HERALD ASSOCIATION, founded in 1878, publishes The Christian Herald Magazine, one of the leading interdenominational religious monthlies in America. Through its wide circulation, it brings inspiring articles and the latest news of religious developments to many families. From the magazine's pages came the initiative for CHRISTIAN HERALD CHILDREN'S HOME and THE BOWERY MISSION, two individually supported not-for-profit corporations.

CHRISTIAN HERALD CHILDREN'S HOME, established in 1894, is the name for a unique and dynamic ministry to disadvantaged children, offering hope and opportunities which would not otherwise be available for reasons of poverty and neglect. The goal is to develop each child's potential and to demonstrate Christian compassion and understanding to children in need.

Mont Lawn is a permanent camp located in Bushkill, Pennsylvania. It is the focal point of a ministry which provides a healthful "vacation with a purpose" to children who without it would be confined to the streets of the city. Up to 1000 children between the ages of 7 and 11 come to Mont Lawn each year.

Christian Herald Children's Home maintains year-round contact with children by means of an *In-City Youth Ministry*. Central to its philosophy is the belief that only through sustained relationships and demonstrated concern can individual lives be truly enriched. Special emphasis is on individual guidance, spiritual and family counseling and tutoring. This follow-up ministry to inner-city children culminates for many in financial assistance toward higher education and career counseling.

THE BOWERY MISSION, located at 227 Bowery, New York City, has since 1879 been reaching out to the lost men on the Bowery, offering them what could be their last chance to rebuild their lives. Every man is fed, clothed and ministered to. Countless numbers have entered the 90-day residential rehabilitation program at the Bowery Mission. A concentrated ministry of counseling, medical care, nutrition therapy, Bible study and Gospel services awakens a man to spiritual renewal within himself.

These ministries are supported solely by the voluntary contributions of individuals and by legacies and bequests. Contributions are tax deductible. Checks should be made out either to CHRISTIAN HERALD CHILDREN'S HOME or to THE BOWERY MISSION.

Administrative Office: 40 Overlook Drive, Chappaqua, New York 10514
Telephone: (914) 769-9000

16

"I CAN'T GO ON"

WRITER'S BLOCK

"Yes for the last two weeks I have written scarcely anything. I have been idle; I have failed."
—KATHERINE MANSFIELD

"When I see a barrier I cry and curse, and then I get a ladder and climb over it."
—JOHN H. JOHNSON, JOHNSON PUBLISHING CO.

WHAT more can afflict the unfortunate wretches who pursue the literary dream? So much struggling to be a writer, croaking to sound like one, straining to soar above the crowd! And just when lift-off seems imminent—the ground turns to quicksand. The writer sinks up to the nostrils in muck. Crawling things awaken. The silent screams begin. This is the nightmare they call . . . *block.*

Block. What a nasty word, this combination of *blah* and *blechh,* this icky reminder of blocked bowels. The eversuggestible writer has only to hear the word to crumple like Woody Allen when someone says "castration."

WORD BLOCK

Discussions of writer's block usually concern the flow of words and how to get words flowing again when the brain seems to shut down. As if a writer's brain could ever shut down or up for more than five seconds. What the brain does is slip away from drudgery and into the writer's preferred pastime, daydreaming. Daydreaming inspires a literary effort and previews its glorious rewards, but it doesn't do the coal-faced labor of research, organization, drafting, and revising. No writer descends willingly to those mines, where words are hacked one by one from the blackness. Facing that dusty pit feels very much like block, whatever else it might be.

Maddening and debilitating, the condition strikes even the most prolific writers. Charles Dickens described his block in terms of "prowling about the rooms, sitting down, getting up, stirring the fire, looking out of the window, tearing my hair, sitting down to write, writing nothing, writing something and tearing it up. . . ." But Dickens, if only to pay his debts, got himself going again. So do most blocked writers, some by riding it out, others by heeding the advice of others. Author Barry Hannah views the condition simply as one more experience to file away. "I had a terrible block against writing this summer," he said in an interview, "and even that I'll look at as subject matter."

Every communications pundit can tell others how to beat word block: Just get *something* down, anything the brain spews out. You can shape and prune later, in revisions and rewrites. Passion first, control second. Shout first, write second. Henriette Anne Klauser splits the artist's mind in *Writing on Both Sides of the Brain: Breakthrough Techniques for People Who Write*. The brain's right hemisphere creates, the left one edits. Play first, then work, she advises; blockage comes from trying to do both at once. (And from thinking about cerebral hemispheres at war.)

FLEDGLING writers want to pump greatness from the moment they have a title in mind. They center that glorious title—
Coming of Age in Kankakee

—skip a space, and enter their byline. They wrestle with an opening line. "This is the untold story of . . ." They watch the blinking cursor. The story dissolves into scenarios of their own fame. Soon they can hear the echoes from posterity—*"It was to be her greatest work"*—when in truth it was to be her biggest block until she gave up writing and went into real estate. Indeed, William Zinsser describes how aspiring writers set out "to commit an act of literature," an impossible task. Journalism-trained authors like Isabel Allende know better. "I don't think of literature as an end in itself," she says. "It's just a way of communicating something."

Reckless bravado may work for some in launching a project, particularly dramatists who thrive on the theatrical flourish. Lanford Wilson, after winning the Pulitzer, is said to have begun a subsequent work with the heading: "THIS IS THE NEXT PLAY BY LAST YEAR'S PULITZER PRIZE–WINNING LANFORD WILSON." Most writers would rise to this challenge with about nine years of creative paralysis.

For the average writer facing a slow start or a temporary block, here are the more conventional approaches to making the words flow again:

- Do a "freewrite" of unedited, unpublishable banter on your topic. Write fast. Try not to stop. Get it down.
- Write yourself a newsy letter or telegram covering the high points; don't bother with beginnings, transitions, or endings but just write chunks that turn you on.
- Begin thusly: "What I really want to say is . . ." or "I would like to write about . . ."
- Begin a difficult passage with a question you want it to answer. Answer the question. Then delete the question itself.
- End the day's writing in midstream, with a passage that's easy to continue rather than with a sealed-off unit.
- Don't get hung up on a word. Write a strings of x's and finish the sentence. Later, perhaps as you walk around the block, the xxxxx word will come to you.
- You're blocked because you're tired and benumbed. Get away

from your desk. Get some rest. Shorten your writing sessions.

- You're blocked because you hate the particular project. Cut your losses by backing out. Spend the time you've gained on jobs you can live with.

- You're blocked because you're disgusted with the pages you've written thus far. Don't look at them. Brian Aldiss, who writes a novel and several short stories each year, says he places completed pages face down and won't backtrack until the first draft is completed. This way he sustains the necessary "vision" and "creative glow." Later, "creative hope mixed with critical discontent" carries him through the rewrites.

- You're blocked because you're distracted. Clear your desk of clutter. Write early in the morning, before the world's distractions begin. Or get out of the house altogether if you can find a work space elsewhere. For San Francisco writer Diane Johnson, "home is home and writing is work." (Better-heeled than most, Johnson chose as her workplace Villa Serbelloni, a historic mansion overlooking Lake Como in Northern Italy.)

- You're blocked not because your mind is blank, but because it's overloaded with all the good ideas that have percolated during the day. Now, as you start to write, they want to pour out all at once and seem to evaporate. If you've written them down, as you must, take one idea at a time and work it through. Keep a notepad handy (on or off screen) even as you write; record the new ideas that shoot by and tend to derail you and deal with them later.

- You're blocked because it's getting you some attention; because you (or someone close to you) romanticize artistic failure and self-destruction. You and your enablers must grow up. Kate Braverman recalls a time when, "for me, art required certain elements of self-destruction. Becoming a mother was the turning point. Then health and sanity began to have the allure that sickness had had."

- You're blocked because you've discovered a problem in premise or structure or some other fundamental aspect that can't be resolved. Annie Dillard's advice: "Every book has an intrinsic impossibility, which its writer discovers as soon as his first excitement dwindles." Accept it and keep writing, she says. Like with a dying friend, you sit up with your book and hold its hand and hope it gets better. Braverman agrees. "Always finish the failure—you'll never know when there's going to be a mutation."

An Idea from the Business World

The business world hates leaving anything to chance, including creativity. Blocked creativity is money lost. So enter Edward de Bono, a learned Brit who turned a technique he calls "lateral thinking" into a worldwide management-training industry. In *Lateral Thinking for Management,* one of his avalanche of books, de Bono offers a process of breaking away from the cognitive patterns ("vertical thinking") people tend to use in solving problems. Such patterns produce blah solutions or dead ends. Lateral thinking gets away from *choosing* the next logical step; it invites completely irrelevant ideas to "intrude" on the continuity of patterned thinking. From these intrusions come disconnected, off-the-wall ideas that seem unrelated to the problem until—bong!—they generate creative and exceptional solutions. Lateral thinking is akin to what writers call intuitive flashes and insights, but more systematic.

For example, de Bono uses the "random word" exercise to introduce discontinuity into patterned thinking. You are blocked. Every idea follows trite patterns. Now, open a dictionary anywhere; the first noun defined on the page (no cheating!) is your unblocking word. Play with all its meanings for about three minutes and see what wild, unchosen connections they might have to your original problem. In de Bono's example, the problem is finding better incentives for a sales force, and the word *gong* pops up. Instead of the traditional incentives, he begins thinking of gonglike proclamations of top performances, loud and brief incentives such as short-term cash prizes, and so on. If de Bono were struggling to create a fictional salesman, the process might be something like: *Gong*—Short, punchy. A son named Bong . . . Bing . . . Biff! *Gong*—Percussion . . . crash . . . car crash . . . suicide . . . car crash suicide and insurance for the family!

*   *   *

THERE are whole treatises on writer's block, including one from the never-blocked advice factory called Writer's Digest. A Wisconsin workshop offers "Twelve Ways to Smash Block" with the cheesy promise, "You never need suffer from writer's block or writer's blank again."

Advice is always easy to give. Jay Parini's essay, "The More They Write, the More They Write," quotes Iris Murdoch and Stephen King, who knock out about a half million words a year between them. "I just keep writing," says Murdoch when asked about being stuck. "I just flail away at the thing," says King. One's own block, however, feels less like being "stuck" than like clinical depression, which it sometimes is. This is the true quicksand, and the harder one tries to climb out the deeper one sinks. Advising severely blocked writers to "write themselves a letter" is like telling depressives to cheer up by joining clubs.

For the big blocks, each writer must find a way to reverse the negative psychic energy that has built up. For Carson McCullers, blocking on *A Member of the Wedding* at the Yaddo writer's retreat, it was lying stomach-down on the ground and beating her fists on the manuscript and calling "Mother! Mother!" Cry and curse, then find the ladder that John H. Johnson talks about (see head of chapter). Use no polite method; borrow the techniques of sports and combat heroes. Pro football coach Mike Ditka developed a unique method of clearing his mind on the sidelines. As sportscaster John Madden described it: "Now you see, you bend over. You put both hands on your knees. And you spit. And good ideas come."

SPITTING won't be necessary in most situations. Ordinary word blockage is the very toil of writing. Some of it results from the contradictions of creating literature, what Harold Bloom calls "achieved anxiety" and what Plotnikov has described as "controlled crying." Always the questions, Is it too much? Not enough? Everything must be in balance, in harmony, but something must tip the scale. The whole writing business is a pretzel of paradoxes, from the philosophical to the technical levels. These are some of the mixed messages that tie writers in knots:

- Just write for yourself; *but* write to sell.
- Just get it down, even if it stinks; *but* don't settle for anything that displeases you.
- Be clever and brilliant; *but* don't show off.
- Avoid big words; *but* don't use too many little words.
- Write with style; *but* don't let style call attention to itself.
- Write something fresh and surprising; *but* don't go off the deep end.
- Tell it as it is; *but* don't offend the wrong people or expose yourself to libel, invasion of privacy, or obscenity.
- Know your subject, write about what you know; *but* don't overwhelm the reader with detail.
- Use forceful words; *but* not too forceful for the thoughts delivered.
- Be sincere; *but* remember Oscar Wilde's admonition that all bad poetry is sincere.
- Know where you're going; *but* don't be predictable.

How do writers handle these conflicts? They don't—not while they compose or they would block until they turned to quartz. In the revision stages they introduce the checks and balances. If an editor insists on further revisions there will likely be more blocks, but at least with some insensitive swine to blame it on.

MOTIVATIONAL BLOCK

Often writers who have tasted some success find themselves unable to face the very idea of writing again. As much as they want to *be* writers, they feel loss of confidence, purpose, and inspiration. Every idea seems to stink because:

- it has already been done;
- other writers know more about it;
- it will be out of date by the time it gets into print.

And so they pace their writing cages wondering, "Why the #@! should I sacrifice another three or four years to a redundant, inadequate, and obsolete pile of uninspired words." It's a good question.

THE week of his birthday in October 1990, Arthur Plotnikov had a dream, only it wasn't a dream. Transported to an unfamiliar city that smelled of *Rippchen mit Kraut,* he was soon caught up among thousands of strangers flowing toward a complex of interconnected white buildings. The strangers, darkly attired and speaking in a mix of tongues, moved through bright lobbies and along walkways and up steep escalators until they reached the mouths of darker interior spaces and were consumed twenty, fifty, a hundred at a time.

Plotnikov moved with them and found himself in the belly of the *Frankfurter Buchmesse,* Germany's international Frankfurt Book Fair—swallowed up for a week with armies of publishing personnel presenting their latest books, some *three hundred eighty thousand* latest books in all.

In the dream that wasn't a dream, Plotnikov was now working in book publishing, assigned by his organization to generate some international business at Frankfurt. He found his stall— No. 936, Floor 2, Hall 4—among thousands arranged in two dozen stadium-sized grids. He got through his business as a publisher. But the three hundred eighty thousand titles overwhelmed Plotnikov the writer. Still trying to make a few ripples of his own, he felt himself drowning in the vast *messe* of books already out there.

Here was evidence to assure even the most intrepid writer that everything of possible human interest had been written and rewritten to death, and that any further utterances were sure to be redundant, unnecessary, and at best, ignored. Plotnikov was working on a book for writers, and, as fate would have it, three stalls away stood a library of Writer's Digest books, enough instructional cream cheese to spread across the world.

Plotnikov had already suffered the literary bends at U.S. book fairs, under tidal waves of up to fifty-five thousand new books each year. The 1990 American Booksellers Association show was enough to intimidate even Kirk Douglas, destroyer of lethal forces on the big screen. But as a writer, "If I had come [to ABA] and seen all these thousands of books, I would never have written mine," he told a reporter.

Writers who enter even a well-stocked bookstore know the gloom of arriving twenty centuries late on the stage of self-expression. But with only ten to fifty thousand volumes, bookstores can leave the impression that something yet remains to be said. Frankfurt dispels any such notion.

Then how do writers go on, knowing they can never say anything new? Sliding into such despair periodically, Plotnikov does what any writer must do: He grasps at anything that can help keep nose above quicksand for another week. He hopes that something will come along to pull him out—a sudden inspiration, a run of good material, a niche that reveals itself. Meanwhile, if he can just keep treading . . .

Three weeks after returning from Frankfurt, Plotnikov found a straw to grasp in a *New York Times* interview with Camilo José Cela, winner of the 1989 Nobel Prize in Literature. Author of eleven novels and numerous other works, Cela said he needed only to look around and not invent anything new to keep writing. He named his themes: "love, life, death, sickness, misery, the same as everywhere else." Then he added (italics mine): *"I think it was Proust who said that everything has already been said but, since no one pays attention, it has to be repeated every morning."*

Can anyone disagree with Cela and Proust, knowing that the world's four hundred thousand new titles in 1990 followed a similar number in 1989? How much new could have been said? Or consider just one 1990 U.S. bestseller, Robert Fulghum's *All I Really Need to Know I Learned in Kindergarten*. If even the lessons of bloody kindergarten bear repeating, then nothing is redundant. More proof? Adjacent to the Cela interview appeared a review of *Sleeping Arrangements*, Laura Cunningham's memoir of growing up in New York in the fifties. No more redundant theme haunts New York publishing offices, yet one more writer tried a variation, and the *Times* adored it.

In his first year as a book publisher, Plotnikov found other straws to grasp. He learned that publishers have no hesitation repeating what's been said, if it will sell again. They may long for something fresh; but since they can't indulge in publisher's block while waiting, they must publish the best works at hand—mainly imitations of previous successes. But publishers don't buy the Proustian rationale that "no one pays attention" to previous works; instead, this is how decisions are made to publish redundant titles—say, another self-help book—when the publishing committee meets in most trade houses:

"It's in the *best tradition* of self-help literature, Tom."

"It's been said before, Bob, but *not by a brand-name author.*"

"There are four million people who read this stuff, Barbara, and *they buy books.*"

"The ideas are the same, Doris, *but times have changed.*"

"Don't forget, Roger, there's a generation of people coming up *who haven't heard it.*"

"Sure it's been published, Frank, but *not by us.*"

"It's been said all right, Joni, *but marketed all wrong.*"

Repeat this scenario in eighty-five hundred publishing houses, and you have half a million books published every year rather than a fifth that many. Writers can take heart at least from the number of authors published, even as they despair at the overcrowded shelves. Still, fear of redundancy is ever with writers; it is the first obstacle to creative output, one that paralyzes new as well as seasoned writers.

To Cela and others, agonizing over originality is a waste of time; only talent, careful observation, and patience matter. Any theme will do for the general reading public, though a writer's temperament may be more suited to one subject than another. Barbara Kingsolver (*Animal Dreams*) says, "The only authentic and moving fiction you can write is about the things that are the most urgent to you and worth disturbing the universe over." Not every writer can generate these cosmic disturbances book after book. Irving Wallace was more practical; he believed choice of subject ". . . has to do with . . . *sensing* what you might be interested in and what future readers might be interested in some years from now."

Expect a certain amount of panic and fear wrestling with these considerations. What *is* urgent to me? Will *anyone* be interested when my work appears some years from now (or in some six months to a year, for magazine writers)? While any theme might do, any subject might not, however great one's talent for bringing it to life. Publishing has its fashions, discernible through observation of the products themselves, the reviewing media, and book-trade media such as *Publishers Weekly*. Every subject will recycle eventually; but if nine submarine thrillers have surfaced in the last two years it might be wise to lower periscope for a while.

WHEN writers finally seize a subject that inspires them, they face Motivational Fear No. 2: that other writers know more about the subject than they. How can I write a war novel if I've never been in a war? How can I write a medical or legal thriller when I've been teaching second grade my whole career?

Writing students advised to "write what ya know about" may feel restricted to parochial settings. But literary history abounds with examples of writers who braved unknown territory. Every American Lit major learns that Stephen Crane had never been near a war when he wrote his Civil War masterpiece, *The Red Badge of Courage*. The task is not to know a subject firsthand, but to be a step ahead of the readers.

Even in nonfiction one needn't be intimidated by the subject masters. Someone who knows everything about Alaska would be a bore; better to read John McPhee, who informed himself enough to bring his sharp eye and storytelling skills to the subject. The outside observer is usually the better reporter than the inside "expert" trapped in meaningless detail and internal distortions, and probably burned out.

In fiction, what counts is not expertise at all, but the illusion of expertise. All art is illusion, accomplished with stage effects that seem more real than reality. With enough accurate detail to stay ahead of the reader, the fiction writer can tackle any subject, including those that seem the province of specialized writers. Some genres have certain conventions that need attention; but the rest is energy, imagination, and a way with words.

As for Motivational Fear No. 3—your book will be out of date by the time it's published—that's properly a publisher's worry, and publishers know three secrets about out-of-date books: (1) If they're the latest out-of-date book on the shelves they're still the latest word; (2) it takes a long time—far longer than writers realize—for subjects to go stale throughout the world; and (3) except for technical manuals, books hold their readership by force of theme and style rather than reference value. Why did millions continue to read John le Carré's Cold War novels after the Berlin Wall came down in 1989? Because a masterful style dates more slowly than politics.

Though much of the technical matter in Plotnikov's *Elements of Editing* became dated a year or two after publication, the unrevised book was still selling briskly after almost a decade. Plotnikov offered to revise on several occasions, but the publishers saw no advantage in it. Nor, apparently, did readers, who kept writing kind letters. Plotnikov wondered if the book had acquired a certain quaintness, like *The Elements of Style*. Eventually he stopped offering to revise and stopped worrying about the durability of his next works. One could only update to the last day of reading proofs; after that, one worried about other matters—such as money.

17

WRITING FOR A LIVING

You Die

"Nothing is more real than nothing."
—Samuel Beckett

Beckett's attachment to nothingness prepared him for the economics of authorship. Writers who expect nothing as the wages of the literary pursuit will spare themselves endless humiliation and perhaps enjoy an occasional surprise. One can cheer Samuel Johnson's eighteenth-century quip, "No man but a blockhead ever wrote, except for money"—and then jump out the window. Where, Dr. Johnson, is the money in a shrinking market glutted with talent? Why on top of everything else, Dr. Johnson, must a nonselling author suffer the indignities of duncehood?

Dr. Johnson's advice needs work. Maybe "No person but a blockhead ever wrote a refrigerator manual except for money," or "only blockheads write for free when they can get paid." Otherwise, it's *okay* to write for pennies or even nothing because that's what half the world's authors do.

A much-quoted Columbia University survey found that working writers averaged about $4.90 an hour in 1979. Today many writers would appreciate even less. If the mean wage is still $4.90 it's only thanks to the Stephen Kings, Jean Auels, and Tom Clancys: For every three hotshots making $5 million a year, figure 1,470 hopefuls earning nothing.

True, a number of authors earn more than nothing and less than millions. In the Columbia survey the median income of twenty-two hundred published authors was $4,775. (In 1990 the Author's Guild put it at about $8,000). The survey also found 28 percent of working writers earning $20,000 or more per year. Twenty grand sounds like something until the costs of professional writing are deducted: $3,000 for agent, $3,400 in income taxes, $2,000 in Social Security and self-employment tax, $2,500 in medical insurance, $2,500 for word processing and fax equipment, $1,500 for writing space, $1,200 for permissions, $1,200 for indexing and other editorial services, and $1,500 in miscellaneous supplies, travel, and utilities—leaving twenty bucks a week for pet and author food.

NUMBERS THAT DREAMS ARE MADE ON

Although some freelancers sneak by with assignments from special-interest media or commercial clients, nothing and next to nothing are the real wages of most literary authors. Only blockheads think otherwise as they moon over the spectacular earnings of name authors and occasional "discoveries." For three decades, Plotnikov has been looking at the economics of writing from every angle outside and inside the publishing industry—and is he ever found mooning over the inflated earnings of a few fortunate freaks?

Constantly.

Because that's what writers do and always have done: Earn little numbers, fuss about them, and moon over the big numbers. Big numbers are intoxicating. They are the stuff of greed and envy, the writer's favorites. Let us wallow in juicy numbers circa 1990:

- *The take:* For all their caterwauling about "slumps," U.S. publishers netted some $15.5 billion in annual book sales. General adult and juvenile book sales alone amounted to some $5 billion. Pretax profits totaled $1.7 billion. Estimated 1994 consumer expenditures on books: $27 billion.
- *The pot:* Annual revenues of the biggest U.S. publishers went something like this: Simon & Schuster, $1.3 billion; Time Publishing Group, $1.1 billion; HarperCollins, $1.1 billion; Reader's Digest Books, $944 million; Random House, $850 million. Another six publishers earned $500 million or more. Royalties paid by all publishers totaled more than $1.5 billion.
- *The deals:* A few hot players reportedly received these advances against earnings: Danielle Steel, $60 million for her next five novels; Stephen King, $40 million for his next four books; Jean Auel, $27 million for three books; Ken Follett, $12.3 million for two thrillers; Barbara Taylor Bradford, $9 million for her next three sagas; Len Deighton, $8 million for four books; Tom Wolfe, $7 million for the book after *Bonfire,* plus $1.5 million in foreign rights; Philip Roth (after switching to a larger, less "literary" house), $1.8 million for three novels; and Amy Tan, $1.7 million merely for paperback rights to her first novel. And speaking of merelys, Ken Follett banked $2.7 million merely for German, Italian, and Spanish rights to his unwritten duo.

Every few months brings another deal that makes the previous megamillions look like beggars' wages. Fueling the cycle are publishers like Joni Evans, who at Simon & Schuster and later at Random House liked to say, "When I have to have it, I have to have it," and superagents like Mort Janklow and Andrew Wylie who convince competing publishers they do indeed have to have it at any price.

- In Hollywood, Joe Esterhaus commands up to $3 million per screenplay. Shane Black got $1.7 million for his next script after the forgettable *Lethal Weapon.*

- Comedy writer Matt Williams, creator of television's *Roseanne,* signed a three-year, $10 million contract with Disney to create more comedies.
- An hour-long script for series like *Hill Street Blues* earns a minimum of about $20,000. Writers of hit comedy series can earn about $1.5 million.
- "The going rate for nonfiction now with a good idea and an author with a track record is $100,000," editor Dan Frank told *Publishers Weekly.*
- Television rights to the sequel to *Gone With the Wind* sold for a record $8 million. Author Alexandra Ripley had already made millions from her Warner Books advance and sales of foreign rights.

Oh, those lovely big numbers—some as fat as lottery prizes but with better-looking odds. About fifty writers are said to command seven-figure advances or fees in the United States. And how many writers are out there? Let's see: U.S. statistics show eighty-two thousand "authors" who are "employed," whatever that means. Nearly one hundred eight thousand people have enrolled in the Writer's Institute managed by World Innovators. Literary agent Scott Meredith maintains a database of one hundred eighty-two thousand professional and aspiring writers. *Writer's Digest* claims a circulation of two hundred sixty-nine thousand. Is it fair to say some half million Americans are pecking away at a hit screenplay or best-seller? If so, then fifty out of five hundred thousand or one in ten thousand will earn a million-plus!

One wrinkle: In the weekly lottery every ticket has an equal chance; in the literary sweepstakes only the thoroughbreds have a real shot. The rest can send a hundred manuscripts a day and it won't better the odds. You become a thoroughbred, *maybe,* after some twenty years of observation, study, research, writing, rewriting, rejection, development, writing, and rewriting; after jumping after any small exposure; after pounding at agency doors and grubbing at editors' feet and writing and rewriting under the guidance of career-shapers; after publishing modestly and promoting madly—only then are you *entered* in the grand prize sweepstakes along with fifty thousand qualified authors who, like you, have paid their dues, goosed their agents, and stand on the brink of their breakaway books.

So much for mooning over big numbers. In the literary pursuit, writing is mainly about little numbers—some of them so small as to be amusing.

"IT'S NOT THE MONEY . . ."

According to common wisdom, when people say "It's not the money, it's the principle"—it's the money. With the average writer, however, it's the principle. It has to be. The money is pure degradation. Even when earning a grand a week as an editor, Plotnikov the writer would fight like a hussar for $35 due from a freelance sale. It was the principle. Call it validation as a writer, call it beating every lousy buck out of the bastards; it was worth doing.

For freelance writers, rates have barely changed in the last twenty-five years and probably won't go much higher in the new millennium. The average newspaper piece earns about $50 to $100; a magazine feature, between $50 and $400. A short story—outside the *Atlantic Monthly, The New Yorker,* and a few other literary lotteries—from nothing to $150. Discounting the blockbusters, the average book contract will earn some $3,000 to $10,000 for three or four years' work. Many books outside trade (general-interest) publishing earn their author less than a thousand overall.

Careful readers will recall that Plotnikov, in his sex-novel days, wrote a nonfiction paperback called *Fetishism in Modern Man* for a flat fee of $1,500. Not a great deal of money today, but it was 1965 and he was only starting out. Besides, *Fetishism* was something less than the definitive study of bloomer fixation. Twenty years later Plotnikov did write a definitive work, a painstakingly researched biography of Jacob Shallus (1750–1796), elusive calligrapher of the original Constitution. Published by the National Archives on the Constitution's two hundredth birthday, the work received national attention and a book award for the Archives. It sold well and established itself in the body of Constitutional lore. Plotnikov's earnings: a $1,500 flat fee. He should have stuck to bloomers.

For a dash of irony, consider the pay scales of certain journals about money. Figure that an average magazine article represents at least two weeks' labor in forethought, research, writing, revising, and querying. The 1990 *Writers Market* reports that *Money World,* with a circulation of two hundred thousand, offers $20 for assigned articles—and for this staggering remuneration writers must wait until a month after the article is published. *Business Age,* circulation one hundred-ninety thousand, coughs up $50 to $250 for articles. *Money Makers,* circulation one hundred sixty-five thousand, pays 20 cents a word, or $400 for a two-thousand-word article. Even *Barron's,* which circulates about three hundred thousand copies, pays as little as $500 for the two weeks' work.

No one forces people to be writers, but enough talented people insist on doing it so that publishers are never in short supply. Major book publishers claim to receive some five to ten thousand unsolicited manuscripts for every one they accept, if they accept any. In a recent survey, 338 magazine editors reported a total of 409,203 unsolicited manuscripts crowding through their transoms. *Redbook* tells rejected short-story writers they were among twenty-thousand losers this year, "but keep trying!" About three hundred thousand scripts and treatments hit Hollywood every year, according to industry analysts. One newspaper syndicate (Creators) received seven thousand submissions in 1989 and used four.

This is called a buyer's market, and the writing business has always been one. In seventeenth-century England, John Milton agreed to a maximum royalty of twenty pounds for *Paradise Lost* and earned about seventeen. Three centuries later the terms are even worse for epic poetry, and those who don't like it can stand aside and let the line through. Of the five thousand markets listed in *The International Directory of Little Magazines and Small Presses,* 1990–1991, Lost Roads Publishers offers one of the most generous deals for a book-length poem: $300 total plus 25 copies. Grab it!

Although publishers enjoy a buyer's market for the average

manuscript, they find themselves in high-stakes bidding wars for the services of bona fide blockbuster authors. The huge advances paid the Kings and Clancys feed the myth of author as valued commodity—the treasured goose that lays the golden egg. The average author, however, is to publishing as egg-laying hens are to the baking industry. Bakers need the eggs, but there are plenty around. The hens, for all their clucking, are long forgotten by the time their output is processed. Money is poured into product management, marketing, sales, and distribution. At the end, the egg is unrecognizable and the hen virtually nonexistent. Who even remembers which came first, the chicken, the egg, or the doughnut? Who worries about the chicken feed?

This scenario is repeated every day in the publishing industry, where overworked editors handle incoming manuscripts like candlers checking eggs for blood clots. Raw product. Reject or produce. Clean it up. Package it. Get it out there. Process is paramount. Content secondary. Creator sloughed off like a by-product until someone—author or agent—starts screaming. Sometimes the author has a role in promotion, a little more clucking—then back to the henhouse.

In newspaper and magazine publishing, once a freelance manuscript is in production the author tends to become a nonentity. Briefly, when the byline is set in type, the author is remembered—then forgotten with a vengeance as the next production cycle begins. Paying writers never advance the careers of editors, so they develop other priorities. Payments are assigned to an administrative assistant who leaves early on Fridays and calls in sick on Mondays.

The surplus of writers and usual cash problems of publishers give rise to hideous payment patterns. Hundreds of magazines still pay "on publication," which can be a year after acceptance if anyone remembers to voucher so small a check. Under most book contracts, publishers have the right to pay nothing—not a penny—if the delivered manuscript is not "satisfactory" according to their own subjective and evershifting criteria (see next chapter). Subsidiary earnings such as book club revenues can be held months before being shared with authors and have a way of being forgotten altogether.

On the side of publishers, it could be argued that they are victims of a narrow-margin industry with a diminishing and unpredictable market; that they are understaffed and over-worked, impoverished themselves by slow payers, shackled by antiquated trade practices, bullied by corporate accountants, and beset by rising costs and unrealistic expectations—but let the publishers argue all that. This is a writers' book.

DUNNING FOR FUN AND PROFIT

To get paid, authors must often honk relentlessly. The honking becomes a second form of creative writing—a controlled outcry that grows less controlled with each dunning letter. Writers become mini–collection agencies, progressing from playful re-minders to menacing threats: *" . . . and my attorney shall seek pu-nitive damages of a magnitude to deter every scoundrel in your brotherhood of evil. . . ."* One tries to balance the desire to be paid with the need to maintain a business relationship, but even-tually one succumbs to pure banshee outrage and sends letters that are passed around the office and turned over to the FBI.

Inside Books, "The Bestseller Magazine," inspired writer Alan Caruba to send creative letters to editors and other writers around the nation urging them to investigate what he called an "egregious and exploitative" failure to pay for articles. Caruba said he had logged twenty years as a published writer and re-viewer and "never encountered such a cancerous situation."

Even such freelance pros aren't immune to lousy payers, but they do develop protective techniques. Among the tips they and Plotnikov pass along (for nonfiction article writers) are these:

- Submit nothing more than brief light features without query-ing first.
- Know what an editor wants and when. Don't rely on pub-lished wish-lists; a week after they appear the editors are swamped with responses. Study the publication. Contact the articles editor by phone, citing your track record in a few words and asking what sort of material is needed for a theme or show issue or to reach a neglected segment of the reader-

ship—these are the toughest acquisitions for editors. Many editors will say, "Sorry, you have to know this field." In response, cite a recent article in the magazine that you could have done better and say why. Be concise and upbeat.

- Find out the pay range *right now.* Don't wait for a nauseating surprise months after acceptance.
- Follow up in writing, then again by phone or fax. Your own fax might be a good investment. Try a few queries. Send a clip now and then, not all at once, and never an ancient one.
- Send the same query to as many publications as might respond, but don't write the same piece for more than one.
- If possible, write only on assignment for a predetermined fee and necessary expenses. Write "on speculation" only if you love doing the piece and have other markets willing to look at it.
- Try to get an agreement in writing, although, unbelievably, some publications don't provide one. Sometimes the terms appear on the back of the check; in endorsing it, you sign over most rights. If no contract is provided, write the editor a note spelling out the terms as you understand them and keep a copy. Try to include in your terms a "kill fee," what you are paid if the article is written as assigned but "killed" before publication. About one out of three magazines pay kill fees, ranging from 10 to 50 percent of the full fee and averaging about 30 percent.
- Don't waste time seeking an agent for magazine sales. Most agents won't bother even for their book clients, and for non-fiction articles agents don't add much clout in the average editorial office. The advice they offer on complicated book contracts wouldn't apply to magazine agreements, which are brief and to the point.
- Magazines don't like to negotiate anything other than fee; but a major article with enduring value deserves better terms than those usually offered. Some magazines want "work-for-hire" arrangements or their equivalent in which the writer surrenders all rights for a fixed fee. Resist by selling specific and limited rights (e.g., "onetime world serial rights," meaning use in the printed magazine for one issue circulated throughout the

world) unless the fee is increased to your satisfaction. Magazines want free rights to reuse the article in their own anthologies or electronic databases. Try for the onetime print rights, with 50 percent of the gross proceeds from all other uses. With magazines that prefer to pay on publication, fight like hell for payment on acceptance. Go for a copyright notice in your name if you expect to go hustling additional uses of the article. Otherwise, let the magazine hold and sell rights and pay you a percentage, with an option for rights to return to you on request. Reprint sales usually amount to peanuts anyway.

- It may be a buyer's market, but if you think you're just what the editor needs and you deliver like a pro, ask for another 25 percent or so. Editors are often prepared to bargain upward a few dollars. And what does it mean to deliver like a pro? A pro *never* misses a deadline, follows the assignment to the letter, submits clean copy in the format requested, researches facts and backs up attributions, and writes with *brio,* not breezy padding. A pro attends to revisions quickly. In short, a pro makes it so easy for editors their grey hairs revert to natural color.

- Submit two copies of a businesslike invoice with the manuscript and keep a copy for tracking. Find out who handles payments and make a personal contact with them when necessary.

As a magazine editor, Plotnikov paid what the market would bear. Like most editors he worked with a bottom-line budget, in which most big expenses—such as overhead and postal costs—are outside the editor's control. Author payments offer one of the few controllable expenses in a publishing budget when production and distribution costs explode. Plotnikov made no author rich, but he made no one wait till the Second Coming to see their check. He reported inside eight weeks and paid on acceptance. Editors who are writers themselves usually have that much compassion. They know that at the other end of a manuscript is a poor live thing with its beak open and skinny neck stretched high. They can hear the cheep, cheeping (or is it "Cheap! Cheap!"?), and they feed it what they can.

18

CONTRACTS THAT KILL

THE BOOK DEAL AND BEYOND

"Writers are like mushrooms: 'They're fed a lot
of horseshit and kept in the dark.' "
—AGENT RICHARD CURTIS QUOTING A CLIENT

"IN what other business," writers wail as they sign their book contracts, "do you agree to take your product off the market for a year and customize it for one fickle buyer—all for nothing if the buyer isn't satisfied?"

"In what other business," publishers groan as they countersign, "do you hand out interest-free loans on a high-risk venture that takes three, four, five years to pay off, if ever?"

In what business is there a document more perverse than a book contract, where the anxieties of humanists meet the phobias of accountants and lawyers? Where one hand gives (". . . the Publisher shall pay to the Author a royalty on the retail price of every copy sold by the Publisher . . .") while the other takes (er, make that the lesser *invoice* price, subtract actual returned copies and a reserve against expected returns, and take away any advances that weren't fully earned on any other books we published by this jerk).

Some contracts read like stock landlord-tenant agreements, always good for a laugh with their one-sidedness. The publisher starts out with just about all rights except the right to be sued, kindly passed to the author. Pages of boilerplate protect the publisher from the "what-ifs" of disappointing revisions, a delinquent author, competing works by the same author, changing trends, market shifts, legal problems, wars, and acts of God.

The author usually retains copyright but agrees to license all meaningful rights for the lifetime of the book in return for (1) getting the book published and (2) a percentage of sales revenues. The author also agrees to deadlines for finishing the work, frequency of royalty payments (commonly twice a year), and maximum time between delivery of an acceptable manuscript and publication (usually eighteen months). Beyond these specifics, the publisher may "publish the work in such style and manner, under such imprint and at such price as it deems suitable," says the usual boilerplate.

When you, the eager author, sign a contract, your editor may muse about big printings in a swell hardcover edition with gold-foil dustjacket and heavy promotion, but these goodies aren't put in writing. Two years later, with the editor long gone and running a bookstore in Aspen, "suitable" publication turns out to be a quiet off-season release of a measly paper edition. There's nothing you can do about it and not much you can find out. No one will tell you the print run or, if any, the marketing budget. Some royalty statements may allude to subsidiary sales, but not always and never clearly. Exactly who bought what when and for how much and under what terms remain the great unknowables.

SHORT-LIVED EUPHORIA

And yet, for all these eventualities the arrival of a writer's first contract is a stirring event. What can compare to the moment when you, the struggling writer, receive from a bona fide publisher those legal-size pages validating the deal? By God, it's a literary sacrament. You have actually "gone to contract" after months of cat-and-mousing with an editor who had to be convinced and who had to convince an editorial group of your publishability.

Only in later days do you understand what's in the contract and how little negotiating room you have as a no-name author, even with an agent. The cat's got the mouse in her jaws, and in most cases the mouse does the natural thing: Goes limp and accepts the publisher's meager terms.

Among university and professional publishers, compensation can be as meager as 5 percent of royalties after enough copies are sold to recoup the publisher's investment. In a normal contract authors do get royalties from the first copy sold— some 10 percent of the hardcover price in trade (general consumer) publishing. But trade hardcovers tend to die within a year or get displaced by a paper edition; in the latter case, royalties drop to about 6 percent of the lower paperback price.

In trade contracts, the average author can expect an advance against future royalty earnings, but not the kind of advance that makes headlines. Publishers base advances on estimates for first-year sales (or first printings), and their estimates will be clinically conservative for two reasons: they favor small, possibly inadequate printings over large warehouse inventories, and they reserve their optimism for the blockbusters that cost a (Stephen) King's ransom to acquire.

Even popular author Cleveland Amory met with pessimism when his second curmudgeonly cat book came up for a print order. "You never get over the frustration of publishing," he told an audience at the 1990 American Booksellers Association show. Amory's original *The Cat Who Came for Christmas* sold 1.5 million copies. For the follow-up, according to Amory, Little Brown wanted fewer words and suggested a first printing of twenty thousand. "Whatever I give publishers, they want less of it," he said. The new book—*The Cat and the Curmudgeon*—was on *The New York Times* bestseller list twelve weeks by year's end.

*   *   *

AN increasing number of books are going directly into "trade" paperback (i.e., a better-quality edition than the mass-market reprint), skipping the hardcover version with its higher royalty and better library sales. If a $10 trade paperback is expected to sell ten thousand copies the first year, the author will be advanced about 6 percent of the $100,000 gross revenue or $6,000. Half will be paid when the contract is signed; the second half when the manuscript is delivered (with required revisions), if it satisfies the publisher. Another arrangement is one-third the advance on signing, a third on delivery, and the final third on publication. In any case, no further royalties will be paid until sales exceed ten thousand or "earn out" the advance, even if it takes ten years. If sales amount to less, the publisher usually takes the loss on the advance (though not necessarily on the book). With a few thousand in earnings, all the author has lost is years of wasted time and credibility as a saleable writer.

Some authors are lucky enough to garner subsidiary sales such as film or foreign rights, which pay a much better percentage than royalties. Authors get some 50 to 90 percent of subsidiary income; the rest goes to the publisher or agent or both, depending on who retains which rights and commissions. An agent may specialize in certain sub rights, such as movie sales, and publishers may be very sharp at selling book club or foreign rights. Ideally these rights would be divided according to strengths, but it doesn't always happen that way.

A literary agent is the best bet for improving other terms of the contract. To the eternal question, "Should I get an agent?" the answer is "yes, if you can," but often you can't until a contract is in hand. Even agents who wouldn't hustle your manuscript can earn their 15 percent negotiating an agreement. A marginal author pushing for another $2,000 up-front starts to smell like trouble. Will he be worth the hassle? a publisher wonders. But when agents ask for more they are only doing business in the comfortable old traditions of publishing. They will ask for $6,000 and get $4,000. More important in the long run, agents understand the subtleties of publishing contracts, which can run to some twenty-five pages of Chancery Court jargon. A sample clause:

> The author shall indemnify and hold the Publisher harmless from any claim, demand, suit, action, proceeding, or prosecution (and any liability, loss, expense, or damage in consequence thereof) asserted or instituted by reason of the publication or sale of the Work or the Publisher's exercise or enjoyment of any of its rights under this agreement, or by reason of any warranty or indemnity made, assumed or incurred by the Publisher in connection with the exercise of any of its rights under this agreement.

In the absence of a trusted agent, some writers turn to an attorney who understands publishing practice. The worst a writer can do is bring the unsigned contract to the family lawyer, who will seek to replace intimidating clauses with inalienable rights and golden parachutes. Not only won't they float, but they can sink the deal. "Publishing law is not particularly arcane," observes former publisher Carol Meyer in *The Writer's Survival Manual* (Bantam), "but it *is* based on accepted ways of doing business and a lawyer inexperienced with these customs and procedures can create a lot of confusion and unnecessary fuss." In his *Beyond the Bestseller* (Plume), literary agent Richard Curtis is less diplomatic: "Whenever a client asks me if he should show a publishing contract to his attorney, I emit a noise not unlike that of a rutting moose whose girlfriend has just trotted into the woods with his rival."

Scores of writers' books detail the elements of a book contract, but Plotnikov's dog-eared favorites are Meyers, cited above, Richard Curtis's *How to be Your Own Literary Agent* (Houghton Mifflin), and agent Richard Balkin's *A Writer's Guide to Book Publishing* (Dutton). All three address the "satisfactory" clause, an area demanding scrutiny. A stock contract says that if the delivered manuscript proves unsatisfactory or unacceptable to the publisher, the author must return the advance received on signing and any other advances.

Feudalism! Publishers should at least be required to detail the reasons for unacceptability and give the author ample opportunity to revise. Better contracts offer an unlimited "first proceeds" clause for unsatisfactory manuscripts, which means advances already paid may be kept unless another publisher buys the rejected work; the author must then pay back publisher number one with the first proceeds from publisher number two. The best deal is a guarantee of nonrefundable advances, especially if the work requires costly research and the participation of others.

THE GOOD FIGHT

Because writers are undervalued as a class, individual authors must battle relentlessly for better terms. In doing so, sometimes allied with their agents, they have fared somewhat better than writers lobbying in groups.

Chicagoan Carol Felsenthal demands up-front recognition of her rising value as a nonfiction writer. A trim, red-haired runner, kibbitzer, mother, and general overachiever, Felsenthal entered the literary sweepstakes near the bottom, doing community stories for a small suburban newspaper. After a brief stewardship at a struggling city magazine, she began writing book reviews for the American Library Association and applied for an editorial post on Plotnikov's *American Libraries* magazine.

Plotnikov liked her spirit, but the career profile was wrong, he thought, for writing on arcane library topics. Plotnikov be damned; Felsenthal plunged forward as chief reviewer and editor of ALA's syndicated book-review column, growing as a writer, looking for article ideas and for people to interview.

Never missing an angle, she began selling story ideas to *Chicago* magazine and to the top national slicks, parlaying one success into others. After panning a book by conservative activist Phyllis Schlafly, Felsenthal drew such a volley of angry mail she decided to look closer—and more objectively—at the woman who could inspire such fervor. Research led to an article that kept growing until Felsenthal decided to go for the book.

Without an agent, she called Doubleday and talked her way to an editor who seemed interested. After a while Doubleday offered a contract with a modest advance.

"I was awed like any first-book author," she told Plotnikov recently, "and I thought, whatever the publisher offers you take. Who was I to bargain? Much later I realized who: A competent author with a subject that could have been shopped around. Writers are always ready to sell themselves short, and publishers can sniff that out."

But at the time the money seemed good. Then as the crushing days and nights of travel, research, interviewing, writing, and revising added up, she began to question why publishers should determine the value of a book assignment and not writers: Only writers can appreciate the cost in life-draining labor and abandonment of normal pursuits.

Felsenthal and Schlafly were political opposites, and it took no little effort just to win the conservative's confidence. As Schlafly raced around the country to rally her followers, Felsenthal ran along. She gathered voluminous notes from observations and interviews and explorations of every likely source.

She met her deadline on the book, *The Sweetheart of the Silent Majority: The Biography of Phyllis Schlafly,* which drew wide attention and sold some fifty-thousand copies plus first serial rights to *Woman's Day.* With a collaborator, Felsenthal wrote a second book for Doubleday, *A Cry for Help: Exploding the Myths About Teenage Suicide—A Guide for All Parents of Adolescents,* also well received and now a fixture in libraries. Felsenthal was on her way and determined that her way would be paid fairly.

That determination was partly driven by her husband, an attorney in general-practice business law. Because they could survive on his earnings if necessary, she could press for fair compensation as a writer. More important, he helped her gain perspective on the writer's value to a corporate enterprise.

Felsenthal was unhappy with Doubleday's promotional efforts and what she experienced as an arm's-length attitude toward authors. "I couldn't even get them to recognize my name when I called." For her next books she found a literary agency

(Sterling Lord) and publisher who did right by her. She signed with Putnam to do *Alice Roosevelt Longworth,* a biography of Theodore Roosevelt's outspoken daughter and Washington's "longest reigning queen." The money was good but the work killing: immersion in Library of Congress family papers and other research sources, tedious acquisition of FBI documents under the Freedom of Information Act, interviews with more than two hundred of Longworth's friends and acquaintances including scores of Washington celebrities and one former president—not to mention the toil of writing and revising on deadline.

In 1991, with two young children and one on the way, Felsenthal felt she must now set terms of compensation based on the value of a mother's time as well as her track record and what she would put into a book project. She was working on a biography of media czarina and Washington power Katharine Graham. Although she will not reveal her specific earnings ("I went to a party of writers where that was all they talked about and it was obnoxious") she allowed that the advance for her new project was some twenty times her first advance.

Felsenthal's stance goes beyond money. If an activity has it's own value, that's one thing. She finds nonmercenary rewards, for example, in teaching a night course on how to get published. But writing is business. She told Plotnikov, "Now *I* determine what it's worth for me to do a book, and that's my price. If I don't get it, I don't write—and thank God I don't have to for survival or self-esteem."

In her night class, Felsenthal offers these tips, among others, for getting published.

- Writers of nonfiction, short stories, and literary novels should look to university presses as a first publisher. There's a trend among such presses to publish short stories and novels outside academia, perhaps because so many universities now sponsor writers' workshops. There's not much money in it—usually no advance—but there's prestige and a good chance of moving to a commercial house with book number two.
- Identify the commercial publishers who are hospitable to

your type of subject or approach. Publishers are constantly turned off by proposals that have nothing to do with their program. A good bookstore is still the best place to see who's publishing what. Read the trade journals such as *Publishers Weekly* and *The New York Times* publishing news (usually strong on Mondays), keeping an eye out for new imprints and programs that will be needing material.

- When you've found a likely publishing house, get the name of the best individual to query there. There are many ways to get a name. One is to call the house, ask for the editorial department, and then, to whoever picks up the phone, "Who would be the best editor to query about (your subject or type of book)?" Another way is to go to that good bookstore and examine brand-new books in the same vein as yours; check the acknowledgments for agents and editors. Biographical reference sources such as *Contemporary Authors* often give agent and editor.

To these tips on getting a foot in the door, Plotnikov adds a brief invocation on patience, the writer's second most valuable asset after talent.

Give us this day the patience to:
Write many long years without promise of compensation;
Endure the months and years of fruitless submissions;
Await each half-year process of decision making;
Sit still between acceptance and publication;
Await replies from editor or agent;
Wait helplessly, sometimes endlessly, for reviews;
Wait and wait and wait for payments due.

"Masochists don't mind waiting, but most people do," says author Leonard Michaels. "It's a miserable, degrading thing, a social torture, inflicted on convicts and dogs."

And every writer.

SEVERAL authors groups seek to improve the writer's lot or at least provide the company that misery loves. Chief among these, the sixty-five-hundred-member Authors Guild (headquartered in New York City) provides financial surveys, a newsletter, seminars, and a model contract to help members nudge publishers their way.

Labor journalist John Tasini helped organize the National Writers Union, which in 1991 affiliated its three thousand members with the United Auto Workers in a three-year contract. The NWU seeks "to change the power relationship between authors and the publishing industry by negotiating fair minimum contract standards." Tasini spelled out four basic issues in *Publishers Weekly* (Feb. 10, 1989): *Comprehensible standard royalty statements,* revealing all printings, sales, and money owed; *timely payment,* within thirty days of the royalty period, with immediate pass-along of subsidiary earnings and a limit on royalties held back against possible returns from bookstores; *nonreturnable advances;* and *compulsory arbitration of contract disputes* as an alternative to murderously expensive litigation.

AUTHORS are beginning to see a few cracks in the feudal system. Penguin U.K. adopted an enlightened contract in 1990. Some U.S. publishers are sponsoring liability insurance for authors, who must warranty themselves responsible for any troubles their works may cause—and in a litigious society troubles come in large doses. Rock Hudson's former lover thought he was troubled $22 million worth by the authors of the star's biography. Such suits don't go away with settlements from a writer's advance.

Writers will welcome kinder treatment and some, like Felsenthal, will hold out for it. But the basic rates of payment are tied to the costs and risks of publishing and aren't likely to change. How much can an author be paid on a $20 book when the publisher sells it to retailers for as little as $10 and spends about $7 for plant costs (editorial and prepress work), printing, paper, sales, marketing, overhead, shipping, and tax? If the publisher hopes to earn even $1 on the $20 investment, that leaves the standard $2 or 10 percent for the author.

Publishers depend on mass sales and reprint and subsidiary

rights for any real profit. Mass sales, in turn, depend largely on the caprice of the chain bookstores in taking the book and shelving it long enough to move or "sell through" as the jargon goes. Some say publishers take a beating on as many as seven out of ten titles. For those seven losers, publishers, like authors, suffer the mockery of Beckett's words: "Nothing is more real than nothing."

DO-IT-YOURSELFERS

Desktop technology has exploded the number of self-publishing ventures and fantasies. Thousands of writers imagine they could publish their books as well or better than the commercial bunglers and keep the bunglers' profit to boot. Self-publishing success stories fill the trade columns: *50 Simple Things You Can Do to Save the Earth* was self-published under the Earthworks Press imprint and headed *The New York Times* best-seller list for ten weeks. *What Color Is Your Parachute?* has sold millions of copies in trade editions since its original self-publication.

Among other successes are self-publications that tell how to self-publish, such as Bill Henderson's *The Publish-It-Yourself Handbook* from his Pushcart Press, and *The Self-Publishing Manual* by Dan Poynter, Para Publishing. Their arguments are seductive: Many of the world's great works were self-published when commercial publishers showed little interest, and self-publishers have hit it big with modest expenditures of $5,000 to $20,000 and extravagant investments of time, footwork, and hype.

And there's the rub. Writers aren't going to become better writers running around as amateur publishers and publicists. If self-publishings were a sure thing, it might make sense to write half as many books to gain twice the control over quality and merchandising. But for every self-publisher who hits paydirt, legions end up staring at three thousand books mouldering in the basement. Distribution is the killer, even with the resurgence of small independent bookstores. After all the bread-and-butter books are shelved—the cat books, the best-sellers, the *proven books,* as the brand-name titles are labeled, and the large-print versions of the best-sellers and proven books—there isn't much room for your *Grandpa Anderson's Country Humor.* Direct-mail sales rarely equal costs. If the title is good enough to attract a distributor, the distributor's discount—as high as 60 to 70 percent—all but wipes out profit. Specialized nonfiction or novelty books may have a shot; literary books, uh-uh.

Plotnikov's advice: Self-publish only because you've exhausted every other avenue and just want the goddamn thing published, or because you're happier playing at publisher, win or lose, than becoming a thoroughbred writer.

Taxing but Tolerable

The universe torments writers when they don't make money and when somehow they do. To the Internal Revenue Service, writing is a business with business expenses when it earns a profit; but if it loses it's a hobby, and you can't take losses on hobbies. Most writers file on Schedule C of Form 1040, "Profit or Loss from Business"; but accounting for the puny credits and debits of creativity on a form suited to wholesale plumbing supply strains even the literary imagination. Every April Plotnikov rubs his scalp raw as he ponders, "What were my 'methods used to value closing inventory' "? "How do I depreciate my desk?" In the late eighties, under a short-lived misguided rule, writers had to link each expense (say, a bookcase) to a specific project and claim the expense only when the project earned money, if ever. The feds finally realized that, duh, a bookcase might be used for *many* projects, some more saleable than others.

For the average writer, the best deduction is the home office, which must be the primary site of the business and used only for business. Some years ago when the IRS had ample staff, an auditor was dispatched to Plotnikov's bachelor apartment to take a look at the home office he claimed for "writing and photojournalism." Forewarned, Plotnikov cleared his small study of baseball mitts and other frivolous matter. An office, he feared, had to look big-time professional. He crammed it with first-class supplies and photo equipment borrowed from the American Library Association. The auditor never looked twice. A Vietnam veteran with longish hair and short beard, he rapped about the war, apologized for his present mission, and wondered if he could add about $50 tax for appearances' sake. He asked what writing was all about. It was beautiful.

AND what *is* writing all about finally, when it comes to money and contracts and translating humanistic values into dollars? While most writers foam at the mouth to tell their horror stories, a significant number consider the writing business a gift from the gods. They write what they enjoy without depending on income, but if money comes it is extra money, mad money! Whatever would they be doing with personal time if not writing? They believe that publishers perform a lovely service, risking many thousands of dollars to actualize the author's dream: a book with an audience.

The unfairness of contracts? Robert Heinlein wrote his agent in 1960, "The contract offered [by Putnam] is gratifyingly satisfactory. But I want one change. I won't take one-half on signing . . . They must delay the entire advance until I submit an approved manuscript. It is unfair to them to tie up $1,500 in a story which may turn out to be unpublishable." The story turned out to be *Stranger in a Strange Land.*

The struggle to start earning? Some have no idea what that means. "The act of writing and getting my stories accepted was not too difficult," says Brian Aldiss. "For me there were few rejected manuscripts, a few rejection slips, no starving in garrets. I should feel guilty but don't."

The economics of publishing? Perfectly marvelous! A book that endures—and many do—earns royalties for years after its creation; an author need only sit back and collect such annuities. Even Plotnikov must admit as $3,000 to $6,000 rolls in annually for his little tome on editing, that the wages of writing do sometimes exceed those of sin. Although each year he must throw tantrums to receive the subsidiary payments due him from one publisher, how else but by writing would he ever see such payments?

Reflecting even on his piss-poorest deals, Plotnikov can usually recall some value that made it worthwhile. Two memories:

- On a freelance assignment for the Chicago *Sun-Times* he profiles the U.S. ambassador to Norway (a Chicagoan) making the rounds in Oslo. His pay for the story is a miserable $100—but for a few golden days he savors V.I.P. treatment at the embassy and the ambassador's fairytale residence. He chews the fat with the ambassador in the residence sauna. "Marvelous!" the ambassador writes when the story appears.
- Plotnikov attends an office outing to watch baseball at Wrigley Field. As he cheers the Chicago Cubs a staff member arrives with a message to call the U.S. National Archives. Plotnikov calls from a phone near a food concession and in the aroma of franks and beer learns that the Archives will publish his book on the Constitution's calligrapher. The financial terms stink; but one day when Plotnikov tallies his life's values, what will compare to such pleasant news on a beery summer day in Wrigley Field with high-fives from his colleagues and the crowds cheering as if for him, a writer of books?

HONK IF YOU'RE A POET

THE SYNTAX OF SUCCESS, WITH BILLY COLLINS

Even if it keeps you up all night,
wash down the walls and scrub the floor
of your study before composing a syllable.

. . .The more you clean, the more brilliant
your writing will be, so do not hesitate to take
to the open fields to scour the undersides
of rocks or swab in the dark forest
upper branches, nests full of eggs. . . .
　　　　　—FROM "ADVICE TO WRITERS," BY BILLY COLLINS

LIKE the writers he needles with this "Advice," poet Billy Collins can usually find some extravagant chore that needs doing just when it's time to face the blank page. He can choose from all the pleasant labors of maintaining a nineteenth-century home in Somers, New York, where he and his wife Diane have settled after a surfeit of urban life on both coasts.

　　Nested in a wooded slope, the house is a comfortable hop from the village center and not far from the reservoirs that feed New York City to the south. Collins heads southward himself a few times a week to teach at Lehman College of the City University.

　　The poet/professor is tall, high browed, soft spoken. In his Gaelic features, crow's feet around the brown eyes, one sees a readiness to tell or hear the good story. He works in a long study furnished with a small desk, heaps of books, and one major distraction: a piano on which he struggles to master jazz basics.

Long an admirer of Collins's work (though indifferent to most contemporary poetry), Plotnikov met the poet through a mutual acquaintance and developed a friendship not particularly focused on writing. But as Collins's stature grew, Plotnikov the editor took advantage, calling on him now and again for poems and advice. In spring 1991, Plotnikov asked Collins— now a successful poet by every measure*—if he would talk about poetry in the context of this unabashed guide. Collins agreed, if only to offset prose-writer Plotnikov's "incredible naiveté" on the subject. The interview follows.

ON BECOMING AND BEING A POET

Plotnikov: What are the first steps on the stairway to the stars? Let's start with your own ascension.

Collins: I came up the usual staircase—a long one with very gradual steps. I started writing poetry in high school, less infatuated with the craft itself than with the image of the poet—who else can wear a cape and get away with it? I wrote imitative poems. At first, bad e. e. cummings, then bad Ferlinghetti, then worse Wallace Stevens. In the next stage my poems became

* With a run of major awards and a book contract from William Morrow, Billy Collins entered the nineties as a rising star in the world of poetry. Recipient of fellowships from the New York State Foundation on the Arts and National Endowment for the Arts (and $30,000 in grants), he was chosen by poet Edward Hirsch as a 1990 National Poetry Series winner, which resulted in the Morrow publication of his fourth book, *Questions About Angels* (1991). In selecting that manuscript, Hirsch called Collins "an American original—a metaphysical poet with a funny bone and a sly questioning intelligence. He is an ironist of the void, and his poems . . . bump up against the deepest human mysteries."

Collins's work appears often in *Poetry* among numerous other reviews. A professor of English at Lehman College of the City University of New York, he is featured at workshops and campus readings across the nation.

All poems and excerpted passages in this chapter are from *The Apple that Astonished Paris,* poems by Billy Collins (Fayetteville: University of Arkansas Press, 1988), reprinted by permission. *Poetry* has given permission for use of "Winter Syntax," which first appeared in its April 1988 issue, © Modern Poetry Association.

interesting to read, but I had no idea what they were about. I sent out blizzards of stuff, some of which landed in little magazines with readerships that would fit inside a two-car garage. *Rolling Stone* was an exception, publishing a lot of my tiny poems back in among the record reviews. Years passed. I grew. Eventually acceptances came from *Paris Review* and *The New Yorker*. Acceptance seems to come easier once you've had some poems accepted—a Catch 22. It's unusual for poets to be accepted by first-rate magazines before cutting their teeth on the wee journals.

P: I'm surprised the weirder "little" mags carry any weight.

C: At least they stamp your parking sticker "published poet" and in the eyes of editors separate you from the great unvalidated. So many people write poetry—children, cowboys, Jimmy Stewart—we need some form of validation. For books of poetry, it's the same sort of progressive credentialing. Small presses such as Applezaba, which published my second book, validate a poet for the next level—even if they don't make cocktail crowds stampede you. After Applezaba came a university press, a big step up for me and a learning experience. Miller Williams of Arkansas accepted the manuscript after sending me to my room several times to write better poems.

P: Published or unpublished, are poets *writers* as the world perceives the term? Philip Roth's fictional writer snaps at his analyst: "And while we're at it, Dr. Spielvogel, a poet and a novelist have about as much in common as a jockey and a diesel driver."

C: Poets aren't writers—they're poets. It might be easier if they could say "I'm a writer" and avoid the fish looks they get when they say "I'm a poet." *Poet* is such a loaded word. A novelist writes novels—that's clear enough—but to most people *poet* implies so much more than writing poems. It's an honorific term. It suggests that you have drunk the milk of paradise, or you're a dreamy layabout, or you swoon at the first crocus of spring. Poetry is a species of writing, obviously, but it's a very specialized craft and one that is not valued by many. Tell a stranger you're a poet and he will first say "Hmm!"—the sound of dull respect—and then, "Have you ever thought of writing a novel? A screenplay?" as if poetry were not enough. Do people ask pianists if they've thought of playing tuba?

But of course the poet and novelist are both writers. One uses centripetal, the other centrifugal force in words. Someone said that poetry is about the poet and the novel about other people. Each expresses a different impulse—to go inside the self, to step outside to others.

P: Still, when you've got the itch to write, why poetry instead of prose?

C: Certain writers take to poetry simply because they have an abnormally intense awareness of language and find they can understand how the form of poetry works. Some people have been successful at poetry and fiction—right now there's Denis Johnson and Steven Dobyns—but this ambidexterity is exceptional. I can *teach* fiction but the few times I've tried to write it I feel I don't know what I'm doing. It's as if I picked up a French horn for the first time. How do you hold it? Where do the fingers go?

P: When *I* try poetry, it's like finding myself in the London Symphony with a bicycle horn and no pants. Other than the time it takes to develop the craft, what's the downside of being a poet—even a successful one?

C: Being ignored, I suppose, although that's a downside of life as an earthling. In effect you are read only by other poets, which is an appreciative audience but a small one. Americans are world leaders in ignoring their poets. Poet Ted Kooser said that if you put name tags on fifty of America's best-known poets and paraded them arm-in-arm down the main street of any town, not a soul would recognize them. I think that's sad . . . and I usually love a parade.

P: I tend to ignore poets I can't understand. Should poets worry about being too obscure—or strive for obscurity to get respect?

C: They won't get much respect for the effort. Even Ezra Pound said a poem should at least be good prose. John Ciardi remarked, "a statement that fails to make sense in prose is not elevated to sublimity just because it is written down in verse." The trouble is that any experiment with language is going to be tagged POETRY. There's just no other word for it. "Poetry" covers so many styles and angles of writing that it ceases to hold much meaning. People complain that they don't read poetry because it's obscure—but maybe poetry is obscure because they don't read it. Ah ha! Why make the effort to be clear if no one's listening? Even so, much of today's poetry is so accessible that we're hearing the opposite objection—"this isn't *poetic* enough!"

P: I find your poems accessible. Does this make you a bad poet or me a bad reader?

C: My poems tend to be plainspoken, though I think reading any decent poem a second time will yield new pleasures. I like the kind of poem David St. John describes as one that gradually reveals itself. Unfortunately, for every such piece there are ten What-the-Hell-Are-You-Talking-About poems that refuse to yield anything even if you sit up with them all night. After a few of these it's refreshing to find something you can catch on the first bounce.

P: What would you say to this popular view: "Poetry is a 'precious' approach to words"?

C: Not the real thing. Yes, poetry is what some people do with their preciousness, those people with first-name initials and multiple WASP surnames. Yes, C. Witherton Warnerhouse, we know every snowflake is different and absolutely miraculous, so let us alone. Again, the umbrella word *poetry* keeps a lot of people dry—everyone from some Neo-Dadaist who bites words out of the thesaurus to Lilly Everhard Crowes and her bleeding blankets of snow.

P: Is poetry such serious business? Your own work isn't known for its seriousness.

C: Not in its tone, true. But I've come to believe that poetry is the most serious business of all. When you think about poetry in the highest sense, an activity that begins before Homer and takes place in all ages in all countries, and when you accept Shelley's definition of poetry as "the record of the best and happiest moments of the happiest and best minds," and when you realize that language is the highest expression of human intelligence—then poetry is a big deal.

P: Is it a way of life?

C: Yes, in the sense that poetry is something you are always doing. That's why poets carry notebooks; the entries are like what a captain puts in a ship's log. And that's why they spend more time looking out windows than other people. The way of life that poetry is, is language. Poets are always curious about how this experience or that impulse would look in language. All the time perhaps one is preparing for the act of composition.

P: Speaking of preparation—how useful are poetry workshops, since you've conducted a fair number? Anne Sexton said they give writers the most important thing: courage.

C: With bad writers, they're just a waste of everyone's time. A workshop helps good writers think about their writing more often, more intensely, even more professionally. The small audience of fellow writers can offer a nice blend of sympathy and criticism, as opposed to your mother, who enshrines all your poems on the refrigerator door, and the public, busily reading newspapers. But workshops are a very recent phenomenon and many poets have matured without them. Someone said the best school for the writer is solitude.

P: You encounter hordes of aspiring poets in your lectures and readings. What do they want to know?

C: Some just want to know how to get published, and I try to steer them to appropriate magazines and directories.* But what the best aspiring poets want to know, indirectly, is how to pull off that special magic of their most admired writers. A good question, and no cute answer.

P: Do you point them to classic texts on writing poetry?

C: I wouldn't touch a how-to on poetry with a ten-foot metaphor. Aspiring poets should read poetry. The library is full of writing masters willing to teach all they know, gratis. They are waiting on the shelves in the dark right now.

P: Waiting to impart skill or envy?

---

* [Including *Directory of Poetry Publishers* and *The International Directory of Little Magazines and Small Presses,* available in libraries or bookstores, or from Dustbooks, P.O. Box 100, Paradise, CA 95969; and *Poets and Writers,* a key bimonthly with information on grants, prizes, and the marketplace, from Poets and Writers, 72 Spring Street, New York, NY 10012.]

C: Envy is a good muse—not envy of someone's success but of their work, as when you read a poem and realize that it is perfect except for one thing: your name isn't at the bottom of it.

WHAT TO WRITE ABOUT

P: Are there some subjects to avoid?

C: Subjects already loaded down with emotion can be difficult. Like the death of children, packed with volatile emotion before you even approach it. So instead of creating an emotion you easily end up just repeating one. Subjects like this are mine fields; one false step and you trigger an explosion of sentimentality.

P: What about topics of social concern? Political poetry?

C: Here lies the old debate about poetry versus rhetoric. A poem has to be at least as interested in its own language as in its subject. There must be a certain surrender to the language as it seeks its own level. How can that be if the subject is abortion, homelessness, drug abuse, and the like? How can a poem surprise if the poet knows and wills the outcome beforehand? The novel is better suited to the politics of contemporary life. In poetry, a little content goes a long way.

P: That's a good cue for reproducing your poem called "Poem."

POEM

Some poems name their subjects.
The titles are *On* this or *On* that,
or they hang like small marquees
indicating what is playing inside:
"Celibacy," "Ostriches at Dusk."

Other poems fall into it as they go along.
You trip over a word while carrying
a tray of vocabulary out to the pool
only to discover that broken glass
is a good topic.

Still others have no subject
other than themselves to gnaw on.
The fly lands on the swatter.
The movie runs backwards
and catches fire in the projector.
This species apes us well
by talking only about itself.

Such is often the case with poems
afflicted by the same plain title
as this one:
a sign by the road announcing a bump.

P: Should poets consider taking on the bigger subjects in long, even book-length poems?

C: As far as I'm concerned, Poe sounded their death knell in modern times when he pronounced that a long poem is really just a number of good short poems separated by stretches of filler. The speed of television information has shriveled the attention span and the audience for sustained poems. It's hard enough to get a roomful of students to sit still for a sonnet.

THE ACT OF POETRY

P: Can poets write without inspiration? Frost says inspiration is mostly animus, hostility toward something. Randall Jarrell talks about poets spending their lives standing in a thunderstorm waiting to be hit by lightning enough times to be great.

C: I prefer to say that if you spend your life in an aviary, eventually a bird will land on your head. Two schools of thought: in the first, inspiration is a species of exotic bird that sometimes perches on your head but otherwise is off in another time zone, maybe on another head; school number two, inspiration is romantic guano; get to your desk and sweat it out. Everyone feels bursts of something—maybe neurochemicals—and stretches of dead time. During a dead time, I can't sit around waiting for the bird, checking the horizon. I have to start laboring and somehow make it look effortless and inspired.

P: But what do you set out to achieve, beyond wordplay? Hirsch called you a "metaphysical poet." Here's what Octavio Paz achieves, according to the Nobel Prize committee: ". . . impassioned writing with wide horizons, . . . seems to incorporate, interpret, and reconstrue major existential questions, death, time, love, and reality." I trust that you strive for no less.

C: That kind of gaseous praise is meant to justify giving $700,000 to a poet. Otherwise, it would make you wonder why the guy isn't a world leader or in line for the Papacy. These high-sounding aims come after the fact, of course. The act of poetry is closer to what Alan Ginsberg called "diddling," or doodling or noodling. Poets are more interested in the technical problems of a specific poem—the "game" of working something out in language—than they are about death, love, or nature. Otherwise, they'd be paralyzed at the keyboard. A poem might end up being "about" death or landscape, but while it is being written, every poem is about its own creation. Auden said that when he was writing a poem he felt like a carpenter.

P: When do you decide on the rhythm of a poem?

C: I try to let the initiating lines suggest the rhythm for the rest. I don't hear a metronome in the background exactly, but every sentence and phrase has its little rhythm. Once the cadence is set, every new line has to be adjusted to keep in step. Modern poetry succeeded in breaking the iambic, as Pound said; but most poetry in English tends toward a roughly iambic beat. Casual talk leans toward the iambic. The human heart beats in iambs (thub-DUB, thub-DUB); by the time we leave the womb our tiny ears have been iambically trained by our mother's heartbeat.

P: Is rhyming out, except in schlock verse?

C: Or in light or occasional verse. Otherwise, it has been out for some time. Like the waltz. One hears a lot of talk now about the New Formalism, but it seems to be taking place on the sidelines. Also, to rhyme well is real talent. Look at Derek Walcott's *Omeros,* with its variety of rhyme-play. Rhyme in such a long poem is likely to thud in our modern ears, but he avoids this through near-rhymes, false-rhymes, split-rhymes, and the like.

P: What about a poet's individual "voice"? Do you find a voice, or create it?

C: That depends on whether you think it was there all the time or not. "Finding your voice" is an unhappy expression, as if you could lose it like car keys and find it under the sofa pillows. But there is this vital moment in a good poet's career, when he—or she—realizes that the poem just written could not possibly have been written by anyone else. Of course, to be capable of such a realization you have to read a lot of poetry; otherwise, unoriginal stuff can sound original to your inexperienced ear. That authentic voice experience, that breakthrough, is the most conclusive way to tell if you have a future as a poet.

FINDING AN AUDIENCE AND OTHER PRACTICAL MATTERS

P: What kind of response do you get to your published works? Are you reaching anyone, do you think? Does it matter?

C: I generally get good, heartening responses, but remember the audience for almost any poet is minute. You could have them all over for drinks at one time. Everyone likes to be stroked, but this doesn't have anything to do with writing. When I write I'm addressing myself to the internal censor that Auden talks about, some Buddha-like figure whose approval I seek. If I can make him wink or raise a finger I know I have done well.

As for public audiences, one is always casting poems into the void, so responses are delightful surprises. One Californian actually mailed me ten dollars because he thought mine was the best poem in a certain issue of a magazine. If you ask me to describe the "ideal reader," you can be sure I'll describe him.

P: I'd like his address. Tell me about the kick of publishing poetry with a major trade house like Morrow.

C: It's like being summoned up to first class. The seats are roomier, the drinks are free, oh, and here comes the hot towel!

P: Yes, as opposed to the crowded economy-class conditions of small press. In *Spreading the Word; Editors on Poetry* [Columbia, S.C., The Bench Press, 1989], little-mag editors point out how "manuscripts never trickle in; they *cascade* in, they *deluge* us." The book gives editors a chance to explain why they chose particular poems out of the deluge. "It was their mystery, offered with impeccable style, that dazzled me," says David St. John of *Antioch Review*. David Wojahn of *Crazy Horse* looks for "an assured sense of style and voice as well as emotional depth." No magic revelations here, but maybe reverse insight into how editors rationalize their rejections.

C: That can be helpful. Many rejections result from not knowing the market—the editorial biases. You have to actually *read* some of these magazines, not just shoot at random. And when one likely prospect turns you down, hot-potato your poems to the next one. That's the best antidote to rejection.

P: Are poetry readings worth the trouble?

C: Readings are a good way to publicize your work—to blow your horn in public—and to give new poems a trial run. Reading aloud will show you where the sour notes are, what might sound inauthentic or excessive. You feel certain seismic reactions from the audience. Naturally some poets can read better than others. Some readings only prove it's possible to write beautiful poems without having a shred of personality.

P: So readings help you revise. How much do you tinker with a poem?

C: In a way it's all tinkering—"fixing" the poem with constantly tinier screwdrivers. Everything is just a draft, except for the occasional, untouchable burst of spontaneous combustion that so infatuated the Romantic poets. Don't believe all their stories. I never quite bought Coleridge's account of writing "Kubla Khan"; I don't care how good the opium was. Someone—Valéry?—said that poems are never finished, just abandoned. The revision process is potentially endless, so you must force yourself to leave the thing alone at some point.

P: A few more practical matters: What kind of cover letter do you send? Do agents ever handle poets? How can poets make money?

C: The best cover letter is like a quick bank heist: in and out real quick and nobody gets hurt; I mention a couple of my publications and thank the editors for their time. As for agents, poetry is too private and ingrown to interest anyone selling audience appeal. "There is no money in poetry"—"and no poetry in money"—goes the chestnut. The way many American poets, myself included, make a living out of poetry is by attaching themselves to a university and maybe hanging around long enough for tenure.

P: What's the secret of winning grants?

C: Once again a Catch-22 syndrome, or let's rename it Schlemieler's Axiom: It is easier to get a grant if you've gotten a grant. If your work is sufficiently developed and you have some track record, then grant-winning depends on the unpredictable dynamics of a committee. I don't believe it's simply who—or even whom—you know. My own grants have been awarded by strangers. The key is whose attention you attract. A single member of the committee, some earnest Henry Fonda who loves your work, might fight hard enough to sway the other jurors.

LIVING WITH ONESELF

P: Reflecting on life at the Yaddo colony, Alfred Kazin said that poets "suffered more integrally" than other writers. "Poets seem to be as specialized in emotional vulnerability as poetry itself. How they pay for their gifts!" What about this suffering?

C: "I fall upon the thorns of life, I bleed!" That's Shelley crying, not this poet. For me, poetry is hardly an expression of personal misery; it's closer to bemusement in regarding the world. This is not to deny the frustration of art, all that striving for a perfection that never comes. Then, too, the most anguished poets stand out in our minds. We ponder the unknowable demons of Berryman, Plath, Sexton, Crane, while in truth there are hordes of happy poets—but who wants to hear about them?

P: We do want to hear what makes the average poet happy, after all the striving, all the rejection, all the sense of having wasted time and perhaps a lifetime diddling over words.

C: Which is the waste, the life away from words or with them? For poets, happiness is capturing elusive meanings from existence and fixing them in certain shapes of words. In the act of composition every good line is gratifying. Just to complete a decent sentence is its own reward. I've said this better, I think, in a poem called "Winter Syntax."

P: Maestro, if you please . . .

WINTER SYNTAX

A sentence starts out like a lone traveler
heading into a blizzard at midnight,
tilting into the wind, one arm shielding his face,
the tails of his thin coat flapping behind him.

There are easier ways of making sense,
the connoisseurship of gesture, for example.
You hold a girl's face in your hands like a vase.
You lift a gun from the glove compartment
and toss it out the window into the desert heat.
These cool moments are blazing with silence.

The full moon makes sense. When a cloud crosses it
it becomes as eloquent as a bicycle leaning
outside a drugstore or a dog who sleeps all
        afternoon
in a corner of the couch.

Bare branches in winter are a form of writing.
The unclothed body is autobiography.
Every lake is a vowel, every island a noun.

But the traveler persists in his misery,
struggling all night through the deepening snow,
leaving a faint alphabet of bootprints
on the white hills and the white floors of valleys,
a message for field mice and passing crows.

At dawn he will spot the vine of smoke
rising from your chimney, and when he stands
before you shivering, draped in sparkling frost,
a smile will appear in the beard of icicles,
and the man will express a complete thought.

THE ELECTRONIC IMPERATIVE

"Technology has revolutionized the business of free-lance writing, enabling me to work better, smarter, and more creatively."
—RICHARD BLODGETT

"I have never touched a typewriter, and still less a word processor."
—IRIS MURDOCH

TWO nonfiction book proposals come before an editor for consideration. Both are well conceived, timely, authoritative. The sample chapters show strong writing skills. But there's a difference.

Proposal A is from an electronically up-to-date writer. The presentation has been prepared on a desktop system with a high-resolution laser printer and already looks like a published work. The typeface is an elegant Caslon. The sample chapters have been composed into pages with crisp headings and boxes and rules. The text wraps around prototype charts and graphs, with captions and labels in bold italic.

Author A's cover letter explains that these mock-ups are meant only to suggest the "look" of the proposed work, not to dictate any choices of typography and layout. And indeed, the editor can already "see" the concept in its published form and demonstrate it to others on the editorial committee.

Toward the end of the proposal, Author A (a bit of a show-off) addresses these notes to production staff:

> **Format:** I can transmit the manuscript in any number or combination of formats, your choice: (1) disk (any size), or (2) transfer of text by modem, each processed in Word Perfect 6.0, spell-checked, grammar-checked, index-keyed, coded according to your specs or the Standard for Electronic Manuscript Preparation and Markup (or ASCII text stripped of codes); (3) scannable hard-copy laser printout; (4) Postscript page files on disk, prepared on Ventura desktop system according to your specifications, with camera-ready pages or film at superfine 1,200-dot-per-inch output, rasterized, high-end graphics. Your revisions can be faxed or telecommunicated to me and I can turn them around immediately, in revised page or film if desired.

The other proposal, Proposal B, looks like a student-typed term paper. There is no mention of disks or desktops. Instead, this added footnote:

> Please forgive the messy corrections and freehand graphs in the sample chapters; I guess I'm a better writer than typist or artist. At any rate, I could finish a rough draft within one year, including research trips, and a revised typescript in perhaps another six months.

The editor lays Proposal B aside momentarily and calls Author A. "How soon could you finish?" Author A replies: "Well, I'm online to all my sources, so I can set up a search strategy, download my data, import some text, fax for permissions, punch out a draft, pull it through the checkers, tag index terms, autoformat the bibliography . . . let's say in about six weeks?"

Farewell, Author B. However talented and dogged, how long can the Bs compete with the electronic wizards who offer to do half the publisher's work, save the production department months of time and a pile of money, and deliver an electronic text translatable into any number of information products?

In judging a proposal, most large publishing houses still consider content and not electronic format to be paramount; a great concept by a masterful writer doesn't have to arrive on disk with laser printout. Nor is the flashiest electronic package worth a damn if the content stinks. But given that even small publishing houses receive plenty of good content, their choices are becoming ever more influenced by the electronics factor: How much can the author contribute to a thrifty finished product?

Between two comparable projects, the one that arrives in clean camera-ready pages is going to look a lot better on cost-out sheets than the standard typescript, which has yet to be keystroked or scanned,* cleaned up, coded, designed, typeset, and composed. Every dollar of increased production costs can translate into a cover price six to nine dollars higher—with less likelihood of consumer acceptance.

In short, the ante keeps rising for authors to get into the game. At one time editors asked only for good ideas, good writing, and a willingness to revise and help sell a book. Now some of them expect adherence to certain convenient electronic standards and even proficiency as a typesetter/compositor. All authors (with the possible exception of poets) now face the *electronic imperative;* at the very least, it will soon be as necessary to write in standard electronic languages as in standard English.

How much further will it go? How technologically advanced must writers become for the convenience of publishers? This remains an issue. Writers should resist having to submit any more than a standard word-processed disk and a legible print-out. One author so balked not long ago in a proposal sent to Plotnikov's publishing house: "I am prepared to provide both a paper manuscript and a disk of that manuscript," he wrote. "The disk would be in 4.2 WordPerfect on an IBM computer. I HAVE NO INTEREST IN CAMERA-READY COPY." At-

---

* Scanners are devices that "read" typed or typeset pages passed before them, converting text into digital, machine-readable form.

taboy. Further electronic services—typesetting, design, composition—should indeed be optional and worth extra pay.

Once publishers accept a proposal, they may want the author to create an electronic manuscript coded to house specifications. The required codes are given in a style sheet which, to writers barely able to find the "Enter" key, may look like a space-age Rosetta stone.

Preparing a short article for *Encyclopaedia Britannica,* Plotnikov had to decipher a nine-part instruction sheet to see if coding text on a diskette would be worth his while. Since only the publisher stood to benefit, Plotnikov chose to submit a paper manuscript, knowing that the editors would receive the article just as graciously. Not all writers enjoy this confidence. When University Press of America first told its many professorial authors they could submit in electronic format and provided instructions for doing so, a great tremor ran through academia. "They asked a million nervous questions," said a UPA executive. "Some seemed afraid they'd make a mistake and wouldn't be published."

Professors are not alone in their anxiety; no doubt half the world's writers fear that publishing technology will get away from them. It will of course, since the technology is so specialized and dynamic that no writer could both stay abreast of it and labor at writing. But why should it matter, as long as the writer's contribution to the publishing process is limited to raw product? High-tech literacy becomes a concern only when publishers demand that authors be manufacturing assistants.

At this writing, most publishers are willing to work with an author's simple uncoded disks or a clean, scannable manuscript. In fact, too much electronic zeal can be a liability: Not every editor is computer-literate, and most editors are turned off by amateur desktop publishing with its generic clip-art graphics. The author's electronic system and the publisher's may be incompatible. Also, authors who submit typeset pages and heavily coded disks tend to resist heavy revision; one big cut and they have to reprogram half the book. Editors don't want to deal with any such reticence.

Circa early 1992, authors did not have to learn desktop

publishing to get published—but without question they had to master word processing simply to be as good and as fast at producing text as their computer-literate peers.

A FEW WORDS ON WORD PROCESSING

For a while there was some charm in the resistance to computer word-processing. Literary Luddites would cite the great writers who managed without computers, and they would sing the virtues of their oh-so-human yellow pads and trusty typewriters. An occasional romanticist still gets carried away, for example, Jay Parini on the advantages of pencil over computer: "You can delete what you don't like with a quick horizontal stroke that both rids you of the unwanted phrase and simultaneously preserves the deletion—just in case it was better . . ." (*Chronicle of Higher Education*).

But most word processors *can* restore deletions, should the author wish to slow the powerful forward progression that word processing allows—that change upon change as fast as the mind works, without a backward glance at the distracting heap of discards. Lost is the trail of rejected text so beloved by scholars, as well as what Parini describes as "the slight rustle of paper, the smell of freshly sharpened pencils or wet ink, the ancient and alluring sensation of text making." Otherwise, portable hardware and clever software have deflated the arguments that computers dehumanize writing.

As most authors now realize, word processing can enhance creativity by reflecting the random activity of the brain. Writing on a screen is like random painting on canvas. Previously limited to stringing out words in a linear mode, now the writer splashes down some words, anywhere on the canvas, top, bottom, middle, no matter. The rough underlayer needn't be erased; it is not a rough draft but a sketch that is overpainted, altered, and smoothed until it looks right.

In *Tools of the Writer's Trade* (HarperCollins, 1990), members of the American Society of Journalists and Authors describe with gusto their favorite word-processing equipment and how they relate to it. Vance Packard was a gradual convert, confessing, "I've always doubted that I had the particular sort of brain required to cope with a computer as a writing tool"; but he progressed from an Olivetti typewriter to an Olivetti ETV 240 word processor and built his confidence.

Even Anne Rice, who writes as if with quills dipped in blood, remarked mundanely in a 1989 *Lear's* interview: "Nowadays I work on a computer, which is absolutely wonderful because it enables me to get past the physical labor the typewriter demands. It makes revision easier and puts a maximum pressure on you to perfect your writing."

Thousands of writers have favorite computer stories, all equally mundane. Does anyone want to hear how Plotnikov confronted word processing through stages of denial, anger, and resignation? Does anyone care about his conversion from Osborne and Kaypro CP/M-system computers to a Hyundai MS-DOS? No! Yet, writers who have struggled through the technological revolution do have hard-nosed lessons to pass along, which makes sources like *Tools of the Writers Trade* so valuable. For example, how *does* one convert manuscripts composed on CP/M into DOS-readable format? *Tools* gives tips on conversion software and services. How does one copy text from the 3½-inch disks of a portable laptop to the 5¼-inch disks of an IBM-compatible? (With a device called The Brooklyn Bridge, suggests Vicky Hay in *Tools.*)

SOME other common tips, gleaned from various sources and Plotnikov's own experience:

- Don't be an iconoclast when it comes to software. Conform! Use a standard word-processing program in a fairly recent version. Publishers will appreciate your compatibility, and you'll benefit from the tips that bubble forth from writer's magazines and other users. What's the best word processor for creative writers? In some respects (such as affordability) *WordPerfect* falls short, but it has established itself across the land as a writer's standard. *Microsoft Windows* has emerged as the standard "graphical user interface" for desktop publishing with

DOS systems. *WordPerfect for Windows* may be the text-graphic interface program to beat.

- Save files as you go along; don't wait until the end of the writing session. In most word processors, text can be saved (i.e., permanently stored) automatically at intervals chosen during a set-up program. Saving what you've written every fifteen minutes is usually safe enough for the pokey pace of creativity.
- Back up your files. This admonition has replaced "straighten up your room!" as the most common nag phrase in human language. Anyone who has lost days of work to disk damage, hard-disk failure, or other electronic calamities needs no reminding. Like brushing the teeth, one simply does it: copies the day's work to backup disks, which are stored safely apart from the original disks or hard disk.
- Revise from printouts. Writers should edit a printed-out version of each chapter as well as the text on screen. What seems right in glowing pixels may look all wrong on paper. It is always useful to revise the printout and test those revisions on the screen. Back and forth, back and forth, until the format that will be read by editors satisfies the eye.
- Don't become a process junkie. Word processing is just that—a process—however alluring the modern programs and their add-on features. Tinkering with process becomes more engaging than inventing content. What marvelous toys, those notepads, split screens, dictionaries, thesauri, and style-checkers, not to mention the whole graphics circus. For writers of certain technical or repetitive materials, these add-on "utilities" do save time and effort or liven up reports with slick graphics; for authors of imaginative literature, they mainly steal concentration from creative thought.

What must the average writer really know to benefit from word processing? Not much more than the basic operations—how to create, retrieve, and copy "files" (i.e., chunks of writing given file names); format a manuscript page; move quickly around a file; transfer or delete blocks of text; automatically delete or replace certain words or phases throughout the text; underline, make boldface, and center; correct an unwanted command; and control the printer. Beyond these functions, writers should perhaps know how to set up a "macro," a simple command that activates a sequence of previously entered instructions. Macros are used for such repetitive tasks as formatting a page—setting the margins, line spacing, page length, headings, and page numbering—all with one stroke.

These basics are learned easily enough from manuals, on-screen "help" tutoring, and user-support hotlines. From the point of view of the writer's efficiency, they should do for a lifetime of happy word processing. But of course, no writer is going to get off that easy.

HIGH-TECH HONKING

The array of high-tech options paraded before today's writers could be viewed as glorious opportunity or further torment, depending on one's needs and disposition. Journalists and others who do large-volume, tight-deadline writing can always use some mechanical help; software utilities, super-fast hardware, portables, scanners, modems, and fax machines deliver it. Those who want to "self-publish" will find it easier than ever to produce handsome pages via desktop systems—but no easier to print, bind, market, and distribute them, which is the real business of publishing. Those who need instant, basic assistance with spelling, word choice, grammar, rhyming, gags, and even ideas, will find sophisticated programs to suit them.

On the other hand, high technology bedevils writers trying to sneak by merely on writing skills honed over a lifetime. If they can put words together skillfully and get them to a publisher, isn't that enough? What more do they need than a telephone, public library, corner mailbox—and, okay, a basic word processor and printer for neatness? Why should they have to keep up with technological fashions? Buy state-of-the-art goods? Become a power user? Equip an "electronic cottage"? Understandably, the electronics industry plays on fears of obsolescence and inadequacy to sell its never-ending output of new models. The compleat writer, we are led to believe, must barrel into the twenty-first century like the high-tech troops of Desert Storm.

Today's writer is one more victim of what Richard Saul Wurman calls "information anxiety," the perception that most new information is indispensable and that without relentless intake one will lose out, fall behind. Since half the publishing world is madly ingesting high-tech information, to some extent the anxiety is justified: Writers who just want to write and not think about chips, disks, cards, boards, lasers, laptops, and a million software modules may be the displaced persons of tomorrow.

What's the answer? Perhaps a middle path between Luddite and hacker makes sense. Wurman's antidote to information anxiety is (more or less) to separate one's real needs from the hysterically perceived needs and act only on the real. Though writers are bombarded with messages to the contrary, they don't *need* to produce manuscripts in 180 type fonts or import high-resolution color graphics into their text. Not yet. Writers need to do what the vast majority of other writers are doing to keep up with publishers. If every other freelancer is using fax, for example, the faxophobes need to get with it or they *will* be left behind.

As communicators, writers actually should keep an eye on new tools being used to create and exchange messages, but they needn't pore through hacker literature or attend $700-a-day seminars. The major innovations spill into the writers' trade literature and popular press. Peter H. Lewis's columns on personal computers (in *The New York Times* and elsewhere) offer one painless alert to new tends. More detailed consumer information is usually available at point of purchase or in libraries. Librarians will guide users to evaluative articles. For subject research, they will also assist in electronic database searching—should an author actually need that level of information.

PLOTNIKOV'S PREOCCUPATIONS

Oh it's easy to talk about beating information anxiety, but Plotnikov suffers all the angst the high-tech devils can whip up—even more than the average writer. As a publisher in the library/information-services field, he is exposed daily to ruminations on high-end research technology. One journal he sees features information "strips" readable only by scanner. In the next office his colleagues sit all day at their computers networking with screen-watchers around the nation. Down the hall a state-of-the-art publishing system sucks manuscript text into an accelerator-like stream of electrons.

At night and on weekends, however, Plotnikov is home with his relatively low-tech setup: (in 1991) a sluggish computer and a daisy-wheel printer that refuses to die. His DOS is 2.11, his WordPerfect 4.2, his chip 8088—versions from a time before time began. The equipment will get him through his present assignments, perhaps, but he feels he is losing ground, losing ground. Like Hamlet, he agonizes but he cannot act: To spring for a bigger hard disk and a laser printer or not to spring? That is the question. What if the technology changes tomorrow? He can't pass a Radio Shack without yearning for the laptop computer in the window. It's cute as a puppy, but how much writing will he do away from his desk? Each Sunday, when the discount-electronics supplement spills from the newspaper, he longs for all those peripherals "at prices so low they cannot be revealed—call for details!" He hesitates.

Plotnikov ponders the special electronic aids for writers that come along. Here at about $400 is "Plots Unlimited," which prompts fiction writers through "theme, conflict, and character"; At some $40, "Write Pro, the Sol Stein Creative Writing Program" offers prompting, mentoring, and "28 priceless tricks of the trade"—$1.48 per priceless trick. "The Humor Processor," about $50, features a database of jokes, plus prompts for "free-associating" new and nutty gags. . . . The comedy-writer's dream, perhaps, but not Plotnikov's. Too much free-associating depresses him.

KEY DECISIONS

In considering an electronic product, the key questions are these: What process is replaced or improved? Do I *want* that process replaced or improved? Some writers would rather look in a print dictionary or thesaurus than press a key for a definition or synonym. It is good to get away from the screen now and then, and good to stumble on to something other than what was sought. Other writers don't want to break their concentration and they enjoy the built-in word guides, including such inventive categorical dictionaries as "Inside Information" by novelist Stephen Glazier.

For some writers electronic style guides may improve the revision process. Plotnikov tried out "RightWriter," a popular style-checker programmed with forty-five hundred rules, and was impressed by its ability to comment on his grammar, word usage, punctuation, and conformity to standard style patterns. However, one of Plotnikov's favorite activities is to do the same—apply to his prose the rules and feelings about human expression gathered in a literary life. "RightWriter" caught a few mechanical slip-ups he'd missed in a chapter, not worth the trouble in his view. Let the copy editors earn their keep.

In a publishing newsletter, Plotnikov read that Strunk and White's *Elements of Style* had been licensed for a software program. What process would be replaced or improved? *Elements* is a pint-sized eighty-five-pager that delights and instructs wherever it is opened. Its index gives quick access by subject. Having already suffered through a video version of *Elements* in which Charles Osgood read the rules, Plotnikov chose to pass on the electronic edition.

Specialized writers can indeed benefit from specialized electronic products. To authors who compile long lists of sources, such programs as "Pro-Cite" and "Biblio-Links" may be godsends. What do they replace? The first replaces the labor of preparing bibliographies and of preparing them in standard formats (such as those of the Modern Language Association); the second, for writers working with electronic literature, replaces the labor of transferring bibliographic information from the sources into one's own manuscript. Here, dozens of tedious work hours are eliminated and the quality of the bibliographies improved.

Likewise, electronic databases enable writers to find and compile information from sources throughout the world in a matter of minutes—searches that would have taken hours, months, or even lifetimes. For a dollar or two a minute on VU/TEXT, for example, researchers can sweep through thousands of editions of some fifty major newspapers to target names or events from the last few years, up to the previous day. If that isn't recent enough, AP ALERT will scan by subject some eight thousand stories a day from the Associated Press wires.

How many databases are there? At least six thousand, according to the 1991 Caudra directories. Some forty-seven hundred are online (accessed by communications lines) and fifteen hundred on "portable" disks, diskettes, and tapes. This much data could justify anyone's information anxiety, especially considering the high cost of most online searching. How important are electronic databases to the average writer? That depends. Writers find them cost-effective mainly in these situations: searching for the needle-in-the haystack item of information; compiling exhaustive recent background on a narrow topic; looking for the very latest writings or findings on a topic; and searching combined and delimited subjects—say, articles mentioning / schizophrenia OR paranoia / AND / writers and writing BUT NOT Plotnikov / /1985–1990/.

WHAT NEXT?

Other than the death of literature that futurists like to predict, the writer has nothing to worry about in the electronic century to come. Instead of warm and fuzzy bookstores and libraries, futurists picture a centralized hive of gigabit (one-billion-bit) chips and optical discs containing all the world's text. This electronic mass will provide specialized and privileged information. The diversions once derived from literature will come from synthetically stimulating forms and devices. Plotnikov envisions some kind of mesmerizing Z-waves generated by a spiked helmet.

As chunks of text are pulled from the master database and repackaged in infinite combinations, intellectual property will be meaningless. No literary individualism, no creative motivation. Goodbye writers, hello anonymous technical drones.

So say the futurists. Futurists flesh out what is technologically possible into the most menacing scenarios imaginable, so that everyone pays attention and buys their books. In 1990 entrepreneur Ted Turner had to offer a $500,000 prize to encourage optimistic scenarios of things to come.

Given the restlessness of human nature, however, one scenario of the distant future is as good as the next. For all anyone knows, writers could be as gods, looked to for salvation from electronic ennui. Literary pursuit could be the new world religion.

The moral: Take the electronic imperative one day at a time. Learn what is needed to meet today's standards and don't look beyond. Hang in long enough to say your piece, cry your cry, honk your honk. For in the long view obsolescence threatens every writer, desktop genius or electronic klutz.

Read on.

21

FACING THE GRIM REAPERS

Obsolescence and Obscurity

.

"Genius past its prime easily turns at times to
nonsense."
—Longinus

"I've always tried to be an éminence terrible
but have succeeded only in becoming an aged
enfant gris."
—Edward Dudley, British editor

If they live long enough, writers eventually lose touch with the general reading public and become outdated. The public changes and a writer doesn't. The public grows old and stops reading. A new public comes along with new values.

Some writers go against the tide of public taste. For a while their very defiance draws attention. One day the tide leaves them ashore like hollow crabs among the seaweed.

This is obsolescence.

Like all writers, Plotnikov dreads the cold inevitability of being out of it. He envisions himself at age one hundred refusing to accept his fate. Some eighty-five years of sitting and writing have given him the look of an ancient fat-bottomed swamp cypress. Yet here he sits in the year 2037 writing a novel he hopes will catch on. Its subject: marital love, based on fifty-four happy years with his wife Mary. No one has published a love story in three decades. In fact, no one has published a book of any sort since 2007, the first year of Helmetvision and its mesmerizing Z-waves. Nevertheless Plotnikov perseveres. He draws a rheumy breath and writes: "Chapter 53: An Episode in the Garden."

WRITERS don't have to be one hundred to feel obsolescent. Not long ago when critics gushed over young Mark Leyner's "rock music in prose," what traditional author didn't feel a touch creaky? Over-forty writers feel obsolescent every time they open *Publishers Weekly* to that page of brightly smiling children—the newly appointed acquisitions editors. What does one *say* to them? "Buy this manuscript and I'll send a puppy"?

Writers tend to hang on to what they knew and could do well. At one time their brand of honking earned at least some of the rewards of being a writer. When it no longer works, they have two choices: adapt to changes in the contemporary audience, or stop writing to that audience. The first requires a buoyancy of spirit and powers of observation that few writers can sustain. Tom Wolfe is a rare example of those who manage to stay interested in and alert to every nuance of change. His work has suited—nay defined—literary fashions over the last four decades. He has dared to berate other authors for tying themselves in self-indulgent literary knots instead of embracing the vitality of the here and now.

To stop writing to the market is a valid choice if one has the means and the will to write for one's own purposes. To hell with Publishers Row and the reading public! One can write for the joy of craft, truth, self-expression, or escape. The public can take it or leave it. Kurt Vonnegut announced in 1990 that he wasn't going to write funny anymore; reality had grown too dark even for his darkest humor. He remarked in *The New York Times Book Review*, "Jokesters are all through when they find themselves talking about challenges so real and immediate and appalling to their listeners that no amount of laughter can make the listeners feel well and perfectly safe again."

Readers can take or leave an unfunny Vonnegut. Many will leave; but Vonnegut apparently will continue to write, if only to articulate "our destruction of the planet. . . ."

As long as writing still addresses the inner search, it makes sense to keep at it. At age seventy, author and critic Doris Grumbach (*Coming Into the End Zone*) sought answers to the bewilderment of advancing age and the death of friends. She told *Publishers Weekly,* "I think writing is an act of healing. It's an exorcism of sorts, to put into words and symbols this almost inexpressible anguish." On the other hand, in 1987, when Holocaust survivor Primo Levi faced mounting distress over the state of the world, he hurled himself down the stairs of his childhood home in Turin, Italy. He had outlived his search for answers. "Not to be onto something is to be in despair," says Binx Bolling of Walker Percy's *The Moviegoer.* Walker Percy's death in 1990 left unanswered questions about his own search.

THE LATEST STYLE

Although some intrepid authors will stick to the old routines hoping the world will come around, most writers believe they can fine-tune their material to current tastes. After all, writers are "with-it" cognescenti with an ear for what's going on, right? Wrong. They are once-with-it people who isolated themselves from the mainstream when they became writers and spent their days in solitary confinement. They have to work very hard to listen again and get in synch with contemporary readers. They have to trade old values for new. If the effort shows, they sound like Barbra Streisand singing rock.

Even the most timeless themes must be delivered within a certain style, and style dates. So do all a writer's fixtures and furnishings, the allusions and references, attitudes and lingo. In 1986 the flamboyant young Tama Janowitz set the literary world on fire with *Slaves of New York,* stylish short stories based on the lower Manhattan art scene. Now she must fight obsolescence. Today's high style is tomorrow's Dubious Achievement

Award. Like vogue words, vogue styles are fastest to go rancid—even as they sit in manuscript.

Of course styles can recycle and often do. Suddenly in 1991 Paul Bowles's langorous existentialism of 1949 was hot thanks to the movie version of *The Sheltering Sky*. Bowles, a well-kept eighty, could enjoy the revival. Most authors are dust by the time they are rediscovered.

Even when aging writers master the contemporary idiom, obsolete values peek out like long johns from an Armani suit. Lovers in a script may talk like their audience, but if they smoke in bed or eat red meat they seem dated. Gonzo self-destructive antiheroes are yesterday's news. Even period pieces must nod to contemporary values, sensitizing cave dwellers and pirates to the new morality.

The AIDS epidemic—and before that a herpes panic—rendered obsolete one of fiction's most powerful devices: sex with a stranger, or the "zipless fuck" as Erica Jong termed it in *Fear of Flying*. What will the Double-O-Sevens now do between kills? The devil-may-care hedonists are finished, and some critics say good riddance. Writers who made literature out of now-unpopular values often join those values on the trash heap.

MINE ENEMY GROWS YOUNGER

Your name is Ken Kesey or Kate Millett or Jay McInerney, and for a while your message and way of saying it coincided with the yearnings and anxieties of a generation, including young hearts along Publishers Row. And the reviews and advertisements trumpeted you as The Voice of a Generation, and as long as that generation was around you knew you were in business. Then suddenly—it always seems sudden—you are forty-something, fifty-something, and what has happened?

Oh, your generation is still around, somewhere out in the subdivisions watching videos and reading the odd book, but it is no longer the hot generation of readers. After age forty a generation loses its clout as a book market. In 1983, some 61 percent of U.S. book readers were thirty-something and under, according to a Book Industry Study Group survey. Only 25 percent were over fifty. A 1985 Gallup report on book buying echoed these demographics. True, the over-fifty set was growing—to 37 percent of the population—but it accounted for only 27 percent of book purchases.

To writers unsure of how to reach the new generations, these figures are daunting—as is the youth of editors judging manuscripts. An inverse proportion seems to be at work; the older the writer the younger the average editor and reader. Plotnikov paranoically estimates that when he turns sixty a corps of eight-year-old editors will be acquiring books for a mass audience of preschoolers.

Those who ride to glory on the shoulders of the young must also face the Grim Reaper—sometimes prematurely. In 1985 critic John Powell observed in *Film Comment,* ". . . some place you've got to find scripts for the Brat Pack . . . that group of young men from roughly fifteen to twenty-five . . ." The hot source, he said, were books by McInerney and Bret Easton Ellis, "the poets laureate of the 'hipoisie.' " Soon these two authors themselves along with Tama Janowitz, Jill Eisenstadt, and David Leavitt were dubbed the Brat Pack, to their short-range benefit.

These voices of their generation haven't quite figured out what to say to the new "generations" that pop up every few minutes with new clusters of interests. Ellis's floundering led to *American Psycho,* a graphic novel of female mutilation that alienated millions even before publication.

STAYING RELEVANT

Aging writers must consider Peter Ustinov's sad observation in *The Sundowners:* "Nothing is more abhorrent to the young than watching their elders at play"—or reading about them at play, he might have added. Turning fifty, Plotnikov mused over what in his present life could interest readers in their twenties—his daughters' generation. His daughters were engaged by the world around them; but Dad's doings put a confectioner's glaze over their eyeballs.

Not a great deal happens to generally contented married fifty-year-olds that has meaning across the generations. A little arthritis in the bowling hand. A decision to remodel the bathroom. A search for the best certificate of deposit. These are not the themes to make young hearts flutter.

Mid-life crises stir some general interest if only because "mid-life" seems to come earlier all the time—the forties, even the late thirties, when life appears to be offering the last chance for reckless adventure. Post-mid-life characters are the real challenge. What makes them interesting? Power—Godfathers who deliver death sentences with a nod. Incorrigibility, as in *The Horse's Mouth*. Humor and sarcasm. Eccentricities and mannerisms. Memories. The last temptation. A plunge from grace: Shusaku Endo's *Scandal* plays on the outward respectability of an aging writer and a venal counterlife.

In repressive societies older characters attract interest by their intellectual and political daring. Such daring falls flat, however, in permissive democracies. In totalitarian states, Phillip Roth has noted, "nothing goes and everything matters"; in his own country, "everything goes and nothing matters."

Yet Roth can immortalize an obdurate old retiree (his father) by sheer strength of storytelling and an eagle's grip on the tragic sense of life. Updike works the same magic with Harry Angstrom in *Rabbit at Rest*. Readers can be made to care about anyone when the author cares enough and can show why.

Whipping up interest in one's aging self is a bit trickier, but there are ways. One of them is curmudgeonism, based on the theory that if you can't join 'em—beat 'em. A good caning by a curmudgeonly coot is always in style, the angrier the more amusing because it needn't be taken seriously. Malcolm Muggeridge—perfectly named to be a curmudgeon—was merely outrageous and irreverent until his later fifties, when age lent the crankiness that gives curmudgeonism its flavor. "It is a minor vexation of growing old," he wrote in his autobiography, "that what seems novel and audacious to the young is stale and already discredited in the light of one's experience."

Another escape from obsolescence is to find subjects that transcend oneself, themes that are always timely or timeless, and to remove oneself as much as possible from the telling. In 1980 Edward Rice, then sixty-one, started writing about a childhood hero: English explorer and scholar Richard Francis Burton. Ten years later Scribner published the biography as *Captain Sir Richard Francis Burton: The Secret Agent Who Made the Pilgrimage to Mecca, Discovered the Kama Sutra and Brought the Arabian Nights to the West.* (With that title, young readers could distinguish Sir Richard from Elizabeth Taylor's Richard Burton.) Rice explained in interviews that people love to read about heroes—especially heroes whose motives remain a mystery and cannot be psychoanalyzed and dated. Sure enough the book took off and gave Rice his first big best-seller, at age seventy-one. It was his twentieth book, and Rice was already at work on another about lost civilizations of Mohenjo-Daro in the Indus Valley. Rice wasn't messing with ephemeral topics.

The downtown style may elude some writers over sixty, but creative powers often reach their height at this time of life. Psychological studies reported by Janet Belsky* have debunked the notion of creativity fading with youth. On the contrary, while mathematicians seem to peak in their thirties and forties, historians and writers blossom as late as in their sixties. Perhaps everything worth knowing is *not* learned in kindergarten. Perhaps Longinus† was right when he said, "Literary judgment is the last outgrowth of long experience." He said it in the third century. It still makes sense.

* Belsky, Janet. *The Psychology of Aging; Theory, Research, and Practice.* Monterey, California: Brooks-Cole, 1984.
† A Greek critic, scholar, and teacher of the third century A.D., Longinus was educated in Alexandria and apparently taught in Athens before becoming advisor to Queen Zenobia of Palmyra in Asia Minor. Through his works and teaching, Longinus was known as a "living library" and "walking museum." What he said counted, and his concise treatise *On Great Writing (On the Sublime)* seems as relevant today as in his lifetime or in the late seventeenth to early nineteenth centuries, when intellectuals revered him almost as a cult figure. *On the Sublime* exemplifies writing that transcends obsolescence and gives worthy advice to that very point.

To writers seeking a higher level of imaginative power, Longinus suggests, "An even greater incentive [than imagining great writers looking over one's shoulder] is to ask the question: how will posterity receive what I write? For if a man is actually afraid to utter anything that looks beyond his own life and time, then his mind's conceptions are destined to be imperfect and blind; they will miscarry, nor ever grow into the perfection which deserves later fame." (From the G.M.A. Grube translation, Liberal Arts Press, 1957.)

Where stamina allows, there seems to be no upper age limit to writing competence, though the light of genius may flicker. Writing may be the very source of stamina. Modern examples abound: Ninety-one-year-old Charles Bennett, author of some fifty-eight produced screenplays, was reworking his *Blackmail* on commission from 20th Century Fox in 1990, pounding out his autobiography, and planning to go on till 120. In 1989, (then) Harper & Row signed up the first book of Jane Goyer, ninety-five, based partly on essays for a newspaper column she was still writing. Barbara Cartland tossed off her five hundredth romance novel at age eighty-nine in 1990. At eighty, Helen Hooven Santmeyer finished *And Ladies of the Club,* a novel filling eleven boxes in manuscript. In 1984 it became a number-one best-seller.

OBSCURITY AND THE VANITY OPTION

In life's last season writers should outgrow the need to publish, but they don't. Like beginning authors, they cry to be heard, risking even more rejection. Now the object is not to escape obsolescence, but obscurity—death without a record of one's outcries. Even if the literary pursuit is foregone, there remains the desperate human need to leave some footprints for posterity.

"I approached fifty-five publishers with my latest novel," confesses Edward Le Comte in "Letters of Rejection: A Personal Experience" (*The American Scholar,* Summer 1988). Though his rejections were far fewer than the Guinness world record of 223 (as of 1987), his tale is interesting because he was approaching seventy at the time, had the tenacity to follow every lead to its conclusion, and probably represents thousands of over-sixty writers in frenetic pursuit of publication.

Le Comte was fortunate. Atheneum published his novel (*I, Eve*) after some last-minute indecision. What of the thousands of elders judged unpublishable by the trade houses and still determined to get into print? Some have the skills and entrepreneurial balls to self-publish. The rest will at some point consider "subsidized" or "cooperative" publishing, otherwise known as "vanity" publishing.

Vanity publishers perform a simple service, though they make it sound like hot stuff. Essentially, they arrange to have a writer's manuscript typeset, printed, and bound into a presentable edition of a few hundred copies. They charge costs plus a substantial service charge and sometimes ask the author to "split" the financial risk of the entire venture. Some do light editing and a press release, which they send with copies to a few reviewers—who recognize vanity imprints at a glance and rarely touch them.

Such vanity "publishing" is not publishing at all, but merely printing. No paying author is rejected. True publication, once a manuscript is selected, includes professional editing and design services, some degree of marketing, and aggressive sales through established channels. Commercial publishers take all or most of the financial risk.

It makes sense to have a manuscript printed if the object is merely to enshrine one's work in some durable form, with enough copies for family and friends and—if they accept such books—the local libraries. A small-run book printer will give a fair bid. Very little more should be paid for the so-called publishing services of vanity presses. In a 1990 class-action suit by twenty-two hundred authors against Vantage Press, such horror stories were heard as, "they took my $6,000 and sent me fifty copies of my book, all of which I had to sell myself."

The allure of vanity publishing is familiar to every writer who has seen the ads, "AUTHORS WANTED BY PUBLISHER." As the author draws closer, the seduction gets thicker than cheap perfume. Jim McCormick, a writer in his seventies, shared with Plotnikov the letters he received from a legitimate but shamelessly seductive "cooperative" publisher.

McCormick has had his ups and downs, from his days as a respected journalist and three-book author to a scramble even for a kind rejection. The usual flak thrown at determined authors, however, has not grounded this wiry WWII bombardier. McCormick established a small publishing firm (Brighton Press) and self-published some of his nonfiction, gaining national publicity. His fiction he prefers to submit to trade houses, humane ones if he can find them. When he spotted a likely prospect in a standard directory, he shipped off his latest novel and waited for a response. It came quickly and was more than a kind rejection. It began:

> *A Far Cry* is a powerful book that galvanizes the mind of the reader and doesn't let go. It's a book that pulsates with life as it deals with love and family associations and the morality of the relationships to hook the reader into time and place. . . . In my minds [*sic*] eye, I believe this would make a good movie. It got several readings in a short span because we were so enthusiastic about it. . . .

After more gushing, the letter got around to what McCormick saw immediately: He'd have to *pay* to play published author. "What would you think of the idea of doing this on a cooperative basis?" the publisher asked. ". . . There is no reason that the partial investor cannot be the writer, if they so choose. . . ."

Feeling mischievous, McCormick decided to play the rube and expressed some interest. The publisher's second letter made an offer of $11,500—that is, a *charge* of $11,500 to McCormick to share the costs and profits of publication. McCormick teased them along, saying he was just waiting for his CDs to mature. Next came a full-blown contract, a call for a "bio photo," and a breathless, "I've already put it on the editing schedule and I can't wait to get started." They were still waiting as McCormick began to get some positive response from trade houses.

LITERATURE ITSELF: OBSOLETE

It isn't enough that individual authors become obsolete and obscure. In *The Death of Literature* (1990), Princeton professor Alvin Kernan sees as obsolete the very concept of author as creator of an immutable statement. In effect he says the new schools of criticism treat an author's work as nothing more than a raw product to reassemble into corrected values. In addition, he notes, electronic media have diminished the central role authors enjoy as creators of books and the very importance of books as "the primary way of knowing something in our society." Finally, if anything is left of literature, the spread of cultural illiteracy will assure its obsolescence.

Kernan's view may be on the dire side—had to be, to get published; yet the chilling effect of revisionist criticism is real. For all one's literary efforts, an ambitious work may be judged only by the unpredictable political values of five years hence. The death of literature grows closer, too, as mainstream publishers trash the whole category of nongeneric quality fiction. Publishers have decided there are many mass markets, not one, and that the literary mass market may be obsolete. In 1991 Bantam divided its mass-market paperback list into six generic categories: women's fiction, science fiction, crime, historical saga, high-tech action, and nonfiction. Where does that leave today's Baldwins or Faulkners or Woolfs?

Unlike Kernan, historian Daniel Boorstin has long argued that electronic media will not make books obsolete. One marvelous virtue of the book as an information/entertainment medium, Boorstin has remarked, is its portability. His remarks came prior to the flood of pocket-sized color television sets in the early nineties. Writers will of course produce the words that crackle from a wrist television, but the words will not be literature and the writers will not be authors as we know these singular entities today.

What can the writer do about the prophesied death of literature? Not much except: (1) write literature so fundamentally overpowering that no one will let it die; (2) write the best possible generic literature and hope it will transcend its form; or (3) stop worrying about it. People who care about literature have been predicting its death since Homer. The same people have managed to keep it going.

Whenever the world stifles the crying that is literature, when word people are denied the irresistible agony of the literary pursuit, all it does is give writers something new to say. Which is one antidote to obsolescence.

Epilogue

HONKING AS MYSELF

The Final Secret

"Before dying, he revealed his secret: 'The grape,'
he whispered, 'is made of wine.' . . . I thought: If
the grape is made of wine then perhaps we are the
words that tell who we are."
—Eduardo Galeano, The Book of Embraces

If we are the words that tell who we are, then I had better remind you quickly that I am the words of Arthur Plotnik and not of Arthur Plotnikov, my doppelgänger for the purposes of this book.

How lightheaded it feels to be using the "I" voice again, as if, with our little play ended, I'd lifted the ass's guise from my shoulders. Was Plotnikov an ass? Somewhat so, braying against the literary world while stubbornly pursuing his way as a writer. But thank God for ass-brained writers, all those thousands who bear the burden of creativity with no more reinforcement than a whack on the hinds. From just such asses comes the lion's share of literature.

Abused writers can take heart from André Bernard's *Rotten*

Rejections (Penguin), a sampling of editorial response suffered by literary lions-to-be: ". . . far too gloomy for us" (of Sherwood Anderson and *Winesburg, Ohio*); ". . . superficial and unconvincing" (of Bernard Malamud and *The Assistant*); "A long, dull novel about an artist" (of Irving Stone, *Lust for Life*); ". . . the American public is not interested . . ." (of Pearl Buck, *The Good Earth*).

Ass-headed authors—they all kept braying!

"THE grape is made of wine." What a fine secret, even if it's the kind of indecipherable flying object South American writers are always uncaging. (Galeano is Uruguayan). *"We are the words that tell who we are."* These secrets whisper to me that unlike most of the world's workers, petrified within themselves, we writers are afloat in some wondrous state of becoming.

Writers are criers, and we are never at peace with what we are; so we cry again to become something else. We are not who we are, but who we will be at our best. In his reflections on writers at the Yaddo retreat, Alfred Kazin observed that "writers, despite the famous hazards of their trade, are optimists. They have to be, for they are usually looking forward to the next book. As the wit said, other people judge us by the books we have written; we judge ourselves by the books we are going to write."

Writing thus becomes both liberation and imprisonment. If we keep writing we exist in the hopeful state of potentiality; if we stop, we have to face the words that tell who we are. Few writers are ready to do so. I look back on all the thousands of words that would define me and, sick to my stomach, race to my keyboard to re-create myself.

I WAS moved recently by the death of poet Paul Engle. I never knew him well, but it was he who admitted me to the Iowa Writers Workshop he founded and then shaped for so many years. It brought me back to those barracks classrooms and frozen fields where birth as a writer seemed more an icy con-frontation with death.

I've kept the letter from Engle that helped trigger a literary pursuit: "... I am determined to have you here.... [Your writings] are lively, interesting, and in need of shaping and pruning. ..." Thirty years later, damn it, I still need so much shaping and pruning I feel like a rogue pear tree. Engle prob-ably felt the same way. He was still writing at age eighty-two, putting together his memoirs and coauthoring a book of reflec-tions with his wife, Chinese novelist Hua-ling Nieh, still becom-ing, still redefining himself.

Any author's death prompts one to mull over the meaning of the writing life. So many important writers have died while I've worked on this book: Samuel Beckett, Graham Greene, Mary McCarthy, Malcolm Muggeridge, Lawrence Durrell, Walker Percy, Jerzy Kosinski. Some were still becoming, late in their eighties; others had lost the ability or saw only in death a transformation from what they were and could no longer en-dure. Yet a common thread ran through their views on writing, as quoted in the obituaries. Graham Greene put it this way (from *Ways of Escape*): "I wonder how all those who do not write, compose, or paint can manage to escape the madness, the melancholia, the panic fear which is inherent in the human situation." In his writings, Greene would admit, too, the absur-dity of the literary pursuit and its obsession with publishing success.

Do we fail as writers if we fail to mesh with the arbitrary tastes of literary arbiters? We fail as workers, perhaps, unable to support families and stoke the American economy. No big deal; so we take jobs selling balloons or editing magazines for the library profession. Without popular acceptance, we may also fail to bring salvation to the masses—and so what? Most of us share the sentiments of Suguro, esteemed writer in Shusaku Endo's novel *Scandal:* "Don't overestimate me, he wanted to tell [his many readers]. ... It's as much as I can do just to deal with my own problems; I can't take on the responsibility for your lives, too."

As a writer I will concentrate on my own problems and try to craft them into literature. *I* intend to be the judge of whether I succeed or not. Will any of my self-proclaimed literature find popular and critical acclaim? Who cares?

I do, of course. But I'm trying not to. I am trying to learn from my own advice, which is the hardest act of all. And what is that advice? That the only failure as a writer is to listen to reason when your heart says *HONK*!

Appendix

THE WRITER'S POCKET ADVISOR

HONK'S PRACTICAL ANSWERS TO SIXTY-FOUR
AGONIZING QUESTIONS

FIRST comes the insuppressible urge to write, racking body and soul. Then the need to do something about it and the first tormented questions—*Who? What? How?* This is no time for Zen and the Art of the Paragraph. The victim is in trauma and needs emergency advice. *The Pocket Advisor* provides it, addressing the most anxiety-provoking concerns of new writers. Should certain answers prove more agonizing than the questions, blame the writing business itself and not this author, who only shares the observations of a long journey through writing, editing, and publishing.

Quick answers have practical value, but they will not allay the long-term agony of the literary pursuit. Nor will a thorough reading of the preceding chapters. The faithful reader will, however, come to *embrace* that agony, once the myths and self-delusions of the literary pursuit have been demolished. From the rubble will emerge the stirring *honk* of a liberated writer at the approach of the twenty-first century. Your own defiant honk.

—A.P.

THE WRITING ENVIRONMENT

Who are all those writers out there?

They come by the hundreds of thousands, calling themselves writers and falling within dozens of categories—novelists, essayists, creative writers, technical writers, trade writers, journalists, genre writers (romance, western, etc.), children's writers, poets, playwrights, scriptwriters, copy writers, and so on. But no one has taken a total count accommodating such variations as full-time or part-time, paid or unpaid, published or unpublished, and recognized or self-proclaimed.

Circa 1991, U.S. Labor Bureau figures show two hundred-nineteen thousand "writers and editors," 40 percent of them salaried; U.S. *Statistical Abstracts* indicates eighty-two thousand "authors" who are "employed." The Scott Meredith literary agency maintains a database of one hundred eighty-two thousand professional and aspiring writers. *Writer's Digest* boasts a circulation of two hundred sixty-nine thousand. A fair guess is that some half a million Americans think of themselves at least partly as writers.

What do they want?

They believe they have a way with words, and they want to trade it for money, attention, and status. They want to express their individuality and validate their existence. They want to purge their hurts and fears by crying out.

They want to "publish" because publishing is a means toward these ends. The degree of wanting varies. Some want only to eke out a living or advance a point of view; others want what Nina wanted in Chekhov's *The Seagull:* "For the happiness of being an author . . . I would bear any poverty, disillusionment,

I'd have people hate me. I'd live in a garret and eat black bread. I'd endure my own dissatisfaction with myself and all my faults, but in return I should ask for fame . . . real resounding fame."

Who publishes writers?

These days just about anyone with access to a desktop computer, including writers themselves, create publications and distribute them to some extent. But true publishers, as the term is generally understood, take a writer's manuscript and develop, edit, produce, manufacture, warehouse, market, promote, sell, and distribute it. They also keep accounts, seek subsidiary sales such as book club rights, and pay royalties. "Trade" or general-interest book publishers perform all these services at their own risk, without fees or investments from the authors. (General-interest magazines are called "consumer" magazines, and provide publishing services for authors as partial creators of the magazine product. They pay fees rather than royalties.)

Professional, scholarly, and specialized publishers provide publishing services on a mini-scale. They receive fewer unsolicited manuscripts than do trade "houses," but rejection rates often run in the 90–95 percent range. Small-press publishers provide basic services, accept a broader range of manuscripts, and sometimes pay only in complimentary copies. "Vanity" publishers accept all manuscripts, do little more than manufacture the book, and charge the author a large mark-up on costs.

How many publishers are there?

No one can keep track, but the evidence shows *masses* of publishing enterprises (and publishing directories) throughout the world:

Bowker's *Publishers' International ISBN Directory* identifies a unique code number for one hundred eighty thousand publishers worldwide. Its *Books in Print* names more than thirty-two thousand U.S. firms in its Publishers Index.

The *Publishers Directory* (Gale) includes some twenty thousand Canadian and U.S. book publishers, including institutions. In its 1991 edition the *Literary Market Place* (Bowker) describes twenty-six hundred North American book publishers (up from ninety-three in 1940) who reported three or more titles for the past year. *Directory of Publishing* (Cassell) details eleven hundred book publishers in twenty-one countries within the United Kingdom's sphere. In Bowker's *Publishers, Distributors, and Wholesalers of the United States,* some six thousand associations and 730 museums report publishing programs in addition to those of the full-scale publishers listed. *The International Directory of Little Magazines and Small Presses* (Dustbooks) describes about five thousand markets. At the 1990 Frankfurt book fair, 8,414 publishers from around the world showed up to buy or sell rights.

The number of "periodicals" (magazines, newsletters, newspapers, etc.) is even more dizzying. *Standard Periodical Directory* lists sixty-five thousand in the U.S. and Canada alone. *Ulrich's International Periodicals Directory* (Bowker) cites one hundred ten thousand. For those who want to explore these lists, most are standard reference items in central public libraries.

Regional directories are also published, mixing book, periodical, and other freelance markets in one area. For example, *The Writer's Guide to Metropolitan Washington* (Woodbine House, Rockville, Md.) details almost one thousand publishing opportunities.

If there are so many publishers, why is it so #@!! hard to get published?

It isn't—if you write highly specialized nonfiction for the special-interest market. Such publications account for most of the numbers in the directories above. Specialize in cat grooming, digital switches, or penile implants and eventually you'll find a regular niche. Write poetry, short stories, and novels and you join a very large crowd fighting for a very few publishers who can bestow money or fame. "Slush piles" of unsolicited manuscripts total tens of thousands along Publishers Row each year. The major houses published fewer first novels (eighty-five) in the fall 1990 season than in any fall over the past decade, reports *Library Journal*. Major periodical markets for short fiction are down to a handful. *The New Yorker, The Atlantic,* and

Mademoiselle groan under some thirteen to fifteen thousand such manuscripts each per year. *Redbook* tells rejected short-story writers they were among twenty thousand unfortunates for the year. Even small-press publishers are besieged. Editor David Wojahn of *Crazyhorse* reports that "manuscripts never trickle in; they *cascade* in, they *deluge* us. . . ."

General-interest markets are shrinking because readers are most enthusiastic about special interests and in response publishers are targeting narrow "niche" markets.

With videos, cable, and every other distraction, are enough people still reading to make writing worthwhile?

Today yes; tomorrow who knows? Americans aren't the world's heaviest readers, but recent surveys show that about 66 percent of the nation's adults have nose to book at least a few times a year. Women read more than men—twice as much fiction, counting romance novels. Folks over fifty account for only some 25 percent of book readers/buyers.

U.S. publishers are issuing forty to fifty thousand titles a year, including textbooks and mass-market paperbacks. No one knows how many individual books are produced, but copies are sold in approximately twenty-five thousand retail stores among other outlets such as mail-order houses. Book-industry sales total more than $13 billion. About 60 percent of American adults borrow at least a book a year from libraries.

So people are reading. Counting mass market, fiction accounts for about 15 to 20 percent of the output—though we didn't say good fiction. People are also listening to books: Audiotaped titles are coming out at about five thousand a year and totaled close to forty thousand in 1991.

GETTING STARTED

I have a way with words and want to be a writer. Where do I begin?

Start at a good public library. There are more ideas, inspirations, and practical tips on the shelves than in a thousand writers' colonies. The library has everything a writer needs except talent and a word processor—and some libraries even lend time on computers. Librarians are writers' saints. Don't hesitate to ask their help, but don't dominate their time.

Mainly, the beginning writer needs to locate these sections in the library: language usage and style; literary reference, including biographical sketches; how-to writer's guides; and market directories (the last are often kept behind the reference desk, available on request). To find your way, search by subject in the user-friendly computer catalogs now in most libraries.

Browse, borrow, bore into some of the titles that turn you on. Read in *Contemporary Authors* or *Current Biography* how other writers have done it. Get familiar with some of the basic tools, for example, *Literary Market Place* (Bowker), which lists agents, editorial services, literary contests, and many other writers' goodies, as well as major publishers. Read *Publishers Weekly* magazine. Look through the latest *Writer's Market* and *The Writer's Handbook* for brief tips from old pros and detailed market data. Be aware that these last two sources, like popular writers' magazines, are pollyannish and lead thousands of eager authors to the same markets.

The library provides not only writers' tools, but a sampling of the market in its periodicals and new books sections. It offers a general reference collection and a window on the nation's information resources through online searching and lending between libraries. Get to know the range of government information sources, often the best and the latest on popular topics. See what special collections the library holds that might serve you; look in the *American Library Directory* for other libraries and special collections available in your area.

In addition to your library visits, haunt the writing section of a good bookstore for the most recent or enduring writer's guides. *How to Get Happily Published* by Judith Appelbaum (NAL Plume) has become a standard primer and is well worth buying; in addition to its lessons and pep talks it describes scores of other standard resources. For nonfiction, William Zinsser's *On Writing Well* (Harper) is the ticket. Theodore A. Rees Cheney's *Writing Creative Nonfiction* (Ten Speed Press) explores the use of fiction techniques for writing "new journal-ism" a la Capote, Talese, and Wolfe.

No one book dominates among fiction-writing guides, but R. V. Cassill's *Writing Fiction* (Prentice-Hall) and Janet Burro-way's *Writing Fiction: A Guide to Narrative Craft* (Little, Brown) are often recommended. Brenda Ueland's inspirational *If You Want to Write* (Graywolf), first published in 1938, sold some eighty thousand copies in a 1987 reissue.

Madeline DiMaggio's *How to Write for Television* (Prentice Hall Press) covers that world-of-its-own thoroughly and read-ably.

WRITING aspirants stuck in a wasteland without good libraries and bookstores might send for such mail-order catalogs as "Tools of the Trade" from Ross Book Service, Box 12093 Sem-inary Post Office, Alexandria, VA 22304 (phone 703-823-1919). The selections cover writing, editing, desktop publishing, and more. A catalog from Writer's Digest Books, 1507 Dana Ave., Cincinnati, OH 45207 (phone 513-531-2222) describes the many specialized titles—such as *How to Write Romances*—of this energetic if uneven publisher.

After immersing oneself in what writing is all about, the next steps are to write and get feedback. Continuing education programs in writing may be available locally. (Ask a librarian.) Be wary of correspondence courses except those sponsored by an established academic program. Writers workshops and sem-inars are listed in several standard guides (see later question) and in writers' trade magazines.

From the day you decide to write, start keeping a notebook of good words and quotes and of observations, large and small—mostly small. Become what Henry James admonished writers to be: someone on whom nothing is lost.

How do I uncork my talent?

Don't set out to "commit an act of literature," advises Zins-ser. Novelist Isabel Allende remarks, "I don't think of literature as an end in itself; it's just a way of communicating something."

In other words, let your talent unfold as a by-product of the story or information you want to convey. The less you try to show your talent, the more it will reveal itself. Writing talent is mainly editing talent. Get it down, clean it up. As Elmore Leonard does, eliminate "the parts people skip." Don't spell out messages; let forceful language and action do the work. Kill every cliché. Dam up the rambling streams of consciousness. Don't worry about an individual voice or style; that, too, will emerge.

Which side of the brain should I use?

Like most writers, beginners are likely to block just when they feel they have the most to say. The head is spinning but the words won't come. Some educators call this impasse a war between the brain's analytical left and artistic right hemispheres—between editor and creator. The idea is to ignore the left brain and write in a free flow of thoughts, then, when you're ready, put the editor to work. Unblocking techniques also include writing oneself a letter: "Dear Myself, I had a terrible time getting started today, when all I wanted to talk about was—" Ah-ha, you've tricked yourself into blabbing away.

Are there finger exercises for beginners?

Always. For example, to force livelier verbs into your prose, try writing or rewriting a page without using the verb "to be" in any form. Hard, ain't (whoops!) it?

Jim Harrison recalls that in school he "was taught to imitate models—to sound like anyone you wanted to. That helps, you know." And it does, just to get that literary syntax into the brain either by close imitation as in parody, or loose approximation of a writer's style. Joan Didion says that as a teenager she typed out passages from Conrad and Hemingway to "see how sentences worked." Most writers' workshop students tend to mimic their instructors on the way to finding their own voices. Half of writing has always been mimicry of one's great predecessors. But to imitate, one has to first read until the voices of good writers enter one's bones—including the finger bones. The prolific Anthony Burgess reminds writers to memorize favorite passages of verse. "Verse is for learning by heart, and that is what a literary education should mostly consist of."

Writing poetry is good practice for other forms. If you can craft a tight line of poetry with powerful words precisely used, words that flow without gushing, you can write a good line of prose. Even if the poems fail as poetry, you are learning.

Real beginners may need a composition course or text with traditional exercises such as "compare and contrast." Exercises in "transactional" or "problem-solving" writing call attention to intended audience and author's purpose. Any exercise that takes the writer from self-indulgent venting to other-directed prose is worthwhile. Some lively exercises are offered in Rita Mae Brown's *Starting from Scratch* (Bantam). Thomas S. Kane's *The New Oxford Guide to Writing* (Oxford) is a nicely organized compendium of fundamentals, creative tips, and practical exercises. Henriette Anne Klauser offers freeing-up exercises in *Writing on Both Sides of the Brain* (HarperCollins).

But there comes the time to go beyond finger exercises. Now passion bids you to write what you're aching to write, fail where you're going to fail, and learn along the way. If the big novel is kicking in your belly, you don't work it out through short stories. Short stories are their own form, made, says Wallace Stegner, "for discoveries and nuances and epiphanies."

How do I turn the gift of gab into writing?

By a process of selectivity that may require hours for a sentence and endless rewrites. Research shows that gabbers communicate about 80 percent through body language. Most of what they say is filler to avoid a silence, and the listener tunes it out. In writing, no tune-outs are allowed; the filler has to be removed and words chosen that simulate the force of body language. Since the listener isn't standing by during the process, writing allows time to agonize over words: choosing them with care to hold and stimulate the listener, arranging them to refresh the listener's mind and ear. If it's done right, the struggle doesn't show.

KEYS TO WRITING SUCCESS

Have I got what it takes to write?
A relative question if there ever was one. What it takes when? According to whom? For what? Did John Kennedy Toole, who killed himself because no one would publish *A Confederacy of Dunces,* have what it takes to write fiction? According to the major publishers, no. According to his mother, and then Walker Percy and a university press, and subsequently millions of readers, yes. But did he have what it takes to face the normal rejections of the writing business?

Harlan Ellison, author of some fifty books and fifteen hundred other pieces, believes "there are writers, and there are authors. *Any*body can be an author. With the demand for material as great as it is today, any poor slob who can write without bumbling over his syntax can sell." His idea of a "writer," however, is that very rare individual who "hears the music," something that can't be taught.

What music? People of such varied traits and talents have become published writers that the usual list—an ear for language, an eye for detail, dedication, fortitude, and something to say—is almost meaningless. Eyes and ears can be sharpened; dedication is driven by hunger and ego, fortitude kicks in as a survival mechanism. And having little to say hasn't stopped thousands of writers. Rather than count your traits, just write when you get a chance and see what happens.

Have I got what it takes to quit my job and be a writer?
You mean, to sacrifice the rest of your life to writing? To make a living at this business? For most people the answer is *no.* In *How to be a Freelance Writer* (Bantam), freelancer David Martindale profiles the writer with an outside chance of success: a gambler, handles rejection, needs no structure in life, persistent, assertive, skeptical, can compromise, secure without money, good business head, strong family support.

To this list, add three key items:
1. Positive self-esteem *independent of* the ups and (mostly) downs of writing.

2. Patience that puts Job to shame. Normally, the literary pursuit takes most of a lifetime, and every aspect of it requires *waiting* to the limits of endurance.

3. Tolerance of isolation. Humans are social creatures, except for writers. Writing is a lonely, inward preoccupation; the writing life takes place mostly in a small room behind a desk. Are you willing to become essentially an observer and dissector of life rather than a participant? Are you willing, literally and figuratively, to work inside while the rest of the world plays outdoors?

Writers without these qualifications should not quit their day jobs. Incidentally, freelancers earn an average of $8,000 a year, according to the Author's Guild.

Are women writers at a disadvantage?

In getting published, no. Publishing may have begun as a man's world, but today women head major trade houses and literary agencies. Female—even feminist—editors have clout. At the helm of some of the most powerful reviewing media, women have evened up the number and prominence of reviews given each sex. Literary fiction is no longer dominated by men, and women writing under their own names have penetrated such male-only genres as sports journalism and spy thrillers. For certain other genres, such as romance, women writers are preferred. Authors such as Jean Auel, a self-described "housewife" some years ago, prove there are no caps on what women can earn by the pen.

By necessity or choice, many women devote what might have been writing time to child rearing. This alone rarely sinks a career, though it may slow it down. Mary McCarry Morris's brilliant debut came a little later than usual—at age forty-five. "When the children were very young, poetry was the most I could grab time for," she says. "When they were in school I was able to find more time to squeeze in writing."

Thriller writer Mary Higgins Clark trained as a secretary. After her husband died, she supported five children partly by writing radio scripts. She sold her first story at twenty-eight after six years of trying. In 1988, at age sixty, she signed a $10.1 million, five-book deal with Simon & Schuster.

Toni Morrison juggled single parenthood with writing, editing, and university teaching. Writing was her Saturday night company, she told *Publishers Weekly*. "I had these little children, and so I wrote at night. . . . I liked the privacy, the interior world that was all mine."

Women writers network better than men. The six-thousand-member International Women's Writing Guild, based in New York, is one link, and there are scores of local connections such as Women Writers West in Santa Monica and the annual Women's Ink in Philadelphia.

Will it help or hinder to identify myself as African American? Hispanic American? Native American?

It won't hurt to mention it and will often help get attention. Most editors would be thrilled to discover a good "minority" writer. Certainly, if you've written a heavily ethnic piece, the editor will want to know your background.

Alice Walker told *USA Weekend* she loves being called a "black woman writer." ". . . It's the best of all possible worlds," she said. "I have the connection to everything absent in the work of a white male writer."

Not every writer of color, however, wants to be labeled an "ethnic voice." Voices, especially strident ones, have their season. Hispanic was hot along Publishers Row after Cuban-American Oscar Hijuelos won the Pulitzer Prize. What's hot tends to get overdone, played out, and stereotyped: "Another growing-up-Latino? We've heard it!"

Writing under any label entails the same risk. Feminist voices, gonzo journalists, brat packers—all rise and fall according to trends and find themselves locked in to type. So-called "regional" writers hate that minor-league label, which New York reviewers slap on any author strong on local color. One has to write what one knows and feels—and holler when anyone starts labeling.

Whom do you have to know to get a book published?

You don't *have* to know anyone, and knowing the moguls themselves won't help if you don't have a publishable work (or an irresistible nonfiction proposal) in hand. Once the goods are ready, however, the task is to get someone to take a serious look—either a reputable agent or mainstream editor. *Now* it helps to know someone who can hand your material to one of those people with an endorsement, "This is worth your time."

You can also blitz the publishing world with copies and hope that some agents or editors are still reading unsolicited manuscripts. Small presses are overloaded and especially understaffed, so you might as well start high. Many legitimate agents offer to read and critique unknowns for a fee, and a pretty stiff one. If money is no problem, try it; otherwise do it only as a last resort.

How do you get to know someone? Attend writers workshops and impress the visiting instructors. Many dozens of unknowns (Anne Rice was one of them) have broken in via this connection. Get the word out among friends, colleagues, and relatives that you're looking to talk to anyone in publishing. Join networking groups such as the women's groups mentioned above or writing organizations listed in the *Encyclopedia of Associations*. For specialized nonfiction, solicit written endorsements from a few leaders in the field; these can bolster your proposal to agent or editor.

Writer Carol Felsenthal (among many others) got to "know" editors simply by calling up publishing houses and asking who would handle manuscripts on her particular topic. She got specific names, then wrote or phoned them directly until—bingo! As a way of finding editors' names, Felsenthal also suggests the acknowledgment pages of favorite new books. *Literary Market Place* and other standard guides in libraries give names of top personnel at publishing houses and agencies. (Some agencies indicate that they will read new writers without charging a fee.) One ambitious source is Jeff Herman's *The Insider's Guide to Book Editors and Publishers* (Rocklin, California: Prima), which names acquiring editors at the major houses and describes their chief interests. Frequent editions will be necessary, since editors dart like swallows from house to house.

THE WRITER'S EDUCATION

What courses should I take in school?

As an undergraduate, take some courses outside the usual English major concentration. Give yourself an understanding of the universe beyond comparative literature. Get a taste of the sciences and their stunning vocabularies—the apogees, chiasmata, and etiolations. Writers with subject specialties outside the humanities—business, for example—are usually more employable and probably happier. Science writers seem euphoric.

Journalism training benefits creative writers as well as aspiring journalists; the line between the two kinds of writing is blurring anyway. Creative writers may not wish to major in journalism, whose curriculum bogs down in ethical theory, but the fundamentals are precious. Tom Wolfe—one of hundreds of versatile authors who apprenticed in journalism—calls the reporter's art "the most valuable and least understood resource available to any writer with exalted ambitions."

Undergraduate creative writing courses are worth a shot, if only as an outlet for the first literary cries. Structured assignments introduce the art of writing on deadline. Such courses are usually confidence builders, encouraging anyone with a sliver of talent to take the literary plunge.

How do I get journalism training?

For academic instruction, through an undergraduate or graduate "J-school" program listed in the *Journalism & Mass Communications Directory*, published annually by the Association for Education in Journalism and Mass Communication at the University of South Carolina, Columbia. Information on two-year programs is available from the Community College Journalism Association, County College of Morris, Randolph, New Jersey.

It's possible to acquire some journalism savvy on the job—if you can land a job in this generally dismal market. Small or specialized media often hire writers with no J-school training but with other qualifications. Here, seasoned house journalists will rewrite your headlines and leads until you get it, and you'll fumble your way through interviews and aggressive news gathering. But you won't learn the sophisticated investigative research techniques J-schools are now teaching. Self-instruction in basic journalism is also an option; hit the library.

Which writers workshop is right for me?
The most sustained workshop experience will come from a university graduate program, with all the attendant costs and commitments. Such programs offer masters of fine arts in creative writing or even doctoral programs, intertwining with the English Department. If you have the funds, ambition, and academic preparation to go this route, consider which type of workshop attracts you. They vary widely, from market-oriented programs parading hot-name writers (and some agents) to the earthier heartland programs, removed from lit-glitz but dedicated to the making of good writers.

Academic institutions also offer nondegree programs, extension courses, and brief summer seminars. In fact, just about every literary organism on the planet runs a summer workshop. For a *Catalogue of Programs* covering 256 U.S. and Canadian institutions, contact Associated Writing Programs, Old Dominion University, Norfolk, VA 23529. *The Guide to Writers Conferences* (Shaw Associates, Coral Gables, Florida) describes some 850 programs, including thirty-two colonies and retreats worldwide. Poets & Writers (72 Spring St., New York, NY 10012) runs scores of ads and announcements for workshops in its indispensable bimonthly, *Poets & Writers Magazine*. It also publishes a guide with some two hundred listings in the U.S. and abroad. The *Literary Market Place* mentioned above lists a number of workshops, as do the spring issues of writers' magazines.

In the guides you'll find specialized workshops that might fit your interests precisely—children's literature, poetry, romance, mystery writing, and every other genre.

What will a writers workshop teach me?
The core lessons of workshops tend to be the same everywhere and could be enumerated in a page or two. Here are a

few principles student Ian Morris took away from the 1990–91 University of Arkansas Writers Workshop: Just tell the story; eliminate and condense; take responsibility for what you say and mean; write what you know. Other universal admonitions include these: show don't tell, understate, surprise, reward, focus, particularize, justify, dramatize. Like most other instructors, A. B. Guthrie would wean his students from reliance on adjectives and adverbs to mastery of nouns and verbs, "the guts of the language."

Good workshops ratchet these lessons into your writing. Sessions include general discussion of writing principles and readings of student works-in-progress. Students criticize one another's works, not always politely, while faculty try to nudge discussion in meaningful directions. Faculty also evaluate and discuss each student's work privately.

Aside from writing principles, workshop students take away a sense of themselves as writers in the community of writers, no longer imposters working in mad isolation. The feeling might be a sense of humility or courage or shared suffering—or likely a combination of the three. But now the fledglings have honked in a flock of writers. They belong.

SETTING UP: PLACE AND EQUIPMENT

Where should I write?

Henry Miller had a simple answer: "All you need is a place to put your ass." Miller put his backside in Paris and Big Sur, overlooking the Pacific. Not bad. But unlike Miller, most of us are tied to the mundane neighborhoods of home, workplace, and research facility. Also, to take advantage of new writing technology, writers need a place for the little butts of word processors and printers.

Romantic writing places and quirky set-ups are the ones that get talked about, not the average or best situations for everyone. Alice Thomas Ellis writes in an old stone "longhouse" in wild Wales, amidst the heathery Berwyn Mountains—perfect, except that the local sheep are said to be radioactive from Chernobyl fallout. Jay Parini composes with pencil and pad at outdoor cafés. Ann Beattie wrote five drafts of a novel on her dining room floor. Voltaire, supposedly, used the back of a lover as a desk. Whatever works works.

For the best odds, seek an uncluttered writing room with good wiring, temperature controls, bookshelves, desk, and large table. Stay away from woods, beaches, and overseas cottages, and close to civilized towns—not writers' meccas!—with modern library systems.

What kind of computer do I need?

Now we're into technological advice, which dates even as it is written. Consider all statements as of early 1992, with an eye toward the mid-nineties.

Writers vary widely in choice of computer brand, but most now agree that computers are (1) helpful in the creative process and (2) essential for meeting the demands of professional writing. Publishers want their material fast, clean, adaptable to electronic handling. They expect quick revisions, instant convertibility from manuscript to type, and sometimes even camera-ready (ready for the printer) typescript from the author. Manually typed manuscripts with tears of dried correction fluid exude so much pathos few editors can bear it.

Although services are available to put any manuscript into electronic form, it's another expense and the author misses the great advantages of word processing on computer: freedom from exasperating mechanical revisions and from linear thinking. Word processing allows manuscripts to be "freewritten" from the inside out, in any direction, expanded or contracted at any point; it allows change upon change as fast as the mind can think, without a backward glance at some distracting heap of discards. Perhaps writers of short poetry can do as well with a pencil; other authors need to process words as efficiently as the competition.

As to what type of computer, an IBM-compatible is the most common choice, although many writers are happy with their Apple Macintosh systems. A safe basic set-up for the next few years would be an (upgradeable) IBM-compatible PC, MS-DOS operating system, one or two disk drives, 286 or 386 chip (486 for high speed), one megabyte expandable RAM memory, and 40 megabyte hard disk, or card. Desk models come with 5¼ or 3½-inch disk drives, or both; laptops (see below) with 3½-inchers. So if you intend to get a laptop in addition to the desk model, you may want 3½-inch drives on the latter for fast interchangeability.

Prepare to spend about $2,500 for the desk model with monitor and the little extras. Mail-order houses give better prices and have a good reputation overall. It also makes sense to buy bargain-priced used computers, but always with a year's warranty.

Do I need a laptop computer?

If you *must* do a lot of writing away from home owing to job or extended travels, a clipboard-size computer could be your best friend. Lightweight models with a back-lit screen, comfortable keyboard, and the latest standard speed and storage cost $2,000 to $3,000. If you expect to do most of your pounding away at home, the desktops are still more poundable. Computers are constantly shrinking—from laptop to notebook to palmtop—and actually increasing in power over their larger predecessors. But until fingers and eyeballs shrink along with them, they can't be as ergonomic as the desk models.

Which word-processing software do I want?

One brand is becoming a standard in the publishing industry: WordPerfect, though there are cheaper and even better-designed programs for creative writers. Thousands of writers use other software, such as Wordstar and XyWrite; but for power, versatility, and compatibility with publishers' programs and all the software you'll ever want, you're safe with a recent version of WordPerfect. The package includes spelling and grammar checkers, thesaurus, and other editorial features. If you buy the program legitimately ($300 to $495) you can pester the twenty-four-hour trouble-shooting help line, probably the best in the business.

What other software do I need?

Need? None, really, unless you write material requiring hot graphic displays or aspire to desktop publishing. For serious graphics on IBM-compatibles, you'll need to acquire such widely used standard "graphic interface" software as Microsoft Windows, with compatible word processing software (here Word for Windows is the leader, WordPerfect for Windows expected to challenge). You'll also need sophisticated layout software and some hardware upgrades to handle it—and that's all we'll say here about desktop publishing, not really part of the literary pursuit.

Beginning and intermediate writers might consider some of the programs designed to coach literary composition. You can keep track of these and other writers' aids through the annual *Software Encyclopedia* (Bowker) and monthly *Software Reviews on File* (Facts on File). Sol Stein's WritePro is one of the better-known literary mentors on disk.

A caution: However seductive, software for writers can become a distraction, drawing too much attention to its own fun self. Do you want to play or write? For writers who play, Stupid Mac Tricks (Addison-Wesley) offers one apt gimmick: a retching noise when disks are ejected.

What's the best printer for me?

Some upscale writers have been using laser printers, which produce the commercial-level typography and graphics associated with desktop publishing. Suddenly all lower-tech printers have become suspect. But why spend $1,500 for laser desktops and accessories if all you need is a $400, 24-pin dot-matrix printer to bang out acceptable manuscript copy? Some writers still swear by their old daisy-wheel printers, which yield crisp letters but are relatively slow.

Another option is the Hewlett-Packard Deskjet, the best of the "ink-jet" printers. Having overcome certain ink-spray problems, the Deskjets produce laser-like quality at about two-thirds the purchase price of lasers. They're fast—and they're quiet, which may be a factor in writer-hostile environments.

Writers need laser printers if they want to produce camera-ready copy at higher speeds (from four pages to seventeen pages per minute) and with the widest range of graphic effects and type fonts and sizes. Few publishers require such production services from their authors, but enough high-tech authors are offering it to raise expectations. The most successful of the desktop lasers are Hewlett-Packard's Laserjets (models II, IIP, III, and IIIP), from about $850 to $1,100. Clean, quiet, and longlasting, the lasers can output gorgeous typefonts in variable sizes, which is great for publication layout but would only junk up the average manuscript.

Should I get a fax?

If you intend to aggressively freelance a great deal of short-deadline, nonfiction material from home, a $600 fax will keep you competitive with other freelancers. You'll want a separate phone line for it. Advice: Use the pay-fax down the street until you get a feel for the volume of use. Use fax instead of writing or phoning when there's more than a mouthful to be said and not a day to waste.

But what if you fax like mad and nobody faxes you back?

What else do writers buy to set themselves up?

Some buy copiers, modems, answering machines, recording equipment, database connect time, clever desktop furniture, and all sorts of toys and gadgets. And some buy a fascinating book called *Tools of the Writer's Trade* (HarperCollins), in which members of the American Society of Journalists and Authors describe all such purchases, their favorites, including hardware and software, books, supplies, services, and even travel.

Which reference books should be on my desk?

An explosion of reference-book publishing in the early nineties has made it precarious to single out classics. The latest editions of the following references, however, will earn their space on or near your desk:

American Usage and Style: The Consensus, by Roy H. Copperud (Van Nostrand Reinhold). Except to enjoy the digressions, why riffle through nine major usage guides when

Copperud has summarized their rulings on thousands of problem words and phrases? He also incorporates current-usage considerations from seven dictionaries.

The Random House Dictionary of the English Language (Unabridged). A lovely dictionary in every way, authoritative, aware of all the good new words and nuances. What else could one expect of a work edited by the late Stuart Berg Flexner? It's large and deserves a dictionary stand. Desk dictionaries or dictionaries-on-disk are okay for a quick look-up, but this lush print version gives a physical experience, like a walk in a word garden. You'll stop and smell the roses.

Roget's Thesaurus of English Words and Phrases (Longman or Putnam/Perigee). As with the unabridged print dictionary (above), this profusion of words and phrases grouped by concept is to be savored and explored. Thesauri that come with word processors punch out lists of words from which to pick synonyms; but, lacking the print version's panoramic view of related and opposing concepts, they seem limited and mundane. The conceptual arrangement rather than the dictionary style stimulates the imagination. Longman first published the classified Roget system in 1852, and latest editions represent 150 years of refinement.

Words into Type (Prentice-Hall). A much-revised classic packed with the editorial savvy authors need. Main sections: Manuscript, Copy and Proof, Copy-Editing Style, Typographical Style, Grammar [master this concise guide and you'll have it made], Use of Words, Typography and Illustration, and a Glossary of Printing and allied Terms.

Beyond these, sure bets include: a current paperback almanac, such as *The World Almanac and Book of Facts;* a few offbeat quotation books enabling you to avoid the tired quotes everyone else uses; the latest *The United States Government Manual* (National Archives), and a dictionary of English idioms for when you can't remember if it's *down* or *up* the river that you sell or send someone, or the *verdict* or the *jury* that's in or out. As for concise encyclopedias—they always seem short on that one name or fact you're seeking; better to get a good inexpensive set such as *Funk & Wagnall's New Encyclopedia* (29 vols.). If money's no object, mount an electronic encyclopedia on your computer system.

SUBJECT AND SUBJECT RESEARCH

What should I write about?

A good question, since it seems that writers have already pulverized every topic on earth. But that doesn't stop a hundred thousand authors a year, so why worry? In workshops they tell you to write about what you know intimately, because you'll put your own twist on it. Barbara Kingsolver advises fiction writers to "write about the things that are the most urgent to you and worth disturbing the universe over." The more practical Irving Wallace feels that choice of subject has to do with "*sensing* what you might be interested in and what future readers might be interested in some years from now [when your book is published, or some months from now for magazine writers]."

In choosing a subject for books, one of the great pitfalls is to write about the hot topic overwhelming you and everyone else at the moment—like the Persian Gulf War in 1991. A book rarely takes less than two years to write and a year to publish. The war will still be of interest years hence, but from a historic perspective, which must be anticipated.

Knowing a subject doesn't necessarily mean you grew up with it or have become the world's foremost expert. It means that you've spent some time observing it as a writer, as John McPhee observed Alaska or Tracy Kidder observed a classroom. Or it means that like biographer Kitty Kelley, you at least have something new and nasty to say.

How much subject background is needed in fiction?

In fiction what counts is not true expertise but the illusion of it. A few researched facts dropped in key places build verisimilitude. "How did you know so much about the guns terrorists favor in the Middle East?" columnist Tom Gaughan asked thriller writer S. K. Wolf. Wolf replied, "You wouldn't believe what you can find in the library." Wolf (Sarah Shoemaker) is a former librarian.

In fictional background, however, the factlike details have to be factual enough not to disturb readers who know better. "Cows can't fly," as they say in workshops—except in South American fiction, where nothing seems nailed down.

How do subjects vary in market value?

Greatly. At a given moment something is always in, something out; the next moment it could be the other way around. Generally speaking, publishers look for fresh subjects that will uncork millions of potential readers. "Recovery" and folksy advice were such subjects circa 1990, but by the time the me-too writers latched on there was a glut of both. The same period saw a lot of terminal-disease fiction, which earlier was the kiss of death. Law fiction was hot—anything with "innocent," "guilty," "trial," or "verdict" in the title. You couldn't keep them straight.

Anthony Burgess says (and many publishers agree), "When book buyers buy books they look for sex, violence, and hard information." He adds, "They get these from Arthur Haley, whose characters discuss problems of hotel management while committing adultery before being beaten up."

Publishers Weekly runs the best trend pieces. It also reports on who's getting the big advances and for what. The common wisdom for magazine writers is, "See what's been published lately and do something entirely different." Otherwise, the best advice is: Write about cats.

How do I find out which books have been done recently on my topic?

That's something worth knowing, so bear with a longish answer. What if you're about to invest three years writing the history of prunes? What if the definitive history is already on press? With major topics it might not matter, but prunes can't sustain more than a book a decade, any more than Asa Briggs *The Pencil: A History* (1990) could be one-upped this millenium.

Unfortunately, there's no foolproof way to do a complete English-language search, including works in progress. That's why, for example, many a publishing season sees the appearance of three or four biographies on one minor individual—as the authors contemplate suicide.

Back at the library, however, you can get a sense of the competition by skimming the spring and fall announcement issues of book- and library-trade magazines, literary supplements, and prolific book review media such as *Booklist,* arranged by subject category. *Publishers Trade List Annual* (Bowker) binds numerous publishers' catalogs and provides a broad subject index.

You can also do some searching in bibliographies. Start with *Cumulative Book Index* (Wilson), which lists all the English-language books reported to it by year of publication (still in print or not) in a very detailed subject breakdown. Some libraries also carry Bowker's *American Book Publishing Record,* weekly, monthly, and annual compilations of the country's publishing output, with subject classifications.

Books in Print (Bowker) includes roughly eight hundred sixty thousand titles publishers report as still available, whatever the year of imprint. Its "Subject Guide" volumes categorize some seven hundred thousand nonfiction works under sixty-five thousand headings. Because many titles begin with a subject word, a search in the *BIP* "Titles" volumes also can be useful—and daunting. One author of a book on writing was shell-shocked to encounter about a thousand books in *BIP* beginning with the words, "write," "writers," "writer's," or "writing." Luckily, most looked awful.

Bowker's *Forthcoming Books* lists titles issued since the last *BIP* deadline, plus books that have been announced up to five months in advance—about one hundred thousand a year all told, with a subject arrangement.

Bowker guides come in quick-search electronic versions, and there are several other high-tech services for looking up works by topic. In the EPIC database, one can search by subject or combinations of subjects through fifty thousand titles in-print and almost-in-print. Such searches might turn up the elusive title.

In specialized areas, the librarian can lead you to bibliographies that might save you from tackling a subject that is already well covered.

Once you've identified some titles on your subject, you might want to check the *Book Review Index* (Gale) and *Book Review Digest* (H. W. Wilson) to see how they were received. The former locates reviews in leading journals; the latter cites reviews and also summarizes them.

One basic approach to browsing a topic is to check the library's main catalog by subject. If you're not sure what terms to look under, ask for the subject-heading list the library uses (the *Library of Congress List of Subject Headings* in most large collections). Try the most specific headings first: "prune—history," not "fruit." Once you have call numbers for some promising titles, see what's on the shelves near them, since the nonfiction shelves are arranged by subject.

Are there subject indexes to fiction?

Yes; ask a librarian. But they are highly selective and designed to match books to reader tastes, not to discourage writers from bringing a new eye to old subjects.

How do I search quickly for articles on my topic?

The cheapest method is to search the printed magazine and newspaper indexes such as *Readers' Guide to Periodical Literature, Readers' Guide Abstracts,* and *The New York Times Index.* But when the need is for a lightning, panoramic search or a very current one, the answer is the array of electronic databases offered by brokers through libraries and by home subscription.

Here, then, is a mini-lesson in modern-day research. Electronic databases, some sixty-five hundred and growing every day, are faster and more flexible than print sources. Often, all you need are a few key words to pull out an instantaneous, up-to-the-minute bibliography on your subject. You tap into these databases by two means: (1) *online,* a direct telecommunications link between computer terminal and a database that is constantly updated, and (2) *CD-ROM,* a compact optical disc containing enormous amounts of recent but fixed information. For online searching, someone has to pay hourly fees to the database broker, and they add up fast. The CD-ROMs, which need a $400 to $1,000 reading device at the computer terminal, are updated by new CD-ROMs received on subscription. In all electronic indexes, librarians and other experienced searchers can map strategies to sort and pull out only the most promising articles from among thousands on your subject.

Once the articles are identified, you need the text. If you can't find it in the library stacks, through interlibrary loan, or in microform, you can usually purchase it from the publisher, the database broker, or a document-retrieval service. Electronic text, microform, and document delivery get pricey. Make someone else pay if you can.

Dialog is the leading database broker. Libraries have catalogs describing each Dialog database and how much it costs. The Wilson indexes (*Readers' Guide,* etc.) are available online and in CD-ROM packages. VU/TEXT and NewsBank provide astounding electronic access to newspaper information. InfoTrac, a CD-ROM index-and-text system for retrieving current articles, is the darling of college students and fast becoming available in public libraries.

If I'm borrowing from sources, what do I need to know about copyright?

In publishing contracts authors take full responsibility for complying with copyright, so it's worth knowing the basics—at least what's in the "public domain," what isn't, and what constitutes "fair use." It gets complicated, but there are rules of thumb. Works federally copyrighted in 1916 and earlier are safely in the public domain (as of 1992). For works copyrighted between 1917 and 1977, subtract seventy-six years from the current year to find the sure copyright-protection cutoff (seventy-five years is the maximum protection, but you would need to know the month of copyright). For example, 1994 minus seventy-six equals 1918. Anything copyrighted in 1918 or earlier would be in the public domain as of 1994. For works created after January 1978, copyright extends for the author's life plus fifty years. A tax-supported government publication may be copied to your heart's content, provided you don't misrepresent large chunks of it as original work. Some works declare themselves in the public domain.

Otherwise, if there's any doubt about copyright, permission should be sought from the copyright holder (through the publisher) *unless the intended borrowing falls within "fair use."* The Copyright Law of 1976 allows certain innocent borrowings or "fair use" so as not to handcuff communications and education. What's fair? According to the law, fair use is relative to the (1) purpose and character of the use, including how commercial; (2) the nature of the copyrighted work; (3) how much is used relative (in size and importance) to the whole work; and (4) the effect of the use on potential sales of the copyrighted work. Publishers will base permission fees pretty much on the same factors: The more crass and commercial your intended use, the higher the fee—if permission is granted at all.

The law provides no numerical guidelines, but in practice you can usually borrow up to three hundred words of material from a book without permission, or about 5 percent of the text from a brief work. But there are all sorts of exceptions: Borrow the last three hundred words of a new mystery and give away the ending, and you're asking for trouble. Or borrow three hundred words and use it in an advertisement—more trouble. Get the idea? In borrowing from poetry, maybe a line is fair. From newspaper articles, a few sentences. From songs, you borrow nothing without permission.

Not-for-profit scholarship, literary criticism, satire, and news enjoy slightly wider boundaries of fair use. Unpublished sources such as letters have been restricted; at this writing, however, it appears the copyright law will be revised to allow fair use of such primary materials under reasonable circumstances.

Fair use or beyond, permission or none, writers should credit the source of every significant piece of borrowed text. The test: Would I want credit if it were mine?

What about copyrighting my own work?

New authors worry too much about protecting their works, typing little "c's" all over the title pages. By law their manuscripts are copyrighted from the moment they're in tangible form. Copyright holders can transfer ownership or license certain proprietary rights for compensation, but until they do so the copyright is all theirs. Publishers usually register transfer of rights after an agreement is signed and register the copyright as soon as the work is in printed form. Before signing a book contract, however, authors should insist that copyright be in their name, even if the publisher is purchasing all apparently meaningful rights. One never knows.

Magazines copyright the aggregate contents of an issue, but copyright for individual articles remains with the authors—unless willingly transferred. For a while magazines were using "work for hire" contracts as a way of gaining proprietorship of articles, assigned or not. This practice has been discouraged, but magazines still want more than onetime North American serial rights; they want long-term exclusive rights, and rights to spin off articles into microform, electronic, and other products, worldwide. You'll probably have to yield these licenses at the going rate if you want to sell your article; it's a buyer's market. You can request some rights to be transferred back to you after the article is published.

Will editors steal my ideas when considering a proposal?

Not likely, so don't post proprietary warnings on every page—this usually signals that the ideas stink. Sometimes if editors have a similar work already under contract, they will inadvertently borrow some of your refinements in polishing that work. There's not much you can do to stop them, so worry about other things.

Where can I find more information on copyright?

Of the dozens of sources, a favorite of authors is *A Writer's Guide to Copyright* (2d edition, 1989) from Poets & Writers, 72 Spring Street, New York, NY 10012. Writers can also go direct to the source by calling the Copyright Office's general information number (202-479-0700) or writing the office at Library of Congress, Washington, DC 20559, and requesting Circular One.

What about libel, invasion of privacy—all those worries?
The best advice: Worry like hell. Your publisher is going to do so, even after you've guaranteed in writing (as you must) that your work is free from such sins.

Libel is published defamation of someone who is identifiable; invasion of privacy usually means exploitation of the private affairs of someone who has done nothing to bring on public exposure. There are defenses, of course, such as truth, but who's going to pay the tens of thousands for a defense? Some authors, especially popular biographers, are taking out expensive libel insurance; a few publishers provide partial coverage. No one wants to face a suit in the first place. Publishers' legal departments are "vetting" manuscripts for possible libel, and even fiction writers must somehow eliminate similarities to identifiable people.

The old notion that "public figures" are fair game doesn't play very well in the courts these days. Public figures are *safer* targets than others, but enjoy certain protections from malicious abuse.

For all these dangers, authors needn't be chilled into writing animal stories and pumping sunshine. Relative to most nations, the U.S. is still a haven of free expression—but not reckless expression. Reasonable caution, responsibility, and awareness of shifting trends in libel/privacy litigation will enable you to tell the story you need to tell. Among the numerous sources of information: *Writer's Friendly Legal Guide* (Writer's Digest Books); *Author Law and Strategies: A Legal Guide for the Working Writer* (Berkeley: Nolo Press); "Libel & Fiction," reprint from Poets & Writers; and lawyer Carol E. Rinzler's articles in *Publishers Weekly*.

SUBMITTING MANUSCRIPTS

Query, cover letter, proposal, samples, manuscript—which do I send when?
For brief items, such as short stories and thousand-word features already written, send a concise cover (or "covering")

letter and the whole manuscript. For longer fiction, the same type of letter becomes a query letter, asking if there is interest in seeing the completed manuscript (editors usually won't consider unfinished fiction, called "partials"); the fiction query letter is accompanied by a sample chapter, plus a synopsis of one to five pages depending on the length of the book.

For nonfiction "projects"—as proposed book-length works are called—you'll need the query letter, a proposal (see below), outline, and writing sample. The book needn't be complete at this stage, but the project must be well thought out and ready to go.

All cover letters benefit from a "grabber" near the opening sentence. Editors or agents want to see the aces only. Show yours as quickly and clearly as possible—"Dear Editor: I lost my virginity at age eight to a Satanic fiend in North Dakota. The saga of my degradation and subsequent climb to political office is detailed in . . ."

After the grabber, the fiction cover letter contains a few sentences on your story and what distinguishes it from the crowd, plus a paragraph on your literary achievements and other appropriate background. Keep the letter lively—but restrained, even though you feel this is your one shot at happiness in life.

In what form do I submit unsolicited proposals and manuscripts?

In such a form as to (1) signal no amateurism, (2) get attention, and (3) make it as easy as possible for the reader. Certain pathetic attempts at gaining attention, paradoxically, do cry "amateur!" Colored paper, gaudy desktop typography, sheaves of clippings, and cartooned happy faces are very sad indeed.

You gain attention from what you say, not from physical format. The writing pro presents a crisp, flawless computer printout on fresh 8½ x 11 white stock, medium weight. Margins are generous. Cover letters are single-spaced; manuscripts double-spaced. Name, address, phone number (and fax if you have one) are on the first page of each item—letter, outline, sample chapter, etc. Last name and a word or two from the title head all other pages, which are numbered.

Do I send the computer disk of the text?
Never, until it's called for. The cover letter might mention the type of software used, unless it's a bizarre type.

What goes into the nonfiction book proposal?
Bear in mind that proposals should run only three to six pages overall, unless the project is enormous in scale and complexity. Within those few pages, include:

1. A heading. Length of manuscript can be indicated here.

FRIEND IN NEED: A HISTORY OF THE PRUNE (WORKING TITLE)
Proposal for nonfiction book, approx. 100,000 words

2. A half-page description of the project: its nature and scope. The description should be informative but enthusiastic. It might include a "high-concept" definition of the book—its essence and style suggested in one lively sentence, e.g., "A new wrinkle on an ancient aliment, a bounty for the culinarian, the curious, and the constipated." Maybe not quite that cute. Don't get into minute detail here; the outline will showcase the contents and structure.

3. The intended audience (potential market): e.g., history and trivia buffs, cookbook buyers, nutritionists, the general reader—whoever is out there reading such books and not impossible to reach. If you know the size or consumer habits of your specialized audience, give that information. "Sunsweet reports that thirty million Americans eat prunes weekly, and that more than two million wrote for a free recipe booklet last year."

4. The relation of your project to similar or competing books. Have similar books done well? Is your approach unique? Will it distinguish the book from the buyer's point of view—e.g., is it the latest, the most complete, the first popular treatment?

5. Your expertise and reputation in the subject field. What

is your authority to write on prunes? What sources will you use? Are you known to prune lovers? Can you help sell books to them? Have you published similar works?

6. Your qualifications as a writer in general. List of major publications, honors, etc. Be brief; you can enclose a resume as further background.

7. Why you have chosen this particular publisher—but only if there's a compelling reason, such as a line of similar titles. Don't invent a reason, and don't get publishers mixed up.

8. Your timetable and other technical details. How much of the project is done, how soon you could deliver the manuscript, what electronic formats you can provide.

9. Any unusual requirements or unavoidable cost factors, such as abundant charts and illustrations. (This is not the time to suggest costly options.)

10. A good closer. A short paragraph to show some writing flair and great confidence in the project. Remind the reader that this sort of work is timeless, a favorite with book clubs, and will "travel well" for overseas rights.

What about article proposals?

When querying for interest in an article not yet written, provide essentially the same information, but no more than a page. Explain why the subject will be hot six months to a year from now. You'll need to peg the proposal to the particular nature and readership of each magazine and give a clear sense of your style and approach. Some authors write a sample "teaser," consisting of the first few irresistible paragraphs of the proposed article. Others send their best recent clip. Don't try to negotiate terms in the query letter. Even if you're willing to work on "speculation"—no promises whatsoever from the publisher—don't say so until you're asked. Usually, an outline isn't necessary if you've described the scope and general contents of the article.

What goes in the book outline?

For nonfiction, the outline can be presented chapter-by-chapter and should quickly reveal the specific elements contained in the project. If the sequence and organization of these elements aren't obvious, use the formal hierarchical outline—but you don't need all the roman numerals and letters. In table-of-contents style, a chapter heading can be followed by the main elements separated by dashes. Give highlights only:

CHAPTER TWELVE: PRUNES AND REGULARITY
Origin of laxative use—references in classical literature—Her Majesty (Elizabeth) and the Royal Prunes—how prunes won the Battle of Waterloo—chemical/biological analysis—the holistic approach . . .

What makes for a good fiction synopsis?
In *The Writer's Handbook,* novelist Serita Deborah Stevens suggests the synopsis must hook the reader, show your writing at its best, and "prove to the editor that you know how to construct a fast-paced story."

In narrative form (present tense gives immediacy), move swiftly through your plot, sketching in characters, emphasizing conflicts, desires, obstacles—building tension. Indicate the major twists and turning points. If flavorful dialogue is key, give just a taste of it.

Don't be coy, advises Stevens, and never hold back the ending. "Editors want to know all the loose ends are tied up and the story is brought to a satisfactory and satisfying conclusion." Agent Richard Curtis points out the difference between the author's own detailed outline for writing the book and the synopsis prepared "to turn on the staff of a publishing company." The purpose of the latter isn't to tell, but to sell.

What should I do about illustrations?
If your project *must* include specific illustrations, you'll need to indicate the approximate number, sources, permissions required, and estimated costs involved. If possible, you should present some rough samples. If you yourself are the photographer/illustrator, submit actual samples—and they'd better be professional and perfectly matched to the project.

If illustrations are optional, make a few brief suggestions in the proposal and leave the rest to the publisher. Don't offer to have your cousin the artist do them.

Should I submit to more than one publisher? How many at once?

Query letters for books or articles may be shotgunned everywhere at once. If a few book publishers ask to see more, should you engage in the once-perverse practice of "multiple" or "simultaneous" submission? Absolutely! Why wait six months for each publisher when there are scores to approach? Book publishers have come to expect the simultaneous approach. Should one house offer a contract, the author has ample time to withdraw from (or bargain with) the others. Book publishers should probably be informed of submissions elsewhere, though it still makes some editors groan.

Magazine editors, who sometimes rush a manuscript into publication, want to be alerted to simultaneous submissions up front—and they don't like the idea. If your article is very hot and time-dated, however, go for the multiple submission and let the editors know they're competing. Otherwise, submit to one at a time but politely suggest a reviewing period of no more than eight weeks. Call after that period, and "regretfully" withdraw the manuscript after twelve weeks. (A manuscript is withdrawn when you declare it so, in writing. Register the letter if you want certain proof.) Someone has to stop editors from sitting on articles for half a year. How about you?

For either books or articles, you must notify all losers the moment a winner has emerged in the race to publish your work. It's only fair.

Agent Richard Curtis advises book authors to multiple-submit to the top-line publishers first, holding less desirable publishers in reserve for a second round. Otherwise, you'll sign a meager deal with the Bug's Ear Press only to be offered a mega-deal from Simon & Schuster a week later. Won't you feel clever?

AGENTS

What exactly are literary agents?

Agents are brokers of creative property. They perform two basic services for writers with something to sell: they find buyers and negotiate deals. To these services good agents bring intimate knowledge of firms and individuals in the market, awareness of market trends and needs, a profound understanding of business practice in the industry, and general entrepreneurial drive. They work for writers according to the terms of a written agency agreement, taking a percentage of the client's earnings under that agreement. The usual cut is 15 percent.

For promising clients, good agents also do some handholding and work with the writer in building a lucrative career rather than simply seeking isolated sales.

Bad agents do little more than charge a fee for reading submissions from unknowns.

Do I need an agent?

For magazine articles, small-press fiction sales, and many nonfiction book sales, no. Write good proposals, follow market trends, and build your modest successes into a track record. Hustle your work at every opportunity.

With few exceptions, you do need an agent to sell fiction to major book publishers, speed up your nonfiction sales, and get the most out of each property. You need an agent for credibility at publishing houses. You need an agent to sell dramatic works. You need an agent so you can say, "My agent," which feels good.

What are agents like and how do I get a good one?

Many agents are former editors with deep roots in publishing. A number worked their way up from the bottom of large agencies. A few were writers. They are doggedly diplomatic people with good instincts and thick hides. Agents get it from both ends—from publishers who don't answer, don't pay, change their minds, welsh on promises; from authors who don't finish books, write something other than what was contracted, call incessantly through every waiting period, and demand attention far beyond their worth.

Each client is another box of headaches, which is why agents don't sign up new writers lightly. In a directory, one leading agency subtly revealed its feeling about new clients: "Writers now handling—50; number can handle—51."

The famous catch-22 is that you can't get a good agent without having published, and you can't get published without an agent. The paradox is truest for general fiction, but exceptions occur every week. What writers must do, simply, is beg agents for an audience the same way they beg publishers for a contract or assignment. The same query letters, proposals, outlines, synopses, and samples go to agents. Instead of "Please consider publishing . . ." the supplication is now "Please consider representing. . . ."

Agents will take as long or longer than most publishers to answer. You'll need to follow up politely but often. It is at least as difficult for a newcomer to get a good agent as to find a publisher, so pursue both simultaneously.

If an agent requests a reading fee (which is legitimate), try other agents or determine whether real instruction is offered or merely a superficial reading.

Query as many agents as you wish, but some agents abhor multiple submissions of the manuscript. "I would prefer to be the only agent reading *Prunes* at this time," is the way they put it.

Agencies vary from one-person shops to international corporations. How does one find them? There are several directories, some evaluative. *Literary Market Place* lists approximately 350 agencies who are "among the most active in the field," requiring each to provide up-to-date references. The descriptions include the range of work handled, major personnel, fees if any, and posture toward unsolicited manuscripts. A fair number of these agencies accept queries from unknowns without charge. Some nine hundred agencies are detailed in *Literary Agents of North America* (New York: Research Associates International). Poets & Writers publishes *Literary Agents: A Writ-*

er's Guide, with general information, interviews with agents, and an annotated list.

Writing acquaintances and instructors may refer you to their agents. It doesn't hurt to ask, unless long silences and sour looks bother you. Biographical directories such as *Who's Who* give agents for most writers listed. Pick out a writer of your ilk and sweep her agent away.

How do I learn more about agents and what they do?

Read agent Richard Curtis's *How to Be Your Own Literary Agent: The Business of Getting Your Book Published* (Houghton Mifflin) and *Beyond the Bestseller: A Literary Agent Takes You Inside the Book Business* (Penguin/Plume). Curtis writes as enthrallingly as some of his clients—Janet Dailey included—and knows the publishing business better than many a publisher. Agent Richard Balkin (*A Writer's Guide to Book Publishing,* etc.) is another articulate voice on agenting and related subjects.

THE PUBLISHING DECISION

What happens when my article reaches a magazine?

It is inadvertently thrown out with the day's junk mail. At least one would expect so, seeing the landfill of paper that chokes most editorial offices. But at properly organized magazines, an administrative assistant records the receipt, sends an acknowledgment card, and routes the manuscript to the appropriate editorial staff, sometimes with a form for recording comments. Often an editor will take a quick glance, just in case the manuscript fills a hole in a forthcoming thematic issue or treats a subject that got white hot in the last few days. A glance will also reveal hopelessly inappropriate manuscripts, which may be quickly returned.

Manuscripts neither white hot nor hopeless now hit the first of several logjams in a slow journey past three or four overburdened editors. Since most magazines are already well stocked with articles and pressed by production deadlines, reading new manuscripts is a low priority. Even those requested in response to a query tend to drift toward the logjams.

As tired eyes finally reach your yearning prose, they look mainly for reasons to reject and be done with one more pile of paper. For nonfiction, a "no" to any of these questions will probably seal your fate: Is it enlightening? Structured with some clear purpose? Fresh and original? Authoritative and intelligent? Fair? Appealing? Clear and concrete? Forceful? Relevant to the core interests of our readership?

Some compassionate editors will send a kind rejection note, but don't get too excited unless acceptance is promised pending specific revisions.

Acceptance, when it comes, will be in the form of a short agreement, unlike multipage book contracts. You will license a cluster of rights, indemnify the magazine against legal damages, and—in most cases—get paid a few weeks after signing. Some magazines still hold payment until publication, whenever that might be and if they still remember you.

How do book publishers reach a decision?

In the average house, say with more than a dozen staff or so, the process goes something like this: A manuscript reaches an acquisitions editor, either by her direct solicitation (in answer to a proposal or following a lead), through an agent, or from a first reader who has judged it a diamond in the slush. The acquisitions editor likes the manuscript enough to get behind it. She believes it "fits the list" of the publisher's particular offerings.

Using the author's proposal for background, the editor works up a written project evaluation summarizing the nature of the book, special production costs, potential market, sales of similar titles, competing books from other publishers, and other profit-loss (P&L) factors. Further input comes from production, marketing, and sales staff: What will each unit (each printed book) cost to manufacture if so many pages and so many copies are printed? How many copies are likely to sell the first year? What marketing costs must be factored in? Unit manufacturing costs may be multiplied by a constant—ranging from six to nine depending on the house and type of book—to determine retail price, which in turn affects estimated sales.

When, you ask, will the *merits* of the book itself have their sway? In two situations: Some publishers circulate the book to outside readers, some to other editors, some to both. Excitement mounts if the book is terrific. In the second and most common situation, the acquisitions editor brings the book to "committee," an in-house group that meets regularly and includes executives from editorial, production, marketing, and sales. Here, merits are weighed against negative factors and decisions made by consensus. Often, the head publisher has the last word.

For swinging a positive decision, nothing beats an enthusiastic and persuasive editor armed with a flawless proposal and a manuscript that can tapdance on the conference table.

THE BOOK CONTRACT

If the decision is "yes," when do I get my contract?

In about two to four weeks. Acting for the publisher, the editor will approach you (and your agent) with a basic offer, including about five or six "deal points" to be decided before the contract is drawn up. Of the deal points, the most important to most new authors are the royalty rates, advance against royalty, payment schedule, and division of subsidiary rights between you, the publisher, and your agent, if any. When you agree that the basic offerings are in your ballpark, a contract will be sent including these provisions and a host of others that you will need to consider. Your incentive not to delay is that you don't get the first part of your advance until you sign.

Can I dope out a contract without an agent or lawyer?

First of all, don't use lawyers unless you have cheap access to an experienced publishing attorney. The field has its own brand of give-and-take, based on practice and not on the literal publisher-oriented text of the contracts. Most general lawyers would cross out every provision in horror, assuring that you never reach agreement.

Agents are the real contract experts, and an excellent time to secure one is when you have an agreement in hand. Shop around by phone, describing your agreement to reputable agencies. Not every agent will increase client load just to get 15 percent of your $6,000 advance; the decision might depend on your long-range potential. But if one of them offers an agreement to represent you for one or two years, why not sign up and send them the publisher's contract pronto?

Lacking an agent, you still have plenty of resources for intelligent analysis of the contract; there's no need to sign within twenty-four hours in fear of losing out. Take a week or even two if you need it. Curtis's *How to Be Your Own Literary Agent* mentioned above, and Balkin's *How to Understand and Negotiate a Book Contract or Magazine Agreement* (Writer's Digest Books) are expert advisors, as is Carol Meyer's *The Writer's Survival Manual* (Bantam). The Authors Guild, perhaps the strongest lobbying group for better contract terms, offers members a model book contract, a detailed guide to it, and other enlightening materials.

Contracts from major houses vary in length from about six to twenty pages, but most of the text is what publishers call standard "boilerplate," which only the hottest authors can melt down. Some of that plate, for example, indemnifies the publisher against libel, copyright infringement, and other harmful content. There's no escaping it.

Here are a few key areas of the standard contract, with some cautionary notes:

Description of the work: This covers the provisional title and required length. *The worst thing you can do to yourself:* Promise to deliver eighty to ninety thousand words with no idea of how those numbers translate into pages or relate to your material. Figure it out first.

Delivery date: This indicates when the final draft of the manuscript is due at the publisher. Publishers take this date seriously, though they may offer brief extensions on request. *Worst you can do:* Agree to a date you're not likely to make;

deliver late enough to have your contract and all advances withdrawn.

Copyright: The clause that declares ownership of the work. The author is the original owner, and only the owner can license rights. *Worst you can do:* Agree to copyright in the publisher's name, as some small houses will suggest "for your convenience." The copyright belongs in your name, period.

The "satisfactory" or "acceptable" clause: Even though your project is under contract, publishers reserve the right to accept or reject your manuscript when you deliver the final version. Despite all your work and good faith, the project can be canceled if in the publisher's view the manuscript is not "acceptable" or "satisfactory" in form and content.

Supposedly, that judgment is based on wording in the rest of the agreement and the author's very clear failure to measure up; but, in truth, rejection might be based on changes in the publisher's financial situation, the departure of your editor, appearance of another title, or simple loss of enthusiasm. Agents and author's groups have fought for a strict set of rules governing this clause, but to little avail. Publishers feel they need to allow for failed manuscripts and changing circumstances. Rejection at this point means all advance payments must be returned, though publishers tend not to chase puny advances unless the author has been especially devious.

The worst you can do: Leave the "satisfactory" clause untouched instead of joining the battle for better terms. In the Authors Guild model contract, the publisher must provide written description of the "unacceptable" problems, allow sixty days (and offer assistance) for changes, and, should the problems remain unresolved, spell out how much of the first advance payment must be returned. Authors should always ask for a "first proceeds" clause, meaning that advances need not be returned unless the work is bought by another publisher. The first proceeds from publisher number two must then be given to publisher number one, up to the amount of publisher number one's advances.

Rights: Although you remain owner of your literary property, within the contract you will usually license the brokerage of all rights with any value. Your share of earnings for each right will be spelled out in royalty percentages or splits of revenues. Ordinarily, the publisher will get the basic "book rights" to print, publish, and sell your work in book form and the "primary subsidiary rights" to license others to publish it. Book club sales, reprints (mass-market paperback editions, etc.), and nondramatic audiotape recordings are among the primary subsidiary rights. To your agent, as a rule, goes the stewardship of "secondary" sub rights, which include dramatizations for performance, British Commonwealth editions, foreign translations, and excerpts or condensations in magazines (before the book is published).

If you don't have an agent, even with contract in hand, should you retain these rights for yourself? Not necessarily, unless you expect to market them aggressively or attract a hot offer. You can continue seeking an agent, or bear in mind that many publishers have excellent subsidiary rights staff and will do well enough by the average author.

Worst you can do: Accept substandard royalty rates and revenue splits as compensation for rights. To some degree, "standard" depends on the author's status and type of publisher and publication, but the sources named above (Curtis, etc.) give a good idea of standard figures in general trade publishing. Chances are you've been had if you get less than a 10 percent royalty on a hardcover edition, a 6 percent royalty on mass-market and trade paperback sales, and 50 percent of book-club, reprint, and other primary subsidiary rights. But for books with real spin-off potential it gets much more complicated, which is why agents flourish.

OTHER QUANDRIES AND USEFUL RESOURCES

How do I help a publisher market my book?

For openers you'll fill out an author's questionnaire providing all the ammunition you can think of to help the book sell. You'll get notable acquaintances, if any, to write blurbs for early publicity. And you'll buy John Kremer's *1001 Ways to Market Your Books: For Authors and Publishers* (Frederick, 51 N. 5th

St., Fairfield, IA 52556) and follow the advice as far as your resources and ambitions take you.

What's a good guide to self-publishing?

Like John Kremer (above), Dan Poynter is a one-man factory of advice for publishers and self-publishers. His *Self-Publishing Manual: How to Write, Print & Sell Your Own Book* is among many resources from his Para Publishing, Box 4232-R, Santa Barbara, CA 93140-4232.

Is there one central guide to the small-press market?

Thanks to editor Len Fulton, an institution in the small-press world, there is the regularly updated *International Directory of Little Magazines and Small Presses,* published by Fulton's Dustbooks imprint (P.O. Box 100, Paradise, CA 95969). It provides details on some five thousand markets. Other Dustbooks titles include *The Directory of Poetry Publishers,* with some two thousand markets.

How do I learn to think like an editor?

Bruce Ross-Larson's *Edit Yourself* (Norton) shows the actual changes that editors apply to weak prose; *The Elements of Editing* (Collier/Macmillan), by yours truly, demystifies a broad range of editorial concerns.

Do I have to avoid sexist phrasing? How can I do it without clumsy alternatives?

Yes, you must master nonsexist writing because (1) it's the right thing to do, and (2) when you offend or simply distract your audience with sexist terms, you lose your audience; the readers think about sexism instead of your subject. An overall apology for using "neuter male pronouns" won't make it any less distracting when readers encounter such phrases as, "every author must fashion his career as he sees fit." Often, the simple solution is to use plurals: "authors must fashion their careers as they see fit." Awkward alternatives such as he/she can be avoided. Practically every sex-specific term (fireman) has acquired a nonjolting neutral alternative (firefighter). Rosalie

Maggio's *The Nonsexist Word Finder* (Oryx) has plenty of suggestions along this line. It takes a while to get the hang of nonsexist writing; eventually it feels (and reads) natural. An excellent guide is *The Handbook of Nonsexist Writing* by Casey Miller and Kate Swift (HarperCollins).

While I'm waiting for my megadeal, where can I apply for prizes and grants?

At the library again, seek out *Grants and Awards Available to American Writers* (P.E.N. American Center), *Literary & Library Prizes* (Bowker), or *Publication Grants for Writers & Publishers: How to Find Them, Win Them, and Manage Them* (Oryx), among other directories. The writer's journals, especially *Poets & Writers,* announce prizes and deadlines as they come along. Expect to pay a reading fee of $5 to $25 for many legitimate competitions—and a few sleazy ones.

Should I join a writers association?

If you feel isolated, as most writers do, associations can help. City and regional groups and the National Writers Club are probably best for beginners; after a few publications you'll qualify for such groups as the Authors Guild and American Society of Journalists and Authors (nonfiction), which offer benefits and lobby on behalf of authors in general. Bowker's *Literary Market Place* and Gale's *Encyclopedia of Associations* list general and specialized (mystery, romance, black authors, etc.) associations.

The question calls to mind a line from *The Yellow Wallpaper,* a play based on a Charlotte Perkins Gilman short story. In a claustrophobic wallpapered bedroom, a Victorian woman observes her sanity slipping away. She had tried writing. "I had thought to join the community of writers," she reminds herself, *"but there was no such community."* Ultimately it is true. You have joined workshops, associations, and shared common experiences with perhaps thousands of writers. But now you are alone in your study and it is time to honk if you're a writer and only you can make it happen.

Good luck.

INDEX

INDEX